SIX WOMEN WHO SHAPED WHAT AMERICANS EAT

NEXUS

NEW HISTORIES OF SCIENCE, TECHNOLOGY, THE ENVIRONMENT, AGRICULTURE & MEDICINE

NEXUS is a book series devoted to the publication of high-quality scholarship in the history of the sciences and allied fields. Its broad reach encompasses science, technology, the environment, agriculture, and medicine, but also includes intersections with other types of knowledge, such as music, urban planning, or educational policy. Its essential concern is with the interface of nature and culture, broadly conceived, and it embraces an emerging intellectual constellation of new syntheses, methods, and approaches in the study of people and nature through time.

Six Women Who Shaped What Americans Eat

Food Choice in an Age of Abundance

Michelle Mart

The University of Alabama Press
Tuscaloosa

The University of Alabama Press
Tuscaloosa, Alabama 35487-0380
uapress.ua.edu

Typeface: Arno Pro

Cover image: © studiostoks / Adobe Stock
Cover design: Sandy Turner Jr.

Cataloging-in-Publication data is available from the Library of Congress.
ISBN: 978-0-8173-2243-4 (cloth)
ISBN: 978-0-8173-6214-0 (paper)
E-ISBN: 978-0-8173-9571-1

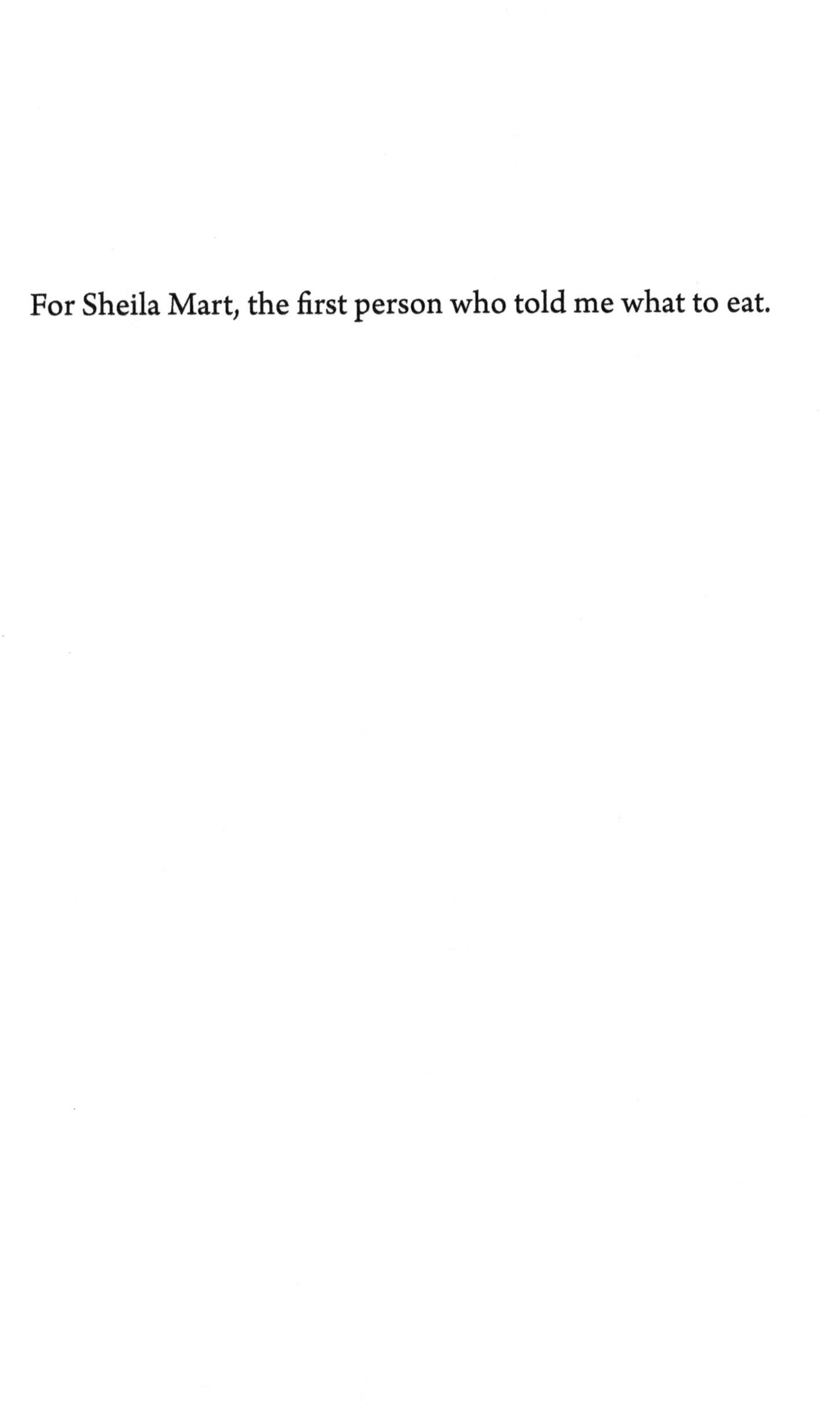

For Sheila Mart, the first person who told me what to eat.

Contents

Foreword

"Where there is much food," goes the adage, "there are many problems. Where there is no food, there is one." Since the creation of the United States Department of Agriculture (USDA) in 1862, the bent of the nation's agricultural policy has been to create an abundance of food—one that would ensure political stability for its republican experiment, plentiful and affordable food for its industrial workers and increasingly urban population, and a base for its economic expansion. The emergence of land-grant universities, agricultural experiment stations, and the Cooperative Extension Service in the late nineteenth and early twentieth centuries all underscored and advanced that policy. And over the course of the twentieth century, new technologies and distribution networks facilitated an increasingly efficient and productive agricultural system, which is marked by the heavy capitalization and economies of scale of industrial production. By the second half of the twentieth century, the United States enjoyed an abundance of food that outstripped even the wildest dreams of the nineteenth-century architects of the nation's agricultural policy. Indeed, having enough to eat became a marker of American identity—the full shelves of the nation's grocery stores provided evidence of its cultural superiority over rivals on the global stage.

Books exploring the developments that facilitated that abundance and the consequences of the transformation of American agriculture that undergirded it—for rural communities, for regional subcultures, for the nation's political trajectory, for its war efforts, for its educational systems, for the fate of its waters and soils, for its foreign relations and domestic policies alike—line library shelves in the United States and around the world. The abundance of food itself, however, has largely been taken for granted or acknowledged in passing as a backdrop for other stories. To be sure, a growing number of food historians have traced various facets of that abundance, following threads like canned food and food adulteration. But historians have evinced little interest in exploring the ways in which that very abundance shaped how Americans thought about food and what they ate. It is into this yawning historiographical gap that Michelle Mart steps with this contribution to the Nexus series.

To do so, she takes up the diverse careers of six women who influenced and embodied broader shifts in how and what Americans ate. Some of the women are comparatively unfamiliar, like Hazel Stiebeling, a USDA chemist who sought to encourage balanced diets by convincing Americans to think about food as the sum of its nutrients, pioneering the notion of recommended daily allowances, and playing an important role in fashioning school lunches along the way. Likewise, few Americans remember Poppy Cannon, a columnist and cookbook author who championed processed foods as a convenient means to make gourmet meals in works like her bestselling *The Can-Opener Cookbook* (1952). Others are quite familiar. Foremost among them is Julia Child, the iconic cookbook author and media personality, who endeavored to convince women that they could make authentic French meals with ingredients plucked from the shelves of American grocery stores. She is so famous a replica of her kitchen is now preserved in the Smithsonian. Nearly as well-known is restaurateur and slow-food movement trailblazer Alice Waters, who self-consciously sought to introduce an alternative to the mass-produced food culture of the 1970s via her restaurant Chez Panisse, which emphasized locally sourced ingredients, selected for their appearance and flavor, and which served as a model for the myriad farm-to-table restaurants that can now be found around the country.

While all six took for granted the abundance of American agriculture, and all sought to influence the specific choices American made about the food they consumed, they diverged in important, even fundamental, ways. The first three women—Stiebeling, Cannon, and Child—embraced the abundance; the latter three—Frances Moore Lappé, whose *Diet for a Small Planet* (1971) helped introduce vegetarianism to the American mainstream; Marion Nestle, an academic nutritionist who updated Stiebeling's guidelines and lamented the degree to which corporations manipulated those guidelines and the food choices that Americans made; and Waters—worried about the downsides of that abundance for human health and the environment and about the unevenness with which its benefits redounded to American society.

The story Mart tells is inevitably inflected by gender, race, and class. The public discourse surrounding food into which these women spoke, after all, was disproportionately shaped by a white middle class, one that seldom challenged prevailing gender assumptions about food. It is also a story permeated by ironies, in which, for example, school lunches designed to set an example for sound nutritional guidelines became evidence of the poor eating habits of many Americans, in which individual choices were repeatedly emphasized in the face of an industrial food system that hindered substantive change and, in fact, sometimes sought deliberately to mislead the public making those choices.

It is not, as Mart readily acknowledges, an exhaustive story or the final word on the ways in which abundance has shaped American foodways. A single volume could hardly capture the regional, subregional, ethnic, and racial aspects of American food choices in an era of abundance. American foodways are far from monolithic. But she does offer a compelling study with which future scholarship will have to contend. By focusing her gaze on the public culture of American food choices, Mart pushes beyond studies that treat quantity and quality—which is to say the desirability—of food independently of one another, and in showing that the two are of a piece, she demonstrates just how powerfully the tensions between them have shaped American culture. Indeed, by placing the food choices Americans have made in their proper context, Mart has given us a story that will make readers rethink why and how they eat what they eat.

Mark D. Hersey
For the Nexus editors

SIX WOMEN WHO SHAPED WHAT AMERICANS EAT

Introduction

In March 1943, *The Saturday Evening Post* featured Norman Rockwell's painting *Freedom from Want* on its cover. The painting was wildly popular and has since endured as an iconic illustration of American identity. A grandmother at the center of the painting presents a large roast turkey to a smiling family and friends around a holiday table. For readers of the *Post*, the joyous scene reflected the increasingly common abundance of food in the United States and how such celebratory meals brought Americans together. But the painting conveyed more than an image of plentiful food and family togetherness; it also carried political and cultural messages. Rockwell's painting was part of a series illustrating foundations of American identity, the "Four Freedoms" announced by President Franklin Roosevelt in his 1941 State of the Union speech: Freedom of Speech, Freedom of Worship, Freedom from Want, and Freedom from Fear. Rockwell's choice to depict Freedom from Want as a large turkey enjoyed by a happy family was apt, illustrating the undeniable bounty of American agriculture in the twentieth century as well as the visceral feeling that people experienced economic well-being through the food widely available to them. In short, being American meant always having enough to eat. It is a cultural association that has continued down to the present day.

Plentiful food presented Americans with an envious dilemma: what to eat? With abundance came *choice*, and questions that were otherwise simple became more complicated. What should one eat and how much, and was that a matter of individual choice? To what extent did government officials, scientists, chefs, and food corporations influence—even determine—what people ate? Moreover, how did American food culture shift in response to individual choice or institutional pressures? The complexities of food choice do not stop there. What factors most shaped individual choice? Taste? Cultural traditions? Cost? Health concerns? Worries about the environment or animal welfare? Or was individual choice illusory in the face of an industrial food system that determined what people would eat?

Two basic assumptions underlie the following discussion of these questions. First, the industrial system that produced abundance was entrenched and dominant in the United States. Second, American food choices were contested, and multiple factors (material and cultural) determined what people ate. From these starting points, this book tells the story of how responses to food abundance determined what people ate.

The story that follows uses six different women to guide us through the thicket of an industrial system that both constrained and encouraged food choice. Each of these women had strong ideas about what Americans should eat, and their opinions were formed by an embrace or rejection of the industrial food system and the abundance it created. The six women profiled here confronted the dilemmas that shaped food choices—and they each came up with different answers. Their impact on American foodways was thus unique and long lasting and integrated into the middle-class, public culture. The women had various professional roles, as government officials, cookbook authors, academics, journalists, and restauranteurs. They were active over many decades, from the early twentieth century to the early twenty-first century. Some were more familiar in the broader public culture, some less so. The following chapters do not attempt to provide detailed biographies of each of these women. Rather, the focus will be on highlights of their professional work that illustrate broader themes in American foodways and the impact of food abundance in the modern era.

The women profiled are the following: Hazel Stiebeling, a chemist and government nutritionist who, beginning in the 1930s, helped shape dietary guidelines and school lunches affecting generations of Americans; Poppy Cannon, a best-selling cookbook author and newspaper columnist who first gained fame in the 1950s by preaching the wonders of processed food; Julia Child, another cookbook author and television personality, who, starting in the 1960s, celebrated French cuisine and made it accessible to American cooks and palates; Frances Moore Lappé, an author and activist on the environmental impact of food in the late twentieth century who was credited with introducing vegetarianism to the mainstream; Marion Nestle, an academic nutritionist, government consultant, and author who decried the undue influence of food corporations; and Alice Waters, a celebrity chef and restauranteur, food activist, and symbol of alternative food movements in the twenty-first century.

As indicated by their different professions, the concerns of these women were distinct. To differing degrees, they highlighted the politics of food, the pleasure of food, the connection between food and health, and the environmental harm of poor food choices. They were all active in an age of food abundance and the industrial production of food—conditions so naturalized in the public culture they were virtually invisible. Importantly, they differed in their reactions to that industrial abundance. The first three—Stiebeling, Cannon, and Child—embraced the benefits of that system, with little question or criticism. By contrast, Lappé, Nestle, and Waters all criticized one or more aspects of the modern American food system, including its cultural, economic, health, and environmental impacts. They argued that abundance—counterintuitively—had its downsides.

Counterintuitive, indeed. What could be a downside of abundant food? The benefits of abundance are obvious. During the decades discussed here, the ability to produce sufficient food for the country as a whole was not in doubt, even if food distribution and access was unbalanced (and indeed lacking for some). Beyond sufficiency, the United States enjoyed plentiful food through an efficient system of industrial agriculture, processing, distribution, and trade. Abundance, then, demonstrated the success of the modern food system. That system did not simply appear in the middle of the twentieth century; it originated in domestic production and processing in the nineteenth century and in global trade and colonialism in the late nineteenth and early twentieth centuries. Nevertheless, this book will begin its discussion in the early twentieth century and focus most on the post–World War II changes to the industrial food system.[1]

Materially, abundance meant that most Americans had ready access to a variety of foods throughout all seasons. Few Americans had to worry about malnutrition, let alone starvation, and the majority could afford sufficient food. But the impact of abundant food went beyond material well-being. It led to what some scholars have summarized as "new ideas about nutrition, health, and sustenance."[2] One of these new ideas was the *expectation* of abundance—abundance that was taken for granted. This was a powerful assumption, both for native-born Americans and immigrants newly arrived. Historian Hasia Diner summarized its impact: "Americans came to believe in their right to an acceptable standard of living wherein hunger played no role. They believed that as Americans they *all* deserved to live free from want."[3] Paradoxically, there were nevertheless intermittent fears about food supply; food scholar Warren Belasco observed: "Even as supermarket shelves groaned with convenience products designed to add value to the land's mounting surpluses, Malthusian worries persisted."[4]

Occasional fears, though, were swept aside by the undeniable evidence of plentiful food. Like other Americans, each of the six women discussed in this book lived with an expectation of abundance; thus, they wasted little time wondering if the American food system could provide sufficient food to support the population. They had other concerns. Hazel Stiebeling, Poppy Cannon, and Julia Child sought to influence the food *choices* that Americans made. Stiebeling wanted Americans to choose nutritious food and a well-balanced diet. Cannon and Child encouraged Americans to experiment with products and recipes to produce desirable meals. Meanwhile, Frances Moore Lappé, Marion Nestle, and Alice Waters encouraged Americans to make food choices that would overcome the problems of the industrial food system. For them, food abundance had created environmental problems and global inequalities, chronic diseases, overly powerful corporate producers, and a hollowed-out food culture dominated by processed foods. Thus, whether these women celebrated the benefits of food abundance or critiqued the problems of the existing system, they all sought to influence Americans' food choices.

It is fair to ask whether questions about food choice—in comparison with the more important achievement of providing sufficient sustenance for all—really matter and why. This book offers an emphatic yes in answer to the first question, arguing that interrogating food choices can shift our framework of understanding culture and the economy more broadly. While assessments of food history are most often reduced to either a story of quantity or of quality (and desire), this book treats both the quantity and quality of food as important and intertwined, and it asserts that the tensions between these categories have political, economic, social, cultural, and environmental effects.

Each of the women discussed in this book had a significant and lasting impact on American food culture, but they were not alone in that regard in their respective fields or eras. Moreover, it is fair to say that these are not the only figures who might have been selected to represent shifts in American food culture; indeed, as the following pages will indicate, and a rich literature in food studies illustrates, there are numerous individuals who have had significant impact on American food culture. The six women profiled in these pages are best understood as exemplars of particular changes and viewpoints, not solitary voices disconnected from cultural trends. Thus, the women were *touchstones,* representative of changes broadly shared by large groups of people and already underway.

Allowing for the idea that the women profiled here were chosen for their ability to illustrate broader cultural trends, why *these* women and *these* cultural trends? The first criterion for selecting subjects was their degree of influence in the broad public culture. Such influence was found in their professional positions, their cultural visibility, and their lasting impact over more than one era.

For instance, Hazel Stiebeling held an authoritative position in the US Department of Agriculture, helping to shape nutrition advice that would impact soldiers, schoolchildren, and ordinary citizens. She is the least well known of the figures today, but she was active over more than thirty years in the USDA, was known in the mainstream press during her career, and received presidential recognition for her work. Poppy Cannon and Julia Child were both best-selling authors, popular and influential, inspiring changes in home cooking that have continued in various forms to the present. Frances Moore Lappé was also a best-selling author whose first book, *Diet for a Small Planet,* remains known as one of the turning points in American food and environmental discourse. Marion Nestle was best known among academics and food activists, though her critiques about food politics filtered out more broadly through the mainstream media. Alice Waters first became well known in the world of high-end cuisine in the 1970s, then famous in the press and among activists as an embodiment of alternative foodways to the present day.

The second criterion used to select protagonists for this discussion was to find women who had something important to say regarding the industrial food system, either embracing its many advantages or critiquing its unintended consequences. The industrial food system has influenced food choice and consumption, shaping food culture; it has also had broad environmental, health, and economic impacts over the past century. Stiebeling, Cannon, and Child worked *within* an industrial food system so ubiquitous and successful that it was naturalized, an unquestioned structure. The abundant food it produced inspired them to believe that all Americans could have optimal, nutritional diets as well as enjoyable cuisine. While Lappé, Nestle, and Waters did not question the desirability of food sufficiency and convenience, they argued that the modern industrial food system fell short in other ways. They—and some of their contemporaries—asked whether the benefits of industrialization were worth the environmental costs, inequality of food distribution, chronic health problems, and what one food historian described as "standardized mass-produced processed dishes" with "predictable homogeneity."[5]

The choice to highlight the impact of these six women raises another important question: why only women and not men? The exclusion of men from this survey is an intentional choice. The relationship between women and food can be taken at face value as a bedrock of American culture, as sociologist Shelley Koch observed: "Cooking as a characteristic of a traditional culinary femininity is an extension of the love and care women provide their families."[6] Yet, such gender observations can also be interrogated as both an affirmation of stereotypes and a challenge to them. This book will examine when food choices and the advice about what to eat was more or less gendered, and whether the impact of these six people was related to their gender.

Along with debates about the industrial food system, the importance of abundance in American food culture, and the impact of gender on American foodways, this book highlights other recurring questions and tensions. Foremost among these is a consideration of whether modern Americans viewed food primarily as a practical necessity for sustenance and survival or as a source of pleasure and a way to fulfill sensual desires. A corollary set of questions is whether food reflected cultural traditions as well as a connection to the natural world or if food was better understood as a demonstration of modern science and technology, measured by the quantities produced and consumed. One other broad, overlapping set of questions used to understand food choices is to ask how class identity and available resources impacted food choices; moreover, did food in the modern era cut across class differences or reinforce them?

That last question raises an important caveat. This book does not seek to present a comprehensive picture of American food culture with all of its regional, ethnic, racial, and class differences. As many scholars have made clear (and any perusal of contemporary cookbooks and cooking shows would affirm), American food culture is not monolithic. It is multicultural and multiregional, reflecting the diversity of a multiracial nation of immigrants, and it has evolved over time.[7] This book does not attempt to capture the richness and variety of food throughout the United States. What is discussed here are changes in American foodways that are found in the broad public culture, as reflected in US government policies, industrial food products, and information appearing in national media and publications. For much of American history, such public culture was dominated by white middle-class values and power, shaped heavily by European, especially Anglo, roots. Thus, for better or worse, the foodways discussed in this book are not encyclopedic.

Nevertheless, the following chapters will range over various topics and issues within the framework described. The first chapter will focus on Hazel Stiebeling, who trained as a chemist and viewed food as a collection of nutrients more than as a reflection of cultural traditions or environmental conditions. As a government nutritionist, she helped to create the recommendations for food groups and portions that shaped dietary advice for much of the twentieth century. Her work on recommended daily allowances (RDAs) also became fundamental to the design of the federal school lunch program.

The next chapter shifts to the recommendations of cookbook author and journalist Poppy Cannon, who in the 1950s instructed middle-class housewives how to use processed food items to create elaborate, modern meals. She wrote more about the pleasurable and performative aspects of cooking than about the nutritional components of the meals served. In the 1960s, Julia Child was also a successful cookbook author and soon afterwards a television personality teaching housewives what to cook. But as the chapter about Child details, she not only emphasized the manifest pleasures of food and its creative potential, but also its deep cultural traditions from France and, later, from various American regions.

Frances Moore Lappé is the third cookbook author profiled here, but she represented a sharp departure from Cannon and Child. As discussed in chapter four, Lappé gained fame in the 1970s with her food and environmental manifesto calling on Americans to shift their diets from meat-based ones to those that were more plant-based in order to fend off a looming humanitarian and environmental disaster. Along with her environmental concerns, Lappé returned to a nutritionist perspective similar to that of Stiebeling years earlier, constructing recipes around nutritional goals rather than around taste or culture. Nevertheless, it became clear that she was more concerned with the political and environmental impact of the food system, rather than with the food itself.

Marion Nestle also viewed food from a nutritionist lens, but her focus was different from that of either Stiebeling or Lappé. Chapter five discusses the work of Nestle, an academic nutritionist who investigated how food access and food systems were manipulated in the marketplace. She consulted with the federal government to update the food guidelines put in place by Stiebeling and others decades earlier. Her work also focused on nutritional components as the measure of food, rather than its taste or culture. Beyond the food itself, Nestle was most concerned with how corporations manipulated both government nutritional guidelines and the food choices of individuals.

The last chapter in the book profiles Alice Waters, who returned to the view that food was a source of epicurean pleasure; but unlike the cookbook authors Cannon and Child, she found that pleasure in fresh ingredients, rooted in particular places rather than in packaged goods from factories or in elaborate recipes. She brought environmental concerns, similar to those of Lappé, back to the fore, as well as the nutritional concerns of Stiebeling and Nestle, asserting that the nutrient value of whole foods was shaped by the environment from which they came. Thus, in Waters's work, pleasure and practicality coexisted symbiotically. The chapter also considers Waters's relationship to "the new food movement" and its legacy.

Surveying several decades and these six influential figures, this book addresses continuities and discontinuities in American foodways and wrestles with their implications, especially cultural, class, and environmental ones. In addition, the chapters discuss the tension between individual food choices and the systemic forces that constrain them. Thus, the story that follows will highlight some of the complexities of modern American food culture and reveal greater understanding about why we eat what we do in an age of abundance.

I

The Bounties of the Modern American Food System

1

Hazel Stiebeling and the Science of Diet Guidelines

In an undated photo in the archives at the National Agricultural Library, three rows of people pose in front of the main building of the United States Department of Agriculture (USDA) in downtown Washington, DC. "Top USDA Administrators during World War II (including Hazel K. Stiebeling)," the photo label says.[1] Of the thirty-six people in the photo, Stiebeling was the only woman. It is an unassuming portrait that belies Stiebeling's impact on what Americans ate.

Hazel Stiebeling was a chemist who treated food as an input—reducing it to its nutrients, devising a set of daily "requirements" that persisted long after her death and continued to shape Americans' relationship to food—without regard for the taste, culture of origin, or environmental impact of that food or its production. Stiebeling's work influenced government dietary guidelines intended to improve the general health in the Great Depression and the readiness of soldiers during World War II. It also became the foundation of the national school lunch program that was launched in 1946, using commodities of the industrial food system to deliver bland meals with sufficient nutrients to children and influencing the tastes of the nation's future generations. Stiebeling, then, had a major impact that reverberates to this day.

Hazel Stiebeling was one among a small number of women nutritionists in the USDA who translated nutritional research into concrete food programs and dietary guidelines that shaped what Americans ate from the 1930s through the early twenty-first century. She and the other nutritionists used scientific analysis to understand the components of food and biological human needs in order to craft dietary recommendations. She and other women worked from within a male-dominated bureaucracy at the USDA to shape what Americans ate. Although she was not alone in her work, she stood out as a leader, becoming the first woman to receive the President's Award for Distinguished Federal Civilian Service—the highest recognition for civilian employees.

This book begins with the story of Stiebeling, because for many Americans, a scientific approach to nutrition shaped how they viewed food and influenced what they chose to eat—or thought they should eat. Government policies remained firmly wedded to a nutritional approach to food, or what one scholar dubbed a "nutritionist" framework.[2] A nutritionist approach was characterized by more than its scientific research. This was a pragmatic view of food, with little attention to its sensuous experience or its sentimental associations. Such a practical approach celebrated the food surpluses produced by the efficiencies of the industrial system and did not consider the environmental and social downsides of such production methods. Yet, as will become clear in this and subsequent chapters, choosing what to eat was often not scientific, practical, or simple.

Hazel Stiebeling's journey from an Ohio farm to becoming an international authority on human nutrition illustrated her ambition and talents in an era when the doors to careers in science were usually closed to women.[3] Born in 1896, Stiebeling showed potential at an early age. Her parents sent her to live with her grandparents more than an hour away in a town called Findlay, since the grade school there was better than in her hometown. In high school, Stiebeling developed an interest in home economics, which led her to pursue a two-year degree in domestic science at Skidmore College. There she discovered the work of her future mentor Henry Sherman in his book *The Chemistry of Food and Nutrition.* Following her graduation from Skidmore, Stiebeling found a job teaching domestic science at her old high school in Ohio. After three years, she returned to New York, this time to complete her BS degree at Columbia University Teacher's College. Upon graduation, she supervised training in domestic science at Kansas State Teacher's College for four years. She then decided to pursue her scientific interests, returning to Columbia first to complete an M.A. in nutrition, then to study chemistry under the direction of Henry Sherman, whose book had inspired her years earlier.[4] By 1928, Stiebeling had earned her PhD in chemistry.

Stiebeling's doctoral studies provided her with a strong research background for her lifelong work on human nutrition. Her thesis examined absorption of Vitamins D and A in conjunction with calcium and phosphorus intake, measuring amounts necessary for healthy development of babies and the prevention of rickets. One journal article observed that the work reflected "careful attention to detail and statistical evaluation," attributes that would also characterize her later work; another author from the 1940s referred to her laboratory work as "brillian[t]."[5] Along with honing her methodological skills, the thesis work resulted in the publication of two papers in the *Journal of Biological Chemistry.*

Stiebeling's graduate work was important for her career in another respect. Henry Sherman encouraged her to take the civil service exam in order to open up more opportunities at the USDA, an agency more receptive to hiring women than other institutions at the time. With the exam credential, Stiebeling was eligible for a position at a new research unit in the USDA; she arrived in Washington as head of the Food and Economics section in the Food and Nutrition Division of the Home Economics Bureau. Thus began Stiebeling's government career. The bureaucratic layers were (and remained) complex throughout Stiebeling's time at the USDA; although her titles and reporting chain changed, as did the autonomy of Home Economics, Stiebeling worked on human nutrition at the USDA from 1930 until her retirement in 1963. Starting as a head of a section within a division of the bureau, by 1942, Stiebeling was the assistant chief of bureau, and then chief of bureau starting in 1944.[6] While serving in that capacity, she held other titles within the Agricultural Research Administration—renamed the Agricultural Research Service (ARS) in 1953—which became the umbrella over Human Nutrition and Home Economics. It is worth noting that the dictates of bureaucratic reorganization changed Stiebeling from a chief of bureau to a director of a subunit of ARS.[7] Nevertheless, in her last two years with the USDA, Stiebeling served as deputy administrator for ARS.

Throughout her career, Stiebeling was recognized inside and outside of government for her research into human nutrition and her ability to translate that research into widely used guidelines. In addition to national and international appointments, she garnered a series of honorary doctorates and the USDA's highest honor, its Distinguished Service Award, in 1952. Her most impressive recognition was the President's Award for Distinguished Federal Civilian Service in 1959—the highest recognition granted to civilian employees—given for her "lasting contribution to the science of human nutrition." As noted, no other woman had earned the recognition before Stiebeling.[8]

Henry Sherman might not have foreseen the acclaim that Stiebeling would earn, but he did harbor an ambition for his student beyond gainful employment. He saw in Stiebeling potential to do important work in nutritional science, perhaps following in the footsteps of W. O. Atwater, an agricultural chemist at the USDA who is known unofficially as the father of modern nutritional science. When Stiebeling left for Washington, Sherman encouraged her: "maybe you are the person to finish Atwater's work."[9]

Long before Hazel Stiebeling went to work there, the United States Department of Agriculture had been concerned with what Americans ate. Since the founding of the department during the Civil War, it had been charged with protecting the well-being of the American farmer—a goal that was for many still synonymous with the well-being of the nation at a time when half of the population worked on the land. And since farmers were responsible for growing the nation's food, the USDA was also charged with ensuring a reliable food supply and with spreading "useful information on subjects connected with agriculture in the more general and comprehensive sense of the word." Within a few years of its founding, such a charge was interpreted as issuing dietary advice for the nation as a whole.[10]

The person most responsible for first realizing this charge was W. O. Atwater, who earned his PhD in agricultural chemistry in 1869 and continued his research during a series of academic appointments, especially at Wesleyan University. While there as a professor, he began a long association with government programs. He served as the first director of the Wesleyan experiment station, conducted research for the US Fish Commission and Smithsonian Institution, was the first chief of the USDA Office of Experiment Stations, and finally became chief of the USDA's nutrition programs. Atwater's research was focused on measuring the energy provided by food (calories) and the individual components of food needed for human health.[11] Atwater's graduate study in both the United States and Germany helped to formulate his view that understanding the human relationship to food was really a quantification equation that could be solved by measuring nutrients, energy, and physical activity; in 1897 Atwater built the first human respiration calorimeter in the United States to take such accurate measurements. Measuring food according to its nutritional components and energy stores fit neatly into an economic assessment of food. Rhetoric scholar Jessica Mudry observed that Atwater thus believed "that the best foods were the ones that yielded the most nutrients for the least money."[12] His moniker as the father of nutritional science was apt, since those who followed in his footsteps—at the USDA and in academia—shared his approach to the study of food and dietary advice.

Atwater completed a series of studies in the 1890s and 1900s that became the basis of dietary guidelines at the time. These guidelines were then paired with departmental recommendations about food budgeting.[13] After his death, other nutritionists in the department took up his work, issuing advice to the public, such as a fourteen-page pamphlet in 1917, entitled "How to Select Foods." The pamphlet, written by Caroline Hunt and Helen Atwater, daughter of W. O. Atwater, organized its recommendations into five groups of food distinguished by the type of nutrition that they provided: fruits and vegetables; meats and other protein-rich foods; cereals and starches; sweets; and fatty foods. This early emphasis on *variety* and on the nutrient *components* of foods remained constant for the next century and meant that all different foods—according to mainstream nutritionists—could find a place in the American diet.[14] Reflecting the Progressive Era ethos of scientifically analyzing a problem (how to ensure that Americans had adequate and healthful diets) and proposing a rational system to solve it, the USDA pamphlet also addressed the goal of assuring adequate access to food when prices had been rising sharply, even culminating in food riots in three cities in February 1917. In addition, once the United States entered World War I, government officials became concerned about providing sufficient supplies, both at home and abroad.[15] Shortages were not the only worry, but so too was an inadequate balance of healthful foods.

Along with wartime pressures, it's worth pausing to consider what else these early twentieth-century guidelines tell us about broad changes in the industrializing United States. The issue of dietary advice took on new importance in the first half of the twentieth century for several reasons. First, with increasing urbanization and fewer Americans growing their own food, people increasingly relied on stores and processors for their food. Being one step removed from food production raised the obvious question of what to buy. Second, in addition to accommodating urbanization, government officials had an obligation to systematize food procurement and nutritional guidelines in order to feed soldiers properly in World War I and then, later, in World War II.

Federal nutrition policies beginning in the World War I era reflected attitudes that would continue for the next century: they were consumerist, pragmatic, and dispassionate. The first characteristic in an urbanizing country appears both necessary and obvious, but it is remarkable how little attention was paid to the possibility of small-scale food production—a sharp contrast, for example, with the renewed interest in urban gardening just a few years later with Victory Gardens and again a few decades after that. Federal guidelines were also consumerist to the extent that they emphasized choice within an abundant supply. The guidelines were pragmatic to the extent that scientists, economists, and policymakers sought to use food as a tool to achieve proper nutrition for the nation's citizens. Food lost its intrinsic cultural or environmental worth and became just one more commodity to be deployed for a particular purpose.

Dispassionate pragmatism, nevertheless, incorporated certain cultural tropes of freedom, modernity, gender, and protective attitudes toward children. Food choice, for example, remained central to federal nutrition policy, referred to as "guidelines." But starting in the Progressive Era, nutritionists and other health experts played a prescriptive role, recommending to Americans what foods they *should* choose. The scientific approach of Progressivism to fields such as nutrition was reflected in the new field of "home economics," which began in the late nineteenth century and was well established by World War I.[16]

There was another essential aspect of federal guidelines and the legacy of W. O. Atwater early in the twentieth century: food choices were more about selecting the right nutrients than about the food itself. The advances in chemistry and medicine that allowed scientists to measure the components of food precisely and the relationship between nutritional deficiencies and disease fed into a paradigm that reduced food to a mere collection of nutrients. Such a paradigm came under attack in the new food and whole-food movements of the early twenty-first century, but it was long the dominant framework of dietary advice in the United States, as illustrated by the work of Atwater, Progressive Era scientists in the USDA, and the generations of nutritionists who followed them.

Several scholars have examined the dominance of this paradigm, especially Gyorgy Scrinis, who dubbed it "nutritionism."[17] The concept is central to twentieth- and twenty-first-century food discourse—and has been both widely embraced and challenged. Scrinis argued that Americans have long sought to rationalize diet in precise, scientific terms far removed from the more difficult-to-categorize natural world. Indeed, Scrinis critiqued what he referred to as a "myth of nutritional precision" based on a "hubris" among scientists who believed their understanding of "the relationships among nutrients, foods, and the body" was far greater than it actually was.[18] Scrinis argued that nutritionism began in the nineteenth century with advances in scientific understanding and could be roughly divided into three periods. The first was the longest-lasting, from the mid-nineteenth to the mid-twentieth centuries, when the greatest emphasis was placed on identifying "protective" nutrients and thereby preventing nutritional deficiencies.[19]

Hazel Stiebeling—along with her USDA colleagues—had a nutritionist outlook throughout her training and government career. She was educated as a chemist, but the direction of her work and reputation placed her firmly within the relatively young field of home economics.[20] Home economics as a discipline had begun in the nineteenth century, especially with the establishment of the land-grant colleges, starting in the 1860s; while these colleges developed extensive agricultural programs, they also offered courses for rural women that developed into home economics or "the rationalization and professionalization of housework."[21] Journalist Danielle Dreilinger described the ethos of the growing profession as one of "pragmatic empiricism."[22] The burgeoning field exemplified the rationalist approach of Progressive Era reformers and established authority for many of its leading women. Yet, feminist arguments in the early twentieth century also challenged the gendered aspect of the discipline that created a separate field for women outside of traditional disciplines. Undaunted, leaders such as Ellen Richards, author of *The Chemistry of Cooking and Cleaning*, argued that food science, bacteriology, nutrition, and sanitation were intertwined. For Richards and other home economists, though, the hallmark of the field was the application of theoretical, scientific knowledge to the practical management of daily living. By World War I, one author observed, home economics was entering its "golden age."[23]

The management of individual homes was central to the field of home economics, and its government practitioners in the USDA sought to teach women throughout the country these lessons, including how to manage the procurement, preservation, preparation, and serving of food. In an assertion of their serious purpose, home economists emphasized that managing food also had a social mission. Historian Megan Elias observed, "In the effort to gain public acceptance, home economists often presented nutrition as a matter of social as well as personal health, claiming that the physical well-being of the nation contributed to its ethical or moral well-being." Elias also observed that home economists demonstrated their own scientific legitimacy by eschewing the issue of food taste, preferring to concentrate on nutrition; they feared—especially as women—that if they talked about taste instead of chemistry, it would undercut the legitimacy of their field. Moreover, their broadest goal was to design a universally applicable diet for good health, regardless of individual tastes.[24]

The social role that USDA home economists could provide became increasingly obvious at the time when Stiebeling joined the USDA. The western drought of 1930 and then worsening depression in the following decade meant that many Americans struggled to get enough food or a healthful variety of food; many Americans were desperately short of money, and even many who remained in rural communities were unable to grow food due to drought or losing their land to creditors. When it recognized the impact of the Great Depression on the nation's ability to feed itself, the USDA, along with other federal agencies, sought to document the state of poor nutrition with a nationwide survey, "Consumer Purchases Study of 1935–36." The survey found that one-third of the nation's families had a poor diet that did not fulfill basic nutritional needs. The dismal results lent support to the movement to enrich flour and bread with iron and three B vitamins and to initiate school lunch programs and more nutrition education. As early as 1938, American diets showed some improvement due to the benefits of enrichment of breads and cereals, active nutrition campaigns, and increases in purchasing power from the depths of the Great Depression. Nevertheless, government surveys showed that many still lacked not only B vitamins, but also A and C, as well as calcium.[25] The problem that Franklin Roosevelt cited in his second inaugural that one third of the nation was "ill-nourished" presented an urgent strategic problem as the United States approached its next world war. Of the first million men called up for military service in 1940, 380,000 were rejected for health reasons, such as having poor teeth, being under- or overweight, or being run-down.[26]

Hazel Stiebeling was one of the government officials assigned to meet the food crisis. Soon after joining the USDA, Stiebeling's work focused on designing inexpensive diets for low-income Americans, particularly diets that would prevent pellagra, which was a serious problem in the American South in the first half of the twentieth century. In order to provide citizens with dietary options, Stiebeling designed four separate dietary plans for families of different sizes and income levels, "Diets at Four Levels of Nutritive Content and Cost."[27] The 1933 guide presented the issue of proper nutrition as an economic and scientific problem that could be solved with rational planning. The diets encouraged the consumption of more milk and fresh fruits and vegetables, as well as more balance overall; but they varied in details: a restricted diet for emergency use; an adequate diet at a *minimum* cost; an adequate diet at a *moderate* cost; and a liberal diet without concern for cost. The sixty-page guide was detailed with many graphs and charts outlining nutritional components and costs of meals, and it described twelve different food groups in menu planning. Stiebeling's work to design nutritious diets accessible to all income levels was driven by an idealistic desire to right the "injustices" visited upon lower-income Americans who suffered from poor nutrition for economic reasons.[28] Stiebeling's 1933 guide had a lasting influence on nutritional guidelines in the USDA and earned her personal recognition for years to come. For instance, a decade later, newspapers described Stiebeling as the food economist who "made nutrition history in her diet plans at four levels of cost."[29]

Stiebeling evaluated foods both on their price per pound and the nutrients each provided and revised diets accordingly. For example, the liberal diet contained more lean meats, fresh vegetables and fruit, fish, and eggs, whereas the budget diets had a higher percentage of calories from dried beans, potatoes, and grain. Stiebeling was concerned with alleviating how poverty could affect health through access to food; yet, she also remained confident that with practical, scientific knowledge and good budgeting anyone could get a healthy diet.[30] Stiebeling's work on food budgeting reflected her strong view that the "nutritive quality of food" was not determined by its market cost.[31] In designing these diets, Stiebeling helped to strengthen the assumption that decided what to eat was a question of choosing the nutritional components needed and then getting "the best return in food values."[32] The impact of her work could be seen in subsequent government food guidelines—and was also recognized when Stiebeling was at the height of her career—in both professional journals and the popular press. One 1944 article in the *Journal of Home Economics* and another in the *Philadelphia Inquirer* the same year observed that her studies of regional food consumption and diet plans at four cost levels had "made nutrition history."[33] Stiebeling was motivated by these dual scientific and social goals, as one journalist summarized her work: "One of Dr. Stiebeling's prime objectives is to give families of all income levels the advantages and enjoyments of the fruits of ingenuity, inventive genius and wizardry of the present era."[34]

The idea of serving nutritionally adequate, low-cost menus got a boost when the newly installed first lady, Eleanor Roosevelt, pledged in 1933 that she would serve lunches in the White House from a low-cost menu as a role model for others. Although Roosevelt told journalists she would not serve such menus when there were guests at the White House, her example was considered important, indicating that such meals would be good enough for middle class or even wealthy Americans. One example of such a White House lunch illustrated its frugality—and emphasis on practicality over taste: hot stuffed eggs with tomato sauce, mashed potatoes, prune pudding, brown bread, and coffee.[35]

Eleanor Roosevelt not only served low-cost, high-nutrition lunches at the White House, she also celebrated the work of home economists and their nutritional research. For example, she invited the founding codirector of the College of Human Ecology at Cornell University to the presidential inauguration in 1933, and in her first interview as first lady, she highlighted the nutrient-rich foods being created at Cornell. At the time, Cornell scientists launched "Milkorno" (and mixture of cornmeal and dried milk), as well as "Milkwheato" and "Milkoato," as inexpensive foods to boost nutrition. That same year, Roosevelt published *It's Up to the Women*, a sort of home economics primer that included recipes for inexpensive, nutritious meals. In the book, Roosevelt noted that just as Herbert Hoover had said that food would win World War I, so would women conquer the Depression as food providers.[36]

Diet planning by Stiebeling and other home economists influenced not only Eleanor Roosevelt, but also many others who were grappling with food shortages in various countries during the Great Depression. Stiebeling's work on diet plans was well respected internationally as well as in the United States. She represented the United States abroad at League of Nations nutrition conferences in Europe and South America in 1936, 1937, and 1939; meanwhile, the dietary framework from the USDA became the international standard in the 1930s. Following World War II and the creation of the United Nations as a successor to the league, Stiebeling continued as an advisor to the Food and Agriculture Organization (FAO) of the UN. In 1946, Stiebeling was appointed to the FAO's Standing Advisory Committee on Nutrition, attending its conference in Copenhagen that year.[37] In the United States, the framework created by Stiebeling in the 1930s continued to shape subsequent government food plans and recommendations and affected disparate policy areas. For example, federal poverty designations in the 1960s were determined in part using economy food plans first published in the 1930s.[38]

Beyond the menu plans, Stiebeling in the early 1930s also sought to establish more complete knowledge about the nutrition needed in general diets across society. In 1933, she published "dietary allowances" for various vitamins (A and C), minerals (calcium, phosphorus, iron), protein, and calories needed by the average adult. Although "dietary allowances" would soon be the standard phrase used to dispense nutritional recommendations in the United States and in other parts of the world, Stiebeling was the first to use the category and organizing principle. Stiebeling drew on her work in Sherman's Columbia laboratory to help craft the allowances. In 1939, Stiebeling and her colleague Esther Phipard expanded the allowances further to include thiamin and riboflavin, as well as recommendations for more age groups, and, importantly, indicated requirements could be increased as much as 50 percent above the minimum recommendation to allow for variability among people.[39]

It is interesting to consider the lasting significance of the "dietary allowances" first put forward by Stiebeling in 1933 and 1939, and what they tell us not only about her impact, but also about the field of human nutrition. These allowances became the basis of subsequent government programs and policies—such as what to feed soldiers, how to design rationing, what to put in school lunches—and popular ideas about a proper diet,including how to advertise food products and educate people about food. The allowances were quantifiable, based on laboratory studies from well-respected scientists, and thus not to be questioned by rational people. For example, a 1944 newspaper article written by Stiebeling observed that people accepted the guidelines due to "the eagerness with which our people have sought and applied to everyday living the offerings of science."[40] Yet, what does it say that there was, in essence, a 50 percent margin of error in the allowances? First, it implied a great lack of precision after all, despite the quantifiable, scientific language. Second, it raised doubts about whether food decisions should be made in such a manner. If dietary allowances might be off by 50 percent, how reliable were they?

Notwithstanding the philosophical and methodological questions about the nature of nutritional standards, the dietary allowances were an important tool for government policymakers faced with imminent war in 1940. In the year before Pearl Harbor, the Bureau of Home Economics at the USDA redirected its work to war preparation, for example working on new recipes addressing possible food rationing.[41] The urgency of the situation pushed official Washington into greater action, with Franklin Roosevelt observing: "food and nutrition would be at least as important as metals and munitions."[42] Paul McNutt, the administrator of the Federal Security Administration, was named coordinator of Health, Welfare, and Related Defense Activities in 1940 to address broad nutritional inadequacies. At the same time, the National Research Council of the National Academy of Sciences established the Food and Nutrition Board (FNB) in order to study biochemistry issues and food and, under the jurisdiction of the FNB, the Committee on Food Habits in order to understand consumption patterns and culture. The FNB was chaired by Russell Wilder of the Mayo Clinic and was commissioned to research how food questions impacted national defense and to make recommendations specifically about the nutrients required for good health.[43] Wilder, in turn, appointed a three-member subcommittee of home economists to develop those recommendations: Lydia Roberts from the University of Chicago, Helen Mitchell from the Kellogg Sanitarium in Battle Creek, Michigan, and Hazel Stiebeling. The three used the idea of "dietary allowances" from Stiebeling's earlier work to devise the "Recommended Daily Allowances for Specific Nutrients," which USDA publications dubbed "a yardstick for good nutrition" and which have stayed with us ever since as "RDAs."[44] Like the earlier dietary allowances, the RDAs incorporated the built-in cushion of outlining *optimal*, not just *adequate* nutrition. The FNB also set up a three-day White House conference on nutrition as a defense issue.[45]

The USDA translated these RDAs into simple advice about food groups and variety. The Bureau of Home Economics of the USDA then published a guide in 1941, "Eat the Right Food to Help Keep You Fit," which categorized foods into nine different groups.[46] The pamphlet listed examples of foods in each category, and included numbers of recommended servings, as well as ways to eat nutritious food for less money, such as "In economical diets use dried beans or peas as the main dish several times a week." In addition to explaining the importance of good nutrition for overall health, the guide encouraged people to follow its precepts—and to urge others to do so as well—in order "to further national defense."[47] Additional wartime guides gave more particular advice, such as a pamphlet explaining the best way to eat out and still get nutritious food, a meal planner with mix-and-match dishes, and a pamphlet showing how to adapt menus and buy economically for only two people.[48]

By 1943, the USDA used RDAs in a new instructional manual for the public, entitled the "National Wartime Food Guide." The 1943 guide streamlined the 1933 diet plans of Stiebeling and the 1941 guide: instead of twelve or nine food groups, the 1943 plan used seven, and, instead of laying out distinct plans for different economic groups, the 1943 plan laid out one set of nutritional recommendations.[49] The "Basic Seven" became the nutritional watchword during the war and after, with easy-to-follow, color-coded groupings and brief explanations of how much to eat from each group. The impact of these guidelines was soon significant for civilians as well as the military; as one author summarized: "Both the RDAs and the food groups immediately became gospel."[50] Stiebeling and Mary Barber, one of her USDA colleagues, used the RDAs and food groups to design diets for US soldiers, prisoners of war abroad, and Japanese Americans in internment camps.[51] Along with emphasizing the importance of proper nutrition, the government pamphlets and other materials asserted that eating right was everyone's patriotic duty to keep the nation "vital": the "U.S. Needs Us Strong."[52] The wartime food guide was visualized in pamphlets and posters as a circle with seven different wedges, one for each food group, a listing and pictures of sample foods within the group, and the admonition to eat some food from each group every day. In the middle of the circle was a nuclear family holding hands. The groups specified as the "Basic Seven" (also written as the "Basic 7") were the following: green and yellow vegetables; oranges, tomatoes, grapefruit; potatoes and other vegetables and fruits; milk and milk products; meat, poultry, fish, or eggs; bread, flour, and cereals; and butter and fortified margarine.[53] The visual chart also included the suggestion "In addition to the Basic 7 . . . eat any other foods you want." The Basic Seven recommendations became widely known through press coverage as well as government publications.[54]

Interestingly, these food guides, were widely circulated during the war with the intent to keep the US population "strong." Although some foodstuffs at the time were rationed (such as meat, butter, and sugar), there was no mention of such policies, and the guides seemed to assume sufficient supplies for all.[55] Separate from any questions of nutritional planning, food rationing in wartime served another purpose. Adhering to the system was a way in which citizens, especially women, could show their patriotism and communalism.[56] Nevertheless, in the case of the United States during World War II, food policies did not seem to impose hardships. Historian Amy Bentley observed that although rationing was ubiquitous, according to wartime surveys, it did not seem to adversely affect meals or food consumption. For example, in 1943, three-quarters of respondents said that the size of their meals was the same as before rationing, and a year later 90 percent of women reported that they could get all of the meat that they needed. Along with such responses, there was evidence that the diets of many Americans during the war actually *improved* in quality and quantity.[57]

In addition, there were no references in these food guides to another government program: Victory Gardens. The success of the Victory Garden campaign was remarkable, reflecting cooperation among the Department of Agriculture, the Office of War Information, the Office of Civil Defense, and the (private) National Victory Garden Institute. In 1943, the peak year of such gardens, twenty million households were growing food, amounting to more than 40 percent of all the vegetables eaten in the United States, as well as 4.1 billion jars of canned food produced. Historian Lizzie Collingham observed that the success of the campaign also led to an increased consumption of vegetables for many Americans. The government agencies charged with overseeing the program were motivated not only by the pounds of food that might be produced, but also by the opportunity to boost civilian morale by encouraging a patriotic and enjoyable recreational activity.[58] Yet, in terms of dietary advice, the widespread availability of extremely fresh produce appeared to be irrelevant to the government's recommendations about what to eat. Vegetables, of course, were included in the USDA food guidelines, but there was little effort to link—or revise—dietary recommendations based upon the increased access to *fresh* vegetables.

The links between patriotism, security, and food consumption illustrated in the rationing program and Victory Gardens continued after the war. Food guides and propaganda admonished, "Food is Needed to Feed the Hungry—Don't Waste It."[59] The issue of waste became particularly urgent due to the food crisis in Europe in 1946 and 1947—as well as the solidifying Cold War that might bring political instability to Europe. Officials in Washington watched with worry the continuing food shortages into 1947, with the worst cases being in Germany, Austria, Italy, and Romania.[60] To gain public support for limits on food consumption even after the guns of World War II had stopped, the president formed a Citizens Food Committee Program to run a campaign to "Save Wheat, Save Meat, Save the Peace." The campaign made appeals on the basis of morality (Europeans were starving, and Americans should not be selfish) and Cold War dangers (starvation in Europe was fertile ground for political unrest and communist advances).[61] President Harry Truman tried to rally citizens to the cause with a speech in February 1946, calling for a reduction of grain used to feed livestock and a decrease of wheat and fat consumption in the United States, so that more could be shipped abroad. Nevertheless, despite the president's entreaties, and the establishment of a Famine Emergency Committee headed by Herbert Hoover, there was no mandatory rationing put in place after the war (except for sugar, which was still under wartime restrictions), so Americans did not decrease their consumption, and the aid targets for Europe were not met.[62]

The work of Stiebeling and other USDA nutritionists was used in this foreign policy crisis to encourage frugality in menu planning and eating. Stiebeling's Bureau of Nutrition and Home Economics published a new forty-eight-page recipe booklet, "Money-Saving Main Dishes" in 1948. The recipes contained the right amount of protein and took account of the rising cost of food and an anticipated meat shortage in the subsequent months.[63] Publicity for the recipe book, as well as other nutritional recommendations, was found in the press; the *New York Times* even offered to send the government booklet and other government handouts free to all who requested them.[64]

The possibility of meat shortages at home and the very real danger of food shortages in Europe reflected the postwar readjustments taking place in many countries. But these shortages were specific and situational. Moreover, they took place against an agricultural situation in the United States that told a very different story. American agriculture and food production in the mid-twentieth century was one of unmatched abundance. This was true even in the depths of the Great Depression, when many Americans could not afford sufficient food despite its availability, and in the 1940s crises of rebuilding peacetime economies. But despite particular crises, there was never a doubt that the American agricultural sector was capable of producing abundant, affordable food sufficient for all its citizens and beyond. Abundance, then, was the most important foundation upon which nutritional guidelines were built in the postwar years; if food abundance was assumed in the largest, wealthiest country on earth, the key issue that remained was to teach people what to eat amid a cornucopia of choices.

One attempt to educate Americans was the first set of guidelines issued after the war. The wartime food guide, though, proved to be durable and was reissued with very slight changes in 1946 as "The Basic Seven."[65] The groups and graphic were unchanged, though references to the country needing people to be "strong" were eliminated, and people were told to "eat this way every day." Added to the poster were serving amounts for each category, some more specific than others. For example, people were to have one or more servings of green and yellow vegetables, one to two servings from the meat category (which now included dried peas and beans), and bread and cereals (which were now advised to be whole grain or enriched) simply "every day." Teaching the population about nutrition and "The Basic Seven" was an ongoing mission. One USDA survey from 1947 found that, while 54 percent of women respondents were familiar with the Basic Seven chart, another 46 percent were not; not surprisingly, the data collected by the USDA showed that those with knowledge of the Basic Seven understood nutrition better than did those without knowledge of the concept.[66] Press stories helped to publicize the reissued government nutritional recommendations. For instance, *Seventeen* magazine reminded its readers that they were probably already familiar with "the famous 'basic seven,'" and, although the war was now over, it was still important for everyone to follow nutritional guidelines daily; the magazine encouraged readers to write to the USDA for their own free wall chart to post in the kitchen.[67]

It's worth noting that the postwar Basic Seven reflected the assumption among many policymakers in Washington that the government had a responsibility to teach Americans what to eat. Beyond the emergencies of the Great Depression, World War II, and European food crises, there was little argument about the need for nutritional guidelines. To bolster such a case, the USDA conducted national surveys about household food consumption, including in 1948–49, 1955, 1965–66, 1977–78.[68] Government nutritionists mined such surveys for information about different regions as well as which specific nutrients were missing from diets. For example, in one 1950 report from Hazel Stiebeling to the secretary of agriculture on diet in urban areas, Stiebeling observed that calorie intake was sufficient, but that people were still in need of making sure they ate enough of particular nutrients, such as calcium. She also reported that diets overall were improving since the disparities in food consumption from low- to high-income groups were shrinking.[69] Stiebeling and her colleagues studied all sorts of foods and their place in the American diet. In another report from 1954, Stiebeling wrote to the secretary's office about the importance of milk, citing what she considered to be the most important textbook on the subject of food and health.[70] USDA nutritionists also translated their research into sample diets for people of different ages and activity levels.[71] One justification among USDA policymakers for continued monitoring of food consumption was to make sure that Americans were physically fit, especially in comparison with people in other countries.[72] Officials such as Assistant Secretary E. L. Peterson concluded that overall the American diet was good and nutritive in the late 1950s, but "we still have a long way to go to bring all family diets up to the recommended nutritional goals."[73]

The framework of the Basic Seven remained—choosing foods within various groups to provide daily allowances and nutritional adequacy—but policymakers in the USDA decided to simplify their advice further in the late 1950s. Apparently, a set of seven food groups was too complicated, so, following a study by Louise Page and Esther Phipard entitled "Essentials of the Adequate Diet" in 1956, the Basic Seven became the Basic Four, comprising the milk, meat, fruits and vegetables, and bread and cereal groups.[74] The "Food for Fitness, Daily Food Guide" was visualized in pamphlets and posters as four brightly colored blocks, with sample foods and minimum servings listed. Importantly, the guide was assumed to be a "foundation," which would be supplemented with other items not listed, such as butter, oil, sugar, and refined grains. Readers were told at the end of the pamphlet that they should add "other foods as needed to complete meals and provide additional food energy and other food values."[75] The Basic Four would prove even more durable than its predecessor, remaining as USDA nutritional advice until the late 1970s. And, just as the Basic Seven guideline was publicized through press stories, so too was the Basic Four.[76]

While the legacy of Hazel Stiebeling's nutritional policies lasted into the 1970s and beyond, she also had an enduring impact on how many Americans viewed advice about diet and who gave it. Stiebeling may have been outnumbered by male colleagues in the USDA at large, but in the early twentieth century, "home economics" within the department was dominated by women, reinforced by the conflation of women and home management. Into the mid-twentieth century, press stories continued to celebrate the home economists of the USDA, especially the women who were "the first choice for the jobs" in the field.[77] The gendering of home economics and nutritional advice was illustrated by the press stories about Stiebeling, starting with the frequent title bestowed on her of home economist, not chemist. For example, one article, instead of straightforwardly listing her PhD credential merely noted that she studied food chemistry in college.[78] Another journalist in 1961 dubbed her "Chief Homemaker of the Nation."[79] Of course, it was not just journalists who treated Stiebeling and her colleagues differently from men, but also people in the government. For example, in November 1946, a *Washington Post* headline read: "Mrs. Truman Entertains at White House Luncheon." The article included the names of guests at this all-female event, with most of them identified only by their husbands' names. Hazel Stiebeling, director of a USDA bureau, was among the guests.[80]

It is important to note that Stiebeling's unequal treatment was not unique among women scientists or home economists. Although home economics might have entered a "golden age" by World War I, it was short lived. By World War II, the USDA's Bureau of Home Economics was renamed the Bureau of Nutrition and Home Economics, highlighting its health mission. Meanwhile, Bureau of Home Economics founding director Louise Stanley was transferred to the Agricultural Research Service to work in international food research. Author Danielle Dreilinger observed that this leader in the field was thus pushed "into the shadows." Although Stanley's transfer led to the elevation of Stiebeling as the bureau's director, its role was soon reduced with a 25 percent budget cut in 1947. Further budget cuts came in the mid-1950s, as the work of the bureau narrowed in response to criticisms that the USDA should not be working in such areas as household management, textiles, and parenting. The bureaucratic reordering coincided with the retirement of many early pioneers in the field, including Stanley and Stiebeling. Shortly before Stiebeling left the USDA in 1963, the bureau had been reorganized as an institute that studied nutrition and was housed within the Agricultural Research Service.[81]

Apart from the bureaucratic pressures on home economics in Washington and long before her retirement, Stiebeling garnered attention in the press. Yet, despite her accomplishments, press stories about Stiebeling used gendered language to praise her and made it clear that she was different from male scientists. One of the frequent descriptions of Stiebeling was that she was "quiet, unassuming" or "a quiet mannered, soft spoken woman" who nevertheless spoke with "dignity" and "sureness which comes from knowing a subject well."[82] Similar difficulties of coming to terms with authoritative female scientists arose a few years later in press descriptions of pioneering environmentalist Rachel Carson, who was also referred to as quiet and unassuming.[83] As with Carson, Stiebeling's unmarried status sometimes came up in articles about her; for example, one 1946 article about her position with the FAO observed: "She is too busy to keep house, but she is fond of the domestic arts and likes to prepare an occasional meal in her apartment."[84] Her physical qualities were also deemed relevant in articles about her work; she was a "tall, slender woman with low voice and smiling brown eyes," an "attractive and charming woman," or "a pleasant-looking gray-haired woman."[85] When Stiebeling won the President's Award for Distinguished Federal Civilian Service, one columnist observed that she was subject to a double standard and almost did not win the award:

> The only reason this piece is being written is that Hazel Stiebeling's name was almost an afterthought in the meager reports of the awards for distinguished service.
>
> She has been working for your federal government since 1930. She is just another one of the tired middle-aged women you see on a bus in Washington when day is done.
>
> But millions of school children who enjoy school lunches today can thank Hazel Stiebeling for her contribution to the program.
>
> St. Stiebeling's research and interest in diet deficiencies in the United States have led to developments not only of school lunch programs, but to increased consumption of milk, fresh fruit and green vegetables.[86]

Several years earlier, in a profile of Stiebeling, another writer quoted veteran (male) reporters who praised her: "Hazel Stiebeling is a swell person. We like her. That is the ultimate expression of masculine approval. It means that Dr. Stiebeling knows her subject, that she is no empty phrase maker, no seeker after the spot-light. It means that she is clear in her thinking, quiet but positive and tenacious in expressing her opinion."[87]

The gendered assumptions in descriptions of Stiebeling and her work reflected broader ideas about all women, thought of more as nurturers who cooked and kept house, not as academics or accomplished scientists. For example, even in a 1943 book by Edna Yost, *American Women of Science*, which praised Stiebeling's scientific work, Yost wrote that "Every woman's first job is in her own home"—an observation that apparently also applied to Stiebeling, whose "brilliance in laboratory work" did not mean that she was "cold or sterile." Readers could rest assured that she had nevertheless had "the kind of human contacts needed for her full development."[88] Stiebeling, at least in her comments in the press, seemed to agree that women played a special role in shopping and preparing food for their families. In an article that she wrote in 1937, "What Price Adequate Diets," Stiebeling noted that "Every woman has a deep interest in the cost of feeding a family."[89] One example of this widely held assumption was a popular radio show, entitled *Aunt Jenny's Real Life Stories,* which was created to advertise the virtues of "Spry" shortening. The show ran from 1937 to 1956, highlighting the folk wisdom of Aunt Jenny whose "every day" recipes Spry published as a separate booklet.[90]

The press stories that dubbed Stiebeling "Chief Homemaker" of the nation highlighted not only the special role that women in general played in feeding their families and children, but also the special role that Stiebeling played in feeding all American children through the school lunch program. As one of the research nutritionists at the USDA, Stiebeling helped to shape the program with her work.[91] The school lunch program revealed important assumptions about the government's role in what citizens ate, how they chose food, and the particular role that women played in feeding the nation.

School lunches had been offered unevenly in various places during the Depression and World War II. Even before the economic crisis of the Depression and the mobilization for World War II, there had been more emphasis on the importance of a nutritious lunch, because large, heavy breakfasts were less common, and lunches more often eaten away from home with twentieth-century urbanization. Thus, there was much support for giving school lunches a steady funding stream by 1946, when the National School Lunch Program was established.[92] From the start, the program was based on competing political interests of providing good nutrition to children *and* providing a market for surplus agricultural commodities. The dual nature of the law was seen in comments from the House Agricultural Committee supporting its passage, noting that it was aimed at both improved health and at "assuring a substantial market" for agriculture. Harry Truman similarly supported this dual mission; when he signed the bill into law, he explicitly said that it was good for the nation's children and farmers.[93] Farm income did indeed go up with the passage of the school lunch program.[94] Historian Susan Levine concluded that between these dueling interests represented by nutritionists and home economists, such as Hazel Stiebeling, on the one hand, and government economists and the agricultural industry on the other, the latter won out. She wrote, "The program was, in its goals, structure, and administration, more a subsidy for agriculture than a nutrition program for children." Historian A. R. Ruis similarly concluded that although the lunch program was "a political triumph," it was "a public health failure."[95]

While great benefits did accrue to the agricultural industry, many children got greater access to healthy food. Such results were illustrated by the example of milk. Beginning in the 1920s, transformations in the dairy industry designed to increase efficiency and cut down on waste of milk components and to meet demands of war efforts in the 1940s had led to increased availability of skim milk after the war—just as dieticians were working to improve nutrition. Thus, USDA cooperative extension agents began to encourage the use of nonfat dried milk in various rural areas. With the passage of the school lunch program in 1946, nonfat skim milk was incorporated into school lunches in isolated areas. Within a couple of years, the USDA was buying large amounts of the dried milk solids from the dairy industry to be used in school lunches—9.2 million pounds in 1949 alone. Dried milk solids would remain an important part of poverty and nutrition programs in subsequent decades.[96] Clearly, USDA purchases of dried milk helped dairy farmers and the industry, but they also helped increase the protein and calcium intake of children in various regions of the country. At the same time, USDA officials continued to see fluid whole milk as important to school lunches, for commercial reasons as well as nutritional ones. For example, in mid-1954, Undersecretary of Agriculture True Morse contacted dairy industry representatives to come to a meeting with program administrators in order to increase milk consumption at schools. Such commercial concerns continued regarding other foodstuffs. For example, in 1964, the secretary of agriculture wrote a confidential memo to the president, proposing that one way to boost sagging beef prices was to increase purchases of the meat for the school lunch program.[97]

Aside from including milk, school lunches followed nutritionist precepts and were designed to be "balanced meals," based on the scientific research taking place at the USDA over many years. One USDA publication assessing the early years of the program highlighted this mission, calling it "one of the world's most extensive programs of applied nutrition" in order to "buil(d) an alert and healthy citizenry."[98] In particular, the lunches drew on the work of Stiebeling and her fellow nutritionists, incorporating the RDA as a measurement and the Basic Seven food groups established during the war. The meals were planned around the seven groups of green and yellow vegetables; oranges, tomatoes, and grapefruits; potatoes; milk and milk products; meat, poultry, fish, eggs, and dried peas or beans; bread, flour, and cereals; butter and margarine. The structure of school lunches was then further refined by the use of RDAs in deciding how much of each group children needed. As measured by the food groups and the RDAs, school lunches were classified as "Type A," which supplied one-third to one-half of a child's RDA and had at least one cup of milk, "Type B," which supplied one-quarter to one-third of the RDA and included milk, and "Type C," which was a glass of milk.[99] Government subsidies to states were then based on what type of lunch was served. The federal reimbursement rate was tied not only to the nutrition rating of the meal (with payments for Type A being highest), but also to the amount of USDA surplus commodities that were used. Thus, the funding model exerted heavy pressure for schools to serve meals that conformed to the Type A model; the success of this pressure was reflected, for example, in the USDA report that, by 1952, two of every three meals served in schools were Type A.[100] Thus, the RDA created by Stiebeling and USDA nutritionists during World War II determined which school lunches would qualify for government subsidies.

Along with the funding model, there was an extensive administrative structure within the USDA to teach schools how to prepare and serve proper meals as recommended by its nutritionists. In addition to pamphlets summarizing the overall program structure and the definition of a Type A meal, the USDA distributed sets of recipe cards and booklets to schools for foods in all categories.[101] In addition to distributing recipes to schools, Stiebeling and her colleagues remained concerned about the use of the recipes in menus, e.g., that thick, filling soups were preferable most of the time since thin soups filled up children, but provided scant calories.[102]

Within the rigid classifications of school lunches and the rules of proper nutrition, the meals were also designed with a cultural purpose in mind. During the war, before the passage of the 1946 act, a Committee on Food Habits, chaired by anthropologist Margaret Mead, advised how to create menus for "national unity." Mead argued that it was important not to offend any group of children, so spices and various other specific foods should not be included. In her recommendations to please as many as possible, the only seasoning allowed was salt; thus, bland foods carried the day. Historian Lizzie Collingham said of the result: "School lunches acted as a powerful force for homogenizing the American diet, subtly creating preferences for innocuous meals which all Americans could share."[103]

By the 1950s, the school lunch program was well entrenched, and the menus continued to be designed around USDA nutritional guidelines. And yet, the dual mission of the program—to feed children and provide a market for agricultural commodities—continued to affect the food served, especially as the percentage of school lunches that came from surplus commodities continued to rise (it was 16 percent in 1949; 26 percent in 1957).[104] Thus, menus were impacted by the surplus commodities available. Menu planning was sometimes difficult; for example, what might a school dietician do with an oversupply of olives?[105]

Even as schools had to deal with the vagaries of which surplus ingredients were available, the program continued to grow, feeding about fifteen million children within a decade and a half of its establishment.[106] As it grew, the lunch program was increasingly tied to the agricultural, or "food service," industry, as opposed to the earlier dominance of the mostly female nutritionists and home economists. By the 1960s, there was a shift in the program and how food was prepared and served. Increasingly, central kitchens sent prepackaged meals to schools instead of having local cooks prepare meals completely in-house.

By the 1960s, there was another change in the lunch program. Twenty years after its establishment, the importance of feeding poor children, rather than supporting farmers rose with the passage of the 1966 Child Nutrition Act, which, for the first time, appropriated money for free meals directly to children in need. Susan Levine argued that this was a major turning point in the main purpose of the school lunch program. Soon after, the school lunch program ballooned in size, enriching companies such as Sysco—its school food service business went from $155 million in the 1970s to more than $23 billion in the 1990s. It became the government's second biggest food program behind food stamps.[107] Participation of children peaked and then fell off after the early 1980s, rising again with the integration of brand name fast foods into cafeterias. Marion Nestle and others have discussed the dire nutritional and health consequences of this shift in more recent years (and the accompanying rise of soda sales in schools), as well as the increased power of the food industry over public schools.[108] This book will return to the implications of this trend in subsequent chapters.

No matter the program's size, the composition of meals, or the bureaucratic administration, school lunches were popular with most Americans. As Assistant Secretary of Agriculture George Mehren observed in a 1963 speech, "There are few programs as widely accepted as this one."[109] One window into this support can be found in the program materials and publicity used in the 1950s and 1960s, when support for the school lunch program was growing and came to be seen as a bedrock government responsibility through the twentieth century. When the National School Lunch Act was passed in 1946, on the eve of the Cold War, one of the justifications for the program was national security. This was a natural continuation of many of the connections made during World War II about diet, nutrition, and the war effort. In the 1946 law, the links were explicit in its statement of purpose: "As a measure of national security, to safe-guard the health and well-being of the Nation's children, and to encourage the domestic consumption of nutritious agricultural commodities and other food."[110] In this way, what one ate—or rather what one fed her children—was a demonstration of patriotism.

A decade later, the tenth anniversary of the program, was a cause for celebration, and there were numerous publicity events to do just that. President Dwight Eisenhower, the secretary of agriculture, and various USDA officials were photographed with children recognizing the occasion. The staged events were covered in various newspapers and television reports.[111] Positive publicity was also in evidence six years later with the designation of an annual National School Lunch Week. Such celebratory attitudes reflected the steady growth of the program in its first decades. For example, the number of participating children doubled from seven million in 1947 to fourteen million at the start of the 1960s; within the first five years of the national program, 30 percent of school-age children participated.[112] In the mid-1960s, Lyndon Johnson celebrated the ongoing school lunch program as a demonstration of American agricultural success: "Our Nation produces food in an abundance greater than any in history—an abundance more than sufficient to provide every American today with a tasty, nutritious, and healthful diet."[113] Johnson emphasized that the benefits of school lunches were clear: "Educators from coast to coast now recognize that good nutrition is as essential to the education of our children as good textbooks." He argued that "dullness and apathy once believed the product of poor inheritance are just as often the product of poor nutrition—and fade away before the onslaught of a few good meals."[114]

Hazel Stiebeling had made similar observations about the importance of the program soon after it began. She also asserted that it had already improved nutrition more broadly. She identified the link between school lunches and diets at home within three years of the program's start. She believed that improved diet trends—including the consumption of more vegetables, fruits, eggs, and milk—was due in part to families learning the lessons of their children's lunchroom. She also linked the lunch program to improved physical, mental, and emotional growth of children. News stories in the following decade continued to echo these judgments.[115]

Along with the pronouncements of Stiebeling and Johnson, the USDA continued its extensive publicity for the school lunch program. In response to various press releases and initiatives, newspapers and magazines published numerous stories celebrating the program, especially around the time of the annual School Lunch Week.[116] In addition to coverage in the mainstream press, stories on the program were also found in the trade press and in supporting materials from the food industry.[117] The USDA emphasized to representatives of the food industry that the program was in their long-term as well as short-term interest. For example, one 1966 pamphlet from the Consumer Marketing

Service of the USDA argued that the school lunch program was "molding both the health and the food markets of the future. . . . The school lunch program has become a huge market for farm products—to the benefit of farmers and the food industry. And it has become the largest institutional feeding service of its kind in the world to the benefit of our whole national economy."[118]

It's not surprising that these trade organizations supported the school lunch program, since their members benefited economically from it. Another argument by the USDA and supporters of the program was that school lunches were economical, modern, and superior to what children might bring from home. For example, a USDA newsletter in 1965 pointed out that the food in a Type A lunch cost fifty cents to prepare, but that the average amount children paid was twenty-seven cents per meal, and that one-tenth of the meals at that time were free or reduced price. That same year, the *Atlanta Constitution* asked, "Where else can you get a well-prepared and balanced lunch for less than half a dollar?"[119] USDA materials often emphasized that meals were balanced, hot, and hearty, made with foods of high quality that were inspected "beyond what the housewife does."[120] USDA ambitions for the school lunch program even ventured into the culture of food. One publication from the mid-1960s, for example, asserted that school lunches taught children how "to eat not only wisely and well but also with pleasure." The pamphlet, like some earlier ones, argued that school lunches would expose children to foods that they might not get at home, thus broadening their experiences, as well as teaching them "social graces."[121]

It is hard to fault the expansion of the school lunch program, which fed more hungry children by the late twentieth century. But the nutritionist design that increasingly relied on prepackaged meals and a food service industry rather than cooks preparing fresh meals in schools, showed that, while the size of the program had grown, some of its original framework and assumptions had not changed. The goal was to provide nutrients to children efficiently within an industrial system, not to consider taste, the nature of food, and its connection to the earth.

It's worth remembering that the nutritionist framework that shaped the school lunch program reflected, in part, anxiety that children might not be eating the "right" foods, even though they lived in a land of plenty. One columnist, for example, observed in 1959 that "a well fed child is not always well nourished."[122] Some articles identified dire consequences, including one that asked, "In the world's richest nation, why must four children out of every five be crippled by partial starvation?" The article included anecdotes from well-off families in which teenagers had suffered severe health consequences, including one death. Although the same *Ladies Home Journal* article allowed that "mothers aren't entirely to blame" for such tragedies, it was clear that they had a special responsibility for their children's diet. Meanwhile, a different article in *Better Homes and Gardens* asked, "Should You Be Ashamed of Your Youngster's Diet?" Lest there be any doubt about who the "you" was, the article continued: "everything dished out by Mother, overseer of the family eating department, is applied nutrition, and you don't need to simmer in the sciences to improve the application."[123] So, while women reading these magazines could rely on school lunches and USDA guidelines to model proper nutrition, it remained their responsibility to execute such formulas within the home.

Several conclusions can be drawn from these two federal efforts—nutritional guidelines and the school lunch program—to shape the foods that Americans ate. Both reflected scientific knowledge about health, viewing food more as a collection of nutrients than as a repository of culture and social values. Both were also predicated on a modern agricultural system designed to maximize output of particular massed-produced and processed foods. The surpluses that resulted from this system were essential to launch the school lunch program as well as provide the economic justification needed to convince skeptics that the government should be in the business of feeding children.

The usefulness of commodity surpluses for supplying the school lunch program points to one other assumption that underlay the program—as well as its nutritional guidelines—and why the connection between food and the environment appeared irrelevant. There was never any question that modern, industrial agriculture was capable of producing all the food that Americans needed. The nutritional guidelines were to help Americans *choose* what foods to eat among their many options. The Type A lunches were to provide children with the optimal meals, beyond necessity. Ironically, Hazel Stiebeling had begun her career at the USDA crafting practical menus according to what people could afford during the Depression; yet, even if many people were cash poor, one of the serious economic problems leading to the economic crisis had been an overproduction of commodities, which made their prices crash. By the end of her USDA career in 1963, Stiebeling was still concerned with the frugal use of food, even as she acknowledged that most Americans were not. She told a journalist: "Wasted food isn't a critical problem now, because we have such an abundance of food. But that might not always be the case."[124]

More than most policymakers, the secretary of agriculture during the Kennedy and Johnson administrations, Orville Freeman, celebrated the widespread agricultural abundance brought by farmers, but seemingly taken for granted by average Americans: "The efficiency and hard work of the American farmers have brought us an abundance that is unprecedented and, to a large extent, unappreciated."[125] Freeman clarified why this might have been the case: "Most Americans take the food abundance we enjoy pretty much for granted. That's understandable. Food, like the air we breathe and the water we drink, is easily available to most Americans."[126] While many Americans took the easy availability of food for granted, Freeman observed that they also did not realize how little they spent on it. In a speech to a June Dairy Month Luncheon on May 20, 1963, he said: "We spend less for this food abundance than any people anywhere . . . anytime . . . in history." In 1953, he explained that Americans spent 23 percent of their income on food, and by 1963 that number had gone down to 19 percent. Meanwhile, in other countries, people might spend anywhere from 30 to 80 percent of their incomes on food. US food was cheap, Freeman concluded, because "the farmer has been, and is, subsidizing the consumer."[127]

Despite the many benefits of abundance, Freeman and others at the USDA were aware that there were downsides to abundance. One was the problem—recognized during the Depression and worsening after World War II—of how to use agricultural surpluses while still ensuring that farmers had a living wage. Assistant Secretary of Agriculture George Mehren observed in a 1963 speech titled "The Challenge of Abundance" that "we must see to it that this abundance is marketed as efficiently and economically as possible," such as in the school lunch program.[128] Another response to this challenge were foreign aid programs over many decades, such as Food for Peace.[129]

George Mehren and Orville Freedman may have been focused on the benefits and challenges of agricultural abundance, but this was not the main concern for Hazel Stiebeling. She took abundance for granted, focusing instead on improving the diets of ordinary citizens through government programs such as school lunches and nutritional guidelines. Importantly, the government programs Stiebeling and her USDA colleagues created were based on the science of food, rather than on its politics and aesthetics, illustrating what has been discussed above as a "nutritionist" approach to food. Not everyone shared this outlook. Poppy Cannon offered different advice, encouraging middle-class women to focus more on the appearance of meals rather than on the nutrients they contained.

2

Poppy Cannon and the Wonders of Processed Food

Poppy Cannon's approach to cuisine was vastly different than that of the pragmatic nutritionist Hazel Stiebeling. While Stiebeling measured the chemical components of foods and designed menus for children and adults that would provide the best nutrition families could afford, Poppy Cannon hardly mentioned nutrition in her best-selling cookbooks. Instead, Cannon encouraged her readers to think more about the impression a meal made: "A chef does not serve a dish, he *presents* it and his presentation is every bit as important as his preparation. Much of the difference between just cooking and epicurean cooking is the *difference in the way the food is served.*"[1] Indeed, beginning with her first book, *The Can Opener Cookbook,* Cannon made it clear that the presentation was *more* important than the preparation—and certainly more than the nutritional content or taste of a meal.

Cannon did not have the political power or scientific qualifications of Hazel Stiebeling. She was not one of the architects of the twentieth-century nutritionist framework that had a lasting influence on US government food programs that shaped available food and how Americans viewed their food choices. Yet, she had a different, but still important, impact on what people ate. More than telling people what they *should* eat, Cannon aimed to shape what food people *desired.* For Cannon, finding pleasure in food was more important than checking off nutrient requirements. Cannon's food advice had a different focus than did Stiebeling's, but both operated in a postwar America in which food abundance and industrial production was assumed, and food was a consumer item to be bought in a modern supermarket. In addition, both assumed that women had a unique role in deciding what people ate. And, in particular, Cannon offered advice about what middle-class white women should cook and serve to their families. Although the recipes in the following pages might elicit ridicule from modern readers, they nevertheless helped to normalize the use of processed ingredients in American cooking, which continues to the present day.

Cannon's influence was felt from different directions. She gained a wide readership through her cookbooks—most famously with her first, *The Can-Opener Cookbook*. She was also a food editor and freelance writer for a number of publications, including *Mademoiselle, House Beautiful, Town and Country, Cosmopolitan,* and *Ladies Home Journal* (the last enjoying the largest circulation of women's magazines in the mid-twentieth century).[2] She also reached audiences through local television and radio programs on food and related topics. Along with her background in journalism, Cannon worked in advertising and marketing, consulting for several food companies and other corporations. As this chapter illustrates, the diverse strands of Cannon's career came together in her celebration of the industrial food industry for which she had formerly worked on advertising campaigns. Finally, Cannon enjoyed a certain amount of fame—or notoriety among some—as the second wife of Walter White, leader of the National Association for the Advancement of Colored People (NAACP), at a time when interracial marriage was rare.

Poppy Cannon's professional background revealed much about her views of food and the messages she conveyed. The 1975 *New York Times* obituary for Cannon began with the ambiguous identity that she was "a widely known authority on food."[3] From the obituary, though, and by surveying Cannon's work, it quickly became clear that she was foremost a writer and advertising professional who gained "authority" because she chose to write about food, not because she had any particular background as a food scientist or chef. Her authority, then, and reputation rested on her ability to communicate to a wide audience and to give advice about food culture, among other topics.

Cannon (born Lillian Gruskin) had been writing since she was a young girl in Pennsylvania, and continued to do so as an undergraduate at Vassar and then in graduate school at Columbia in journalism and short story writing.[4] In Cannon's early career, she began work as a freelance writer for various newspapers and magazines on different topics; this work would continue throughout her life, even as she took on other professional positions. Beginning in 1934, she worked in the consumer service department of General Foods. From this perch in an industrial food corporation, she moved into advertising with Maxon Inc.

and later Peter Hilton Co. She worked on various types of accounts, some related to food, some not. Cannon began a long-standing relationship with H. J. Heinz Co. (she continued as a consultant at Heinz when she was no longer an account executive), but she also worked on accounts as diverse as Gillette, Elizabeth Arden, Hitz Hotels, the government of Haiti, Burton's Frostings, Colonial Trust Co., and Seabrook Farms Quick-Frozen Foods. Thus, until about 1950, Cannon was an advertising and marketing executive, *not* a journalist or cookbook author.

Among her varied clientele, it is worth noting that Cannon worked on advertising the products of several industrial food companies—the kind of processed foods that would later become integral to her cookbook recipes. She celebrated her relationship to food products, writing in her résumé from the early 1950s that she had been the first to name particular brands in her food columns on easy-to-fix meals beginning in 1938. Her approach to food marketing would find its way into her cookbooks in other ways as well. Cannon boasted in the résumé that her ads for foods at Maxon Inc. went in new directions, writing that she "was one of the first to use the romantic, nostalgic, hunger-rousing approach to food copy as contrasted with the nutritional theme formerly in vogue among advertisers." Even in her first job at General Foods, she recounted that she worked in different ways to bring "a gourmet point of view to General Foods promotion."[5]

Two other observations from Cannon's résumé bear noting. First, even in this document sketching out her professional accomplishments in journalism and marketing, she included a reference to some of her creative writing, such as a poetry book, *Enchantment on Your Lips,* she was working on which was a combination of poems and recipes for people in love and who loved food; yet, the creative works also had a practical purpose: she wrote that most of the poems had already been seen in Heinz ads for the Pittsburgh Symphony. Cannon also included poems in the book she wrote about her husband shortly after his death, and there were drafts of other poems found among Cannon's papers.[6] The inclusion of these brief poems spoke to Cannon's creative aspirations, which informed her approach to food in general.

A second observation from Cannon's résumé and papers is also noteworthy. Her identity seemed to be very much defined by her relationship with Walter White, longtime executive secretary of the NAACP.[7] She listed her marriage and White's position on her résumé, and that relationship dominated the content of her papers deposited at Yale University; in fact, there was very little about her own professional work in the collection (which ended nineteen years before her death). One conclusion from this omission (and from the content of Cannon's correspondence) was that she viewed White's work as much more important than her own.[8] Cannon demonstrated her devotion to White soon after his death in the 1956 biography she wrote, *A Gentle Knight.* The book recounted their courtship and marriage (tip-toeing around the timing of their extra-marital affair), and was a paean to White's accomplishments and character.[9] In addition to the book, the many love letters between the two illustrated their close relationship.[10] (Interestingly, food was seldom a topic in their correspondence, even when Cannon was traveling to exotic places.)

Cannon's stories about her personal life with White and the extent to which she seemed to define her life by her marriage to him reflected some of her assumptions about gender and women's domestic roles. And these assumptions, in turn, shaped who she believed was responsible for providing and preparing food. But rather than begin our discussion of Cannon's influence on American cuisine with the role of women in provisioning (more on this below), it makes more sense to start with the food itself. *What* should Americans eat in the mid-twentieth century? Cannon's answer to this question had deep roots in her professional background in marketing and advertising.

The central premise of Poppy Cannon's food advice was that prepared ingredients—processed foods—could be used in multiple, imaginative ways to create "gourmet" meals. Cannon not only gave permission to her readers to use processed ingredients, but she celebrated their possibilities: "At one time a badge of shame, hallmark of a lazy lady and the careless wife, today the can opener is fast becoming a magic wand."[11] The metaphor of a magic wand was telling, and one that Cannon used often. It conveyed the idea of creating something with little work. She told readers of *The Bride's Cookbook,* "A is for Abracadabra—that special type of magic that transforms a can or packet of ready-made food into a thing of joy to savor."[12] Thus, she encouraged brides to serve meals that were out of the ordinary and whose methods of creation were invisible. A close reading of some of Cannon's recipes illustrated these points.

At the start of her first and most famous book, *The Can-Opener Cookbook,* Cannon laid out the ground rules of her approach: "Every recipe includes a short cut—a canned or quick-frozen food, a mix or a new and simplified way to arrive at a particularly delectable result."[13] Cannon's references to canned soups summed up her approach at its most straightforward—and they appeared to be her favorite prepared ingredients. She pronounced the quality of modern canned soups, ranging from bouillon and broth to complete soups, to be good and easily substituted for homemade. She told readers that the secret between what might be a bland soup served straight from the can and something special was spicing. She preached the wonder of dressing up a canned soup with extra spices, condiments, or toppings.

Some of her "recipes" consisted of a rather simple addition to a reconstituted can of condensed soup, while others veered off in more elaborate, puzzling directions. For example, Cannon's "Black Bean Soup Guatemala" added a teaspoon each of meat extract, onion juice, and Kitchen Bouquet Browning & Seasoning Sauce®, along with a couple of tablespoons of sherry to the reconstituted can of soup. Each of these ingredients (except the sherry), of course, was another processed item to add to the soup base. Kitchen Bouquet was a frequent addition in many of Cannon's recipes that added color and flavor with a vegetable base, caramel coloring, and salt. Cannon's similarly simple recipe for "borsch" [*sic*] consisted of opening a can labeled as such and topping it with sour cream; with this soup, she also included a quick do-it-yourself version (based on canned beets, consommé, and cabbage) if your store did not happen to carry the premade borscht. Similarly, Cannon's recipe for scotch broth consisted of reconstituting the canned soup, adding canned kidney beans, and a little sherry.[14]

Some of Cannon's other soup recipes included either more elaborate or more unappetizing combinations.[15] She recommended reheating clam broth from the store with a tablespoon of catsup, topped with whipped cream: "A spoonful of tomato catsup or tomato sauce stirred into the broth gives it an appetizing pink glow." Similarly, she thought reheated (or cold jellied) consommé with a little claret and red food coloring would make a special soup. An example that focused more on blending flavors rather than colors was "Split-Pea Garbure" from dehydrated split pea soup mix, with cut up cocktail or Vienna sausages added. Another example that used complete products to create something new was "Vichyssoise" from quick-frozen mashed potatoes and condensed cream of chicken soup.

Moving beyond simple soup recipes to entrées, side dishes, and sauces, Cannon made elaborate use of prepared ingredients to create more substantial meals.[16] Some of these recipes did not stand the test of time, such as Quick Crab Meat Mornay, which called for reconstituted chicken soup to be baked with a beaten egg and crab meat, or Blushing Bunny, which combined condensed tomato soup, milk, cheese, mustard, egg yolks, and beaten egg whites served on toast. Others became standard quick dinners using canned ingredients: canned macaroni in cream sauce, mixed with cheese and then baked (i.e., macaroni and cheese) or Venetian Spaghetti with Clam Sauce (canned minced clams mixed into canned tomato sauce and served on pasta). The emphasis remained on using some ready-made product or short cut to save work or achieve the desired results. Cannon relied on such products instead of telling her readers how to learn the proper cooking method for a particular dish. She cautioned, for example, "Because it's so easy to achieve perfectly cooked rice *every time,* we suggest using quick-cooking rice."

In all different food categories (and in all her different books), Cannon had simple recipes that were little more than serving methods for processed foods and ones that were more elaborate, with multiple steps. For example, appetizers might range from a bowl of packaged potato chips served with a dip of canned deviled ham mixed with cream cheese, to "Haitian Pâtes de Poulet," which entailed making little puff pastries from a pie mix and filling them with a chicken-based pâté.[17] Her recipes also ranged from ones that sound perfectly acceptable to a modern middle-class cook to ones that have made 1950s and 1960s cookery the object of ridicule in the decades after. For an example of the former, take "Salmon Steaks au Vermouth," which began with frozen steaks and had only a simple marinade with vermouth, lemon, and herbs.[18] For examples of the latter, Cannon recommended recipes such as Creamed Frankfurter Slices (browned, sliced franks, combined with condensed celery soup and milk and mustard), Pizza Hash (canned corned beef hash mixed with cheese, shredded American cheese, canned tomato sauce, canned mushrooms, parmesan, and spices), and New Wave Mince and Pumpkin Pie (canned mincemeat, mixed with juice, spread on a store-bought pumpkin pie, with melted marshmallows on top).[19]

Acclaim in the press for Cannon's *Can Opener Cookbook* reflected the appeal of her methods. For example, an article in the *New York Herald Tribune* celebrated her use of "ready-to-serve foods and modern techniques" that took "a third of the time" of other recipes. Another *Herald Tribune* article the same year detailed some of her quick tips, especially important for Cannon as a busy career woman with three children and a husband. The article also advertised her twice-weekly cooking show, *Cook and Win,* on a local New York station. The press release for another local television show, *What's New,* similarly celebrated her philosophy that "cooking can be easy, economical and glamorous."[20]

It is worth pausing to remember that Cannon's recipes—as foreign as some of them may seem to modern foodways—were similar to others found in books and magazines through the 1950s, 1960s, and beyond. Cannon was as much a cultural touchstone as a pioneering force. For instance, some recipes—although less elaborate presentations than some of Cannon's dishes—combined packaged goods to become staples of postwar meals. For example, Mary Drake

McFeely described tuna noodle casserole, in different variations, as "the emblematic dish of the postwar kitchen."[21] Cannon and her contemporaries, then, helped normalize processed ingredients and make them a ubiquitous part of American cooking. Meanwhile, other authors went far beyond Cannon (who often tried to recreate classic dishes) in their innovations. The juxtapositions of packaged goods found in some booklets or magazines invited derision by later middle-class generations, with offerings such as pancakes made with 7 Up, a football-shaped molded chicken confetti salad, and hard-boiled egg penguins decorated with black olives.[22]

Poppy Cannon had some favorite products that appeared in many of her recipes. Along with Kitchen Bouquet Browning & Seasoning Sauce, Cannon often turned to a trio of condensed soups—cream of chicken, cream of mushroom, and (a little less often) cream of celery. These soups were especially important as the basis of sauces that she felt elevated every meal: "The perfect sauce is the zenith the ne plus ultra of gastronomic accomplishment and appreciation." Yet, the perfect sauce remained difficult to achieve on one's own; thus, "in a small inexpensive can of condensed soup it is possible to find almost the same concentration of flavor, the same blending of ingredients—all done for you!"[23] When it came to breads and desserts, Cannon often relied on various mixes as the basis of a recipe; in her *Bride's Cookbook*, for instance, she organized those chapters by sections such as "Things to do with muffin mix," "Things to do with popover mix," "Things to do with devil's food mix," etc., as well as highlighting the various recipes that used custard or pudding mix.[24] In an effort to be comprehensive about her recommendations of various food products, Cannon drafted a "guide to the Bride on Buying Food" as a follow-up to the *Bride's Cookbook*. The alphabetized listing went from A to Z (e.g., A-1 Sauce®, Almonds, Anchovy Fillets, etc.); every item included a brand recommendation with just one exception (garlic).[25]

Some of Cannon's favorite products became staples in the American kitchen, even if some of her combinations sounded odd to later generations. For instance, many an American cook continued to rely on condensed soups as well as quick-cooking rice, not to mention various baking mixes. Moreover, some products that seemed novel in Cannon's day, such as tomato sauce in a can or jar, jarred mayonnaise, or frozen or canned vegetables, became more common over time. Other products did not stand the test of time and disappeared.[26] Foremost in this category were canned meats (such as canned hamburgers) and canned poultry (including chicken and turkey pieces with bones). In one menu section, Cannon even gave directions for how to accomplish a quick

Thanksgiving dinner using a whole canned turkey. She observed that canned poultry was more economical than fresh, even though fresh and quick-frozen poultry parts were increasingly available, and a poultry meal was less of a luxury than it once had been.[27]

Not surprisingly, food processors were happy to produce recipes that encouraged use of their packaged goods. Four years after *Can-Opener Cookbook* appeared, the test kitchen for Campbell's Soup came up with a dish that continued into the twenty-first century to be prepared by many American families at Thanksgiving: the green bean casserole. This recipe included canned green beans, cream of mushroom soup, and canned fried onions, with a little soy sauce added. Campbell's reported that it was the most popular recipe it had ever produced and that roughly 40 percent of cream of mushroom soup sold was used to make it. Historian Anna Zeide summarized that the dish "displayed canned foods in all their glory, as they came into their prime." To encourage other creative uses of their products, in the 1960s, Campbell's put out one of its most popular booklets, "Cooking with Condensed Soups."[28]

Whether or not a particular processed ingredient stood the test of time, Cannon's reliance on an array of such products reflected a shift in how middle-class Americans viewed food in the postwar and later periods. When fewer people lived on farms or worked in agriculture and fewer middle-class households employed servants who cooked and prepared food for the family, food was increasingly something that had to be *bought* rather than made. The trend of buying readymade food ingredients was not new. Campbell's, for example, had been selling twenty-one different canned soups starting in 1904.[29] Aside from the success of Campbell's soups, which made them a staple ingredient for Cannon and other postwar cooks, it's worth pausing to consider how the rise of industrial manufacturing permanently changed Americans' relationship to food.

With the industrialization of food processing in the late nineteenth and early twentieth century, the purity of food became a key concern for many people. As more food was produced in factories instead of on one's own farm, could consumers be sure that the food in a package (or can of soup) matched the description on the label? Could buyers be sure that a particular product was safe to eat? Policing purity became one of the earliest charges for the USDA; chief chemist Harvey Wiley made a career of investigating food "adulterants" for safety and labels for veracity. He gained much publicity with his volunteer "poison squads," who ingested various processed foods to test the safety of additives. Historian Benjamin Cohen observed that in the late nineteenth and early twentieth centuries, the debate over purity evolved as most Americans came to accept that all industrial foods were manipulated to some extent; food emerging from a factory could not be exactly the same as that grown on a farm. Thus, discussion in the public culture focused on which kinds of manipulation were considered acceptable and which were not.[30] Due to the efforts of Wiley and other Progressives in Washington, responsibility for these decisions was given to USDA scientists, whose authority was codified in the 1906 Pure Food and Drug Act.

A second transition in Americans' relationship to food was increasing dependence on industrial products. This was due to two related developments: the decline of people working on farms, and the rise of industrial food as an economic sector. At the start of the nineteenth century, 75 to 80 percent of Americans worked on farms. Over the next two centuries, the share of Americans working in agriculture would continue to fall, in inverse relationship to the rise of an industrial economy. By 1900—amid the pure food debates—40 percent of Americans worked in agriculture; by 1950, the figure was down to 12 percent, and, by the early twenty-first century, less than 1 percentt (0.67 percent in 2013).[31] Americans, then, were undeniably dependent on the food produced by others and mainly on a vast industrial food production and distribution system.

The sheer size of the industrial food system also reshaped Americans' relationship with food. Since the early twentieth century, as Campbell's soup found its market, manufactured food products of all sorts had been growing. Production got a big boost with the demand for nonperishable foods for the military and others in World War II.[32] Following the war, the industrial food infrastructure grew even more dramatically. More than one historian has referred to the mid-twentieth century as "the golden age of food processing."[33] This golden age rested on several pillars. Since the early twentieth century, Americans relied on agricultural and processing systems that were increasingly industrialized, as well as on a government system of regulation and inspections to ensure safe foods. Upon these foundations, the postwar food system entered a new period of growth due to technological advances in processing, on the one hand, and rising affluence and an expanding middle class, on the other.

Successful methods of canning, freezing, and preservation had been established earlier in the twentieth century. But after World War II, processing was transformed with the help of hundreds of new chemical additives that extended the shelf life of food and improved taste. For example, calcium propionate made packaged bread last longer and sulfur dioxide gas preserved color in frozen food. Hydrolyzed starch made baby food creamier, while newly synthesized dyes and flavorings enhanced the appearance and taste of processed foods.[34]

Together, processing methods and additives increased the value of foods. The value of these "convenience" foods was especially appealing to working women, who made up 32 percent of the labor force by the mid-1950s.[35]

Convenience foods were appealing not only for their intrinsic qualities, but also for their affordability and widespread availability in grocery stores. Although self-service grocery stores dated from the early twentieth century, they—like most other parts of the food system—experienced a growth spurt after World War II. Grocery stores increased in size, as did the market share of large corporate chains.[36] It is not surprising that consumerism became the organizing principle of the food system, especially with the increase in suburbanization and per capita income in the twenty years after World War II.

Such easy access to convenience foods had political implications. The industrialized food system that produced abundant food to be purchased at inexpensive prices became the premier example of US superiority in the Cold War. Many scholars have discussed the powerful propaganda created by abundant industrial food; and, even more, as Shane Hamilton argued in *Supermarket USA*, industrial food became a global system that long outlasted the Cold War.[37] In *A Consumer's Republic*, Lizabeth Cohen wrote that, in addition to Cold War propaganda and the economics of globalization, consumerism came to reshape the American postwar political and economic identity; indeed, consumerism reshaped what it meant to be American.[38] The rise of consumerism coincided with an increase in per capita income in the two decades after World War II. The confluence of these two developments was tangibly demonstrated for most Americans on their trips to well-stocked grocery stores. In addition, newspaper headlines, such as "1954 Food Supplies Plentiful," reinforced what was self-evident.[39] Broadly, then, the ability to purchase such food came to symbolize political as well as economic freedom. In such circumstances, the changing nature of food was clear; food was a product of factories, not nature. As historians Gary Cross and Robert Proctor argued in *Packaged Pleasures*, food in "nature is ephemeral," but "containerization liberated us from nature, at least a little."[40]

The golden age of industrial food sketched out above is revealing about many aspects of American life at mid-century, including consumerism, affluence, Cold War ideology, changing gender roles, technological innovation, and agricultural abundance. This, then, was the atmosphere in which Poppy Cannon wrote her books preaching the wonders of canned goods.

Similar to most Americans in the 1950s and 1960s, Cannon assumed that food was something to be bought—one more consumer item among many. Along with her consumerist approach to food, another way in which Cannon reflected the contemporary zeitgeist was in her celebration of modern technology. She often praised the innovations of modern food products, as did many others. For example, authors of the *Women's Home Companion* in 1954 wrote: "Best of all—canned foods know no season: January, February, June, and July—who ever stops to think nowadays whether anything is in season! They're available all year long and offer a wealth of variety and excellence that were never dreamed of by our grandmothers and that help make us the best-fed nation in the whole wide world."[41] Cannon praised the quality of many prepared ingredients that could be substituted for homemade with equivalent taste and texture; indeed, many of her recipes assumed that otherwise ordinary meals would achieve gourmet status due to magic flavors from a bottle of Kitchen Bouquet or the ability to get quick-frozen fish from the local supermarket. Her recipes and commentary made it clear that industrially processed ingredients were not only equivalent to homemade ones, but sometimes even superior—especially for the housewife who was not professionally trained. Indeed, an ordinary housewife who had a "magic wand" at her fingertips needed little experience in the culinary arts; she just needed a well-stocked supermarket nearby.

Just as Cannon's recipes reflected prevalent attitudes about food and meals in the 1950s, so did her embrace of processed ingredients. Such views also found their way into contemporary literature as seen in Mary McCarthy's 1954 novel *The Group*. One character, for example, expounds on the virtues of Campbell's soups, some of which "were better than anything the home cook could achieve." Another adds that canned corn niblets were "Almost like corn on the cob."[42]

Characters from *The Group*, along with other women in the postwar period, probably got their food advice, including the adoption of new products, from one of the best-selling mainstream cookbooks that sought to answer all cooking questions for everyday use. Many women reported that they, or their mothers, had a favorite that they turned to for basic (and sometimes more elaborate) advice.[43] Four were most often cited as being akin to a cooking bible: *The Fannie Farmer Cookbook* (which first appeared at the end of the nineteenthth century as *The Boston Cooking School Cook Book*); *The Better Homes and Gardens Cook Book* (first published in 1930); *Joy of Cooking* (appearing a year later in 1931, and greatly expanded in 1943); and the relative newcomer, *The Betty Crocker Cookbook* (it first appeared in 1950). Each of these books was large, comprehensive, and had multiple printings throughout the postwar decades. Cannon's books fit comfortably with many of their recommendations, such as one, from *Joy of Cooking*'s Irma Rombauer, who wrote of canned soup in the 1930s: "a finer product than canned soup was never produced."[44] Nevertheless, Cannon was not competing directly with these books, since she never attempted to be as comprehensive and held to a more narrowly-focused set of themes.

Along with her celebration of processed food ingredients, Cannon highlighted the modern technologies increasingly found in the home. A decade after the best-selling *Can-Opener Cookbook* was published, Cannon wrote *The Electric Epicure's Cookbook*. The book was a celebration of various small electric appliances designed to make meal preparation both easier and more modern; she saw electric appliances as no less than a revolution in cooking, with which one could "work miracles."[45] The first part of the book had a separate chapter for each appliance (what she labeled "utensils"), while the second half consisted of various recipes, all making use of at least one of the appliances. Some of the appliances became commonplace in modern kitchens, while others either disappeared or became special occasion items. She discussed the blender, beater or mixer, roaster oven, portable oven, rotisserie, broiler, skillet, deep-fat fryer, saucepan, pressure cooker, griddle, hot tray, slicer, ice crusher, and ice cream freezer. Some of Cannon's recipes were also designed around appliances that fell into disuse or disappeared entirely. *The Electric Epicure's Cookbook* had countless recipes using appliances which would be replaced by manufactured food products. The electric slicer disappeared from homes because people bought ready-sliced packages of meat or went to a delicatessen. The ice cream freezer became a gourmet novelty in the face of an explosion of manufactured ice creams, ranging from humble, inexpensive brands to gourmet fare. Meanwhile, a number of small electric appliances seemed unnecessary if one had an oven-range that could roast, broil, and fry.

Cannon praised each appliance for the labor it would save housewives, as well as the machines' ability to improve the texture or presentation of various dishes. For example, she extolled the wonders of the electric blender: "There need never be another curdled Hollandaise! With the magic of a blender a perfect Hollandaise equal to that served at the best French restaurants can be made in less than a minute. The recipe is foolproof." Cannon was so taken with electric tools that she often recommended them in a gratuitous way. For example, she discussed how an electric portable oven could be used to bake various frozen items, such as a ready-made pie; why this could not be done in a conventional oven was never explained. Similarly, she talked about the ease of using a blender to make garlic butter to spread on a readymade loaf of Italian bread. Several items had precise, electronic heat controls and were also compatible with a removable electric probe, which she encouraged all readers to get. For several items, Cannon highlighted the modernity and scientific precision of "thermostatically controlled cooking."[46] Gone would be a cook guessing at the right temperature or needing experience for particular recipes; the electronic dial would ensure success.

On first consideration, it might have appeared as if portions of this new book went against Cannon's earlier reliance on readymade ingredients. This was seen most clearly in her sections on the pressure cooker and soups. She laid out the ease with which one could make stock, bouillon, and broth instead of having to buy it in a can. Another example was her explanation of how the magical blender made mayonnaise almost as easily as opening a jar. Yet, on second glance, it soon became clear that the book used almost as many prepared or canned ingredients as the earlier one and represented an almost seamless blending together of two modern food technologies—processed ingredients and electric home appliances—to achieve "gourmet" results. Thus, putting aside the electronic aids included for each recipe, many of the ingredients and overall sorts of dishes remained similar to those in her first book. And, as in her first book, Cannon had favorite processed ingredients that she included in many recipes. For example, in *The Electric Epicure's Cookbook,* just about every recipe with beef extolled the wonders of meat tenderizer to improve the end result.[47] This was an example of her conviction that the quality of the ingredient one began with was less important than the ability to improve it with a chemical addition or modern technology.

Another similarity between *The Electric Epicure's Cookbook* and *Can Opener Cookbook* was the extent to which each emphasized the importance of *presentation* for a successful recipe, over and above taste or nutrition. And, not merely presentation, but a sometimes dramatic spectacle. Cannon's simplest presentation tricks involved adding a little food coloring to a dish to make it appear more appetizing at the table. She might use a spice to impart color, citing the appearance more than the flavor, such as "Gilded Rice," made with saffron and curry or turmeric: "Rice with a golden glow adds a party touch to any meal."[48] Rice dishes had other positives, such as "Ring of Rice": "Nothing is dressier than rice molded in a ring—filled with Chicken à la King, Lobster Newburg, or any creamed vegetable."[49] Cannon also included the stereotypical gelatin-infused dishes—such as "Jellied Ham Mousse": "For a buffet supper nothing could be more dramatic than this ham mousse piled into a hollowed cabbage, with the leaves spread out all around. . . . Incredibly beautiful with the pink mousse!"—and decorated meats, such as ham, for which she recommended using more imagination than the hackneyed pineapple and maraschino cherries: "you might try fresh or canned slices peaches, or apricot halves or sweet pickles, or watermelon rind cut into designs."[50]

The performative aspects of Cannon's recipes often involved guests either watching as a dish was finished at the table or participating in a final assembly themselves. At times, the ritual was very detailed, as with Smoked Salmon with Trimmings: "Place one of your prettiest napkins on a plate, arrange the toast on the napkin, covering it to keep warm. Pass toast along with a small platter of well-chilled, thinly sliced salmon. Have on the coffee table a pepper grinder and a tiny bottle of the very best olive oil. Each person lays his salmon on the toast, pours on a golden dribble of olive oil, adds a grind of fresh black pepper. This salmon ceremony is most appropriate when you're serving cocktails to a small group around the coffee table."[51] More commonly, Cannon outlined less elaborate rituals that required guests sitting at the table to sauce their own dish, such as Honeydew Melon in the English Fashion, which called on guests to pass sugar (to sprinkle) and a pitcher of lime juice mixed with syrup from the canned fruit (to pour).[52]

By far, Cannon's favorite dramatic dishes were those that were set aflame in front of guests. She summarized to readers: "Any dinner no matter how simple takes on distinction when it comes with a flambé dessert." Many of her desserts in *Can Opener Cookbook* included a flambé presentation, ranging from the classics such as Crêpes Suzette ("one of the most dramatic desserts") and Baked Alaska ("the ultimate in blaze-of-glory desserts"), to others less familiar, such as Ring Cake for Anniversaries ("a white cake baked in a ring topped with a 'golden frosting' and served with flaming brandy set in a cup inside the ring"). Cannon's flambé fetish went beyond desserts to other courses, such as Roast Canned Chicken Flambé with Black Cherries and Steak Maxim Flambé, and continued to later books as well.[53] At times, the flaming dishes even seemed to pose a fire hazard, such as Flaming Onion Soup, which appeared in Cannon's 1968 book, *The New, New Can Opener Cookbook*. Cannon explained: "This is one of the most dramatic first courses you can serve. It should be served with theater—the toasted bread flambeed on a heatproof platter at the table." The method included setting to flame a small pitcher of cognac to be poured while burning over the whole platter of toast, creating a large flaming platter in the middle of the table.[54] Cannon was not alone in her embrace of flambéed dishes, which became widespread in elegant restaurants in the 1960s.[55]

Finally, it's important to explain that Cannon's focus on presentation and drama was intended not for just one dish, but for a whole meal, for an event. The second chapter of *Can Opener Cookbook* was about menu planning. It was full of advice about selecting complementary dishes, paying attention to all their characteristics. She discussed the importance of setting the table, selecting utensils, décor, and glassware. Her message made it clear that one would be judged for the final product. She summarized the importance of "Drama at the Table" thus: "If your food is basically good and if you have contrast in texture, color, and flavor, that's more than half the battle. Add drama and you're sure to make yourself a reputation. All of us in our lifetime have eaten honest, nourishing food that is dull as dishwater."[56] Elsewhere, she talked about drama at the dinner table stemming from the cook's "good sense of theater"; often her sections calling for dramatic presentations were closely tied to a sense of adventure and experimentation.[57]

Cannon's ideas for making meals dramatic events suffused all of her food writing. For example, she wrote the editor of *House Beautiful* Elizabeth Gordon with the idea of a new monthly feature for the magazine, "Modern Epicure's Almanac," which would be linked to historical events for a given month, such as in October an almond-flavored custard for the Feast of St. Francis and a Columbus Day Buffet. Interestingly, for this proposed almanac feature, she also suggested recipes each month that would include foods that the USDA suggested to be featured in a given month—presumably those expected to be most in abundance.[58]

There was another implication of Cannon's embrace of drama and spectacle in her cooking recommendations: they alluded to a particular elegance that was both nostalgic and aspirational. For example, one reason for praising modern appliances such as a blender and pressure cooker in *Electric Epicure* was because they allowed one to "achieve some of the elegant and formerly elaborate dishes of the turn of the century" such as soufflés, timbales, and molded custards.[59] Such nostalgia for the elegant fare of the rich also reflected middle-class aspirations to gourmet meals formerly out of reach. As with most mainstream cookbooks in the twentieth century, Cannon's were aimed at white middle-class women with hopes of enjoying sophisticated culture. Historian Laura Shapiro argued that within Cannon's own career this aspirational side grew stronger over time, as reflected by the move of her column from *Mademoiselle* to *House Beautiful* in the 1950s: "she had always considered herself far above the marshmallow-salad school of quick cooking, because her business was imitating great cuisine. Now she started revising her approach to greatness."[60]

Although Cannon emphasized drama and presentation, she did not ignore taste; she made occasional references to the flavor of various dishes (as reflected in her many recommendations to spice up canned ingredients on one's own). Yet, overall, taste never seemed as important as presenting a completed dish and meal that looked wonderful at the table. Certainly, there were almost no references to fresh foods and ingredients and why they might be desirable. An example from her 1968 book illustrated this view. In the chapter on salads, Sliced

Tomatoes Basilica is made with canned, sliced tomatoes; Cannon remarked: "The new sliced salad tomatoes, canned, are an excellent product and fill a long-felt need." This concoction was followed by Sugared Tomatoes with Lemon Slices, using the same canned tomatoes. Rather than commenting on the bland taste of canned tomatoes, Cannon instead recommended doctoring the product. Her praise for canned, sliced tomatoes is a reminder that when Cannon did discuss "taste," her definition of what was good differed from many other cookbook authors or dominant views in subsequent decades. For example, it's hard to imagine any modern cooks agreeing with Cannon's views on taste such as the following: "A can of macaroni and cream sauce is the beginning of great wisdom for the hostess in a hurry. Merely sprinkled with cheese and heated in the oven, it is excellent. Dressed up in the manner of old Virginia [by adding chopped ham], it's superb."[61]

In one specific and oft-cited area, Cannon's prescriptions for taste and presentation meshed: she was very concerned about serving foods at the proper temperature, especially hot foods. Many of her recipes included specific admonitions along these lines. For example, discussing the benefits of serving soup from a tureen at the table into heated soup bowls, Cannon wrote: "There is all the difference in the world between a really hot, *hot* soup and one that is wanly lukewarm."[62] Here and elsewhere, she explained how it was perfectly safe (and a good practice) to heat china dishes in a turned-off oven (about 150 degrees) or on an electric warming plate next to the table. In *The Bride's Cookbook*, she counseled: "There is nothing more depressing than a lukewarm chop or a tepid soup, a gravy of bath temperature and congealing grease."[63]

If we put aside for the moment the idea that tastes genuinely differ and evolve, we are left with three important conclusions from Cannon. First, she enthusiastically embraced how modern technology processed foods that were readily available and easy to use; she did not question this transformation or that food was a product of the factory, not of nature. She did not criticize the tastiness of processed foods overall—though she did caution cooks to sample different brands, since some were better than others: "Some of the quickies [readymade products] . . . are wonderful, some are passable, some are terrible. You have to pick, and as you go along, remember the brand name that pleases you."[64] Many of Cannon's recipes sang the praises of various manufactured ingredients, never hinting that they, as a category, were inferior to fresh foods in terms of taste or texture. For frozen foods, she offered extra praise in her rare references to nutrition; she wrote that frozen vegetables retained more vitamins than other choices, even calling them "fresh": "Quick-frozen vegetables are the freshest vegetables you can buy, and the finest."[65] One of Cannon's books, *The Frozen-Foods Cookbook,* was devoted entirely to them.[66] In organization and types of recipes, it resembled her other books, though of course with increased use and prominence given to frozen ingredients. Many of the recipes might have felt more familiar to a modern reader, since items such as frozen chicken parts, cuts of meat, fish fillets, and vegetables remained in common use decades later. Other ingredients have since fallen into disuse (e.g., frozen soups instead of canned soups and frozen mashed or whole potatoes). Reflecting her belief in the wonders of frozen vegetables, this chapter on vegetables was the longest in the book.

A second important conclusion from Cannon was that whether frozen or otherwise processed, readymade ingredients allowed the cook to make fancier, more elaborate meals, a form of cultural expression and individual creativity. Such expression seemed more important than sustenance; in a society of abundance, Cannon and many others took the ability to find ample food for granted. Cannon's embrace of drama, as discussed above, was not only for mere spectacle, but also to foster creativity and artistry. Indeed, Cannon explained that with her can opener, she was transformed: "I become the artist-cook, the master, the creative chef."[67] Many of her asides about presentation often contained some reference to the creativity of the cook; for instance, when praising the quality of prepared ingredients, she counseled, "All that remains for you is to translate them in your own inimitable fashion, and with your sweetest smile."[68] She encouraged her readers to express their creativity—balanced by a certain amount of good taste: "Fantasy and Imagination play a large part in successful salads but nowadays it is well to remember that the most effective salads are casual. Ornate and overdecorated salads are no longer smart."[69]

A third important conclusion from surveying Cannon's work was that she reinforced widespread ideas about the role of women and food, while at the same time gently challenging some aspects of that role.[70] Cannon's audience unmistakably comprised wives who were expected to provide food for their husbands, children, and guests. Cannon made the common assumption that women were primarily responsible for the procuring, cooking, and serving of food. Sometimes this assumption was unstated, sometimes explicit. *The Bride's Cookbook,* of course, left no doubt about who would be doing the cooking in a family. Cannon made it clear that cooking for one's husband was an expression of a wife's love; she promised in the book to combine "romance with practicality."[71] Reflecting common gender mores, Cannon reserved one task in the book for men: carving. Under one heading, "How to Carve Chicken or Turkey," she stated: "This is your husband's prerogative . . . we won't go into it." Instead, she listed one reference for a book that a husband could consult if he was in need of some advice on the subject.[72]

On the other hand, Cannon's assumption that women were the primary home cooks did not mean that she assumed they were stay-at-home wives, and her books were full of praise for the skills needed to be a successful cook. In her *Bride's Cookbook*, she provided tips for working women: "If you are a working woman as well as a bride, you will find it convenient to write out your meal plans for a whole week . . . and shop for staples all at one time." She also encouraged her readers: "Don't check your brains at the kitchen door. The kind of thinking that gets you an A in English or Economics will stand you in very good stead when you cook. Taste your food analytically. Read recipes carefully. Examine labels."[73] Nevertheless, even if she encouraged women not to hide their brains and wrote from the perspective of a working woman, Cannon and press coverage of her reinforced gendered ideas about the role of wives in the kitchen and in a marriage. For instance, the press release for her television show *What's New* included the following: "'And,' adds Poppy with an impish grin, 'a dash of femininity never hurt any household. Dressed-up meals and dressed-up meal planners usually add up to a happy home.'"[74]

Such advice coincided with Cannon's frequent allusions to creativity. She did not call on women to use their brains, to dress up themselves and their food to be mere props, but to be artists. With their creativity, Cannon believed that women could make mealtimes an expression of their individuality, as well as pleasurable for all. Nevertheless, her celebration of artistry also reflected the contemporary expectation that successful wives and mothers *were* creative, especially since they had the luxury of time that allowed them to be creative. Through the first half of the twentieth century, the wide adoption of electric appliances and packaged foods in the United States lessened the time needed for individual household tasks, while simultaneously changing the expectations for women's domestic roles, a situation that Ruth Schwartz Cowan dubbed "the ironies of household technology."[75] Thus, a mere dinner was no longer sufficient. As scholar Sherrie Inness summed it up: "The 1950s ideal was for a woman to transform a humdrum meal into a memorable event."[76] Such pressure led some women to worry whether or not they were doing enough to live up to the ideal, a dilemma illustrated in the evolution of the modern cake mix. A number of scholars have written about the initial failure of modern cake mixes to sell widely, since they required only the addition of water, apparently leaving some women feeling as if they were not actually "making" a cake. Food manufacturers released new products requiring women to add an egg as well as water, helping to make cake mixes widely used and popular.[77]

The "ironies" that manufactured and processed foods presented regarding the role of women in the kitchen were also reflected in the scholarly discussion of the period. Some historians focused more on the pressure that women felt to meet a creative ideal, while others argued that women enjoyed cooking more than food manufacturers assumed; they debated about to what extent women were pushed down a new path or to what extent they chose it.[78] In many ways, the role of Poppy Cannon illustrated that there was no simple way to resolve this tension. She embraced the idea that women could make delicious meals after a day's work at the office, they could give free rein to their artistic yearnings, and they also shouldered the responsibility for feeding the family.

Even while Cannon was attempting to revise the expectations placed on women in the kitchen, she embraced other aspects of gender roles wholeheartedly: some foods were favored by men, though men's role in food preparation was narrow indeed. Along with her admonition to new brides that carving should be left to their husbands, she titled another chapter in the same book: "Meat for your Man to Eat."[79] As many scholars have affirmed, "Meat is perceived as intrinsically male in American culture."[80] Cannon reflected this assumption in her recipes; for example, she recommended in *Can Opener Cookbook* how to improve upon a salad for men: "Practically anything in the way of meat, cheese, and salad greens can go into a chef's salad. It is basically a mixed green salad made hearty—and hence much more acceptable to men—by the addition of solid food usually cut into julienne strips."[81] It should be no surprise that men's apparent love of meat was reflected in increased meat consumption in the 1950s, with a whopping 150 pounds per capita among all citizens per year, almost all of which was beef and pork.[82]

Cannon was not alone among authors who shared common gender assumptions, as shown in particular in the small subgenre of cookbooks aimed at men. Such books reassured readers, as did one from *Esquire* magazine, that "you won't find doily tearoom fare here"; this book and others like it "carefully spelled out which foods were appropriate for women and which were appropriate for men."[83] Paramount to this distinction was the idea that men not only preferred meat, but were the ones best equipped to cook it. *The Life Picture Cook Book* (1958) declared, "Steak is a man's job."[84] This was especially true if the steak was cooked outdoors. James Beard and Helen Evans Brown told readers in their *Complete Book of Outdoor Cookery* (1955): "We believe [charcoal cookery] is primarily a man's job and that a woman, if she's smart, will keep it that way."[85] It is interesting to note that, although men might be in charge of steaks on the grill or of carving the roast at serving time, cookbooks and columns (except those few explicitly directed at men) continued to assume that women were still responsible for meal planning, shopping, and the other dishes and courses to accompany a slab of meat. In other words, women needed to do the behind-the-scenes work, even while male prowess was on display for guests at a backyard barbeque. As several observers noted, this distinction reinforced the idea that women were responsible for the daily, mundane tasks of cooking, while men were celebrated for their special-occasion contributions.

The distinction between women's ordinary and men's extraordinary cooking was also embedded in another widely held belief that men were intrinsically better cooks than women. There was a Catch-22 at work here: women shouldered the day-to-day burden of providing family meals, whereas men cooked because they wanted to. The expectation placed on women, then, in a circular fashion made them less creative cooks. The apparent gender difference in cooking was assumed, as one historian summarized, "in the spirit of improvisation" and confidence that men brought to the kitchen, while women slavishly followed recipes.[86] This stereotype was dramatized by two of the characters in Mary McCarthy's *The Group*. Shortly after their wedding, the husband combined various canned ingredients with a Poppy Cannon panache, and as their relationship began to sour he criticized his wife's approach to cooking: "She had no imagination, following recipes with her glasses on and measuring the seasonings and timing and everything: Cooking was a lively art and she made it academic and lifeless." Meanwhile, the same husband became enraged if he arrived home, and his wife did not have dinner prepared after her own day on the job.[87]

The gendered approach to food was also reflected in *Gourmet*, which began in 1941, aimed at an audience of sophisticated men. The magazine followed from a long European tradition that assumed the best chefs to be men, while women were utilitarian home cooks. *Gourmet*'s approach, moreover, was in opposition to the nutritionist framework built by scientists and home economists in the early twentieth century. Home economics was clearly gendered, as historian Megan Elias observed in her discussion of *Gourmet*'s early years: "The association of women with food science and nutrition and the construction of these branches of knowledge as being in opposition to alcohol and pleasure led to the rejection of women's abilities as cooks."[88] *Gourmet* also called women's abilities into question because they represented a mainstream approach to food which eschewed not only pleasure but prized speed over taste.[89]

Interestingly, the widespread gendered ideas about food preparation were both reflected in Poppy Cannon's work but also challenged by her in a subtle way. Her call on women to be creative, to become artists in their kitchens, was what most people assumed to be the purview of male chefs. In addition, she encouraged women to make the service of meals a performance, again encroaching on the territory of men, whose cooking prowess was occasionally on display at the grill while women did the behind-the-scenes preparation in the kitchen. And, finally, Cannon subtly challenged traditional assumptions by giving advice to women working outside the home, not just to housewives.

Most of Cannon's books were similar to each other and reflected a common philosophy and method: manufactured ingredients were to be embraced; presentation was most important; fresh food was irrelevant. Changes she inserted over time were sometimes minor, and probably a reflection of foodways around her. For example, *The New, New Can-Opener Cookbook*, published seventeen years after the original, included more vegetable recipes and more references to international recipes that Cannon had adapted, as well as inspirations for dishes that came from famous restaurants.[90] The international flavors, though, were not necessarily what a modern cook would expect and certainly did not embrace the use of fresh ingredients. For example, a recipe for a doctored, canned minestrone was improved as follows: "Canned minestrone is a fine product, but if you want to achieve something really akin to the great soups of northern Italy, try this one, complete with basil-blessed *pesto*." Cannon's pesto, though, was a mixture of olive oil, butter or margarine, salt, Parmesan, garlic, and *a half teaspoon of dried basil*.[91] Hardly what most Italians would recognize as pesto. Cannon's limited changes for the book also seemed to go in the opposite direction of internationalization and gourmet cooking. Indeed, the book contained a number of additional recipes based on manufactured products and ornate presentations that gave it an old-fashioned feeling by the time it appeared in 1968. Some recipes read almost as self-parodies for stereotypical recipes of the 1950s and 1960s, including Lucianian Eggs au Gratin (canned cooked macaroni in cheese sauce mixed with sliced, hard-cooked eggs and topped with grated cheese); Ham in Champagne Sauce (canned sliced ham topped with a sauce from water, cornstarch, consommé, lemon, and champagne); or Strawberry Flummery (canned strawberry pie filling baked on buttered, sliced white bread).[92]

Despite these obvious limitations and the lack of "authentic" flavors in her core books and recipes, Cannon's interest in international cultures and cuisine seemed genuine. On an obvious level, this was reflected in her prose and recipes, beginning with *Can Opener Cookbook*, which had many references to

European-based dishes, and occasionally to ones from Mexico and the Middle East. Sometimes Cannon encouraged her readers to doctor a readymade product to give it a European flair. For example, in reconstituting a canned fish chowder, Cannon recommended substituting white wine for a quarter or half of the milk in the recipe in order to make the chowder taste "very 'French.'"[93]

Along with her books focused on American cooking, Cannon published two cookbooks devoted exclusively to European cuisine: *Eating European: Abroad and at Home* (1961) and *Italian Cooking* (1975). Each of these was distinct from most of her other books, though for different reasons. The earlier one was the longest of Cannon's, with each chapter full of cultural insights as well as recipes; it reads more like a travel memoir than a straight recipe book. Cannon's acknowledgment to TWA for making her travel for the book possible indicated that she had sufficient upfront sponsorship to allow her to include chapters on thirteen different countries. Unlike her other books that never mentioned the seasonality of food and that encouraged the use of processed ingredients, here Cannon lamented "standardized eating," encouraging her readers to leave their hotels, be adventurous, and eat in local markets, restaurants, and outdoor stands. She wrote that the book was deliberately a travelogue, written for actual as well as armchair travelers. Despite her uncharacteristic advice to embrace the local instead of familiar American cuisine, she added a helpful hint to the weight-conscious traveler, worried about so much culinary indulgence: she recommended bringing along powdered meals that could be mixed with water (or instant coffee) in the hotel room to replace a daily meal with a low-calorie, processed alternative.[94]

Cannon's other book exclusively on European cuisine, *Italian Cooking*, was her shortest. The eighty-page paperback, unlike her earlier ones, included many drawings as well as black and white photos. She emphasized the familiarity of Italian cuisine for most Americans, as well as its popularity. Aside from taste, she seemed to have embraced Italian cuisine due to its simplicity. The book emphasized the variations of cuisine from different regions of Italy, and many of the recipes included more fresh ingredients than were found in her earlier books. Many recipes, though, continued to use processed ingredients as well. This last book of Cannon's (written the year that she died) indicated that some of the new culinary sensibilities of the 1970s were shaping her interests. For example, reprising an earlier recipe for pesto-topped minestrone soup, she still used butter mixed with olive oil for the pesto, but unlike the earlier version, which must have been bland if not tasteless (made with just a half teaspoon of dried basil), this one used four tablespoons of fresh basil.[95]

In addition to *Italian Cooking* and *Eating European*, Cannon ventured outside of her formulaic books in three other instances. A brief book in 1958 sought to capitalize on the growing interest in losing weight and substituting diet foods for more familiar alternatives. *Unforbidden Sweets: Delicious Desserts of 100 Calories or Less* set out an ambitious goal: she told readers that, while staying under the one-hundred- calorie limit, she aimed to provide good flavor, texture, and form, while still focusing on "glamour." The book was a departure in that Cannon did not discuss calories in any of her usual recipes, though of course her call for glamour, as well as the many processed ingredients used, would have been familiar to those who knew her other books. One of the other big departures in this book was Cannon's liberal use of "liquid nonnutritive sodium cyclamate sweetener" (going by the brand of Sucaryl) throughout.[96]

Cannon's two other books that fell into different categories were collaborations. Neither seemed to reflect Cannon's sensibilities. Cannon cowrote *The Presidents' Cookbook* with Patricia Brooks in 1968. Yet, reading the book, it appeared to have very little of Cannon in it. With no introduction or conclusion from either author, it was a straightforward tome with one chapter for each president. Each chapter included some historical background and events of the era, anecdotes about the president and his wife, and recipes that might have been prepared at that time, though it was not always certain that they were served in the White House.

Her collaboration with Alice B. Toklas was very different. *Aromas and Flavors of Past and Present* (1958) was written by Toklas, with an introduction and comments by Cannon. The unexpected "collaboration" between two cooks whose styles, sensibilities, and values regarding food could not have been more different resulted in a disjointed book, with the recipes written by Toklas faithfully reproduced, though framed and commented upon by Cannon. The schizophrenic quality of the book was particularly apparent when compared with Toklas's single-authored *The Alice B. Toklas Cook Book* (1954).[97] Moreover, this ill-conceived "collaboration" revealed much about Cannon's work as well as her aspirations; it also laid bare some of the clashes between mainstream postwar American cooking as exemplified by Cannon and non-industrial, French cooking as exemplified by Toklas.

Toklas's 1954 book was part memoir, part cultural history of France (and the United States), and part recipe book. The recipes were arranged into chapters with particular themes, stories of friends and travels, and social observations; each chapter had appropriate recipes interwoven with the text. The recipes had clear narrative directions, though were sometimes vague on the quantities of ingredients. The recipes used only fresh, nonprocessed foods and traditional methods (i.e., no electric appliances), never mentioned how to accomplish a recipe more quickly, and assumed that readers would have a basic familiarity with cooking techniques. Little was said about presentation of the food, and more about its taste and the occasion of its enjoyment. In short, this was a love story about food, and its role in the lives of Toklas and her friends.

Four short years later, *Aromas and Flavors* appeared with a different tone and without the essays embedded in Toklas's first book. The newer book was short and divided into eighteen straightforward chapters on distinct courses or groups of food. Toklas's recipes were varied and mainly French and appeared in her earlier style, but there was no other writing from her outside of a brief preface. In this, she recounted a childhood of bland food and the revelation of experiencing new tastes when she became older. She also included two important recommendations. First, she emphasized that the quality of ingredients was of the utmost importance and that one should always choose the best quality possible, changing the recipe if necessary to achieve this. So, for example, if one could not afford top-quality ingredients for a particular recipe, it was better to switch to another recipe with less-expensive ingredients, but ones of top quality. She repeated that the best ingredients made the best-tasting dishes, period. And, the best-tasting dish was most important, because it would give you and your guests the maximum *pleasure.* Toklas's second guiding recommendation was to pay attention to the menu and how foods went together in order to achieve "a climax and a culmination," neither of which need be dramatic: "Come to it gently. One will suffice."[98]

Cannon's leading role in shaping *Aromas and Flavors* was somewhat puzzling. The two first met in 1953 while Cannon was on a culinary trip to Europe with her *House Beautiful* editor, Elizabeth Gordon. Meanwhile, Toklas had met and become a supporter of Cannon's husband, Walter White, years before.[99] Cannon and Toklas became friends, with Cannon admiring Toklas and apparently convincing her to undertake the unlikely collaboration. Cannon viewed Toklas, in the words of one biographer, as "elegant and feminine."[100] The result was what another writer labeled "a publishing fiasco." In the end, Toklas distanced herself from the final result, while many of her friends also condemned it.[101] The unexpected collaboration made sense for Toklas's publisher, Harper. The manuscript for Toklas's first cookbook had been submitted with many mistakes, recipes with too many exotic ingredients, and was a sloppy production overall; having Cannon as a collaborator would fix these issues. In addition, Toklas had been motivated to accept the collaboration with Cannon since she was eager to quickly fulfill her outstanding contract with Harper for a second book, so that she could embark on the memoir she really wanted to write for another publisher.[102]

The book itself, though, was more interesting than the reasons for the odd collaboration itself. Before each recipe, Cannon inserted an introduction to the recipe in italics, often with recommended shortcuts using processed ingredients. The juxtaposition of perspectives was jarring. Toklas had clearly laid out in her preface the importance of using the best-quality ingredients and deliberately recommended no manufactured ingredients in the recipes. Moreover, reading Cannon's instructions, it seemed as if she did not give Toklas the courtesy of discussing her insertions. For example, before Toklas's recipe for White Soup of Artichokes, Cannon recommended: "A package of frozen artichoke hearts and a can of Swanson's chicken broth make an admirable version of this soup. If you use a blender you needn't bother about sieving or straining." In a cake recipe Cannon wrote that one need not bother adding "very, very strong coffee drop by drop," as Toklas's recipe recommended, since tossing in a spoonful of instant coffee would do.[103] Cannon spoke directly to the reader instead of to her collaborator. For a recipe called Vegetable Coronets, Cannon observed: "Despite her lightly veiled disdain of deep freeze vegetables, I have a feeling that Miss Toklas would approve of frozen artichoke hearts. They are very convenient to use in this recipe."[104] For a classic onion soup recipe, she confided: "Consider that this is said in a whisper: You can use Miss Toklas' ideas even though you resort to canned or packed dehydrated onion soup."[105] And for a cake frosting, Cannon admitted that she never discussed processed mixes with Toklas: "Whether or not Miss Toklas would approve I can't tell, having never discussed the question of frosting mixes. But may I suggest that an excellent 'icing' for this or almost any other cake can be made from a packaged frosting mix."[106] In one other way, Cannon's insertions would have been familiar to readers of her other books; she sometimes included recommendations regarding serving presentation, such as with Duck in Delicate Aspic: "This is the recipe to serve by candlelight to the strains of a minuet."[107]

To be fair, some of Cannon's recommendations were included to help American cooks substitute ingredients that might have been hard to find in the United States. For examples, for crème fraiche, she suggested sour cream with an egg yolk mixed in (for color), quick-frozen rabbit in serving pieces instead of a whole young hare, or quick-frozen chicken breasts if raw pigeon breasts were not to be found.[108] Although Cannon offered suggestions to improve the execution of Toklas's recipes, she was generous with her praise of particular dishes, such as one soup, which she pronounced "extraordinary—extraordinarily good, novel, nourishing and sustaining," or a fish dish which she praised as "without a doubt, one of the most interesting and attractive fish dishes that I have ever encountered."[109] She was also generous in her praise of Toklas's taste; with regard to a stewed apples recipe, she wrote: "This is another instance where Alice Toklas uses ordinary ingredients to achieve a notable and unexpectedly different result"; to achieve this result, she agreed with Toklas to be careful about the apples chosen, providing some recommendations of ones available in the United States, cautioning "So-called Delicious apples will not do."[110]

This brief pronouncement about respecting the taste of ingredients and understanding that the produce of supermarket shelves might be wanting hinted at Cannon's respect for good food and her admiration of Toklas. Indeed, Cannon's lengthy introduction praised Toklas on many levels, explained in self-conscious detail how their approaches were different, and yet described all that Cannon had learned from Toklas.[111] Cannon called Toklas "At the same time an intellectual, an epicure and a practical cook, [who] can cook at the same high level as she talks about and writes about food." Cannon pronounced Toklas's multiple identities to be a product of changes in the twentieth century and believed that Toklas's Americanness (despite many years of living in France) was what allowed her to combine the roles of epicure and cook. Cannon described the discussions the two had, and how Toklas disdained all processed or prepared ingredients, and asserted that fast cooking could not be good cooking. Toklas argued there was no such thing as an epicure "in a hurry." Cannon presented as a triumph her getting Toklas to try several American cake mixes, finding success with a yellow cake mix and a devil's food one; and she also took credit for introducing Toklas to an electric blender, which was embraced with much excitement. Cannon wrote explicitly about her admiration for Toklas ("I had adopted many of her ideas") and their collaboration process for the book, confessing that she held Toklas in "awe" and that they spent many hours together trying to work out terms to use (e.g., beat v. stir) and the importance of indicating how many servings a recipe made.

In her appreciation of Toklas, Cannon also underscored some of the differences between American and French approaches to cuisine. Cannon observed that many French food experts believed Americans juxtaposed food improperly, lacking tradition. Cannon, though, asserted that "We still believe, as citizens of the world, we have a right to make such juxtapositions." All the same, Cannon made it clear that she agreed with the consensus that France was the "gastronomic capital . . . of the world."[112]

There are two other remarkable topics that came out in Cannon's introduction. One was that Cannon explained how Toklas made her reconsider her devotion to the idea of "creative cooking." Cannon recalled that Toklas had scorn for the idea that something always needed to be "creative" or original. Instead, Cannon learned from Toklas the value of the French attitude about the importance of executing a classic recipe well as opposed to assuming that it must be new: "Little by little I began to understand that there can be value in giving a fine performance of another's composition . . . that an exquisite interpretation can be in its own way just as creative, just as imaginative as an invention." All the same, Cannon did add that the French love of tradition and seasonality could lead at times to monotony in food and eating.[113]

The other remarkable meditation in Cannon's introduction was her consideration of women's relationship to food and cooking; her discussion of gender roles read like a forerunner to Betty Friedan's *The Feminine Mystique*. Cannon praised Toklas as an "intellectual cook," an approach that she believed could make cooking and housework more fulfilling. Not only was Toklas's exercise of the intellect fulfilling in that regard, but also one that would "lif[t] the heart and stimulates the spirit." Moreover, although Cannon was always a proponent of processed foods and new appliances as time savers for women, she realized that the result could be opposite to that intended. This was a rare moment of considering the gendered pressures placed on women: "Perhaps the way of Alice B. Toklas is the way out—the liberation—for these women in America who are being forced willy-nilly into what might be the arid isolation of housework and child-raising. This desert often extends through a number of years while children are young. For it is not true that our modern mechanical appliances free women from domestic responsibilities. They help to make her more efficient but at the same time they load upon her more responsibilities, rather than fewer. They make it possible for her to do more and more. But more and more is required of her."[114]

In other places, Cannon had revealed her understanding of gender roles, especially the pressures that white middle-class women might feel. Two years before *Aromas and Flavors*, in her memoir about life with Walter White, Cannon acknowledged that her own life did not follow the path of the lives of many other white middle-class women: "My own pattern of living, which combines job and family, appears to be more usual among colored women of middle and higher economic brackets than it is among white families of comparable standing . . . among the colored professional group—teachers, lawyers, doctors, newspaper editors and government officials—working wives are not at all exceptional."[115]

Just a year before her death, *Poppy Cannon's All-Time, No-Time, Any-Time*

Cookbook was both an attempt to trade on the source of her fame and a return to core principles. As she explained in her foreword to the book, it included pieces from five of her previous books (*The Can Opener Cookbook, The New Can Opener Cookbook, The New, New Can Opener Cookbook, The Frozen Foods Cookbook,* and *The Electric Epicure's Cookbook*), repeating some of the same recipes, suggestions, and philosophies that defined her approach to food and cooking. This last book was also an implicit acknowledgment that her efforts outside of her tried-and-true formula were not as successful financially nor as well-known.[116] Cannon made a nod to some of the changes in food culture that had taken place in the twenty years since her first book appeared, such as renaming some chapters to acknowledge that a meal need not be built around meat ("The Meatless Mainstay: Cheese, Rice, Pasta") and by explaining that some "convenience" foods came directly from nature, not a factory (an egg, a banana, an apple).[117] But aside from such slight re-framing, seeking "convenience" remained her goal, just as it had been in her earlier books. For Cannon, convenience meant saving time ("the most precious commodity in our day and age—perhaps in *any* day and age") and elevating food to an "epicure level." Here, for example, she offered her version of chilled Peach Soup Glace Charente, the origins of which stemmed from several European countries, with heavy French influence. The classic approach included careful peeling, cutting, stewing, sweetening, and sieving fresh peaches, as well as obtaining ingredients such as crème fraiche; Cannon's version dispensed with such work, making the soup out of canned peach pie filling and yogurt.

As in her earlier books, Cannon explained that every recipe had some sort of short cut (a canned or frozen ingredient, or the use of a new appliance). She repeated her familiar argument on the importance of "seasonings" in order to improve taste and reprised her section on the ease of making good-tasting stock in a pressure cooker. But her brief nod to taste was, as usual, overshadowed by her emphasis on presentation ("presentation is every bit as important as . . . preparation . . . the difference between just cooking and epicurean cooking is the difference in the way the food is served.") and her reliance on processed ingredients.[118] The book included a Dinner Table Souffle ("Great drama for the guests to watch!"), Glamourized Hot Dogs ("dainty canned Vienna sausage nestled in small finger rolls"), and a "recipe" for serving olive-oil-brushed frozen pizza as an appetizer or entrée.[119] Cannon tempered her enthusiasm for processed ingredients slightly by acknowledging that the quality could vary, especially in canned chicken products. Canned meat also had its drawbacks, but Cannon provided a solution: "Many canned meats and gravies are not particularly attractive to look at. They may have a grayish or drab brick color, but this can be easily changed into the deep glossy brown of a French ragout by the addition of widely available bottled gravy darkeners, such as Kitchen Bouquet or Gravymaster."[120] Resourceful, as always.

Poppy Cannon's elaborate meals, made from the manipulation of canned goods were not celebrated for their taste or their creativity—either in the 1950s or by those looking back at the recipes half a century later. Nonetheless, Cannon left an important imprint on American food culture. Her embrace of canned ingredients—along with many contemporaries who wrote cookbooks and magazine columns—helped to normalize processed foods in American cooking and to demonstrate the many uses of abundant products found on supermarket shelves. The cookbook author discussed in the next chapter—Julia Child—also fully embraced the offerings of American supermarkets, though the ways in which she used these ingredients were completely different, as was her reputation and her legacy.

3

Julia Child and the Elevation of American Cuisine

In the foreword to her co-authored book, *Mastering the Art of French Cooking,* Julia Child wrote that the "excellence of French Cooking, and of good cooking in general, is due more to cooking techniques than to anything else" and that "All the techniques employed in French cooking are aimed at one goal: how does it taste?"[1] Thus, Child summarized the ideas that would animate the book and her long career that followed: taste and proper technique were paramount in good cooking.

It is no exaggeration to say that Julia Child revolutionized American cooking and eating in the late twentieth century. Indeed, countless writers, food scholars, and chefs have made such an observation. She elevated cooking to a creative, self-actualizing pursuit, not merely a domestic duty, and taught her audiences to approach eating as an epicurean pleasure, not just a source of sustenance. One gauge of Child's impact is her fame, which was and remains legendary. She is the best known of the six figures profiled in this book, and her status as a pop cultural icon is secure. With this fame, many came to feel that they knew her intimately—due in part to her self-effacing television personality and style of writing—leading most people to refer to her initially by her full name, but thereafter simply as "Julia."[2] There have been countless affectionate parodies of her on television shows, such as *Saturday Night Live,* and the internet, and her biography has been portrayed in films, such as *Julie & Julia* (2009). Many books, chapters, and articles have profiled her work and influence. What follows here will not attempt to revisit all that has come before, but rather to discuss her unique influence—in comparison with the other women profiled in this volume—in shaping what Americans chose to eat and why.

Julia Child's *Mastering the Art of French Cooking* was published ten years after Poppy Cannon's *Can-Opener Cookbook*. Each became bestsellers and brought fame to their authors. Yet, the resemblance between Julia Child and Poppy Cannon appeared to end there. While Child encouraged her readers to use raw ingredients, learn proper cooking techniques, and create delicious meals from classic French recipes, Cannon encouraged her readers to believe in the magic of a can opener and processed ingredients over the work entailed in learning cooking fundamentals in order to create good-tasting meals. First impressions, though, rarely tell the whole story. Cannon and Child had more in common than one might assume. First, they wrote for a similar audience: middle-class or upper-middle-class housewives with a certain amount of education, sophistication, and experience of European travel. Second, they both reflected a postwar United States that enjoyed unprecedented food abundance and assumed that virtually any desired ingredient could be found in an American supermarket, either in the fresh food aisle or among the canned goods. Neither seemed to give a thought to the origins of food or the environmental impact of food production. Both Child and Cannon embraced and helped reinforce America's industrial food system in their approach to cooking. Although Child did not promote the use of canned processed foods to the extent that Cannon did, she adapted France's legendary cuisine to supermarket offerings available to American housewives, including frozen foods, but also soup stocks and certain condiments. Third, Cannon and Child both ignored the nutritional content of food; Cannon cared more for the presentation of a meal, and Child cared more for the taste of a dish than whether it delivered particular vitamins or had many calories. And, finally, while Cannon more explicitly discussed the presentation of a meal, Child also cared about such questions, and became, literally a performer, first on her show *The French Chef* and in other television shows to follow.

Another similarity between Cannon and Child—and something true of all the women profiled in this book—is that they each reflected ongoing trends in food preparation and food choices; they were representatives of their respective periods. Their lasting influence lay in the number of people they influenced and in how they helped to accelerate existing trends, turning them into bedrocks of American foodways.

Acknowledging what Julia Child had in common with other influential figures in American food culture does not answer the question of why Child's fame was so great and her influence unique. Any consideration of Julia Child's lasting impact should start with the book that made her famous, *Mastering the Art of French Cooking*, a volume that was by 1974 named one of the best-selling cookbooks of the century and that was reprinted many times after its initial publication.[3]

Child's encounter with French food was—as retold in many stories about her postwar arrival in Europe—an unexpected revelation.[4] Child, who had no professional cooking experience, fell in love with French food beginning with her first luncheon of *sole meunière* when she and her husband arrived in France in 1948. As one writer recounted, "Child later credited that simple but extraordinary combination of finest Dover sole and finest Norman butter with forever changing her appreciation of food." Another writer added that the "blissful feeling" Child experienced at the meal started her lifelong appreciation for French cuisine.[5] Immersed in the flavors and culture of French food, it was not long before Child enrolled in the well-respected Le Cordon Bleu cooking school in order to learn the techniques of French cooking. Thus, the roots of *Mastering the Art* were planted.

Along with Child's relocation to France and the commencement of her formal training, there is another lesson to be taken from this biographical sketch: the extent to which the experience of eating and the pleasure it produced made Child want to cook. *Pleasure*—as derived from good-tasting food—remained Child's goal and motivation throughout her career.

From their earliest days in France, Child, along with her husband, Paul, set out to enjoy French food. They went out often and had elaborate meals at different restaurants. They avoided the usual restaurants that Americans frequented in Paris, seeking out ones that served the best-prepared, high-quality foods.[6] Love of such meals led Child to enroll in Le Cordon Bleu, and later to join a women's eating club, Le Cercle des Gourmettes. Child's enjoyment of food—then and over many years—was reflected in her frequent letters to friends as well as in her journal, often recording details about meals and restaurants. For example, her journal entries for one trip contained comparisons of three risottos from different restaurants in Italy, as well as a course-by-course critique of one disappointing meal at a French restaurant.[7] Her many letters to chef James Beard, who seemed to take as much pleasure in food as she did, were filled with detailed references to foods and meals. For example, writing to Beard about her visit to The Four Seasons restaurant in New York, Child effused: "I shall never forget it; I still weep when I think of that fish monté, and even describing it brings tears to my eyes."[8] Another letter to Beard about food she encountered in

French markets was equally vivid: "The markets are délirants! I go mad in them, and want to buy everything I see. Oh, those charcuteries, those fish, those fresh pastas. Those wonderful little collections of fish one buys for a soupe de poisons, etc., etc."[9] Here, and elsewhere, Child's pleasure was palpable. And, early in her career, it was inextricably tied to French food culture. Her affection was apparent in the name she used for France, in letters, writing, and in the dedication for *Mastering the Art:* "La Belle France." The dedication read in full: "To La Belle France, Whose peasants, fishermen, housewives, and princes—not to mention her chefs—through generations of inventive and loving concentration have created one of the world's great arts."[10]

It is worthwhile to note that Child was not alone in her admiration for French cuisine. Long before *Mastering the Art* was published, many Americans had admired French cuisine; indeed, throughout the West, French cuisine was widely considered to be the finest in the world. Beyond the ideal of fine food, though, French cuisine represented sophistication, refinement, and worldly knowledge; it represented the aspirations of many Americans, who felt that, in comparison with Europeans, theirs was a young, less-developed culture. For many educated Americans, the time was ripe to fulfill such aspirations. At the end of World War II, the United States was the wealthiest country on earth, and its political, economic, and military leader. Perhaps it was even a leader in popular culture, which was increasingly exported. But when it came to high culture, such as gourmet food, Americans remained conscious of their junior status. Gourmet food, thus, was an appealing representation of high culture. The aspirational interest in such food created fertile soil for Child and *Mastering the Art.*

Child's love of French cooking rested on three pillars: taste; seriousness of purpose; and proper techniques. As historian Laura Shapiro summarized: "Julia never doubted for a moment that the quintessential taste of France was portable, that it could be realized by any cook, anywhere, with the right instructions."[11] Child's allusions to taste were found throughout all of her books, personal writings, and television shows. *Mastering the Art* began with the admonition that it was directed at those who wanted to produce "something wonderful to eat," while Child's television shows became famous for usually including a sequence in which she tasted a cooked dish and showed her enjoyment on camera. Shapiro described a typical tasting sequence thus: "Julia's whole countenance shut down as she lifted the spoon and focused inward, then she opened up again and, most often, look pleased. 'Mmm, that's good.'"[12] Beyond the sensual experience of taste, though, Child embraced *French* food not just because it was good, but because it had *rules.* She told an interviewer in 1972 that French cooking was the best because its rules meant "you know what you're doing. The French cooking language is very precise." She asserted that the rules and skill they encouraged were paramount: "There isn't anything special about French cooking. It's just good cooking done by people who know what the hell they're doing."[13] Child formed this opinion from her days at Le Cordon Bleu, learning that fundamental techniques were the building blocks of all cuisine, to be repeated with different ingredients, in order to create different meals.[14]

Since Child's starting assumption was that good food was a function of proper technique, she had no doubt that the purpose of *Mastering the Art* was to teach that technique and, with hope, impart to her readers skills that would, over time, make them less dependent on any particular recipes. This attention to teaching basic skills made the book feel like a series of cooking classes reproduced on paper. From the start, it was clear that Child took her role as a teacher seriously. Child reassured her readers: "Cooking is not a particularly difficult art, and the more you cook and learn about cooking, the more sense it makes."[15]

It's important to pause here and say something about Child's coauthors, Simone Beck and Louisette Bertholle. Much has been written about what was, at times, a difficult collaboration. The three women met at Le Cercle des Gourmettes, after which they started a small cooking school run out of Child's apartment in Paris, L'École de Trois Gourmandes. Beck and Bertholle had already been working on a French cooking book for an American audience and invited Child to join them, bringing her knowledge of American culture to the project. It soon became clear that Child and Beck would be the dominant partners, in part because neither had children and thus had more time, in part due to Bertholle's work ethic, and in part due to their fruitful friendship and ability to collaborate. Child and Beck, indeed, became lifelong friends. As the division of work became more lopsided, the three twice renegotiated the contract among them; Bertholle's share was reduced to one-fifth, and then later to 10 percent of proceeds.[16] Although the roles of Beck and Bertholle were certainly important in *Mastering the Art*—the former more so—the following discussion will stay focused on Child, whose English writing and American voice were essential in communicating to home cooks in the United States. Moreover, the cooking lessons contained in this volume, and the voice that animated them, shaped Child's long career and legacy.

The seriousness with which Child viewed the pedagogical mission of the book was reflected foremost in its tone and organization. Methodical is the description that first comes to mind. Moving beyond her opening reassurance to readers that they were perfectly capable of learning how to cook French food,

Child backed up her promise by explaining that all unfamiliar French terms and assumptions would be translated. The book then began with several short chapters to introduce techniques, equipment, measurements, and other topics that might have been unfamiliar to a cooking novice.[17] The "Ingredients" chapter included explanations for some transatlantic differences (e.g., crème fraiche vs. sour cream vs. whipping cream), as well as the repetition that all the recipes could be made from foods bought in an American supermarket (with just a couple of exceptions, such as foie gras or truffles). The chapter "Measures" provided several detailed tables of conversions for American, British, and French measurements, as well as liquid vs. dry. Meanwhile, the chapter "Cutting" attempted in a few illustrated pages to describe the proper way to hold a knife and prepare ingredients, encouraging readers to practice these techniques for themselves.

The last prefatory item before the recipe chapters also indicated the careful organization that would follow. The table of contents listed ten chapters, one each for a different category or course of food (e.g., entrées and luncheon dishes, poultry, vegetables), and all except for one was divided into subsections also listed. The division of chapters and subsections was a familiar format shared by the majority of cookbooks, though the particular choices reflected French categories, as well as Child's determination to teach readers fundamentals. For example, the poultry chapter was subdivided into the following: roast chicken; casserole-roasted chicken; sautéed chicken; fricasseed chicken; broiled chicken; chicken breasts; duck; goose. The divisions in the sauce chapter were also notable: white sauces; brown sauces; tomato sauces; the hollandaise family; the mayonnaise family; vinaigrettes; hot butter sauces; cold flavored butters; stocks and aspics. Such detail—as well as the placement of "Sauces" as the second chapter—reflected Child's pronouncement: "Sauces are the splendor and glory of French cooking, yet there is nothing secret or mysterious about making them."[18]

The recipes in each category were no less detailed, sometimes resulting in lengthy expositions for each dish, since the authors were determined to break down all steps for proper teaching of technique. Child allowed in the foreword that it might make the recipes "a bit longer than usual."[19] Many observers have commented on the length of recipes in *Mastering the Art*—and the benefits of such a choice. Historian Paul Freedman observed: "One of the virtues of Julia Child [was] that she took nothing for granted. If you followed her admittedly long but not unusually difficult recipes, the souffle or the boeuf en daube would turn out as planned."[20] In addition to step-by-step instructions, the recipes were also printed in a careful format that listed all ingredients for a given step on the left side of the page with actions to be taken printed on the right.

Child's meticulous attention to detail was found throughout the book, reflecting her belief that the more detail she provided, the more knowledge about French cooking she would impart. She interspersed the step-by-step directions with little asides about French foodways. For example, she cautioned readers, "A sauce should never be considered as a disguise or a mask."[21] In her description of a basic French dressing (what today would be called a vinaigrette), she also included possible variations, but made it clear that the French and Americans had very different ideas about salad dressing: "sugar is heresy" in France.[22] She gave other examples of different tastes in the two countries. For instance, while introducing the section on poultry, she observed: "While an underdone chicken is not fit to eat, it is a shame to overcook chicken, allowing the meat to dry out and lose its juice and flavor. However, we have noticed that the French criterion of doneness seems like under doneness to some American palates."[23] In the introduction to the meat chapter, Child explained that it was difficult to decide which recipes among the many to include, so the authors "picked those which seemed to us especially French, or of particular interest to American cooks."[24]

In their efforts to teach readers authentic French recipes, Child and her coauthors made it clear that techniques were, in the end, more important than ingredients. For example, in introducing both the Hollandaise and Mayonnaise "families," Child allowed that both could be quickly and easily made with an electric blender, making them almost "fool-proof." She nevertheless advised that everyone "should" learn to make each by hand "as part of your general mastery of the egg yolk." Child confidently asserted that once readers learned the basics and practiced, they would be able to "easily and confidently" make the sauces in just a few minutes. Child included the blender method for each, but made no secret of which should be chosen by real cooks; regarding hollandaise, she observed: "If you are used to handmade hollandaise, you may find the blender variety lacks something in quality; this is perhaps due to complete homogenization. But as the technique is well within the capabilities of an 8-year-old child, it has much to recommend it."[25] In other sections of the book, readers were similarly advised that there were certain foundational recipes that they "should" master, such as béchamel sauce or pâte à choux.[26] And, while it might have been acceptable to use a blender for some recipes (e.g., mayonnaise), for others, only traditional methods would do. For example, Child cautioned that a food mill, not a blender, should be used to puree soups: "There is something un-French and monotonous about the way a blender reduces soup to universal baby pap."[27]

Although frequent references to proper technique, and what should be mastered, might have come across as condescending to readers, the affection with which people viewed the book indicated otherwise. The tone of *Mastering the Art* introduced the warmth and joyousness that would characterize Child throughout her career. Far from being a scold, the voice of Child was of a cheerleader who conveyed the confidence that anyone could cook wonderful French meals as long as they followed the directions. No inborn talent or other secrets were needed. And, in what would also become a signature of Child's later television career, even this first book allowed that sometimes things do not go as planned. For example, the recipe for Fish Quenelles (pâte à choux with fish puree poached in the center) was followed by "Fish Mousse, In Case of Disaster: If by any chance your quenelle paste turns out to be too soft to poach as quenelles, it will taste every bit as good if you declare it to be a mousse"; this pronouncement was followed by clear and simple directions of how to cook the mousse if needed.[28] Child kept this easygoing attitude toward mistakes throughout her career. For example, in *Julia Child and Company*, Child told readers that if their meringue layers cracked while assembling a cake, not to worry, the "San Andreas faults" could be "disguised" with filling.[29]

Child's occasional reminders that *Mastering the Art* was designed to teach basic cooking within everyone's capability was conveyed in references to haute cuisine and more elaborate recipes. For example, in the introduction to brown sauces, Child noted that brown sauces could take a very long time of simmering, reducing, and additions: "This may take several days to accomplish, and the result is splendid. But as we are concerned with less formal cooking, we shall discuss it no further."[30] Occasionally, the inclusion of a more complicated recipe was labeled as such. "Fish Soufflés from the Haute Cuisine" began with the distinction: "These are only more complicated than the preceding soufflés in that each requires fish *filets* poached in white wine, and each is accompanied by a delicious type of hollandaise sauce called *sauce mousseline sabayon*."[31] One particular recipe (Canard en Croûte) stood out for its elaborate procedure—something so intimidating that it might have led readers to distrust Child's assurance that these were simple recipes; but it was an exception, thus not impugning Child's trustworthiness.[32]

The detailed steps and serving flourishes of Canard en Croûte hinted at the performative aspects of mealtime that had been central to Poppy Cannon's recipes. Indeed, Child and her coauthors did not shy away from dramatic presentations. But it was striking how infrequent such descriptions were in *Mastering the Art*. Most of the limited references to presentation at table were confined to the "Desserts and Cakes" chapter. Introducing the section on sweet soufflés, Child wrote: "Many people consider the dessert soufflé to be the epitome and triumph of the art of French cookery, a glorious and exciting finish to a great meal."[33] Thus, Child, in part, seemed to be answering the expectations of American readers by highlighting the presentation of soufflés and other desserts. And, with a dish that would make Poppy Cannon happy, the authors included "Tarte aux Cerises, Flambée: For a spectacular entrance, sprinkle sugar over a cooked fruit tart, caramelize it briefly under the broiler, pour on liqueur, and ignite it as you enter the dining room."[34] Such a flambée was all the more striking for its rarity in the book; drama always took a backseat to taste in *Mastering the Art.*

For Child, the time it took to prepare a dish also took a backseat to taste. One of the messages found throughout *Mastering the Art,* which Child continued throughout her career, was that cooking should always be measured by its taste, not the speed with which it was accomplished. For example, a little later in her career, she wrote to James Beard in the midst of a series of experiments with different flours and recipes for breads, apparently responding to the pressure to come up with a faster method for bread making. She concluded with exasperation: "All the quick methods I've experimented on give a bready look but an immature and uninteresting taste. I am tired, anyway, of all this quick-quick business; all I'm interested in is something damned good to eat and I don't care how long it takes."[35]

There was another important guiding principle in *Mastering the Art.* In Child's foreword, she reassured her readers that no out-of-the-ordinary ingredients would be needed. In fact, she wrote that the book could well have been titled "French Cooking from the American Supermarket."[36] In the recipes that followed, Child was true to her word, with only the rare recipe having an exotic ingredient, such as truffles or foie gras. Yet, when Child pledged to use widely available ingredients from American stores, she did not recommend using overly processed or prepared foods. Almost all of the ingredients listed were whole or single ingredients, such as cuts of meat, butter, milk, fruits, or vegetables. The default assumption throughout the book was that whole and, when appropriate, fresh ingredients would be used and that sauces, stews, and cakes would be made from scratch. The contrast between Child's and Poppy Cannon's assumptions about ingredients could not have been greater. And, yet, Child included a few exceptions to this rule, primarily in two categories: canned bouillon or broth and frozen vegetables.

The use of canned bouillon or broth was described as acceptable if homemade stock was not available. Child was not judgmental in putting forward this option, though she made it clear that it was the second choice, since there were detailed instructions about making different types of stock. If that was not possible, Child explained the proper method to make the canned version acceptable; for example, "canned chicken stock may be substituted for homemade white stock if you give it the following preliminary treatment." Such treatment included simmering the product with measured amounts of onions, carrots, celery, white wine, and three different herbs for thirty minutes, after which the mixture was to be strained and was then ready for use.[37] Similarly, if homemade fish stock was not available, "emergency fish stock—clam juice" would be acceptable following doctoring and recipe adjustments for its excessive salt.[38]

The other category of acceptable prepared foods was frozen vegetables. The numerous references to frozen foods was concentrated in the vegetable chapter, with only one or two frozen ingredients cited in the rest of the book. The striking contrast between this chapter and the others in this regard led to a couple of possible conclusions. Child might have been making key assumptions about the quality of fresh vegetables in US supermarkets as well as the great quantity of frozen ones available. She might also have assumed that many home cooks were used to or would want to use frozen vegetables. The content of this chapter might also have been a reflection of how Child and her collaborators viewed vegetables—they were not considered the centerpiece of a meal—making the frozen version more acceptable. Indeed, the recipes in this chapter were often little more than cooking methods.

Even so, it was still clear that fresh vegetables were preferable to frozen. Child began the chapter with a lengthy explanation about why Americans so often remark on the tastiness of green vegetables, such as beans, in France. She wrote that the key was the French method of quickly blanching vegetables and then stopping the cooking with a plunge into cold water: "This is the great secret of French green-vegetable cookery."[39] Beyond disclosing this secret, Child indicated that fresh vegetables were preferable. For example, in her reference to green beans, she wrote: "Fresh beans take time to prepare for cooking, but have so much more flavor than frozen beans that they are well worth the trouble."[40] Regarding asparagus, she observed: "Frozen asparagus will always be limp however you cook it; the following method is as good as any we have found."[41] The frozen vegetable that earned the most praise was spinach: "Although it never has quite the lovely taste of fresh spinach, frozen spinach is certainly one of the great inventions."[42] This chapter was also the only place in the book where a few canned vegetables were included (namely, peas, onions, and mushrooms); the descriptions included ways to doctor the vegetable disguising its taste, though canned onions ("unpleasantly sweetish and over acidulated") were allowed only "in an emergency."[43] One last indication that the authors placed less value on vegetables (and grains) than on the other food groups and recipes was the casual insertion of "converted rice" and "packaged precooked rice" at the end of the chapter. Although clearly not vegetables, ways to improve these two processed rice products were added here, almost as an afterthought.[44]

Processed products such as these were the exception in the recipes presented in *Mastering the Art*, as was the allowance for canned or frozen ingredients; the reader could have had no doubt that fresh, whole ingredients were to be used in the recipes. Yet, embedded in the dictum that everything needed could be obtained in an American supermarket was the assumption that the *origin* of ingredients was immaterial. That the season was often unimportant. That "fresh" was a relative term. And, finally, that the raw ingredients themselves were far less important than how they were transformed into a meal.

The recipes did not specify particular *types* of ingredients, except to explain to readers how to substitute American for French variations (e.g., how to adjust recipes because crème fraiche was usually not sold in the United States).[45]

Similar to most of her contemporaries, Child wrote with the assumption that the ingredients listed in the book were always available from the abundant stocks of an American store, no matter the season. One brief mention of seasonality was notable because it was unusual. In the introduction for Soupe au Pistou, Child explained: "Early summer is the Mediterranean season for soupe au pistou, when fresh basil, fresh white beans, and broad mange-tout beans are all suddenly available. . . . Fortunately, this soup is not confined to summer and fresh vegetables, for you can use canned navy beans or kidney beans, fresh or frozen string beans, and a fragrant dried basil." Thus, Child both pointed to this as a seasonal food, but noted that Americans need not worry and could use canned ingredients if needed; the recipe was written for fresh ingredients, but also listed the canned alternatives.[46] Along with its lack of interest in seasonality, *Mastering the Art* also did not discuss a sense of place. The whole book, of course, was dedicated to the foods of France, but there was only an occasional reference to any regional differences in food.[47] Thus, there was an irony at the heart of *Mastering the Art:* it was a book celebrating traditional French foodways but paid little attention to time and place; it was, in its own way, a book of the American industrial food system.

One final observation can be made about the triumph of technique over raw food that was evident throughout *Mastering the Art:* Child and her coauthors approached cooking as a science as much as an art. On first glance, this assertion seemed to fly in the face of Child's persona and values. In this book and throughout her career, Child made it clear that the object of cooking was to produce delicious, lip-smacking food—and that the best source of such food was a rich French food culture going back centuries. Her description of various tastes and dishes often had a sensual quality to them. And for Child, closely related to achieving delicious taste was the *joy* that a good meal brought. Child also wrote about cooking as a "creative art." Moreover, her disinterest in a scientific approach to food seemed apparent in her refusal to discuss nutrition and nutritional components of meals. Hazel Stiebeling's plans of meals as balanced nutritional packages could not have been more different from the way that Child wrote about food. Indeed, in her introduction to vegetable cooking techniques, Child made fun of such American assumptions: "The French are interested in vegetables as food rather than as purely nutrient objects valuable for their vitamins and minerals."[48]

Thus, Child's sensual approach to food was clear. But, did this make her less "scientific"? Like good scientists, Child and her coauthors emphasized over and over the importance of proper technique. In the foreword, Child told her readers to pay attention to directions and carry them out with precision and to make sure that all tools and utensils were in good working order.[49] Exacting descriptions in various recipes included, for example, wrist movements to make a proper omelette.[50] In places, there was a scientific explanation for the characteristics of particular foods that would bring the desired result (e.g., beaten egg whites need a little acid to be stabilized, which could be obtained from a proper copper bowl or cream of tartar if necessary).[51] Child and Beck's preparation for the myriad recipes in the book meant countless hours spent testing and trying out different versions and experimenting to find the proper formulation: clearly, they were using a scientific approach.[52] One final observation: the book's acknowledgments indicated that Child consulted with scientists in government as well as trade organizations to answer particular questions about ingredients or utensils. The seeming combination of a scientific and sensual approach to food found in *Mastering the Art* and Child's subsequent career prompts us to rethink the oppositional idea that food was seen either from a nutritional or sensual perspective, that cooking was either an art or a science.

However we describe Child's approach to food and cooking, it found a ready audience in the United States. As noted above, Americans had long admired French cuisine; morevoer, in the postwar period of spreading affluence, some had the means to embrace gourmet food and the high culture that it represented. The now-shuttered *Gourmet* magazine began publication in 1941.[53] It started small, reaching a circulation of 30,000 at the end of World War II, but by the time *Mastering the Art* was published in 1961, it had a circulation of 173,000.

In addition to the magazine, the publishers reprinted many of the recipes in a two-volume cookbook in 1950 and 1957, as well as other gourmet recipe books on particular themes.[54] The magazine was initially aimed at sophisticated men, those who might continue in the tradition of elite male chefs, and those who had primed their interest in gourmet food with membership in upper-class, male dining clubs that had formed beginning in 1934.[55] Signaling this gendered intention, the magazine used a professional male chef to demonstrate cooking lessons to readers. Unlike what many assumed to be the utilitarian, nutrition-based cooking of the average American housewife, *Gourmet* conveyed the message that fine, pleasurable meals could be made by creative men who learned from elite chefs. Yet, it was clear from the outset that women were actually the principal readers of the magazine. In addition to assuming that the great chefs of the world were male, the publishers of *Gourmet* also assumed that those chefs would be French. The content of the magazine was not only recipes, but windows on French culture, art, and places. *Gourmet* was tapping into a growing interest in the United States, as symbolized by the popularity of crêpes Suzette as a chic restaurant specialty in the 1930s and 1940s.[56]

Gourmet was not devoted exclusively to French cuisine and culture. It contained what Ruth Reichl referred to as "an international cornucopia," ranging from "Indian dal, lasagna with handmade pasta, mushrooms stuffed with snails, empanadas, Viennese boiled beef, even home-brewed vinegar."[57] The cross-section of international recipes appealed in particular to upper-middle-class women (and those who aspired to the upper-middle- and upper-class) who wanted to improve their social standing and knowledge through food. In addition to *Gourmet*, there were other indications that social aspirations were tied to cuisine. *Bon Appetit* began publication in 1956; at first it was sold only in select liquor stores to show the connection between liquor, wines, and gourmet cooking; its appeal was to a similar type of readers as those who read *Gourmet*.[58]

Subscriptions to *Gourmet* and *Bon Appetit* were just one indication of increased interest in gourmet foods. Clientele for elite French restaurants, especially in large cities, such as New York, also rose in the 1950s.[59] Government officials took note of this changing food landscape in the 1950s and beyond. For example, Assistant Secretary of Agriculture Clarence Miller wrote in 1959: "There appears to be a growing market for specialty and gourmet foods. This is probably due to a number of factors such as higher real income for many Americans, increased travel, and the urge for new and novel foods." He added that although data on the historical growth of the market was spotty, the department had collected information about food retailers and wholesalers who were stocking specialty items.[60]

Food writer Betty Fussell wrote about the heady excitement of post–World War II educated, white American women who were discovering a new world of exotic flavors. She wrote how she and her contemporaries were inspired by trips to Europe and were eager to recreate their meals at home, especially at dinner parties with a competitive edge: "everything had to be French. We women were discovering with excitement how to upgrade our Irish stews into boeuf bourguignonne and boeuf en daube. . . . Now we planned out dinner parties like surveyors exploring new land. . . . . The ritual presentation required responsive aaaahs." She also made it clear that, along with the expectation that one would serve an impressive French meal, was the unquestioned assumption that the labor would be one's own, even though the final result should look effortless.[61] Filmmaker Nora Ephron had similar memories of the excitement middle-class women experienced when they discovered international foods—as well as the pressure they felt to serve more sophisticated cuisine: "food acquired a chic, a gloss of snobbery it had hitherto possessed only in certain upper-income groups. Hostesses were expected to know that iceberg lettuce was déclassé and tuna-fish casseroles *de trop*. . . . The American hostess, content with serving frozen spinach for her family, learned to make a spinach soufflé for her guests."[62]

Child's embrace of classical French recipes and the importance of proper cooking techniques did not mean that she aspired to *elite* meals. Although she widely sampled and enjoyed haute cuisine in France, it quickly became clear that her mission was to teach people how to make delicious food. The food was paramount, not the social trappings that went with it. While many Americans might have automatically assumed French food to be fancy, complicated, and something eaten by the wealthy, Child repeatedly made it clear that food was not restricted by class. *Anyone* could prepare delicious French meals once they mastered the proper techniques.

Child did not only ignore elite food pretensions, she actively scorned them. For example, the cooking school that she started with her coauthors in Paris in the 1950s was named "École des Trois Gourmandes," reflecting preference for this term over "gourmet." "Gourmand" had been used by the legendary French food writer Jean Anthelme Brillat-Savarin to denote a connoisseur of food. Child rejected the label "gourmet" as one that denoted a picky or pretentious eater. Child followed in the tradition of Brillat-Savarin, writes historian David Strauss, assuming that "A gourmand, by contrast, enjoyed satisfying a lusty appetite while appreciating fine dinners."[63] Her disdain for other people's pretensions was also illustrated in some of her letters to chef James Beard and food writer M. F. K. Fisher, which included references to "Haute Kweezeen" when discussing haute cuisine—apparently making fun of those using the exalted name in a heavy accent.[64]

Child also expressed her frustration with pretentious restaurants. In 1968, for example, writing to James Beard from France about not going out to eat as much as in the past, she concluded that some restaurants had become overly fussy: "I would far rather have something quite simple and perfect than something fancy."[65] She made a similar criticism of pretentious restaurants a few years later when she complained that a long-standing favorite near her house in France was being upstaged by a new restaurant run by "a big cheese from Paris."[66] Similarly, she wrote to her friend M. F. K. Fisher in 1972 about the restaurants in France that she favored: "The little places remain the most pleasant to us, where they have 10–12 tables, and are not trying so damned hard to be chic."[67] Child's disdain for gourmet pretension informed her approach to *Mastering the Art.* She later explained to *Time* magazine that her intention was to "take French cooking out of cuckoo land and bring it down to where everybody [wa]s."[68]

Child's message that good food should be accessible to everyone was clear in *Mastering the Art.* What was also clear was the assumption that home cooking was a woman's job. If pressed, Child would certainly embrace the idea that cooking could be done by either men or women. Yet, her own biography indicated that, like others of her generation, she had internalized the gender roles surrounding food and cooking. For example, when asked by an interviewer in 1972 about why all haute cuisine chefs were men, she responded: "Certainly you have to be big and tough for restaurant cooking. It means long hard hours and working over a very hot stove. This is difficult work for a woman unless she's a great big butch of a girl."[69]

But professional chefs, of course, were not Child's main audience, neither for her books nor television programs. As noted above, the intended audience—beginning with *Mastering the Art*—was similar to that envisioned by Poppy Cannon for her books: middle- to upper-middle-class, educated women, with a certain amount of international sophistication. There were many reasons that the book resonated with postwar white middle-class women. It confirmed the assumption that the best food in the world was French. It assured women that, even if they were educated or had disposable income, it was *their* responsibility to provide their families with tasty meals. It underscored the idea that modern Americans should become more culturally sophisticated. And it spoke to the idea that cooking was creative and fun; it was an art. Betty Fussell explained: "We didn't want to be professional chefs. We wanted to be artists, and

Julia was there to show us how cooking could be elevated to an art."[70] Added to these assumptions was another: that the woman who used *Mastering the Art* liked to cook and cared about taste; for such a woman, the speed with which she could put dinner on the table was irrelevant. Child summarized her assumptions in the foreword to the book: "This is a book for the servantless American cook who can be unconcerned on occasion with budgets, waistlines, time schedules, children's meals, the parent-chauffeur-den-mother syndrome, or anything else which might interfere with the enjoyment of producing something wonderful to eat. Written for those who love to cook, the recipes are as detailed as we have felt they should be so the reader will know exactly what is involved and how to go about it. This makes them a bit longer than usual, and some of the recipes are quite long indeed."[71]

There were many assumptions imbedded in this brief statement of purpose—ones that Child would hold throughout her career. For a reader such as Betty Fussell, the intertwined appeal to class and gender seemed most significant. Looking back on her embrace of Child, Fussell wrote that part of the attraction was to immerse herself in what was viewed as a superior European culture: "In food terms, we middle Americans were all nouveaux riches, giddy with a cornucopia of goods and techniques that poured in from Europe."[72] Such riches, though, Fussell knew were not available to all: "This was no undertaking for the poor. Such equipment cost money, and we weren't looking for bargains. All we wanted, like Jacqueline Kennedy, was the best. Julia warned us away from cheap pots. She taught us that a pot with a copper bottom less than one-eighth inch thick was worse than useless."[73] One can easily assume from reading about how many women identified with Child after *Mastering the Art* that Fussell was not the only one who felt the pressure to acquire the proper tools to become a master cook. There is no doubt that Child was utterly sincere in her scorn for pretension and her assertion that *anyone* could learn good cooking with proper technique and practice. Yet, Child, inevitably, also wrote from a particular vantage point and social framework.

Child grew up in Pasadena in the interwar period. Her mother came from a wealthy family, and her father made money in southern California real estate. Child went to elite schools, including Smith College, and by the time she relocated to Europe after the war, she already had assets worth millions of dollars.[74] In Paris, she met Simone Beck and Louisette Bertholle at Le Cercle des Gourmettes, a food and wine club for upper-class women.[75] As Child learned more about especially upper-class French food culture, she became more motivated to make it accessible to American women.[76] Thus, Child's background and experience of French food rested on the easy access to whatever foods and ingredients were desired, as well as the ability to outfit a kitchen with various tools and equipment. Moreover, Child and her fellow authors were wealthy enough that they did not worry about preparing dinner following a day of full-time employment; they felt no time pressure in their cooking. In sum, while Child had disdain for class pretension and believed that anyone who wanted to learn to be a good cook could do so, her book appealed to people with disposable time and income. Child quipped: "French cooking is not for the TV dinner and cake-mix set."[77]

Along with Child's assumption that her readers had the time to enjoy cooking was the assumption that finding pleasure in the process of cooking and producing good food were worthwhile goals. Fussell—like other readers who embraced Child's instruction—also accepted that food and pleasure were intertwined. Fussell wrote that before World War II, food in American culture seemed dull, mundane, certainly not associated with pleasure. But after the war, "We began . . . to take food as seriously as we took other pleasures."[78] It is important to remember that Child, too, took pleasure seriously, assuming that pleasure could be derived from hard work. Historian Laura Shapiro made it clear that there was no contradiction between Child's devotion to proper technique and enjoyment in cooking. "Cooking was fun for Julia," she wrote, "and she wanted everyone else to experience it that way, too, but fun didn't mean frivolity to her."[79] Such an understanding of pleasure, invites a reconsideration of Child's gendered assumptions about cooking. While Child may have internalized the assumption that home cooks were women, she saw such a responsibility as pleasurable, not a burden to escape. Just two years after *Mastering the Art* appeared, Betty Friedan's *The Feminine Mystique* articulated the protests of many middle-class women against oppressive, domestic drudgery.[80] And although it may seem at first glance as if Child and Friedan had very different views of women's empowerment, they had both, as scholar Mary McFeely concluded, "argued for empowerment of the individual."[81]

Whether or not readers of *Mastering the Art* considered the pursuit of cooking pleasure as an assertion of women's empowerment, the cultural impact of the book was profound. When it first came out, the book sold well; but sales really took off when it was selected for the Book-of-the-Month Club in August 1962. Child's book was not the main selection, but a "dividend selection"; nevertheless, it became the most popular in the dividend category in the club's history.[82] But the impact, of course, went beyond the numbers. The book and Child as a figure encouraged a whole new attitude toward French food, gourmet sensibilities, and the pleasures of the table. Writers have made pronouncements such as it being a "watershed" in American cuisine.[83]

It is difficult to define a "watershed." Some have tried with very specific examples. Writer Nora Ephron recalled that following the publication of *Mastering the Art* more and more specialty foods became available: "Cheeses, herbs, and spices that had formerly been available only in Bloomingdale's delicacy department cropped up around New York, and then around the country."[84] *Time* magazine attributed the increased number of cheeses available in supermarkets in the 1960s (going from about a dozen to roughly fifty) to Child's influence.[85] Another writer offered that, following publication of the book, there were more cooking schools and new cooking equipment stores as a result. Similarly, hostesses made their dinner parties more elegant: "Chocolate mousse, Grand Marnier souffle, coq au vin, and boeuf bourguignon, all became standard dinner party fare, thanks in great part to Mrs. Child."[86] Measuring the exact impact of Julia Child might be difficult, but there was certainly a consensus that the availability of gourmet ingredients exploded in the 1960s. Food writer Mimi Sheraton recalled: "Before the sixties . . . a fancy food department consisted mainly of packaged foods, imported canned soups from England and France. . . . It was so disgusting, you can't imagine."[87]

Such vivid anecdotes, though, might not always be reliable. For example, historian Megan Elias observed that the number of American books on French cooking was roughly the same in the decade before and the decade following the publication of *Mastering the Art* (roughly fifteen in each).[88] And, it is hard to imagine that most American supermarkets outside of certain large cities actually carried fifty distinct cheeses in the 1960s. Thus, part of what the anecdotes speak to are the particular *people* who were most affected by the publication of *Mastering the Art* (white, upper-middle-class, educated women in cities such as New York). And, yet, the impact of Child was long-lasting, moving beyond her initial audience.

One way to think about the initial and then long-term impact of Child is to consider the other cookbooks used in kitchens across America. There were a few bestselling cookbooks that had earned authoritative status; these books were the most frequently used in many kitchens, and the basic references for various cooking questions as well as a wide compendium of recipes for different courses and occasions. In sum, these lengthy books were encyclopedic when it came to the average American kitchen and defined what could be called a general, mainstream American cuisine that cut across various regions, classes, and other groups. The three most widely used of these kitchen "bibles" were *The Joy of Cooking*, *Betty Crocker's Picture Cookbook*, and *Better Homes and Gardens New Cookbook*.[89] Each of these had multiple printings and editions and were still being sold by the second decade of the twenty-first century.

The *Joy of Cooking* was the most popular American cookbook.[90] By the end of the 1960s, its various editions had sold more than eight million copies.[91] It was the least corporate of the three, first published privately in 1931 by a single author, Irma S. Rombauer. Within five years, the second edition had acquired a publisher, Bobbs-Merrill, and by the fourth edition in 1951, Irma Rombauer's daughter, Marion Rombauer Becker, was coauthor. Marion Rombauer Becker authored two of the most popular editions (1964 and 1975), and, though both hers and her mother's name remained on the book, the later editions were revised by a grandson and then great-grandson.[92] Among the qualities that made *Joy* a favorite with many readers was the conversational, warm tone of Irma Rombauer, which was preserved in most of the editions. Julia Child often noted that she admired Rombauer's writing style—which was something she hoped to achieve in *Mastering the Art*.[93]

A brief survey of the *Joy of Cooking* published in 1964 revealed many differences with Child's book. The number and variety of chapters in the table of contents covered every course and category of food an American housewife could imagine serving, adding up to an amazing thirty-eight chapters; along with the expected topics, there were also more unusual ones, such as methods for preserving food. The longest chapter in the book was "Know Your Ingredients," which discussed whole categories of food as building blocks in cooking, for example, explaining the differences between particular milks and creams, as well as discussing vegetable and nut milks. The chapter also had recipes for some basic ingredients, such as different types of stock or how to make cream cheese, as well as asides about some processed ingredients. The authors were critical of monosodium glutamate (giving a "certain deadening similarity in foods"), artificial color ("resist the impulse to add color to food from little bottles"), and processed cheeses (which have a "gummy texture and insipid taste").[94]

The recipes in *Joy* used mainly fresh, whole ingredients, as opposed to processed ones.[95] Processed ingredients appeared occasionally in the book, but usually with acknowledgment that they were not ideal; for instance, a subsection of the soup chapter is on "Quick Soups" based on canned, frozen, or dried soups doctored in a way that Poppy Cannon would recognize. But in contrast to Cannon, *Joy*'s recipes *de-emphasized* presentation. For example, the authors cautioned: "Artificial coloring, rigid aspics, fussy detailing abound. These techniques for presenting food in fancy form are unpleasantly obvious and eating quality is sacrificed. Don't torture the food. Instead, play up its gustatory highlights and allow its natural subtle colors and textures to shine."[96]

Comparing *Joy of Cooking* with *Mastering the Art* revealed clear differences in approaches—as well as a few similarities. The most obvious difference, of course, was that *Joy of Cooking* was not an instruction manual for French cooking and culture. Its recipes reflected mainstream American cuisine (with a heavy influence of New England roots), with a smattering of international recipes included, especially French, and a few complicated dishes, such as quenelles. Reflecting assumptions about a typical American diet, some sort of meat, fish, or poultry was assumed to be at the center of most meals. Although the authors gave careful advice about using fresh vegetables cooked properly, the vegetable chapter was rather short compared to the total contents of the book, and the recipes were clearly for side dishes. In contrast, there were separate chapters for fish, shellfish, meat (this chapter was quite lengthy, and including detailed drawings of animal carcasses and cuts of meat), game, and poultry and game birds.

American cuisine had long emphasized consumption of large amounts of meat—even during the Depression and World War II. Before the war, average meat consumption was 126 pounds per capita, per year; this figured *increased* during the war, never falling below 139 pounds per capita, per year. American wartime rationing allowed 6 ounces per day in comparison to British rationing, which allowed only 16 ounces per week. Demand for and availability of meat went up after the war, reaching 155 pounds per capita in 1947.[97] Thus, American housewives in the 1960s grew up assuming that meat was the centerpiece of most meals.

Unlike Child, Rombauer and Becker introduced their book with references to nutrition ("To present these essential nutrients in the very best state for the body's absorption is the cook's first and foremost job") and the importance of providing for one's family ("Never forget that your family is really the most important assembly you ever entertain").[98] Rombauer and Becker told their readers that taste was important, but usually this was when they were making occasional comparisons between fresh prepared and processed food. For example, along with their condemnation of processed cheese, Rombauer and Becker urged readers to make bread instead of settling for "the pallid commercial bread loaf in general use today," to make cakes from scratch since mixes were for "emergencies," and to figure out how to cope with supermarket produce ("less than perfect vegetables we are often forced to buy," including tomatoes that are picked green and "often become mealy and almost tasteless").[99] One key difference between the books was the attention paid to sweets. While *Mastering the*

Art had one chapter on desserts and sweets, *Joy of Cooking* had separate chapters on fruits; yeast and quick breads and coffee cakes; pies, pastes, and filled pastries; cakes, cupcakes, torten, and filled cakes; cookies and bars; icings, toppings, and glazes; desserts; dessert sauces; ice creams, ices, and frozen desserts; candies and confections; and jellies, jams, preserves, and marmalades. To be fair, the book was intended as a comprehensive treatment of all sorts of cooking, but such a profusion of recipes for sweets also reflected something about American cuisine and the expectations of modern housewives.

The two other widely used encyclopedic cookbooks at mid-century—*Better Homes and Gardens New Cook Book* and *Betty Crocker's Picture Cookbook*—shared a basic assumption about American cuisine with *Joy of Cooking*, though also had some clear distinctions. Like the other books, *Better Homes and Gardens* was intended to give readers a broad, comprehensive instruction for a variety of dishes and meals.[100] The 1953 version of the book was published in a loose-leaf binder, with cardboard dividers to make it easy to use in the kitchen. Similar to other books, it too was clearly intended for housewives, as reflected in the writing and numerous drawings throughout. Most recipes called for fresh, whole ingredients, with occasional processed ingredients, especially in a section for "Jiffy Cooking." Menu planning assumed that meat, poultry, or fish would be at the center of most meals (and the book included diagrams and pictures of animal carcasses and meat cuts) and that sweets were important in cooking (five of the sixteen food chapters were for sweet foods). In addition to the drawings, there were many poor-quality photographs scattered throughout the book to show step-by-step cooking as well as the finished dishes. The photos ended up portraying at times quite unappetizing-looking food, including a few whose recipes were ripe for parody. For example, one appetizer at the center of a party table was "Liver-Sausage Pineapple," which consisted of liver sausage mixed with a few spices and mayonnaise, along with gelatin and yellow dye, all decorated with stuffed olives and topped with pineapple leaves stuck in the top.[101]

Similar to the *Better Homes and Gardens* book published by the company that put out the mainstream magazine with a similar name, *Betty Crocker's Picture Cookbook* was also a corporate creation. The character Betty Crocker came from the advertising department at General Mills, which used the figure on printed recipes, magazine ads, and a radio show to embody an adviser for home cooks.[102] Historian Megan Elias commented that the popularity of *Betty Crocker's Picture Cookbook* in an age that celebrated convenient processed foods was apt: "Americans apparently even preferred their cookbook authors prepackaged."[103]

Betty Crocker's Picture Cookbook also included various photo spreads, along with pen-and-ink drawings to demonstrate techniques; the book also appeared in a binder format to encourage ease of use in the kitchen. The introduction to *Betty Crocker's Picture Cookbook* reminded cooks that it was their job to provide proper nutrition for their families, but also invited them to choose dishes and preparations that would not be too difficult for them. The cookbook also gave readers choices in recipes, for example comparing a traditional method and a quick modern one in baking.[104]

In sum, then, these three bestselling, encyclopedic cookbooks, although distinct, shared key approaches and assumptions. They were all lengthy and covered all meal courses and types of food, thus aspiring to be everyday guides for a home cook. They all assumed that meat, fish, or poultry would be at the center of family dinner, as well as other meals, and that sweets were an important part of the American diet. The recipes in all the books relied mainly on fresh, whole ingredients, with some occasional use of prepared foods. And, finally, they all made assumptions that their readers—and the person responsible for feeding the family—was a housewife. Thus, beyond cooking instruction, as Sherrie Inness wrote, these books were celebrating "the ideal of the Happy Housewife."[105]

There was another encyclopedic cookbook "bible" that greatly influenced American home cooking before these three tomes appeared—and then again later in the century: *The Boston Cooking-School Cook Book*, which became known as *The Fannie Farmer Cookbook*.[106] Fannie Farmer's book became a bestseller at the start of the twentieth century, encouraging home cooks to focus on the importance of food for physical health. It lost its primary place among cookbooks only when *Joy of Cooking* appeared in 1931. Farmer was significant for first instructing American home cooks about the importance of precise measurements and uniform recipes; in short, the book helped to teach women that cooking was a *science*. Thereafter, cookbooks were written in a similar style with particular ingredients, carefully measured. Julia Child recalled that her mother frequently used *The Boston Cooking-School Cook Book* and that she herself cut her teeth on its recipes.[107] One can readily connect the call for good technique and precision in *Mastering the Art* with Child's introduction to cooking by *The Fannie Farmer Cookbook.*

The Fannie Farmer Cookbook remained a best seller throughout the twentieth century, with several revisions along the way. One particularly well-regarded version was that done by Marion Cunningham in 1979.[108] The Cunningham version was so admired because it preserved recipes from earlier versions—some revised after careful retesting—dispensed with many of the processed ingredients that had found their way into revisions at mid-century, and reintroduced some of Farmer's older recipes, which had been lost in various updates. The broad range of chapters each began with an introductory essay about a particular food group, followed by the recipes, and accompanied by intermittent pen-and-ink drawings to illustrate ingredients and techniques. As it happened, Child became friends with Cunningham in the mid-1970s, writing to her with admiration about her revision project, with special praise for her systematic method of retesting all the recipes.[109]

To better understand the impact of Julia Child, comparisons with other authors are in order. The celebration of quick cooking with processed foods that made Poppy Cannon famous in the 1950s continued into the 1960s, though *not* always with the assumption that housewives wanted to become artists with their can openers. Peg Bracken's best-selling *I Hate to Cook Book,* published in 1960, appealed to a different instinct. Bracken spoke to women who felt obliged to get through the daily chore of cooking for their families—whether they wanted to or not. She encouraged readers to make liberal use of manufactured products and simply doctor them up.[110] Bracken even counseled that cooks could keep such use of processed foods secret for example, by not telling their husbands that the rolls served with dinner were actually frozen ones, heated in the oven. As Megan Elias summarized, "Bracken's cuisine was based on the art of deception."[111] Bracken's acknowledgment that some women were forced to cook spoke to frustrations similar to the ones Betty Friedan would write about a few years later in *The Feminine Mystique.*[112] Bracken was not alone in her assertion that not all women liked to cook; she was just particularly well known for her evocative title and best-selling status. To be fair, though, as Laura Shapiro asserted, Bracken's book seemed to indicate that she did not really hate cooking; what she *did* hate were the heavy emotional and technical demands placed on women to cook for everyone, every day.[113]

Far from Peg Bracken's sensibility were other influential figures who shared Child's love of cooking. Bracken and Child clearly appealed to different types of readers—and influenced different aspects of American food culture. Two particularly interesting food writers were M. F. K. Fisher and James Beard, both of whom became close friends of Julia Child. Each had a great influence on modern American cuisine, especially with the upper-middle-class cooks to whom Child appealed. As Betty Fussell recalled when she was describing the biggest influences for her and her friends: "In the postwar decades, these were our masters: Fisher in the forties, Beard in the Fifties, [Craig] Claiborne and Child in the sixties and seventies."[114]

M. F. K. Fisher was the most famous writer of gourmet style in the mid-twentieth century. Like Child, Fisher was from California and had also been shaped by her time in France, where she lived in the 1920s. (Decades later, Alice Waters would share a similar California and French culinary influence with Fisher and Child.) Fisher was a much-admired writer, known for her individual voice and her focus on the *experience* of food. She celebrated French foodways and had a disdain for American cuisine.[115]

This experiential approach, of course, was also essential to Child (as well as Waters). Child and Fisher met in mid-1966 and were soon exchanging descriptive and affectionate letters.[116] Child's husband, Paul, was part of the correspondence, and both Child and Fisher frequently used pet names for each other. Letters were addressed, for example to "Notre C*H*E*R*E AMIE & F*R*I*E*N*D." Child and Fisher shared stories of travels, changes in foodways, and critiques of different restaurants. They seemed to enjoy most talking about France ("La Belle"), both clearly sharing a love for the country and its food.[117]

Another significant "food friend" of Child's was James Beard. Beard, author of many cookbooks, took on a special role as an authority on American cuisine starting at the end of the 1940s. Unlike many contemporaries who had an inferiority complex regarding American food in comparison with French, he celebrated American and regional food traditions, encouraging readers to "take time to both cherish the old and investigate the new" in American food. His 1972 *American Cookery* was very much a celebration of a wide-ranging cuisine. Beard was one of the leading forces behind the 1959 establishment of The Four Seasons restaurant in New York; the upscale restaurant became famous for its celebration of seasonal cuisine, changing menu, décor, and even uniforms with each season.[118] Decades later, this celebration of seasonality would become a cornerstone of the new food movement. Beard's friendly, joyful approach to delicious cuisine in the 1950s set the stage for Child.[119] Judith Jones, the editor at Knopf who worked with Child on *Mastering the Art*, recalled that the pleasure Beard took in cooking was his great appeal: "He exemplified what cooking should be, which is fun and creative and something you enjoy, not something that you think of as a chore."[120]

Child and Beard had a long-standing, increasingly close friendship beginning in 1961 until his death in the mid-1980s.[121] Beard, at the center of the American food world, met Child soon after *Mastering the Art* was published. He was well known for bringing people together in the field; Child told him in 1976 how important his role was: "I have always said that it is because of you that all of us (with a few unfortunate exceptions) in the cooking world get along so well and can help each other when needed."[122] Their affectionate letters covered a wide range of topics, including travel stories, discussion of books, and restaurant critiques.

As her career progressed, Julia Child soon grew more famous than her good friend James Beard. This was due largely to the wild success of Child's first television program, *The French Chef*, and her many shows and appearances on television thereafter. Child's carefully written cookbooks changed American foodways and brought her great respect, but her television persona created a cultural icon.

The French Chef first appeared on the air in February 1963 on WGBH in Boston. By the fall of that same year, more than a dozen other public television stations had picked up the program; by January 1965, all ninety PBS stations carried the show. New episodes of the show were produced for ten years, and repeats continued after 1973. The early and growing popularity of the program, in turn, increased sales of *Mastering the Art*. Child began the series with recipes that were already familiar staples of American French restaurants at the time: beef bourguignon, onion soup, lobster a l'Américaine, and crêpes Suzette.[123] As many have observed, the show became an immediate success not necessarily due to the popularity of the French dishes, but because of Child herself. As she had done in *Mastering the Art*, Child took her pedagogical role seriously, breaking down each recipe into carefully explained steps. She was just as encouraging to her viewers as to her readers, making it clear that anyone could succeed in making delicious meals. On television, Child was both an effective pedagogue and an unintimidating cooking friend. A number of people have observed that one reason Child did not intimidate viewers was that she seemed authentic. Betty Fussell described it this way: "In a world of frozen sets, dehydrated jokes, and canned laughter, Julia is so spontaneous, freewheeling, relaxed, and utterly real that many Americans are convinced she's either loony or drunk."[124] Others have observed that the relaxed atmosphere also came from the rudimentary technical qualities of the early shows, which helped to make Child more approachable. In its early days, *The French Chef* was an inexpensive production, with a small crew, little editing, and single takes.[125]

Child's spontaneity was also reflected in her willingness to make mistakes on camera. Just as she had counseled in *Mastering the Art* that unsuccessful fish quenelles could be turned into fish mousse with guests none-the-wiser, on television she encouraged viewers to improvise if something went wrong in a recipe. Sometimes the mistakes were dramatic, as recalled by Betty Fussell, when episodes featured a potholder catching fire, a fish falling, or a dessert unintentionally melting.[126] As a number of writers have observed, Child's motto was "never apologize."[127] One example of Child's approach in action was during her first season in an episode called "The Potato Show."[128] Among several potato recipes she was making, she had a mixture of soft potatoes in a sauté pan that she intended to flip with a sharp wrist action. Although she looked at the potatoes and said they looked a little too runny to flip, she decided to try anyway, looking at the camera and telling the audience that "When you flip anything, you really need to have the courage of your convictions." Child jerked the pan back to flip the mass, only to have about a quarter of it land on the stovetop; she calmly used a rubber spatula along with her fingers to scoop the pile back into the pan, patting it to blend in with the rest, observing, "You can always pick it up and when you're alone in the kitchen, who is going to see?" Noting that the dish was not as browned and cooked as planned, she counseled, "Anytime something like this happens, you haven't *lost* anything, because you can always turn this into something else." Thereupon, Child sprinkled grated cheese on the mixture, poured some cream on it, and explained that she would either bake or broil it to complete the dish.

Along with her spontaneity and authenticity, there were other parts of Child's persona that were distinctive and soon well-known. She spoke in a warbly, booming voice, with an upper-class, transatlantic accent. Although patrician-sounding, her relaxed approach to cooking made her warm and inviting. Child made it clear, though, that being relaxed did not mean being sloppy or unprepared. On *The French Chef* she wore a plain blouse with an emblem from her former cooking school in Paris ("L'Ecole 3 Gourmandes") attached to the front breast; her outfit was often completed by a short necklace, such as pearls. Each episode ended with a presentation of the dishes cooked, ready for serving, and with a joyous "Bon Appetit" as a send-off from Child.

There was one other distinctive aspect to Child's television persona: she seemed to defy gendered expectations for women. Child not only spoke in a booming voice, but she was also physically imposing, standing at six feet, two inches, with a large frame. Historian Laura Shapiro summarized, "There was nothing dainty about Julia Child and nothing stereotypically feminine about her kitchen." Megan Elias added that "Although female, she was not feminine and indeed behaved toward food in a way that was exuberantly rough, grasping wet lobsters, playing games with chicken carcasses." Moreover, she easily used foreign terms (like professional French chefs) and invited women to become masters of the kitchen.[129] These aspects of Child's personality that came across in the earliest episodes of *The French Chef* became familiar and remained in place for later shows. For example, a reviewer for Child's new show in 1979 (*Julia Child and Company*) praised her "authenticity" and "brisk, busy manner." These were clearly qualities that he expected to see: "Mrs. Child's attack on these dishes is the same as always: vigorous and cheery. She takes hold of those hunks of meat with the authority of a German masseuse and shapes them to her will."[130]

Child seemed to enjoy not only her fame, but also the good-natured parodies of her. She said as much in 1988, when she told an interviewer that she did not mind her current publicity tour for a new book remarking, "I'm a ham," which she demonstrated by recreating Dan Akroyd's 1978 imitation of herself on *Saturday Night Live.*[131] Child realized her own comic potential and was willing to use it, such as in appearances on *The Late Show with David Letterman*; Child appeared on the show eleven times from 1983 to 1994, in brief segments making a particular recipe on a hot plate with Letterman as her assistant.[132] During her third appearance on the program, Child displayed her talent for improvisation when the hotplate she was using did not work; so she turned a raw hamburger into "beef tartare au gratin" by using a blow torch to melt cheese on top of the meat.

In addition to such guest appearances, Child was a regular fixture on American television for roughly forty years, including her ten years of *The French Chef.*[133] Along with her popularity, she earned honors for *The French Chef:* a Peabody Award in 1965 for educational television and an Emmy in 1966 (the first educational show to win one).[134] Betty Fussell dubbed her "a television queen" by the 1980s, and David Letterman called her "the most recognizable chef in the world" in 1994.[135] In addition to *The French Chef*, she had twelve other programs, some were one time programs, though most were series; some of these were tied directly to one of her books (such as *Julia Child and Company*) and some were made particularly for television. Child also began doing short cooking segments for *Good Morning America* starting in 1980.[136] One of her less-successful series came in the late 1980s, *Dinner at Julia's*; many felt as if it did not reflect the familiar Child persona, because it highlighted upscale dinners at a large Santa Barbara estate.[137] One of Child's frequent collaborators on television was fellow chef and author Jacques Pépin. Editor Judith Jones observed that, although both had been trained in French cooking, Pépin, the native-born Frenchman, had ended up becoming more American in his approach to cooking than Child. Pépin was more willing to improvise in recipes and try anything, while Child remained more traditional in her approach to recipes; the two would sometimes have good-natured disagreements during their television segments.[138]

Child's varied television shows moved far beyond the traditional French cuisine of her first, longest-running program. The same was true of her books following *Mastering the Art.* Clearly, Child began her career by falling in love with French cuisine and cooking and became successful because she was able to convey that infatuation to many Americans. But Child was more concerned with encouraging Americans to learn good cooking, rather than to denigrate American cuisine. She allowed that many Americans had their own fine traditions, including her family: "My grandmother and my Aunt Annie, too, were wonderful hen cookers and I have only the most delicious memories." In addition, she observed that many Americans were more experienced in the kitchen than were many French, who relied on professional chefs in restaurants or cooks in home kitchens.[139] As early as 1963, she was approached by a friend on behalf of Barrows and Company Publishers to undertake a book on American cuisine along the lines of *Mastering the Art.* Although Child begged off since she was busy with her television show and the second volume of *Mastering the Art,* she allowed that the idea was "very appealing," and she might revisit the issue in a couple of years. She was, though, convinced that such a book would be short: "it couldn't be too long, as there aren't that many recipes—Virginia ham, Southern fried chicken, Indian pudding, etc., and fish chowder, and corn breads."[140]

During the 1960s, with the success of *The French Chef* and the sales of *Mastering the Art* (in its eighth printing by fall 1964), Child became more confident about her talent, which was reflected in the dominant role she played in *Mastering the Art of French Cooking, Volume Two.* Moreover, with the second volume, she knew that her audience would already be more sophisticated and knowledgeable about food than that for the first. Child narrowed her focus and added two new chapters (baking and charcuterie). The book—although less known than the first—reflected careful preparation by Child and was widely praised.[141] Meanwhile, her fame grew, leading Time Life to engage her as a consultant for its series on foods of the world, and she appeared on the cover of *Time* magazine in 1966.[142] Thus, Child was in a position to broaden the types of books that she wrote. Betty Fussell observed that in the books written after *Mastering the Art,* Child became "ever less French and ever more American."[143] Child said that *From Julia Child's Kitchen,* which first appeared in 1975, was the favorite of her books. In 1982, when she had six books to her name, she told her friend M. F. K. Fisher, it was "entirely my own, written the way I wanted to do it."[144] Another author observed that in the book Child "made no apologies for being American."[145] Child told her editor that she felt freer with this book: "Now I don't have to be so damned classist and 'French.' To hell with that. I am French trained, and

I do what I want with my background."[146] Nevertheless, it is important to note that Child maintained that her French training was essential. In other respects, she remained self-confident about how she chose to express herself. When her longtime editor Judith Jones had encouraged her in the early 1970s to be "more personal" in her next book, Child strongly resisted the idea; she wrote to her friend James Beard, "Just because everyone else is being personal, why do I have to follow suit? NO."[147]

Throughout her career, Child held on to her French training as well as her strong opinions about what she believed was correct. For example, in 1973, following her first food column for *McCall's* magazine, she told James Beard that, although the staff were nice, she was "somewhat aghast at their recipes—they never cook the butter and flour for a roux, for instance. I don't understand that!"[148] Following her monthly column for *McCall's*, she reached an even larger audience when she became food editor of *Parade* magazine in 1981. The food articles that appeared there in the early 1980s—reaching forty million readers—were described by one writer as "some of the finest culinary articles then appearing in American newspapers."[149]

Meanwhile, her books also continued to be popular and eclectic in their offerings. For example, *Julia Child and Company* appeared in 1978 and was organized around the premise of providing recipes for complete dinners on particular occasions (e.g., a birthday dinner, a VIP lunch, a Sunday night supper). There were thirteen meal chapters, along with an introduction, and six additional miscellaneous advice chapters (e.g., on rice, on tomatoes, on foods to bring to other people's houses). Child completed the book with a collaborator (E. S. Yntema). The book had a selection of dishes from different cuisines, with Child explaining: "that really is the American way of doing things."[150] Each chapter began with a brief essay to describe the menu and why it was organized the way it was; the tone throughout was conversational and in the first person (similar to what Judith Jones had suggested several years earlier). Such a casual approach was also reflected in the recipes, inviting readers to use alternative ingredients when needed for freshness or cost. The book concluded with a whole chapter on "menu alternatives."

Throughout her career, Child encouraged the idea that cooking was a creative art and, thus, that cooks should feel empowered to choose alternatives when they wanted. For many cooks, the desire to be more creative led by the 1970s to a whole new approach to cooking. The revolution—dubbed "nouvelle cuisine"—was started by French chefs, but soon influenced professionals and home cooks across the Atlantic as well. The definition of nouvelle cuisine was not rigid, but it had certain hallmarks, including lighter, simpler dishes in comparison with traditional nineteenth-century French cuisine, eliminating many flour-based sauces; use of more fresh vegetables and herbs and lighter meats; and more regional and local foods.[151] Child's reaction to this revolution was complicated; after all, it was a challenge to the traditional French cuisine that was the basis of her training and very successful career. Yet, if she wanted to continue to be relevant in the food world, she needed to adapt to some of these changes.

At first, Child was more obviously critical of nouvelle cuisine. For example, she wrote a letter to the editor criticizing a 1975 *Newsweek* cover story that celebrated nouvelle cuisine. She questioned the depth of the movement beyond a short-lived trend and a public-relations campaign.[152] At the same time, she sent a letter to William Rice, who had written an article in the *Washington Post* critical of nouvelle cuisine. Child praised his article, explaining that the *Newsweek* piece "really got my goat—so full of errors and ignorance." She also ridiculed the interest in nouvelle cuisine as a fad: "God, what a bandwagon, and everybody's on it, from *House and Garden* to *Redbook*."[153] In *Masters of American Cookery*, Betty Fussell quoted Child's summary judgment of the new cuisine: "I don't really like it because the food looks FINGERED. It doesn't look foody to me."[154]

Within a few years, Child realized that she could no longer simply ignore or condemn this cooking trend. In her 1978 *Julia Child and Company*, she outwardly praised the "joyously anarchic *nouvelle cuisine*," but in a backhanded way and by redefining it in a way to suit her cooking. She named one of the leading figures in the nouvelle movement, Michel Guérard, and praised the liberation he and others had brought to cooking but noted: "His unprecedented combinations and piquant menus have inspired some bizarre travesties." Ouch. Yet, Child followed this comment with the assertion that she too was joining in the movement: "Several of the recipes in this book are *nouvelle* in a restrained way, like the little composed salads which serve as appetizers, of the Choulibiac and the Chicken Melon, both of which, though classical in flavor, are untraditional assemblages."[155] This last recipe might not be described by others as a nouvelle dish: it was a boned chicken, remade into a paté, and then stuffed back into its intact skin and shaped to resemble a melon, and then cooked. The complicated dish was part of the menu for a "Holiday Lunch."[156]

The year before the book was published, Child discussed this same recipe in a letter to M. F. K. Fisher as well as her opinions of nouvelle cuisine. She concluded that "nouvelle" was simply "using established techniques to cook up what you want." She gave the example of her new chicken melon recipe, which she had given a fanciful French name implying that it contained both melon and cheese—although it had neither; she told Fisher that she found this amusing. In the same letter, she turned to another criticism of nouvelle adherents who say you cannot use flour in sauces: "I think that is a lot of talk drummed up for nouvelle cuisine by journalists who don't cook. What's wrong with a perfectly executed béchamel or velouté?" Changing opinions again, Child praised and criticized nouvelle cuisine and organic food in the same sentence: "However I do think the talk has been useful because it makes one far more conscious of light versus heavy cooking, just as the organic food craze (whatever that means?) has made us all far more aware of additives and adulterations."[157]

Child's discomfort with these new food movements was still in evidence a decade later in two more letters to Fisher. Child sounded frustrated that she was out of step with a new generation's approach to cooking. In a 1987 letter to Fisher, she discussed planning for a new television show, but observed with disappointment, "Cookery shows have now so proliferated you can't do straight cooking anymore and hope to get on prime time."[158] A year later, her frustration at not fitting in remained. She wrote to Fisher once more in a plaintive tone: "Big question—does anyone want to do real cooking anymore? . . . This is a pasta age. I am just hoping there are still those who enjoy the mechanics of cooking as a hobby, and who like to eat food type food."[159]

There are other reasons in addition to Child's age and self-confidence that would have led her to distrust nouvelle cuisine, organics, and other new approaches. These movements not only focused on achieving new tastes, but also implied criticisms of the industrial food system and conventional diets and aspired to "healthier" food. Child trusted the American food system and the abundance of the modern supermarket. In her first book, she told readers that anything they needed could be found in an American supermarket and maintained the same assumption throughout her career. She trusted the advice of government extension agents as well as trade organizations about particular foods that she planned to highlight on television shows.[160] For example, Child wrote to the Director of Information Services for the USDA Extension Service Walter John—among other officials—over a few years with questions on the scientific differences between beet and cane sugar, the composition of cream of tartar, and more detailed information about the characteristics of tripe. John not only answered her questions, but sent further information and referred her to other sources. While Child turned to the USDA for basic chemical and nutritional questions, USDA officials also realized that they could use Child to their advantage. For example, in 1970, the USDA Consumer Marketing Service wrote to Child asking her to help "promote" rice in November and December in cooperation with the Rice Council. Child readily agreed that she would include rice in her show on November 4. In addition to her relationship with the USDA, Child also sent questions to trade organizations about foods and their characteristics. She never saw the food industry with the critical eye that many in the new food movements later did. Her trust in the industrial food system and the abundant food that it produced was implicit in her books and television shows, as well as in her professional relationship with the USDA over many years. And, when it came to the organic food movement, she was skeptical, continuing to trust the food industry instead.[161] As historian Laura Shapiro summarized: "Unless there was incontrovertible evidence of danger, she was wholly opposed to any measure that restricted food choices, or ruled out a particular category of food, or put any kind of food in a bad light."[162]

Similarly, Child was impatient with the yearning for healthier foods. She was critical of what she believed to be an American obsession with nutrition, concluding, for example, "I think one should get one's vitamins in salads, and raw fruits, and what is cooked should be absolutely delicious and to hell with the vitamins."[163] Not surprisingly, Child did not hold nutritionists in high regard. Marion Nestle observed of Child: "She was . . . famous for her disdain of nutritionists, who, she frequently stated, were ruining food for everyone else."[164] As always for Child, taste was the measure of good food and good cooking, not nutritional contents. Not surprisingly, Child was also dismissive of the obsession with weight and the urge to eat "lighter." Although Child called herself a "compulsive eater" who used will power not to overeat, she concluded that as long as one ate in moderation overall and remained moderately active, watching weight was unnecessary. She said that if she and her husband had "a greedy spell," they simply counted calories for a short time, and then forgot about the issue. She made clear, though, that no one should resort to so-called diet products, what she called "fake food."[165] Even if one were counting calories, taste remained paramount.

Throughout her career, Julia Child's devotion to delicious food—achieved through proper techniques and creativity—never wavered. She encouraged fellow Americans to respect cooking as an art on a par with other disciplines. For example, when her friend James Beard died, she was one of the driving forces behind the James Beard Foundation because she hoped it would help "to establish gastronomy as a recognized art and bona fide discipline."[166]

The figures profiled in the next three chapters turned their attention elsewhere. Rather than focus uncritically on the creative possibilities arising from American supermarkets, they questioned how American farmers produced food in such abundance—and at what costs. They also criticized constraints on individual food choice by corporate interests and government policies. As a result, they pushed American foodways in new directions. We'll turn first to Frances Moore Lappé, who viewed food production in a global context.

II

The Hidden Costs of Abundance

4

Frances Moore Lappé and Criticisms of the Global Food Industry

For Frances Moore Lappé, food was political. More important than the taste of food, the ease of its preparation, or its nutritional content, was whether the production of food was democratic or anti-democratic. Did the production of and access to food privilege some groups over others? Lappé believed that it did. In her first and most famous book, *Diet for a Small Planet*, she wrote: "It is the poor that pay most for an agricultural system geared to the production of steaks for profit instead of cheap food for us all."[1] Lappé—still writing and working as a political activist in the second decade of the twenty-first century—has spent her career trying to right this social injustice, working toward what she described as "living democracy," by dismantling the global industrial food system. And the first step in achieving this goal was to change what Americans ate.

Lappé and *Diet for a Small Planet* represented a sharp departure from the assumptions made by the three women discussed thus far in this book. Although the preceding chapters have highlighted the differences among the utilitarian, nutritionist approach of Hazel Stiebeling, Poppy Cannon's celebration of easy modernity, and Julia Child's call to savor the pleasures of delicious, properly prepared food, the three agreed on some basic ideas. They never questioned, for example, the obvious abundance of food in modern America and that abundance was not equally shared. Nor did they think a lot about the connection between the food one ate and the environment where it was grown. They also assumed that meat or animal protein was the centerpiece of most dinners. And, finally, they did not consider that the production of food and diets was political. Lappé reached a different conclusion on each of these four assumptions;

she considered food in a broader political and social context, not just a personal or home economic one. She first articulated these ideas in 1971 with *Diet for a Small Planet.* The book's impact was great. It was a touchstone for a growing environmentalism in the 1960s and 1970s and a rallying cry for what would soon be a burgeoning vegetarian movement. Her challenge found a cultural resonance in the 1970s and beyond, and thus had a lasting influence on American diets ever since.

There are various ways to understand why France Moore Lappé rejected the most widely shared assumptions about what Americans should eat and the system that produced their food. One explanation might be that Lappé was merely responding to widespread recognition of environmental degradation, the obvious problems of the American food system, and a global food crisis, all of which were evident in the early 1970s. Yet, the origins of Lappé's critique go further back. Domestic and foreign policymakers had for decades tried to address "the agricultural problem" (surpluses), indicating that the status quo was unsustainable. Thus, there were many precursors to the crisis of the early 1970s hiding in plain sight.

Lappé's call to change the American diet reflected longstanding political debates. It makes sense, then, to start by considering these problems, before turning to the solution that Lappé proposed.

One of the greatest successes of modern American agriculture was the production of abundant food. The agricultural system was most celebrated for its ability to produce vast quantities of food efficiently for relatively cheap prices. The twentieth century agricultural model stemmed from nineteenth-century technological changes (such as mechanical reapers), greater emphasis on specialization (monoculture), and expanding output, as well as growing industrial markets for food processors. By the early twentieth century, these trends were magnified by changes in demand, technology, and agricultural organization. Growth of industrial food processing and the needs of World War I increased demand for food, while at the same time efficiency and output were boosted by the widespread availability of gasoline-powered tractors and reorganized farms, which were more akin to factories than small family farms.[2] The result of all of these changes over almost a century was unprecedented agricultural abundance. Commodity surpluses were not only produced in the United States, but in other countries that adopted similar agricultural technologies in similar climates, including Canada, Australia, and Argentina; wheat production, for example, in the United States and those three other countries increased threefold from 1870 to 1920, although the population in the countries only doubled.[3] And while such bounty was celebrated—especially since it brought cheaper food—it was also responsible for what was referred to by many as the "agricultural problem" for much of the twentieth century: surplus.

The downside of agricultural surpluses was felt first by small farmers in the 1920s, many of whom saw their incomes plummet along with falling commodity prices. During World War I, agricultural production had expanded greatly to meet the demands of the war, but when the fighting stopped, the glut of grain could not find a ready market, and prices fell. The emphasis on efficiency of output had always benefited large farmers over small ones, and this discrepancy was increased by declining prices, which necessarily favored producers with the greatest economies of scale (large farms). The agricultural crisis of the 1920s—excess capacity, oversupply, and collapsing commodity prices—was one of the structural weaknesses that ushered in the Great Depression of the 1930s.[4] The severe, long-lasting economic crisis affected not only income but many people's access to sufficient food. As discussed in chapter 1, despite the abundance of food, malnutrition became widespread and a serious concern of USDA nutritionists, such as Hazel Stiebeling, who issued guidelines for well-balanced diets even for low-income Americans. The widely cited statistic that 40 percent of the first one million military inductees on the eve of US entry into World War II in 1940 were unfit for service due to a decade of poor nutrition demonstrated that Stiebeling and other nutritionists were not always successful in solving the problem of food access.[5]

The falling prices that had accompanied grain surpluses in the 1930s were no longer a problem once World War II began.[6] Indeed, the great amount of food produced in the United States was important for military supplies and for maintaining morale at home. Following government nutritional recommendations, soldiers received 5,000 calories a day, including more meat than the average civilian consumed during the war; thus, historian Harvey Levenstein observed that many soldiers ate better than when they were civilians, in terms of quantity, quality, and variety of foods.[7] Meanwhile, on the home front, most civilians were still eating quite well. Although the government initiated programs such as a "Share the Meat" campaign in 1942 to limit civilian consumption to 2.5 pounds per week and instituted rationing for sugar, coffee, and many other foods in 1942 and 1943, the impetus for such programs was due more to a limited supply of tin, rubber, and glass needed for packaging rather than any actual food shortages.[8] Total US food production continued to increase. By the end of the war, food production was one-third more than it had been when the fighting began, and the United States was producing one-tenth of the world's food supply.[9] In addition, Americans were encouraged to grow their own food in Victory Gardens—and many did—thus increasing vegetable output even more during the war. The amount of food available to Americans indeed was ample. By way of illustration: the generous 5,000 calories allocated to soldiers, in 1942, included 360 pounds of meat (mainly beef), while the per capita meat consumption that year was still an ample 125 pounds of meat (working out to more than one-third of a pound of meat per day). Even with this lopsided allocation of meat, the military only used 12.5 percent of the beef produced—as well as 25 percent of canned vegetables, 4 percent of eggs, and less than 5 percent of dairy.[10] Overall, then, it is fair to say that despite occasional complaints about rationing (and especially its continuation until late 1946, with sugar limits continuing into 1947), Americans ate well during the war, illustrating both the relative nature of food abundance and widespread expectations of it.[11]

Although many Americans might have expected that the end of wartime rationing would bring normality or at least the end to the sense of a food emergency, such hopes were dashed. The United States emerged from the war as the preeminent world power and an occupier of war-torn Europe and other places with severe food shortages, especially in the winter of 1946–47. Historian Amy Bentley labeled the contrast between American consumption and severe shortages elsewhere as "embarrassing" and a "painful discrepancy," since most Americans were eager to enjoy their abundance following years of Depression and war; the demand for red meat was so high that grain in the United States was diverted to animal feed, and pledges for food aid abroad went unfulfilled.[12] Although Truman and others in his administration worried about the dire situation in Europe and Asia, they also knew that opposition to rationing in the United States was strong. So, administration efforts in 1947 to siphon food to those who needed it abroad relied on a newly formed group, the Citizens Food Committee, and a propaganda campaign to encourage less food waste and more conservation.[13] Arguments appealed to sympathy for starving Europeans, as well as to American self-interest to protect all that the country fought for in the war, summarized in a slogan: "save wheat, save meat, save the peace." Thus, the campaign raised the idea that food shortages might even lead to another war; in some of the proposed propaganda, the danger was clearly described as communists who might extinguish freedom in Europe unless Americans provided needed food: "Our security, our way of life, our very existence depends on it."[14] A year later, such security concerns, illustrative of the growing Cold War, would cement support for the $13.5-billion-dollar, five-year Marshall Plan. The plan was a broad-based initiative to rebuild the European economy, which was the largest trading partner for the United States; more than one-quarter of the dollars came in the form of food aid or help to rebuild the continent's agricultural capacity.[15]

Beyond the specific reconstruction effort, the Marshall Plan can also be understood as an effort to harness America's "food power" and to establish an intertwined domestic and international food system that would remain in place for a quarter of a century. Post–World War II American food power rested on surpluses attained through continued use of chemical and mechanical technologies, as well as further consolidation of small, family farms into large, often corporate ones as a result of the increasing cost of farming. From the start of World War II until the mid-1950s, operating costs of the average American farm tripled, while the number of farms fell 40 percent from 1939 to 1959, and fell almost 50 percent again from 1950 to 1970. Over the same period, the average size of farms increased by two acres each year. The consolidation of the number and growing size also meant a consolidation of earnings; by the end of the 1950s, earnings by the top 6 percent of farms were equivalent to the bottom 94 percent. Not surprisingly, this consolidation of earnings was mirrored in production, so that by the 1980s, 50 percent of food in the United States was produced on 4 percent of the farms. And, finally, the number of Americans employed on farms went from 25 percent in 1945 to 6 percent by 1965 and to 2 percent by the end of the century.[16] As these statistics indicate, this was nothing short of a revolution in American agriculture.

While this remade agricultural system produced great bounty, this was not an unalloyed good, as demonstrated previously during the Great Depression. The New Deal solution to rescue the agricultural sector in the 1930s was to manage the supply of commodities and thereby increase farmer income. Scholar Bill Winders observed that, although the details of administration policies might have changed, over time, "the basic tenet of U.S. agricultural policy remained relatively constant" throughout the twentieth century.[17] Increased yields, decreased crop prices, and reduced earnings for farmers produced what historians Nick Cullather discussed as a "paradox of plenty" and Sarah Phillips described as "the perplexing state of permanent plenty."[18] The downsides of such surpluses were obvious to postwar Americans as well as historians looking back on the situation. Editors of *Time* magazine referred to the double edge of this "golden glut" in 1953, and a *Newsweek* journalist called it a "tyranny of plenty" in 1954.[19] Solving the financial side of this plenty, which resulted in reduced crop prices and reduced farm income, was an ongoing problem in the 1940s,

1950s, and 1960s. Sarah Phillips explained that, by the end of the 1950s, the US government had run out of storage capacity for surplus grain, despite spending huge amounts of money for commodity storage; largely due to such costs, Phillips noted that "agricultural expenditures made up the *third largest item* in the federal budget, following only defense outlays and interest on the debt."[20] In 1949, the secretary of agriculture under Harry Truman, Charles Bannan, had tried his hand at solving the problem with a proposal to replace the New Deal era program of parity payments with direct payments to farmers based on average income, which was intended to increase farmer income and keep food prices low. There was little political support for Bannan's proposal, so the old system continued with a revised formula of how to figure parity. Dwight Eisenhower's secretary of agriculture, Ezra Taft Benson, also wanted to dismantle the elaborate payment system to farmers and to reduce surpluses. He, too, failed in his goal. The Kennedy and Johnson administrations also failed to eliminate surpluses through their farm policies—although they did reduce them.[21] In sum, then, as each administration failed to eliminate surpluses at their source, they found new uses for them.

Starting in the Truman administration, as discussed in chapter 1, food surpluses were used for the school lunch program. This was no afterthought. Indeed, the goals of finding a use for surplus commodities and feeding children were equally important in the creation of the federal program. By the 1960s, the federal government increased its use of surpluses with more aid programs, including the launch of the food stamp program and the increase of free and reduced-cost school lunches. Support for such programs increased as the needs of many Americans became more apparent, especially in the context of Lyndon Johnson's War on Poverty in the mid-1960s. Senator Robert Kennedy, for example, on a fact-finding mission in the Mississippi Delta for a Senate antipoverty subcommittee, was shocked by the widespread hunger that he found there, observing, "My God, I didn't know this kind of thing exists. How can a country like this allow this?"[22] In addition to domestic programs that sought to alleviate hunger (such as free school lunches), both the Kennedy and Johnson administrations expanded the use of food surpluses to achieve foreign policy goals. Historian Bryan McDonald observed that "Food power as a kind of strategic policymaking came to its maturity in this decade, and the persistent farm surpluses of the postwar years slowly began to decline."[23]

The use of surpluses and American food power abroad, though, started before the 1960s. It had been integral to the Marshall Plan and a symbol of American superiority in the Cold War. A year after the Marshall Plan ended, Congress passed the Agricultural Trade and Assistance Act, better known as Public Law 480 (PL-480), in 1954. Under this law, the government could use surpluses to increase international trade and stabilize American markets; it allowed countries without dollars to pay for commodities in their own currencies and empowered the president to expand the use of commodity surpluses for emergency aid. These export subsidies were integral to domestic agricultural policy as well as foreign policy, becoming what Bill Winders referred to as "the third pillar of supply management policy, alongside price supports and production controls."[24] The law also established a Food for Peace Office that, in the words of Bryan McDonald, "would become the foundation of American humanitarian assistance programs" over the next two decades.[25] Nevertheless, until the law was revised in 1966 as the Food for Peace Act, its primary motivation was political, not humanitarian. The new law removed the requirement that only surplus commodities could be used for aid and gave dollars to countries with which they could buy American crops of their own choosing.[26] PL-480 and its subsequent iterations were also assertions of American superiority in the Cold War. As historian Shane Hamilton discussed in *Supermarket USA*, economic and propaganda efforts, such as the American displays at the 1957 Zagreb International Trade Fair and at the 1959 American National Exhibition in Moscow (which became famous in news coverage as the "kitchen debate" between Richard Nixon and Nikita Khrushchev), highlighted the success of American agriculture and the bounteous food available for purchase in the United States.[27]

Another pillar of postwar international American food power was the Green Revolution.[28] The Green Revolution, which did not receive its name until 1968, grew out of a Rockefeller Foundation research program in Mexico in 1943 designed to increase agricultural output. The initiative relied on new hybrid plant strains, as well as mechanical technology, chemical fertilizers and pesticides, and increased water. It spread from Mexico to other parts of Latin America, as well as to Asia and Africa in subsequent decades. Although it grew out of private foundations, its principles and methods were soon adopted by government-assistance programs. Ironically, in the decades when the United States had unmanageable food surpluses, the Green Revolution model exported throughout the world was designed to boost grain output elsewhere. By 1970, the success of this agricultural revolution was celebrated by governments and international organizations, such as the UN's Food and Agriculture Organization; and that year, Norman Borlaug—the scientist responsible for creating a high-yielding, dwarf wheat hybrid essential in the Green Revolution—won the Nobel Peace Prize.

The Green Revolution, though, had a darker side—as Frances Moore Lappé and other critics argued.[29] The new agricultural systems did not just increase yields of grain, it also remade whole economies and societies. Fields devoted to new grain varieties created commodities for a global market, using expensive technologies not affordable to small farmers. Moreover, farms that had previously provided varied foods for local markets switched to growing commodities for export. This switch in crops had important consequences. Diets changed because some crops were no longer grown; at the same time, since large amounts of agricultural output was slated for export, many people in these developing countries became dependent on expensive food imports instead of using locally grown food. In addition, with the adoption of new agricultural technologies, many rural people lost their jobs and migrated to overcrowded cities to compete for other forms of employment. In her study of the Green Revolution, Marci Baranski summarized that one of its fatal flaws was the assumption "that crops can be widely adapted across both physical and agroecological environments."[30] The Green Revolution, then, strengthened the global food system, but lessened the control ordinary people had over their food and increased its cost for the poor.[31] Thus, the primary, stated goals of the Green Revolution—to export agricultural technologies, increase output, and solve global food shortages for millions of people—were only partially achieved, while the initiative had unintended negative consequences on economic, social, environmental, and food systems.

The failure to provide cheap, accessible food abroad underscores the difficulty of defining what was cheap and for whom. If many of the costs of producing food were externalized—as they were in modern, industrial agriculture—was the abundance that resulted actually "cheap"? Examples of externalized costs included pollution from chemicals and petroleum, negative health effects of unbalanced, less fresh diets, loss of local control over domestic food production and access, erosion of rural communities, and low wages for agricultural workers.[32] Many critics, such as Vandana Shiva, have cited massive subsidies for grain production from the United States and other Western governments as another externalized cost, making food look "cheap" when it was not.[33] Considering such externalities, the American bounty might not be as cheap as many assumed. Externalized costs and other downsides of the American food system were key concerns of Frances Moore Lappé—and we will return to them shortly—but it's worth pausing to remember that most Americans in the twentieth and twenty-first centuries *ignored* such issues. As we have been discussing thus far, the miracles of agricultural abundance were both celebrated and assumed in the mid-twentieth century. Hazel Stiebeling and other government policymakers crafted food recommendations to achieve optimal nutrition from abundant foods available; and cookbook authors such as Poppy Cannon and Julia Child made food recommendations to achieve optimal convenience and excellent taste from unlimited choices in the supermarket available year-round. Moreover, when they stopped to consider what was cheap and affordable, they looked to the price in the supermarket and no further. Such a narrow measure of affordability, though, masked the high externalized costs of food.

Abundant food—indeed surpluses—had pushed down the price of food in the 1920s and 1930s to the point that many people were driven off the land. The double edge of abundance thus became the perennial problem of twentieth-century agriculture, all while ever greater efficiencies and yields per acre continued to increase. Nevertheless, in the mid-twentieth century, as processed food became more widespread, the value added in such products made food more expensive for a period of time with a greater share of food dollars going to processors, not farmers. Thus, in the midst of plenty and with easy access to what by any international measure would be cheap food, Americans complained that a higher percentage of their income was spent on food from the early 1940s through the 1950s.[34]

Intermittent "high" supermarket prices became a political problem for Washington policymakers. For example, there were widespread protests in 1966 by consumer and housewife groups for lower supermarket prices.[35] Secretary of Agriculture Orville Freeman, who served under both John Kennedy and Lyndon Johnson, sought to counter the impression that food was overly expensive with his "Food is a Bargain" campaign. Freeman made various arguments to bolster his position. In 1965, he summarized in a memo to President Johnson that people should not just look at the price tag of an item, since "In terms of its real cost, food is a bargain."[36] Freeman explained that, although the cost of food increased in a store, wages had increased faster, so the percentage the average worker spent on food declined. And for the needy and children who might not have rising wages, the federal government was expanding food-assistance programs. Moreover, he also asserted that some food prices had been leveling off and even decreasing. He celebrated the productivity that made abundance possible and assured the president that he and his department had been working for five years to publicize the message that food was a bargain. The wide-ranging campaign was a collaboration between the food industry and the USDA. Harold Lewis, the director of information of the USDA, reported with satisfaction in 1965 that housewives were internalizing the government's message;

for example, the percentage of those surveyed agreeing that food was a bargain went from 29 percent to 40 percent in just a few years. One message repeated by the campaign was that of all countries, the United States had the lowest ratio of food cost to income. To drive home this point, the USDA awarded shoppers with food coupons in a game called "Only 19" to publicize that Americans spent just 19 percent of their income on food.[37] Secretary Freeman also argued that food was a bargain because modern processed or prepared foods had added value, since a certain amount of the preparation work had been done for consumers, or what he termed a "built in maid service." Thus, the price tag included labor that a housewife no longer needed to perform. Finally, Freeman also argued that food prices may have gone up 13 percent since the late 1940s, but in that same period of time other costs of living had gone up 32 percent.[38]

The ongoing debate over the cost of food was only one of the controversies surrounding food in the decades after World War II. As discussed above, the cost of food was intimately connected to its abundance, which was both a blessing and a political curse. Various efforts to address the so-called agricultural problem included using the Green Revolution and other means to bolster the "food power" of the United States to achieve Cold War political goals and to enrich a global food industry. Frances Moore Lappé wrote her first book as a rebuke to the assumptions of this interwoven food system and its consequences. *Diet for a Small Planet* was published in 1971, just as the industrial agriculture system faced new challenges, leading to what would soon be dubbed "the food crisis" when in the early 1970s grain supplies plummeted, demand increased, and prices skyrocketed. In particular, Lappé criticized the social consequences of a system that failed to fairly distribute abundant food. Lappé's critique of the American food system and the food choices that Americans made remained relevant more than half a century later, even though there had been much confusion about the arguments she made.

Lappé, in a long career as an activist and author, is best known for *Diet for a Small Planet*, a decidedly unconventional book. It was surprising in its format, its interdisciplinary argument, and its strident call to understand that food was not merely sustenance, but a link to politics, the environment, and justice throughout the world. The book's breadth and ambition to change how people thought was illustrated in the epigraph: "This book is about protein—how we as a nation are caught in a pattern that squanders it: and how you can choose the opposite—a way of eating that makes the most of the earth's capacity to supply this vital nutrient." Her wording was significant. The book was ostensibly about food, or rather the lack thereof in different parts of the globe. Yet, her thesis statement did not mention "food" directly. Instead, it talked about "protein" and "the capacity of the earth."

A consideration of this paradox leads to several observations about Lappé's famous book.

First, Lappé was inspired by environmental warnings and countercultural values, yet she used a traditional nutritional framework (à la Stiebeling) instead of talking about food itself. Second, Lappé was alarmed that the earth would not long be able to feed everyone, yet she sometimes wrote more about the politics of food than about the environmental aspects of its production. And, finally, Lappé wrote that she started the book believing that the exploding population would lead to world hunger, thus following in the neo-Malthusian footsteps articulated by Paul and Anne Ehrlich in their 1968 best-selling *The Population Bomb.*[39] As Lappé's views evolved in the process of writing her book, she concluded that world hunger was caused by wasteful diets, not just population numbers. Nevertheless, the theme of dwindling resources due to overpopulation remained a popular interpretation of the book.

Lappé's starting point was the countercultural urge to challenge established norms (for instance in diet or dress) crossed with increasing concern about environmental degradation. She argued that many people wanted to avoid polluted foods as well as waste that hurt the environment. In her argument, then, individuals would benefit from eating uncontaminated foods, and the earth would benefit from less wasteful food-production methods. She discussed both of these themes (purity and waste) at the outset of the book and focused much of the book on how to dismantle the existing food system. Yet, if we dig down further to consider Lappé's framework, much of her argument discussed not the waste of *food*, but the waste of *protein*. Thus, the first paradox of *Diet for a Small Planet:* the crusading book emblematic of the counterculture reinforced instead a traditional, utilitarian view of the food system, the success of which was described in the scientific language of protein production. To unpack her argument, it helps to recall the nutritionist framework described by Gyorgy Scrinis that was discussed in chapter 1; if one views food through a nutritionist lens, it makes perfect sense to focus on the components of food, such as protein.

Diet for a Small Planet was a blueprint for how to prevent world hunger by ending the waste of protein. Thus, Lappé's main argument was based on the assumption that protein was the most important nutrient human beings needed—no matter the *food* in which it was found. Moreover, she argued that people were in trouble because the industrial food system in place in 1971 in many regions—and spreading all the time—was highly inefficient at producing protein. Lappé, of course, was not alone in her concern for getting adequate protein to everyone who needed it. For example, six years before her book appeared, USDA policymakers discussed department experiments into the "biosynthesis of protein from petroleum" to alleviate what the administrator of the Agricultural Research Service called "the world protein shortage."[40]

The first part of Lappé's book laid out the argument for why the waste of protein was a serious global issue: too much grain was used to feed livestock instead of humans. Lappé argued that the imbalance made no sense because getting protein from meat—especially beef—was highly inefficient. She included in the book protein conversion ratios in order to support her argument (e.g., three pounds of grain produced one pound of chicken, while sixteen pounds of grain and soy produced one pound of beef).[41] Lappé argued that this inefficient system had been built recently with the rise of feedlots to raise meat and the global trade of grains; thus, she placed much of the blame at the feet of the industrial food system built for the enrichment of large corporations, not for the purpose of feeding the greatest number of people.

Throughout the book, Lappé's political and economic argument about the injustice of the industrial food system was evident. For example, in her critique of the meat-centered American diet, she wrote: "It is the poor that pay most for an agricultural system geared to the production of steaks for profit instead of cheap food for us all."[42] *This*—in sum—was the heart of Lappé's concern in the book and indeed in much of her writing and activism over the more than four decades that would follow.[43] She was not focused on food itself, nor on the state of the environment for its own sake. She was instead focused on how the food *system* was used against the poor throughout the globe to block their self-determination and self-sufficiency, or what she would later call "living democracy." But this radical linkage is not what Lappé became best known for in the mainstream culture; she became best known as an advocate for vegetarianism in modern America. Yet, to be fair to those who distorted her argument, there is much contained in *Diet for a Small Planet* that fits neatly into the nutritionist framework that also provided ample support for a budding countercultural, vegetarian movement.

In part 1, Lappé's focus was mainly on waste—specifically the connection between a meat-based diet, the inefficiency of meat production, and waste. Parts 2, 3, and 4, in contrast, were first and foremost about protein. She was concerned with the physiological need for protein (broken down by weight); the definition of protein (and the distinction among the twenty-two amino acids, eight of which could not be made by the body), where protein could be found outside of meat (including very detailed protein tables with the precise amounts of protein in different foods), and finally, how to include protein in one's diet without meat. The instructional, scientific breakdown of Lappé's argument was clear throughout these three sections. She wrote about the digestibility and biological value of proteins absorbed in the body and included another chart on the "food protein continuum," classifying foods only according to their place on the continuum. Her data continued with another chart on calories per usable gram of protein in different foods. Ever practical, she added a chart of protein foods with the monetary cost of each.[44] Parts 1 and 3 were notable for the extent to which they hardly mentioned food per se, but mainly discussed "protein."

In part 4, Lappé shifted her focus again, turning the book more into a primer for preparing meatless meals with sufficient protein. She began with a cultural appeal to question the idea that meat needed to be at the center of every meal. She included a brief appeal to those seeking to lose weight, since lessening meat in the diet, she argued, meant fewer calories per meal. She tried to entice readers with the idea that meals without meat would "free" cooks and encourage more creativity and more pleasure. For example, "There are other non-health related returns from non-meat-centered eating. For one thing, it can be more fun. You will find a greater variety of textures, colors, and tastes in plant foods that are more satisfying to handle, touch, and smell than that slab of meat."[45] Following her quick nod to creativity and pleasure, Lappé was back to business with another set of scientific protein charts, this time detailing complementary protein relationships and proportions that could be used to create complete proteins in the absence of meat.[46]

Having laid the groundwork with the concept of complementary proteins and a list of ingredients always to be kept in the pantry or refrigerator, Lappé then launched into various recipes for non-meat dishes and meals. Her more than 150 pages of recipes—almost half of the book—were divided into categories of types of meals, how they were cooked, what occasions they should be served on, etc. Thus, Lappé's critique of the American food system and the global consequences of the American diet turned into a cookbook of meatless recipes.

The collection of recipes was remarkable in a number of ways, foremost in its obsession with protein. Each recipe included how much protein it contained as well as the percentage of the recommended daily protein allowance that it represented; in addition, each included the complementary protein combination in the dish. This utilitarian collection of recipes was more focused on protein levels than on taste, and frequently had optional tips for slipping extra protein into a dish, such as the following: brewer's yeast added to a vegetable sauté, dried milk put in latke and falafel recipes, wheat germ sprinkled over a spinach rice pot, and chocolate chip cookies with chopped peanuts, sunflower seeds, and dried milk added. These were the types of recipes that led to parodies of vegetarian cooking in the 1970s and 1980s. The reputation was enduring, as reflected almost fifty years later in a survey of American food by historian Paul Freedman, who dismissed the recipes in *Diet for a Small Planet:* "they didn't taste particularly good."[47] They were about the ingestion of protein, not the taste of food. To put a final point on it, the section header for appetizer recipes was "Appetizers That Count"—presumably by the protein yardstick, no matter what the taste.[48] Despite the extensive list of recipes, Lappé could not resist providing further scientific, nutritional instruction in thirty pages of appendices, on a wide range of topics from basic cooking tips for non-meat ingredients to protein cost comparisons to comparisons of different grain, flours, and sweeteners.

Lappé's approach to protein may have been obsessive, but it was not simplistic. One might speculate that, for rhetorical purposes, she could not completely disavow the accepted nutritional wisdom about the importance of protein if she hoped to convince readers to embrace a new diet. Her goal was to get Americans to eat more alternative proteins instead of meat, not to deny the nutrient's importance. Whether or not she had a deliberate rhetorical strategy regarding protein, there is no indication that she doubted the importance of protein—especially as illustrated by her detailed recipes. Overall, then, she challenged the dominant ideas about diet and nutrition but nevertheless reinforced them by reducing meals to being a vehicle for protein. Finally, it is worth noting that, although Lappé began the book with a powerful critique of the global food system that served the interests of large corporations and squandered the earth's resources, there was very little discussion of land, farms, and how food was grown in the rest of the book. Protein, then, seemed to be a distraction from the broader political and environmental issues that motivated her.

Looking at some of the mainstream press articles about *Diet for a Small Planet* gives clues about its lasting impact. First, *Diet for a Small Planet* was a common reference in press articles about vegetarianism not long after the book was published, and Lappé became known as an authority on vegetarianism. References to Lappé in the 1970s focused on the benefits of vegetarianism, primarily arguing that such a diet was lower in calories and less expensive than a meat-based one. For example, a discussion of vegetarianism appeared several times in the pages of *Cosmopolitan* magazine with such titles as "Cosmo Girl's Guide to

Vegetarianism," "What Vegetarianism Can Do for You!," "Dieter's Notebook," and "The Virtues of Vegetarianism."[49] The first and second articles, from 1972 and 1975, began with full-page images of beautiful, blonde women, one a photograph and one a drawing, posed provocatively with bare legs, long hair, and holding or sitting atop vegetables and grains. "The Virtues of Vegetarianism" also began with a smiling photo of a blonde woman standing over bowls of vegetables and grains and biting into a piece of fruit. The articles explained the different categories of vegetarianism (ovo-lacto, lacto, vegan, modified—including fish and "occasionally poultry") and how such a diet could benefit individual readers by helping them to lose weight and save money (and presumably turn into beautiful blondes). Three of the articles began with observations about the large amount of beef that Americans ate on average, which had increased dramatically in recent decades; two emphasized the point that such an increase rested on a wasteful use of grain. They also asserted that people who ate little or no meat were healthier and lived longer. In addition, the articles mentioned other reasons that people became vegetarian (including ethical, evolutionary, religious, and ecological ones).

Even though the articles referred to the ecological consequences of meat-eating, the dominant argument remained one about the benefits of vegetarianism for individual readers. Each article mentioned Frances Moore Lappé and her book as a key instructional manual for those wanting to try vegetarianism. One called *Diet for a Small Planet* "helpful," while another gushed that she "miraculously" found it in her bookstore, another referred to it as "the modern classic that teaches you how to derive complete proteins from plant foods," and finally one called it "the veggie bible."[50] Following Lappé's lead, the articles all discussed the question of how best to get protein on a vegetarian diet, and the importance of protein; one even asked whether a vegetarian diet was "safe" with respect to protein amounts.[51] Another expressed initial surprise that *Diet for a Small Planet* did not discuss fruits and vegetables much, but then observed this made sense since "they contribute almost nothing in the way of proteins."[52] Along with *Cosmopolitan*'s articles introducing the concept of vegetarianism and its benefits, *Seventeen*, also directed at young women, carried an article echoing similar themes and conclusions, and citing *Diet for a Small Planet* as the source to find out how to get enough protein as a vegetarian.[53]

Beyond mainstream press directed at young women, Lappé seemed widely known as the godmother of modern vegetarianism, based on scientific, nutritional principles of eating enough protein. For example, in 1992, *Essence* magazine ran a how-to article for parents, "Raising Vegetarians: Vegetarian Meals are the Smart Choice for Families Concerned with Health and Well-Being."[54] The article explained the benefits of vegetarianism, and directed readers to the twentieth-anniversary edition of *Diet for a Small Planet,* since Lappé provided many recipes of complementary proteins that were "high-quality meals rich in usable protein and adequate nutrition for a growing child." In different contexts, Lappé became known as an authority on the question of protein for budding vegetarians when the book first came out and for decades afterwards.[55] Discussions about tofu as a source of protein and a symbol of countercultural cuisine sometimes included references to the famous author, sometimes mentioning her environmental argument. For instance, a 1985 article in *Natural History* cited Lappé's argument "that soy and other vegetable protein sources are the frugal, sensible route to nutritional sufficiency for all human beings."[56]

Lappé's authority remained secure, although later her work was brought into some of the debates about vegetarianism; some authors criticized her nutritionist lens and others her failure to focus on the quality of food in question. For example, one 1999 article in *Midwifery Today* took Lappé to task for the "myth" in her book about the complex system of complementary proteins, which required careful planning and measuring for vegetarians. The author noted that many people still believed this to be true, although Lappé herself had revised her emphasis in the twentieth-anniversary edition: "I gave the impression that in order to get enough protein without meat, considerable care was needed in choosing foods. Actually, it is much easier than I thought."[57]

A few years later, *Diet for a Small Planet* was also cited as evidence for why environmentalists should be vegetarians due to the waste of nutrients when animals grazed on marginal lands and grain was fed to animals. Meanwhile, other critics cited Lappé's argument to support the opposite point. An article in *Alternatives Journal,* for example, argued that for years too many people focused only on Lappé's pro-vegetarian conclusions, while leaving out her important critiques of the corporate food system. In other words, it mattered whether you got your meat from an industrial feedlot or from a local farmer who grazed animals, and grain from industrial farms was not better than local sustainably produced meat. "Lappé's allegations have been narrowly and simplistically framed by well-known writers," the article said.[58]

Press stories that appeared when *Diet for a Small Planet* was first published as well as those in subsequent years revealed why Lappé became known as a godmother for modern vegetarianism. Yet, small but committed groups of vegetarians had long existed in the United States. Historian Adam Shprintzen showed that vegetarianism had strong supporters beginning in the early nineteenth century United States.[59] These advocates supported dietary reform for nutritional and social reasons; their agendas were radical in the nineteenth century—such as Sylvester Graham telling followers that alcohol, processed bread, masturbation, meat, and tobacco were all overly taxing on the body.[60] Although modern sensibilities might lead one to scoff at Graham's extreme pronouncements and the inclusion of masturbation in the list of what damages one's health, many modern scientists would probably agree with the idea that excessive amounts of the other substances on his prohibited list impaired health. As the nineteenth century proceeded, vegetarians became more organized, including a meeting of a World Vegetarian Congress at the 1893 Columbian Exposition and the establishment of the Vegetarian Society of America, which remained in existence until 1921. Vegetarianism among a small minority of Americans continued through the twentieth century. In the middle of World War II, when American meat consumption had increased dramatically, about 2 percent of the country identified as vegetarians.[61]

Meanwhile, the remaining 98 percent of Americans enjoyed their meat, with per-capita consumption ranging from 150 to 200 pounds from the eighteenth to the mid-twentieth centuries.[62] The meat-centered diet of Americans revolved around three types in particular: pork, beef, and chicken. The changing place of each in terms of importance reflected economic and social changes, not just the evolution of taste. Before the twentieth century—in a pre-urban, preindustrial America—pork was the dominant meat consumed.[63] Pigs made sense in an agricultural America since they were relatively easy to raise, slaughter, and preserve. As urbanization increased in the twentieth century, pork consumption declined relative to beef and chicken. By the early 1950s, per-capita beef consumption had surpassed that of pork. In an attempt to regain their market share, many pork breeders switched to leaner breeds, especially to compete with the lower-fat chicken; their efforts though were in vain, as pork remained decidedly in third place among American meats.[64]

Even while pork producers were trying to lower the fat of their products amid health news about the dangers of excessive animal fat, the desirability of beef remained unchanged; historian Roger Horowitz concluded that "beef has held a remarkably constant place in the nation's symbolic food universe" with steak at the "pinnacle" of desirability since the eighteenth century.[65] Food scholar Warren Belasco argued that the obsession with beef continued into the twenty-first century dominating the discussion about possible food shortages: "I am struck by how much the Anglo-American discussion of our future prospects has really been about our right and ability to eat meat, especially beef."[66]

Steak might have been the object of greatest desire, but the most significant change in modern American meat eating came with the revolution in how chickens were raised, packaged, and sold, so that in sheer pounds consumed, chicken overtook all other meats by the early twenty-first century. By 2002, Americans consumed 81 pounds of chicken per capita per year, compared with 68 pounds of beef and 48 pounds of pork; writer Jonathan Safran Foer summarized the dominance of chicken in the first decade of the twenty-first century thus: "Americans eat 150 times as many chickens as we did only eighty years ago."[67] Chicken had gone from being a special occasion meal to a convenient, inexpensive, prepackaged ingredient in many different dishes. There were three primary reasons for the revolution surrounding chicken eating: the adoption of different breeds that grew meatier, more efficiently; the adoption of new technologies and business models (including processing and prepackaging and raising chickens indoors with the regular use of antibiotics); and extensive publicity regarding the health dangers of beef and fattier meats. Whether or not Americans ate more chicken, beef, or pork, they continued to embrace a meat-centered diet decades after Frances Moore Lappé became a godmother of vegetarianism.

How then do we evaluate the impact of *Diet for a Small Planet*? As indicated by the discussion in the mainstream press, the book was both an inspiration to and instructional manual for budding vegetarians in the early 1970s and after. Other vegetarian cookbooks would follow (such as the best-selling *Moosewood Cookbook*), and those who embraced the new cuisine were further inspired by the broader countercultural and health food movements, emphasizing their political goals more than the taste of their food.[68] Yet, it would be a mistake to evaluate *Diet for a Small Planet* as merely a call for vegetarianism or any sort of appeal to individual health. Many made this mistake, which dominated the popular memory of the book. Lappé's goals were broader and more ambitious. Her book was nothing less than a critique of American food power and the global food system of which it was a part, in the form of a handbook for counteracting that system.

Shortly after her book appeared, the world food crisis laid bare the inadequacies of the system built after World War II. The food crisis unfolded from 1972 to 1974, with decreased grain supplies and sharply increased prices that sparked political and economic instability. It had multiple causes, especially the elimination of American grain surpluses.[69] Although policymakers from the 1930s to the 1970s had worked to eliminate surpluses, or to solve what was often referred to as "the agricultural problem," many people had all the while come to rely on those surpluses. Surpluses had kept prices for American consumers low and increased the amount of meat available; they had also been used to supply domestic programs, such as school lunches and poverty relief, as well as strengthen US power abroad, alleviate acute shortages, and stabilize global prices.

Following the Kennedy and Johnson policies in the 1960s that had diminished the size of surpluses, the Nixon administration made several key decisions to lessen surpluses further. In an effort to lower the storage costs of surpluses for the federal government, the Nixon administration pushed farmers to further reduce grain production from 1970 to 1972, while at the same time increasing food distribution to domestic and foreign-aid programs, and for the first time opening up the US grain market to the USSR and other communist countries. Demand for US grain increased sharply, and supply was reduced accordingly. As a consequence, wheat prices skyrocketed in the United States in 1972, although the USSR continued to benefit from cheap prices subsidized by the US government. Meanwhile, supermarket prices rose across the United States—up 20 percent from December 1972 to January 1973—leading to grassroots protests.[70] A year earlier, the Nixon administration had introduced more instability into the economy with the decision to withdraw the country from the post–World War II Bretton Woods system, which had stabilized world currencies and pegged them to gold and the US dollar; the end of Bretton Woods affected food prices as well.

The food crisis was further exacerbated by growing demand due to world population increases (an average of 80 million people per year in the early 1970s), extreme weather events (including drought in India, China, Australia, Russia, and West Africa) that had reduced world harvests, and the oil crisis of 1973–74. In addition, increased affluence in different parts of the world put more strain on food supplies due to rising demand for meat, the industrial production of which was dependent on using vast amounts of grain for feed. For example, in China in the early 1970s, the average person consumed 450 pounds of grain annually, 350 directly and 100 as feed for occasional meat, whereas the average American consumed more than 2,000 pounds of grain annually, 90 percent of which was fed to livestock to produce meat.[71] Such an inefficient use of grain in the midst of a food crisis was precisely what Lappé had warned about in *Diet for a Small Planet*. Her other warnings about the instabilities and inequalities of the world food system were also borne out by the crisis. The dangers of worldwide shortages and runaway prices in the United States were brought under control with broadly successful crops in 1975 and 1976, but the old agricultural problem of surpluses on the American market, which had been a policy focus for decades, also returned.[72] Thus, the food crisis was a temporary blip rather than a wake-up call to rethink the structural problems of the international food system. Scholar Bill Winders argued that these structural problems were twofold. First, "The essence of the U.S. food regime was a system of trade protections and farm subsidies that resulted in agricultural surpluses that were largely dumped in the periphery as food aid." Second, he concluded that market imbalances were exacerbated following the Green Revolution: "Nations around the world adopted surplus-inducing policies and then clogged world markets using export subsidies."[73]

As it became clear to Frances Moore Lappé that few Americans were ready to address structural problems in the food system, especially its political and environmental impacts, she published a follow-up to *Diet for a Small Planet*, beginning more than forty years of activism. Over the years, she refined the arguments laid out in her first book, though she kept her focus on the intersections of food production, global politics, and the environment. She believed that the most important reason to replace the existing food system was to build meaningful democracy in the United States and around the world. For Lappé, democracy was both the goal of a new food system and the means to achieve it; thus, an ideal system would offer equal food access for all and would increase equality in daily life. For such an ambitious goal, she needed to convince her readers that there was something wrong with the industrial food system.

The first book she published after *Diet for a Small Planet* was *Food First: Beyond the Myth of Scarcity*.[74] She cowrote the 1977 book with Joseph Collins and Cary Fowler; the lengthy book sought to explain in greater depth the economic and political arguments that undergirded *Diet for a Small Planet*. Lappé was explicit that the book was to counter the neo-Malthusian argument that hunger existed because population growth—especially among poor, developing-world people—was out of control. Food aid was not the solution, but instead "the redistribution of control over food-producing resources." She made it clear that the rich along with the poor suffered under the industrialized food system run by governments, landed elites, and corporations, because it endangered food security. Instead, "Democratizing the control over food-producing resources is the only road to long-term agricultural productivity for others and for us." In this book, as in all her subsequent ones, Lappé's passion was clear: "Hunger exists in the face of abundance; therein lies the outrage." As in *Diet for a Small Planet*, Lappé denounced the wasteful use of grain to feed animals in order to produce industrial meat; yet, meat eating itself was less of a focus than it had been in the earlier book. In *Food First,* she criticized the wastefulness of grain-fed meat, but highlighted other problems with the food system. In particular, Lappé criticized the legacies of colonialism, which left many ordinary people on marginal land and led to systems based on maximizing exports and yields that benefited the few. Lappé argued that the Green Revolution illustrated the flaws of such values, since it encouraged the switch to mechanized, chemical-based agriculture, the decline of traditional diets in favor of export crops, and the disappearance of meaningful agricultural jobs. To replace the wasteful and unjust system in existence, Lappé called instead for a food system that would strengthen rural communities, protect the soil, and not view food production as merely a "speculative investment."

Nine years later, Lappé made another attempt to explain why the world food system created insecurity and hunger. Again, using the framework of puncturing myths, Lappé, along with Joseph Collins, Peter Rosset, and Luis Esparza, published in 1986 *World Hunger: Twelve Myths.* The tightly organized book, which included one chapter for each myth, reiterated the arguments she made in the longer *Food First,* but it was more accessible and more clearly a call to action for ordinary citizens. As with many of her books, Lappé ended this one with a clear listing of what individuals could do to undercut the current system (including speaking out against the myths, choosing a life that expressed values, and using spending power to support alternative systems). She reprised the didactic tone of *Food First,* a style that she would return to again and again. Her frustration was clear, as she tried to figure out what to say that would change people's beliefs and actions.

A decade and a half later, Lappé wrote another book explicitly critiquing the world food system, this time working with her daughter, Anna Lappé, as coauthor in *Hope's Edge: The Next Diet for a Small Planet.* This 2002 book was an ambitious effort to compare and contrast the food system on five continents, highlighting its biggest problems as well as the greatest possibilities for change. The book was an eclectic mix of styles and goals, moving back and forth between first- and third-person voices, between anecdotes and systematic critiques. Some parts had a sentimental edge as well as New Age language (e.g., referring to "Thought Traps" and "Liberating Ideas"). Similar to *Diet for a Small Planet,* this book also included recipes for vegetarian, whole food, and organic cuisine. The authors talked about not only making the food system more democratic, but also about satisfying the senses to create delicious food. The didactic tone was familiar, though the grab bag of topics and components was overwhelming. It ended with several sections on resources and recommended actions.

Although Lappé's books provided powerful critiques of the food system, her activism seemed most animated not by food itself but by a broader, underlying goal: to build meaningful democracy and repair world systems. Working with her coauthor Joseph Collins, she cofounded the organization Food First to educate people about the causes of hunger and its solutions. Food First published numerous books on these topics, including *Food First* and *World Hunger*, as well other titles by Lappé: *Betraying the National Interest* (coauthored with Rachel Shurman and Kevin Danahar) and *Taking Population Seriously* (coauthored with Rachel Shurman). *Taking Population Seriously* was a short book that critiqued the neo-Malthusian explanation for world hunger; *Betraying the National Interest* also addressed world hunger but focused on the reasons that US food aid was ineffective and merely part of a broader, ineffective system of military aid and development assistance.

As Lappé refined her ideas about world food systems and creating a "living democracy," she continued to experiment more in the rhetorical structure of her books and how best to articulate her political philosophy. In *Rediscovering America's Values: A Dialogue that Explores Our Fundamental Beliefs and How They Offer Hope for America's Future*, she wrote a literal dialogue between opposing positions, trying to define values such as freedom, democracy, and fairness. She introduced the book by explaining the connection between her work on food systems and values: "Hunger became my measuring rod. My first test of any economic or political system would be whether or not all its people are eating. This decision and these subsequent realizations have led to almost twenty years of work to understand and to communicate the causes of poverty and hunger."[75] The structure of a philosophical dialogue was creative, though ultimately awkward and somewhat a patchwork of ideas.

In another experiment with format, Lappé cowrote with Paul Martin Du Bois *The Quickening of America: Rebuilding Our Nation, Remaking Our Lives.* This 1994 book not only provided a listing of resources but was structured as a workbook with pages to be used for writing and exercises. Its goal was to discuss democracy as a way of life, to explain the meaning of a "living democracy." In this book there was no mention of food systems. Lappé continued her focus on democracy in later publications. *Getting a Grip^2: Clarity, Creativity and Courage for the World We Really Want* (first in 2007 and then revised in 2010) continued to discuss many of the themes in *Quickening of America*, also including concrete recommendations for people to help create a living democracy. The arguments and tone were familiar from her earlier books, dividing chapters into three sections labeled clarity, creativity, and courage.

In *EcoMind: Changing the Way We Think to Create the World We Want,* Lappé focused on the environmental crisis, which had been worsened by a consumerist outlook that exploited the earth instead of working within its systems. She used food and agricultural systems as examples of this destructive approach to the earth. In this book, then, she was most explicitly returning to some of the themes from *Diet for a Small Planet,* though her tone and solutions had evolved since then. Avoiding the political and scientific tone of *Diet for a Small Planet, EcoMind* was organized by the concept of "thought traps" and how to overcome them with "thought leaps." For example, she wrote: "We can change the norms and rules of our societies to keep negative human potential in check and to elicit these powerful, positive qualities we most need now."[76] And instead of calling on people to eschew meat or to become vegetarians, she criticized industrial meat production and called for food production that cooperated with nature ("agroecology").

As an activist and prolific writer, Lappé did not confine herself to authoring books; she gave speeches and wrote numerous articles in left-leaning publications, such as *Sojourners, Mother Earth News,* and *Tikkun.*[77] Her articles also appeared in more mainstream and academic publications, such as *Harper's* and *Development.*[78] Articles in those publications were similar in topics and in the proposed solutions that were laid out in Lappé's books, though of course they were narrower in scope. Her concerns in various journals were often international, critiquing the global problems of exploitation and the poor distribution of food. In addition, press articles about and interviews with Lappé continued long after *Diet for a Small Planet* had been published.[79]

In addition to her books, articles, and speaking engagements, Lappé sought to broaden the reach of her message by cofounding three different activist institutes. In 1975, she and Joseph Collins started the Institute for Food and Development Policy (Food First), which focused on the causes of world hunger. In 1990, she collaborated with Paul Martin Du Bois to found the Center for Living Democracy with the goal of helping citizens create meaningful democracy in the United States. And, finally, in 2001, Lappé along with her daughter, Anna Lappé, started the Small Planet Institute, which combined the goal of creating a living democracy in the United States and abroad while also addressing how the industrial food system was antidemocratic and an environmental threat. Each of these institutes published books and articles, sponsored speakers, and brought together activists to work toward the stated goals. The scope of Lappé's work was ambitious from the start, even if in many people's eyes her association with vegetarianism remained paramount, as illustrated in a 2004 article, which indicated that Lappé's *Diet for a Small Planet* "introduce[ed] many Americans to the concepts of protein complementarity and the politics and economics of vegetarianism."[80]

As noted above, Lappé's books reflected the broad political and economic goals of the institutes, encouraging readers to also become activists. Her books were not highly theoretical, but instruction manuals for readers on how to take *action* in the political sphere and improve the world. They contained resources at the back, appendices with lists of organizations and contact information, as well as lists of specific actions that one could take. Related to this mission, the books also bordered on self-help literature, which instructed people how to help themselves and thus society as a whole. In that vein, Lappé's books were never subtle and often had a didactic tone that could either be rousing or off-putting, depending on one's perspective. Lappé's determination to reach readers with a singular message also meant that her books were repetitive in their arguments and material. And, like any good activist, Lappé used whatever tools were at her disposal; in her case, this was the fame and credibility that she had gained as author of the best-selling *Diet for a Small Planet.* The introductions of her subsequent books invariably made a reference to that book's message and impact. Nevertheless, even while citing her first book that had brought her fame as a food authority, it was clear that, for Lappé, the *politics* of food was always more important than the food itself.

Thus, an assessment of the decades of Frances Moore Lappé's writing and activism points back to the area for which she was most known: challenging the meat-centered American diet. While her advocacy for democracy and more sustainable food systems are often overlooked, her arguments in favor of vegetarianism gained new currency in the early twenty-first century with the growing alarm over climate change. As was clear in *Diet for a Small Planet,* and continuing through her many books and career, Lappé argued that there was an inescapable environmental consequence to what Americans chose to eat. And, by far, the greatest environmental impact was made by a meat-based diet. In the years since *Diet for a Small Planet* first appeared and Lappé became the godmother for modern vegetarianism, many others made arguments to reduce or eliminate meat from the American diet. Two main strands of thought dominated these arguments: a moral one and an environmental one. The arguments were distinct but nevertheless intertwined.

The best-known voice articulating the moral position for veganism was that of Australian philosopher Peter Singer, first in the 1975 book *Animal Liberation: A New Ethics for Our Treatment of Animals.*[81] Writing at a time when many people were condemning racism, Singer likened the "tyranny" of humans over animals to the tyranny of whites over Blacks. He argued that the pain inflicted on animals—in experimental laboratories and on factory farms—stemmed from prejudice against nonhuman creatures or "speciesism." Instead of making distinctions based on species, Singer argued that the moral and objective distinction should be made on the basis of whether a living thing felt pain; that animals felt pain (excepting perhaps certain sea creatures, such as mollusks) was indisputable. Part of the book was used to criticize the ways that animals were experimented upon for scientific and commercial purposes, though the majority focused on convincing people not to eat animals, seemingly the first way to achieve animal liberation. In particular, Singer criticized the modern factory farm as cruel and abusive. He allowed that it might be possible in a rural area to find meat raised well on a small farm, but that for most people getting access to such farms would be difficult, so it was better just to give up meat altogether. He encouraged readers with the idea that they could move to veganism gradually, first foregoing animal flesh and factory farm eggs, and then moving toward veganism, since it was difficult to change eating habits all at once. But to change them was the only moral choice: "Flesh taints our meals. Disguise it as we may, the fact remains that the centerpiece of our dinner has come to us from the slaughterhouse, dripping blood."[82]

To bolster his argument against speciesism and in favor of veganism, Singer anticipated critics who might have argued that factory farms were necessary in order to feed the world. He drew on the arguments of Lappé in *Diet for a Small Planet* to explain how eating meat, especially from factory farms, was actually very inefficient, since twenty-one pounds of plant protein in grains was converted into one pound of animal protein for humans. He quoted Lappé's apt description of a factory farm, "A protein factory in reverse!"[83] Five years later, Singer returned to the argument of inefficiency made by Lappé in the book he coauthored with Jim Mason, *Animal Factories*. The authors discussed the inefficient conversion of plant protein to animal protein and the amount of fossil fuel energy wasted in the production of meat from a factory farm. In addition to inefficiency, Mason and Singer highlighted the cruel treatment of animals on factory farms and the extensive pollution created by such farms. Another important theme was to contrast a traditional small farm with the modern-day factory operation, which hurt small farmers (or drove them out of business altogether) in addition to hurting animals. Their criticisms of consolidation and cruelty, especially, were bolstered by graphic photos of caged animals enduring horrific conditions.[84]

Mason and Singer praised Lappé's "brilliant book" and likened her pathbreaking role for the American diet to that of Rachel Carson's for the environment. They accurately observed that Lappé had revealed "the relationships among Western diets, world hunger, and environmental despoliation," but like many others, they also implied that her primary message was calling on people to be vegetarians (not merely to eat less meat).[85] They ended their book by asking readers to take action, experimenting with vegetarianism, finally suggesting: "Why not just go vegetarian?" which "is on the rise all over the country." Moreover, they pointed out that decreasing meat and dairy, and increasing vegetables, fruits, and whole grains was better nutritionally, as outlined in the 1977 "Dietary Goals for the United States" from the Senate Select Committee on Nutrition and Human Needs.[86]

A quarter of a century later, Singer and Mason collaborated on another book to convince Americans to go vegetarian: *The Way We Eat: Why Our Food Choices Matter.*[87] Not surprisingly, the authors used a number of arguments from their earlier book, but they reframed them. Instead of talking about factory farms in general or the importance of liberating animals, they detailed the food choices of three families to illustrate why "what we eat is a matter of ethics."[88] The personal stories drew the readers in, but they also reflected trends, especially since the 1990s, to assume that individual choices—consumer choices—could solve broader cultural or environmental problems. What Americans chose to eat and chose to buy mattered, since all were empowered to "vote with our fork," in popular parlance. Although Singer and Mason were sympathetic and respectful of all of their subjects, the introduction to the lower-income family of Jake and Lee was judgmental in the way their diet was described (heavy in meat, dairy, fried foods, refined carbohydrates, all from the industrial food system). Connected to their story was the tale of increased American meat consumption and the intensification of factory farming. The story clearly moved up the ethical ladder when the authors switched to the "conscientious omnivores," Jim and Mary Ann, who were chosen for a profile because of their "ethical principles." Alas, though, Jim and Mary Ann's ethics were also found wanting, since they tried to balance purity and pragmatism in their food choices. Finally, Joann and Joe were profiled. They had chosen to be vegan, which satisfied their ethical concerns—and clearly those of Singer and Mason as well. In the last section, Singer and Mason asserted that they were not trying to be absolutist about the ethics of eating, and argued that eating fish was preferable to eating other animals, that organic, local and fair trade choices were better, and that humanely raised animals were better than ones from factory farms; yet, they also asserted in this section that domestication of animals was *always* oppressive and that choosing to be a vegan is the highest ethical position.

Other authors also made the ethical and moral case for vegetarianism and veganism. Historian James McWilliams took up the arguments of Singer in his 2015 book, *The Modern Savage: Our Unthinking Decision to Eat Animals.*[89] He asserted that animals were sentient beings who are capable of suffering, although critics often dismissed such assertions as emotional and childish anthropomorphism. He criticized the attempts of ethical omnivores to escape responsibility for immoral factory farms by eating meat from small family farms or an "agrarian landscape of the imagination, a nonindustrial idyll where happy animals play on happy farms." Instead, he wrote that people could not escape the fact that even on supposedly humane family farms, "animals are raised for the ultimate purpose of being killed and turned into commodities." In addition to the moral implications, McWilliams said that small family farms could not be an alternative to the industrial system, since they would not be able to produce the same volume of meat. Such an argument did not allow for the possibility that if Americans ate *less* meat, industrial farms could be eliminated without widespread veganism.

Other writers in the early twenty-first century also continued in the footsteps of Singer, making moral arguments against factory farms, although not meat eating per se. Dan Imhoff observed that CAFOs (concentrated animal feeding operations) were "a wicked concept that's really only about money." Imhoff argued that Western religious traditions, starting with the Bible, have taught that animals must be treated respectfully even if they were going to be eaten; such respect, he observed, "Defines us as a species. It defines us as a society." CAFOs, though, destroyed any respect between humans and animals.[90]

Jonathan Safran Foer also argued the moral case against eating animals, but more urgently by asserting that it was the only way to stop climate change. In his 2009 book, *Eating Animals*, Safran focused on the immorality of eating animals. A decade later in *We Are the Weather: Saving the Planet Begins at Breakfast*, he returned to the issue of eating meat but focused more on the environmental crisis than on morality.[91] Foer, thus, echoed the arguments of Frances Moore Lappé about the environmental implications of meat-eating, as well as the moral and ethical position of Peter Singer and others. Foer, though, added something more to the pro-vegetarian arguments: he wrestled with the cultural aspects of food choice that defied moral sermons and scientific data. Foer acknowledged that the cultural aspect of food could not be wished away: "Food is not rational. Food is culture, habit, and identity."[92] For instance, he described the centrality of food in his own family experience, as well as in the identities of other Jewish families. Moreover, Foer addressed another association sometimes ignored or overlooked by food activists: pleasure. He described in detail the pleasure he took in fried chicken and sushi, a distinct loss in his decision to become a vegetarian. And, while his decision for animal welfare took precedence, he did not pretend that he found the same pleasure elsewhere: "A vegetarian diet can be rich and fully enjoyable, but I couldn't honestly argue, as many vegetarians try to, that it is as rich as a diet that includes meat. . . . I love sushi, I love fried chicken, I love a good steak. But there is a limit to my love."[93] Similar to other activists, Foer argued that choosing what to eat was like voting with your fork: "One of the greatest opportunities to live our values—or betray them—lies in the food we put on our plates," since making that choice was a "social act."[94] This last acknowledgment, in part, led him to conclude that, although his real objection was to factory farms not to small, humane farms, it became untenable to live out that distinction; for example, as a social practice, being a vegetarian could be accommodated whereas rejecting a host's meal based on the farm where its ingredients came from could not.[95]

In *We Are the Weather,* Foer took up more directly the legacy of Lappé, who had denounced the hidden costs and cruelty of factory farms but focused her greatest attention on the environmental and global consequences of a diet based on industrial meat. Foer provided detailed data about the outsized impact that factory farms had on the climate crisis as measured by the CO_2 and methane produced, and the land, water, and fuel resources squandered on animals raised for human food. He wrote that the link was undeniable and urgent: "We cannot keep the kinds of meals we have known and also keep the planet we have known. We must either let some eating habits go or let the planet go."[96] Part of the book also read as a confession of Foer's own shortcomings or what he labeled "pathetic" "hypocrisy": he ate meat a number of times on his travels in the previous decade, including factory-farmed burgers. Foer was reflective about what he saw as his failure: "Eating consciously will be one of the struggles that span and define my life . . . not as a reflection of my uncertainty about the right way to eat, but as a function of the complexity of eating."[97] Understanding that complexity, Foer still had no doubt about the way forward for the American diet.

By the second decade of the twenty-first century, many Americans felt the same urgency that Jonathan Safran Foer did. They understood that the environmental consequences of industrial food production—including factory-farmed meat—were real, measurable, and a significant factor in escalating global warming. Whether or not they shared Foer's moral opposition to meat eating, an increasing number of Americans and Westerners came to believe that they should eat less meat—or at least earnestly consider such a change. Thus, the embrace of new meat alternatives beginning in 2019 went far beyond earlier alternatives of homemade or store-bought veggie burgers composed of nuts and grains.[98] The real breakthrough came with the popular brands Impossible Burger and Beyond Burger, sold in supermarkets and offered in various fast-food and chain restaurants. The products were a triumph of technology and food science, producing plant-based burgers that seemed to "bleed" just like beef ones. In one case, the blood came from beet juice, in the other from heme, made from genetically modified soy protein added to genetically modified yeast. Even if these foods had a smaller carbon footprint than beef burgers (one study of the Impossible Burger, for example, said it had an 89 percent smaller footprint than a beef burger), they were nevertheless highly processed industrial foods that fostered little connection with the environment.[99] Meanwhile, following the market success of nonmeat burgers, other companies were hard at work creating meat in laboratories grown from the stem cells of cows; the eventual cost and carbon benefit of these products was not yet clear by 2020.[100]

When Frances Moore Lappé recommended in 1971 that Americans eat less meat, there was little indication she was imagining a diet of Impossible Burgers and laboratory-grown beef. Her goal was to change the global food system by encouraging Americans to change their eating habits, not to encourage the industrial production of imitation meat. Similar to Lappé, Marion Nestle also wanted Americans to change their eating habits. But she did not see the biggest impediment to healthier diets as the American fondness for meat. Instead, Nestle argued that large food corporations were intent on manipulating food choice for their own benefit.

5

Marion Nestle and the Battle against Big Food

Similar to Frances Moore Lappé, Marion Nestle spent a career critiquing the downsides of the American industrial food system. Although the women agreed on much—including the observation that food was political—the focus of their research and activism differed. Lappé examined how the global food system produced abundance that was unevenly distributed, while exploiting workers and damaging the environment. Repairing such a system, Lappé argued, would be the manifestation of true democracy; she was more focused on democracy than on food. Nestle, instead, was most concerned with what Americans ate, how much they ate, and how this impacted their health. She argued that their food choices were manipulated—even more, subverted—by large corporations whose primary goal was to make money. Yet, despite the depressing record of these manipulations and of citizens failing to heed nutrition advice from health experts, Nestle remained a true believer in the power of education and science to win out—if only it was a fair fight. She gave evidence for such optimism in an interview with *Fortune* magazine in 2002. She explained that little money was spent to market good nutritional advice, whereas much was spent to market junk foods such as candy. For example, Nestle observed that the corporation that sold Altoids mints had an advertising budget "five times what the National Cancer Institute and the Produce for Better Health Foundation spent to encourage consumers to eat five fruits and vegetables a day."[1] It was hard for nutritionists to be heard when they were outspent five to one.

The following chapter will examine what Marion Nestle tried to teach Americans—even if she and her fellow nutritionists were competing with the vast marketing power of food corporations. Nestle was an influential voice in academia, government, and the media for decades. She was a trusted source for journalists and a well-known public face for mainstream nutritional guidelines, earning such monikers in the press as "America's nutritionist." A perusal of Nestle's correspondence in the 1990s and 2000s indicates that academics and journalists frequently sought her opinions on general as well as on specific dietary and policy issues. For example, an initiative by New York City authorities to reduce salt and sugar consumption elicited a request for comment in 2010 from city papers. Her correspondence also shows that she maintained active relationships with many public figures in the world of food culture, including many in the new food movements as well as other prominent figures. For example, restauranteur Danny Meyer wrote in 2011 to say that a dinner he hosted for her was "my way of saying thanks for the profound contributions you've made to our industry." Nestle's authority in the mainstream food culture even made it into high school Advanced Placement exams in 2011. One mother wrote to say that her son told her an essay prompt was an excerpt by Nestle about the local food movement: "You are everywhere!" she gushed."[2]

Throughout her career, Nestle was remarkably consistent in the lessons she taught about nutrition. In her 2006 book *What to Eat* she summarized: "The basic principles of good diets are so simple that I can summarize them in just ten words: *eat less, move more, eat lots of fruits and vegetables.* For additional clarification, a five-word modifier helps: *go easy on junk foods.*"[3] Behind this simple precept, though, were complex, difficult to solve problems. Corporate manipulation of nutritional advice was predictable, since the overabundance of food produced by the industrial system created a constant pressure to convince Americans to eat more and to eat the wrong types of food. In such a food environment, corporate actions were rational if ethically suspect at best, and contemptible at worst. Nestle believed that government policymakers and professional nutritionists *should* be the necessary counterweight to food companies, through regulations and education. Unfortunately, policymakers and nutritionists too often failed to do their jobs to use science to protect American health. As a result, Nestle argued, Americans ate the wrong food and too much of it, leading to chronic health problems that were serious for individuals and costly for society as a whole. Despite Nestle's incisive diagnosis of this situation, she remained optimistic that scientific knowledge would eventually lead people to make rational choices about their diets. Nevertheless, as the following discussion makes clear, Nestle's confidence in people's ability to make rational choices about their diet might have been misplaced.

Marion Nestle was a scientist by training and retained a scientist's outlook through her many years dissecting the politics of the food system. Her academic credentials, accomplishments, honors, and affiliations were extensive, and would take many pages to detail; they can be found on the website she maintained, foodpolitics.com.[4] Nestle earned her PhD in molecular biology in the late 1960s, after which she taught biology at Brandeis University and biochemistry and biophysics, medicine, and family and community medicine at the University of California San Francisco School of Medicine. Nestle retrained and refocused her research and career in the mid-1980s with the completion of a master's degree in public health, focusing on nutrition, and she gained a licensure in nutrition and dietetics in New York State. She began her long association with New York University in 1988, chairing the Department of Nutrition and Food Studies and Public Health, and affiliating with other departments and colleges in the university, as well as establishing a long-term visiting relationship with Cornell University. Nestle became the Paulette Goddard Professor of Nutrition, Food Studies, and Public Health at NYU in 2004 and Emerita in 2017, while still continuing to teach, lecture, and write at NYU and elsewhere.

Nestle's academic success increased her influence within the nutrition and food studies fields. She trained many other scholars in nutrition and food studies and influenced federal government food guidelines. She helped to remake the NYU nutrition department with a broader food studies approach, summarizing part of the goal to a popular magazine in 1999: "We want to make food studies an academically respected field."[5] Nestle was proud of this academic role, writing in 2022: "I do have a tangible legacy. It includes . . . the now-burgeoning field of food studies."[6] But Nestle's greatest impact on the American diet was from her books, aimed at both an academic and a trade market, speaking engagements for a similar audience, and mainstream press interviews, articles, and other popular distillations of her research. Nestle has written twelve books, eight of them as a single author, and she has edited or co-edited three additional books. She first gained fame outside of her field and academia in 2002 with *Food Politics: How the Food Industry Influences Nutrition and Health.*[7] This book was later revised and expanded and became a staple in university food studies and nutrition curricula. Her other books include: *Safe Food: Bacteria, Biotechnology, and Bioterrorism*; *What to Eat*; *Pet Food Politics: The Chihuahua in the Coal Mine*; *Feed Your Pet Right*; *Why Calories Count: From Science to Politics*; *Eat, Drink, Vote: An Illustrated Guide to Food Politics*; *Soda Politics: Taking on Big Soda (and Winning)*; *Unsavory Truth: How Food Companies Skew the Science of What We Eat*; *Let's Ask Marion: What You Need to Know about the Politics of Food, Nutrition, and Health*; and *Slow Cooked: An Unexpected Life in Food Politics.*[8]

Along with this brief biography, there are two important points to remember that frame how Nestle sought to influence what Americans ate. First, she never left behind her scientific training and nutritionist perspective that food was, foremost, something that impacted health, for good or ill. Second, Nestle's commitment to nutrition education and communication was passionate. A quick perusal of her blog, even without reading any of her books, or the list of her speaking engagements, makes this obvious, especially since the blog is integrated with a well-produced, easy-to-use website packed with information about all topics related to food. Before turning to the specifics of her advice, it makes sense to begin by trying to understand the public role of nutritionists that shaped Nestle's outlook.

Nestle began her academic career teaching in and working as an administrator in biology programs in the 1970s and 1980s. But when she shifted her focus and earned an additional degree in public health nutrition, she left academia for two years to work in the federal government at the Department of Health and Human Services in the Office of Disease Prevention and Health Promotion. She was staff director for nutrition policy and senior nutrition policy adviser, as well as the managing editor for the 1988 *Surgeon General's Report on Nutrition and Health.*[9] Based on her work in government as well as subsequent writings in which she described her field as "nutrition policy," it is clear that Nestle believed the government could and should play an important role in shaping diet.[10] Moreover, the government's policy, Nestle believed, should be guided by scientific knowledge about food, not by politics.

Nestle's government work followed in the footsteps of other nutritionists dedicated to helping Americans decide what to eat.[11] Nestle was conscious of this legacy, writing about the work of W. O. Atwater at the United States Department of Agriculture (USDA) ("the father of modern nutrition") in *Food Politics* and *Why Calories Count.* Indeed, she and her coauthor Malden Nesheim dedicated their 2012 book, *Why Calories Count,* to Atwater.[12] Similar to Hazel Stiebeling's work on designing diet recommendations for all different income levels, she and Nesheim praised the model that Atwater established in this regard, writing: "Atwater stated repeatedly that the purpose of his experiments was to devise the most economical diets that could meet the nutritional needs of people of various ages, occupations, and social classes."[13] Nestle observed that Atwater's nutritional recommendations were not always heeded in his lifetime (e.g., he advised people to limit fat and sugar intake, though others at the USDA ignored this), but the system he established of selecting a variety of foods from among different nutritional groups rather than any particular foods, stood the test of time.[14] As much as Nestle praised the work and legacy of Atwater, she also recognized that his work and the early recommendations of the USDA encapsulated the contradictory mission of the agency. The Department of Agriculture was charged with ensuring a reliable food supply *and* with diffusing useful information on agriculture and related topics (thus, dispensing nutrition advice). The central dilemma was that the interests of agriculture and food producers were not necessarily the same interests as those of citizens buying and eating food for sustenance and good health. Nestle spent her career addressing this dilemma in one way or another, observing that the interests of food producers usually trumped the nutritional interests of citizens; it was her goal to right this imbalance.

The inherent conflict between the interests of big agriculture and food companies, on the one hand, and those of citizens, on the other, solidified with the overwhelming agricultural abundance that characterized the twentieth century United States. Along with other observers, Nestle identified that the "eat more" approach to diets took hold and strengthened in the nineteenth century with the increasing industrialization and processing of food. As discussed in earlier chapters, much has been written about the economic dilemmas of food surpluses that, by the 1930s, produced a *market* crisis even while many poor Americans experienced severe food shortages during the Depression. Meanwhile, the surplus of food following World War II was celebrated as a demonstration of American success, although it continued to bedevil Washington policymakers trying to stabilize the agricultural economy. Abundant food, though, was not just an economic dilemma. What to do with all that food when producers faced what historian Bryan McDonald, Nestle, and others referred to as "fixed stomachs" (or the biological limits for food)? Thus, what resulted was the ongoing, and increasingly urgent need of "Big Food" to reprocess and create value-added foods, and to convince Americans to buy such new products.[15] In other words, one way the food industry dealt with excess supply was to get Americans to eat more in the form of processed food.

Luckily for food producers, the establishment of food abundance took place at the same time that consumerism became a bedrock of American culture.[16] What better way to increase food sales than to turn food into one more consumer item with "value-added" and processed foods? The cuisine of authors such as Poppy Cannon celebrated this transformation. Cannon and others found new uses for packaged, value-added products, seeking to make food a new source of excitement and pleasure. They took their cues from different social and economic changes, but they were also building upon fundamental ideals of consumerism designed to elicit pleasure. Historians Gary Cross and Robert Proctor observed that consumer technologies in the twentieth century were aimed at "sensory intensity to compete with satiety and boredom" and "optimization" of "subtle sensual encounters." Engineering food pleasure and attending to "flavor mixes" and "mouth feel" was illustrated by packaged foods, such as a Snickers candy bar.[17] Deliberate engineering for pleasure to maximize sales was just the sort of consumer manipulation that Nestle decried, since this was done, as Cross and Proctor observed, "With so little regard for social and bodily consequences."[18] Nestle rejected these sorts of formulations, since they hid the nutritional and health issues at stake in food selection. Lappé had also rejected such a consumerist formulation as it reduced food access to available wealth.[19]

In *Food Politics: How the Food Industry Influences Nutrition and Health*, Nestle indicted the consumerist approach to food primarily because it harmed people's health.[20] The book made her known outside of academic and government policy circles and introduced most of the topics found in her subsequent books. Nestle's starting point was an acknowledgment of the "overabundance" that characterized the American food system. Although she asserted that this was a "great unspoken secret," it was clear that most Americans at the start of the twenty-first century had a regular food supply that was "so plentiful, so varied, so inexpensive" in "a society so affluent that most people [could] afford to buy more food than they need." Inevitably, then, food companies were forever competing for customers in this buyers' market, hoping to convince Americans to "eat more." Meanwhile, modern scientific and nutritional research repeatedly demonstrated that many health problems were caused by eating too much and eating too much of the wrong foods. Thus, Nestle argued, the advice of nutritionists routinely clashed with the interests of food companies: "The 'eat less' message is at the root of much of the controversy over nutrition advice . . . food companies work hard to oppose and undermine 'eat less' messages." The motivation for food companies was clear, Nestle argued in this book and throughout her career; she summarized in her 2022 memoir: "Food companies . . . are not social service agencies. They are businesses required by stockholders to prioritize profit above all other values—human, social, and environmental."[21]

Nestle argued that the controversy between the advice of nutritionists and the interests of food companies came to a head in 1977 with a set of government recommendations entitled *Dietary Goals for the United States.* In these goals, government nutritionists called for a reduction in fat, saturated fat, cholesterol, sugar, and salt in daily diets and an increase in fruits, vegetables, and whole grains. The backlash from food producers, especially the beef, egg, and dairy industries, was immediate and formidable, resulting in a revision of the goals within a few months that softened or obfuscated many of the original recommendations.[22] For example, the January version included the directive to "reduce consumption of meat," but by the end of the year it was replaced with the confusing passage to "choose meats, poultry, and fish which will reduce saturated fat intake." Nevertheless, Nestle pointed to this report as a landmark signaling the end of the "eat more" phase of American food culture and the start of an "eat less" one. She summarized: "Despite the compromises, the *Dietary Goals* proved to be a turning point; the report set a standard for all subsequent dietary recommendations and change[d] the course of nutrition education in the United States." Yet, as Nestle's own argument in *Food Politics* made clear, the "compromises" were significant, replacing clear directives with soft suggestions that assumed citizens would know what saturated fats were and where they could be found. The turning point, then, was really in the consensus *among nutritionists*, some of whom worked in the USDA, trying to sneak sound nutritional advice into public policy without triggering industry ire. Other scholars, not just Nestle, agreed that the 1977 *Dietary Goals* was a significant turning point in nutritional advice.[23]

Nestle detailed the political competition over government nutritional advice, both before and after the *Dietary Goals*. She described how the "eat more" message that dominated most of the twentieth century was not just a commercial one, but for nutritionists such as Atwater and Stiebeling stemmed from the real concern that Americans might not be getting all of the nutrients they needed for optimal health. Yet, the "Basic Seven" and "Basic Four" (discussed earlier) were clearly obsolete in an age of obvious overabundance of food and rising dietary-related chronic diseases. Nevertheless, Nestle made clear that, after the 1977 *Dietary Goals*, the food industry remained on high alert, engaged in a constant battle to soften nutritional recommendations and protect their customer base. In this battle, Nestle concluded, industry efforts were usually successful. For example, a set of guidelines from the Department of Health, Education, and Welfare in 1979 ("Healthy People"), Nestle explained, was "the last federal publication to explicitly advise 'eat less red meat.'"[24]

Although lengthy guidelines from the federal government were not read by average citizens, they nevertheless impacted what was taught in schools and accepted by the medical establishment.[25] Some guidelines were summarized, presented to the public, and became easily recognizable. The 1992 Food Guide Pyramid was soon ubiquitous in schools, media, and elsewhere. As scholar Jessica Mudry noted, the 1992 pyramid was so significant because it widely publicized the nutritional recommendations of the 1977 *Dietary Goals*.[26] The pyramid represented a victory for nutritionists, who wanted to present food in a proportional hierarchy; yet, its recommendations, similar to those in other policies, were also softened after a barrage of lobbying from food producers.[27]

Nestle's discussion of the pyramid and other guidelines explained that food lobbyists inevitably wanted food advice to emphasize variety and moderation and never to demonize any foods as intrinsically bad. Nestle concluded that this relentless pressure created guidelines "that disguise 'eat less' messages with euphemisms" and "make dietary advice more positive despite the lack of compelling evidence that this approach is more effective in helping people eat more healthfully."[28] A perusal of federal nutritional pamphlets and guidelines bore out Nestle's assessments. The government educational materials were almost always positive, repeatedly used the words "moderation" and "variety," and invited people to "choose a diet" with many vegetables or diets low in fat or low in cholesterol.[29] The impact of food industry lobbyists was reflected in the emphasis on *choice* and the often vague language in place of specific advice. Nestle argued that such language made it difficult for ordinary people to understand dietary advice from the government. For example, she critiqued the directive "Choose beverages and foods to moderate your intake of sugars": "Well what does *that* mean? Nobody knows . . . people [do] not understand what it is they're supposed to do with food. They talk about sugar, they talk about saturated fat, they talk about salt. They don't talk about soft drinks. They don't talk about beef. They don't talk about salty snacks."[30] She also linked the obfuscations of such language with the unfair burden placed on individuals: "The guidelines are not helpful because the whole thing is based entirely on personal responsibility. It's up to you as a consumer to know what a low-fat food is, what a high-sugar food is, the difference between whole grains and refined ones. . . . And unless you can parse a food label—which most people cannot do—it's very difficult."[31]

Throughout *Food Politics*, Nestle detailed how industry lobbyists (who had exploded in number from the 1950s to the 1990s) succeeded in watering down sound nutritional advice with euphemisms. In the section titled "Working the System," Nestle described the revolving door for food lobbyists and government officials, the "softball" lobbying of educational seminars and social occasions, and last-resort legal challenges. Nestle observed that academic colleagues were not immune to lobbying: "Co-opting experts—especially academic experts—is an explicit corporate strategy. . . . This activity requires a modicum of finesse; it must not be too blatant, for the experts themselves must not recognize that they have lost their objectivity and freedom of action."[32] Nestle reserved particular condemnation for corporate lobbying and marketing efforts aimed at children and their schools, especially by soda companies. Nestle revisited each of these topics—the manipulation of academics and children—in greater depth in her subsequent books, *Unsavory Truth* and *Soda Politics.*

Unsavory Truth (2018) was both a familiar reconsideration of how corporate lobbyists targeted academic nutritionists, but also a nuanced discussion of an apparently insoluble problem, namely, how to prevent lobbyists from compromising scientific objectivity.[33] It was an investigation by a mature scholar who was both critical of experts who compromised their objectivity, but also defensive of colleagues and the ideals of scientific objectivity in the face of political and cultural challenges. Nestle began the book with comparisons of the food industry to the tobacco and drug industries. She detailed how tobacco and drug companies routinely co-opted scientists or cast doubt on science that was detrimental to their reputations, used even small gifts to influence experts, and argued that personal choice and responsibility were sacrosanct values; in many examples, she illustrated how the food industry used the same "playbook" with equal success. Some instances of food industry manipulations—and hence of "public policy and public health"—were obvious and easy to condemn. For example, Nestle described various industry-sponsored studies designed to prove the magical powers of a single food product, such as pecans, POM Wonderful juice, or chocolate milk. She also gave examples of when nutritional organizations (not just individual academics) were compromised by industry ties, such as the Academy of Nutrition and Dietetics (formerly the American Dietetic Association), which allowed its seal of approval for healthy eating to appear on Kraft Singles ("a prepared cheese product," according to the company). Other examples of corporate manipulation were less obvious, especially for those outside of the fields in question. Nestle carefully explained differences among the academic subdisciplines concerning food and nutrition, as well as among the various professional organizations in each, including their size, influence, and reliability. She indicated that the food industry was often keen to blur the distinctions among these subfields and eliminate the idea that some may be more scientifically objective than others. For example, Nestle explained that the field of "food science developed as an arm of the food industry," so food science departments were "closely aligned" with the industry. Meanwhile, "the purpose of nutrition science [as a field] is to improve public health," so nutritionists who condemned certain foods might end up in conflict with the food industry.

In the field of nutrition, one of the best-known examples of academic success—and industry co-optation—was the case of Fredrick Stare. Stare was a singular figure, representing both conventional scientific authority and nutritional advice in the 1960s and 1970s and the dangers of corporate influence. Stare was the founder of the Department of Nutrition at the Harvard School of Public Health and served as chair from its start during World War II until his retirement in the mid-1970s. From this authoritative perch, he garnered industry donations and support and was in demand for media and other appearances, dispensing common sense advice and warnings against "cranks." He was increasingly criticized for his close ties to the food industry, and many detractors charged that his advice was thus tainted.[34] Nevertheless, he was prominent in his field as well as in public culture, as demonstrated by the many nutrition columns he wrote for newspapers. During his tenure, he raised millions of dollars for his department from industry funders, leading to the creation of an endowment generating $800,000 a year by 1990. Stare asserted that corporate contributions never compromised his scientific independence because they were all "pooled" into one fund and not designated for any particular purpose. Nevertheless, by 1976, he was labeled as a "food-industry apologist" in a report from the Center for Science in the Public Interest. Nestle wrote that new documents found in 2016 showed his industry ties to be more extensive than previously thought, and he was less independent than he claimed. For instance, the documents showed he skewed research findings at Harvard to favor the sugar industry, which he had long supported—and which had long supported him.[35] Nestle strongly condemned Stare's record as well as his impact on public health and the integrity of the field of nutrition, even if she understood the motivation to accept industry support.

Few scientists were in a position to receive millions of dollars in donations from industry sources, although as Nestle made clear, even small gifts could bias people. Nevertheless, Nestle asserted that nutrition professionals had no choice but to "engage with food companies." She argued such engagement was a professional necessity for a few reasons: academia was highly competitive and public research funding was in short supply; professional organizations needed contributions for conferences and publications; and individuals, such as herself, were expected to give lectures and participate in seminars. Nestle argued that scientists could avoid the perils of industry funding with a commitment to "a three-step process: recognize, disclose, and manage."[36] Nestle used her own approach as a model. She made clear that she was ever watchful for bias in her work, relying on a scientist's training to be objective. She also noted that she disclosed any funding she accepted and limited its scope and purpose. Nestle explained that she accepted expenses for travel and speaking engagements, and any honoraria for lectures were deposited in a library or scholarship fund at her university. Nestle did not imagine that a three-step, rational process was simple or 100 percent successful, though she reasoned: "Imperfect as my policy may be, it requires me to think carefully about every interaction with a food company that involves payments or gifts."[37] Nestle admitted that such guardrails against undue influence did not always work—even in her own case. In *Slow Cooked*, she recounted her relationship with Oldways Trust, an organization that supported the benefits of the "Mediterranean Diet" in the 1990s—which happened to have heavy sponsorship from the olive oil trade association. Nestle wrote, "Knowing what I know now," she would not have been so deeply involved with the organization.[38]

In *Unsavory Truth*, one can feel Nestle's conflicts: she believed industry cooptation was a constant danger; yet, she accepted industry money and asserted that "financial ties with food companies are not necessarily corrupting." She laid out in detail the financial ties between the American Society for Nutrition and its positions, which "appea[r] to favor industry over public health," but she continued as a member of ASN and worked on some of its committees.[39] She argued that calls to ban all industry funding were unrealistic and proposed the possibility of pooling all industry donations to be administered by an independent party; yet, right after describing the proposal, she wrote that it had not worked in the case of Fred Stare and Harvard. On this and related questions, Nestle was introspective and sincere, though finding no neat solution to a complex issue. In her memoir, Nestle confessed her disappointment that *Unsavory Truth* received little attention in the mainstream press and almost none from academic colleagues. Perhaps this was not surprising, since it raised difficult questions about objectivity, even for well-intentioned academics.[40]

In contrast to her views of the food industry's manipulation of academics, which could be subtle, Nestle judged the manipulation of children to be obvious—and reprehensible. The section in *Food Politics* on marketing food to children was titled: "Exploiting Kids, Corrupting Schools." It gives equal attention to the marketing of junk foods, which led to obesity, and the business plans of soda companies to insinuate themselves into the budget planning of cash-strapped schools. Nestle argued that children from a very young age were subject to advertisements of all sorts of junk foods on television and on the internet; under this barrage, they were influenced to use their own money to purchase such foods or pressure their parents to buy the products. Nestle was incensed that such marketing was also found in schools in three areas: commercials on a service called Channel One (mandatory viewing in many schools for almost twenty years from the end of the twentieth to the beginning of the twenty-first centuries); school lunch programs that had been taken over by fast food companies in many districts; and vending machines with junk foods, especially soda. The complicated relationship between soda companies and school districts came under an umbrella called "pouring rights," which entitled a particular company, such as Coca-Cola or PepsiCo, to have exclusive presence in vending machines in exchange for various types of sports equipment or other supplies, ranging from furniture to sound systems to computers, and financial subsidies tied to consumption from the vending machines. Nestle sympathized with schools that lacked sufficient funding, but she found the arrangements insidious because of the undeniable health consequences for children: "the relationship between soft-drink consumption and body weight is so strong that researchers calculate that for *each* additional soda consumed per day, the risk of obesity increases 1.6 times."[41]

More than a decade later, Nestle continued her case against soda companies in *Soda Politics: Taking on Big Soda (and Winning)*.[42] As in the earlier book, she condemned the tactics of the soda industry, which she likened to those of tobacco companies in their relentless promotion of their product and in the way that they sowed doubt about medical research. Despite what the soda companies argued, Nestle pointed to the big increase in calorie intake with soda consumption, primarily calories of sugar, since each twelve-ounce can contained about ten teaspoons of the sweetener. Nestle cited research that demonstrated increased obesity with increased sugar consumption, but her health criticisms of soda went beyond obesity. She also outlined research that found a correlation (not a cause, Nestle was careful to specify) between sugar consumption and diabetes, independent of obesity. Indeed, Nestle described research that found a correlation of sugar intake with many other chronic conditions, including heart disease, stroke, dental disease, bone disease, gout, asthma, cancers, rheumatoid arthritis, behavioral problems, psychological disorders, and premature aging. Among these conditions, Nestle noted that dental cavities were the "single most common chronic disease in children and adults worldwide." Nestle recounted that nutritionists had long known that soda caused tooth decay. For example, she described the work of Cornell nutritionist Clive McCay, who testified to congress in 1950 about his experiment of dropping teeth into a glass of Coke and watching them dissolve. For his trouble, Coca-Cola labeled him a "faddist" and enlisted the testimony of Fred Stare to assert that soda did not hurt teeth.

Others, in addition to McCay and Nestle, had criticized the damaging effects of too much sugar. Nutritionists, doctors, activists, and scholars had long been documenting the effects of the growing consumption of sugar on health and culture and its ubiquity in processed and convenience foods. Anthropologist Sidney Mintz, who traced the international production and consumption of sugar over centuries, observed that one notable aspect of modern American food was how sugar and fat consumption both went up and were often paired together in processed foods, appealing more to "mouth feel" than to taste.[43] Health journalist Gary Taubes, who wrote two books about the danger and ubiquity of sugar in American diets, observed, "By far the most significant and consistent change in human diets as populations become Westernized, urbanized, or merely affluent is how much sugar they consume."[44] While Nestle agreed that Americans ate too much sugar and that sugar impacted health in particular ways, her main focus remained on the excessive sugar *calories*, which resulted in obesity.

Of all Nestle's books, *Soda Politics* was most explicitly an advocacy primer for citizens to take action against large corporations—here, soda companies. Nestle outlined the mixed record of federal nutrition guidelines when it came to sugar and soda, thus making the case that more action was necessary.[45] Although nutritionists at the USDA and the Department of Health and Human Services had been recommending reduced sugar intake since 1980, Nestle gave examples of continuing pressure from industry, especially the soda producers, which weakened those guidelines. If government guidelines were weak and failed to discourage soda consumption, Nestle proposed different ways that citizens could act on their own. Many chapters ended with bullet-point lists summarizing research and actions that people could take, such as meeting with school officials and school boards to argue for banning soda in schools, writing letters to the editor about the issue, and working on campaigns already started by nonprofit advocacy organizations (Nestle provided a list of them at the back of the book). She also praised the campaigns to prevent the Supplemental Nutrition Assistance Program (SNAP) from being used to purchase soda, New York City Mayor Mike Bloomberg's attempt to limit the size of soda bottles in convenience stores, and the efforts of New York State (and others) to pass a tax on sugary drinks. Nestle brushed aside criticisms that these campaigns were paternalistic or took away people's freedom, countering that industry manipulations of science and marketing already compromised freedom of choice.

Nestle's criticisms of soda companies were closely related to her most important health concern over the course of her career: obesity. She argued that an "eat more" food environment resulted from the deliberate strategy of food corporations in pursuit of profits to cajole, pressure, and trick people into consuming more calories than they needed. The inevitable consequence of an "eat more" environment and overconsumption of calories was obesity.

The increase of overweight and obese Americans in the late twentieth century became an epidemic and a health crisis, according to medical authorities, policymakers, and nutritionists. The incidence of obesity was clear from the statistics. For example, CDC data indicated that the percentage of obese adults tripled from 1960 to 2000, going from 11 percent to 33 percent, with the biggest rate of increase in the 1990s, when it went from 23 percent to 33 percent. Meanwhile, in the same decade, overweight Americans jumped from 56 percent to 65 percent of the population. By 2007–8, the combined number of overweight and obese adults reached 68 percent of the population. The CDC said that the health consequences meant that almost as many people would die from poor eating and lack of exercise in the 1990s as from smoking in the same decade. The data for children and teenagers was also discouraging, with the number of overweight children ages six to eleven in the 1990s measured at 13 percent, and overweight teens at 14 percent; other experts argued these estimates were low and that 25–30 percent of children were overweight or at risk of becoming so. By 2007–8, the percentage of obese children ages six to eleven was estimated at 20 percent and ages 12 to 19 at 18 percent. These statistics predicted an increase of chronic diseases when these children became adults, including hypertension, diabetes, and some cancers.[46]

The increasing percentage of overweight Americans beginning in the late twentieth century and the increase of chronic health conditions associated with this trend became a central focus of Nestle's writing, activism, and the advice that she offered Americans about diet. Nestle shared these concerns with many nutritionists and doctors, especially when it came to obesity and heart disease. Starting in the 1970s, the issues came to be seen as more serious in the public culture. The accumulation of research led the National Research Council to lower the number of calories in the RDA, and the American Heart Association recommended in 1974 that all Americans lower their meat consumption by one-third in order to lower their cholesterol.[47]

From Nestle's point of view, rising obesity illustrated the health consequences of large corporations relentlessly pushing an "eat more" approach to food; the situation also illustrated that citizens were not armed with clear information to help them make the right food choices in the face of a political and economic environment that did not serve their health interests. Rising obesity, then, was the predictable result of corporate manipulation and individuals lacking sufficient nutritional information. Along with her nutritional expertise,

Nestle's concern about the health consequences of obesity perhaps stemmed from her childhood. She wrote in *Slow Cooked* that her father was seriously obese and died of a heart attack at the age of 47.[48]

Since obesity was one of the health consequences of poor diet, discussions of the issue were found in many parts of Nestle's writing and food advice. She discussed the issue most directly and extensively in the 2012 book that she co-authored with Malden Nesheim, *Why Calories Count*. The book began with the assertion that the number of calories consumed was "arguably the *most* important cause of public health nutrition problems in the world today." The authors were careful to translate the scientific details of calories and their biological uses for lay people, for instance, using the following concrete image: "100 calories is the amount of heat needed to bring a quart of water to the boiling point." Nestle and Nesheim argued that not only were definitions important, but also the scientific measurement of calories and nutrients as established in the work of W. O. Atwater. They defended Atwater's work and also the motivation behind it to recommend the most economical, nutritional diets for diverse groups of citizens.[49] The authors, then, took exception to the arguments of historian Nick Cullather and communication scholar Jessica Mudry, each of whom questioned the legacy of Atwater and his emphasis on *counting* calories.[50] While Cullather and Mudry argued that Atwater focused on the quantification of calories and ignored the cultural and political consequences of such an endeavor, Nestle and Nesheim charged that the two were "anti-scientific," since Atwater's studies of energy metabolism were conducted without any political motivations. Mudry argued that her concern was understanding how *rhetoric*, not quantification, shaped what people ate; she wrote: "Understanding food through quantities and talking about food using a discourse of quantification undermines the sense of taste that is employed when we eat."[51]

The brief critique of these two humanities scholars discussing the consequences of a nutritionist perspective is noteworthy on two fronts. First, Nestle and Nesheim agreed that "calories have political dimensions," even if they disagreed that the work of a scientist such as Atwater had political dimensions. And, second, elsewhere in the book, Nestle and Nesheim made it clear that the average person should not have to think much about counting and measuring calories: if people have access to adequate and varied diets and eat only when they are hungry, they are likely to get sufficient nutrients and not too many calories.[52]

Many people, though, did not eat according to this straightforward biological guidance. Beyond the question of scientific definitions and the mechanics of nutrition, the most important message of *Why Calories Count* was that Americans consumed too many calories, and many had thus become overweight or obese.[53] The authors noted that in 2007, per-capita calories available to Americans was 3,750—far beyond what was needed.[54] They gave detailed statistics about rising obesity in the United States and the number of excess calories that created body fat. They had no doubt that people were consuming the excess calories available—"research shows that if food is at hand, people will eat it"—in part due to shifting social norms that had increased the number of times and places that people ate. This dysfunctional situation resulted in the common desire of many Americans to lose weight, a goal that Nestle and Nesheim clearly supported. They ended the book by encouraging readers to take action by choosing smaller portion sizes as a first step toward lessening calories and losing weight.

For some people, Nestle's solution for the obesity crisis ("Diets are about calories. Eat too many, and weight goes up. To lose weight, you have to eat fewer calories.") was misguided.[55] This simple equation, critics countered, misunderstood the issue on multiple levels. First, in popular and academic culture, there was growing alarm in the late twentieth century about the rise of eating disorders, such as anorexia and bulimia, especially among young women, who felt extreme pressure to conform to unrealistic, gendered expectations of weight and appearance. Press articles and television melodramas illustrated the apparent consequences of worrying too much about weight. By the early twenty-first century, coinciding with increased levels of obesity, the cultural focus shifted to "fat acceptance" and "body-positivity" instead of eating disorders.[56] Many overweight Americans asserted that, although they did not have eating disorders, their weight had been unnecessarily pathologized even if they had healthy diets, were active, and in good health; they rejected the ubiquitous bullying and "fat shaming" they faced in popular culture and professional life.

A related criticism argued that since weight gain and obesity had become unnecessarily pathologized, such an attitude thus reinforced an unhealthy obsession in American culture with dieting. As historian Helen Zoe Veit detailed, a slender body became the ideal for white, middle-class women starting early in the twentieth century, representing not just an aesthetic preference, but a manifestation of self-control, morality, science, modernity, and progressive reform.[57] The power of this association lasted over the next century and affected society as a whole, beyond white, middle-class women. From this beginning, an industry arose around dieting, which continued to highlight similar ideals. Historian Warren Belasco summarized these ideals as a faith in the ability of individuals to perfect their bodies through willpower and self-denial.[58] Based on such ideals, dieting consciousness permeated American culture and became big business, spawning books, television programs, careers for advice gurus, processed diet foods, supplements, and more.[59] It is worth noting that, although Nestle was deeply concerned about increased obesity, she was highly critical of diet formulas that purported to "solve" someone's weight problem quickly or easily. In addition, Nestle criticized the obsession with diets that complicated the issue of what to eat. Instead, Nestle counseled that weight would never be a problem if one only ate when hungry and not more calories than the energy expended.

Beyond the criticisms of fat shaming and a ubiquitous diet culture was a more complicated critique, charging that efforts to diagnose and solve the obesity epidemic ended up blaming overweight *individuals*, rather than holding the modern food *system* responsible. Geographer Julie Guthman made the most thoughtful of these arguments.[60] Unlike some critics who argued that obesity was not really increasing and that it had no effect on health, Guthman stipulated that obesity was indeed becoming more widespread and that it could impair health. Moreover, she acknowledged that nutritionists, such as Nestle and food activists like Michael Pollan, were highly critical of the industrial food system that subsidized unhealthy food and served the interests of large corporations rather than citizens. Nevertheless, Guthman argued that Nestle, Pollan, and others, by focusing on nutritional education, food choices, and "voting with your fork," placed the burden for poor diet and obesity on individual actions and individual responsibility. The heart of Guthman's argument was that, since 1980 neoliberalism has dominated economic and political thought in the United States, and it has affected many aspects of American life—and encouraged a food system based on producing an abundance of cheap food, using cheap labor, and taking advantage of government policies that ignored health and safety concerns. In addition, a neoliberal outlook prized individual choice and responsibility; Guthman summarized: "Neoliberalism has thus contributed to the idea that health is a personal responsibility more than a social one, which has allowed intensified social scolding of the obese."[61]

Although Guthman did not dispute the statistics regarding rising obesity and its corollary health problems, she questioned whether the situation was indeed an "epidemic" as widely asserted in the press and argued that there was too much reliance on the "crude measure" of body mass index (BMI). As many critics pointed out, BMI was merely a ratio of height to weight, ignoring frame, bone density, composition of body mass, and other individual differences.[62] Other scholars joined Guthman in questioning whether obesity really was an "epidemic." Historian Charlotte Biltekoff, for example, described how the century-long obsession with dieting and proper eating was shaped not only by W. O. Atwater's science of measurement and quantification, but also by a set of moral and political values of middle-class virtue and citizenship. Biltekoff summarized: "Nutrition provided a rational justification for the imperatives to be frugal, thrifty, and economical with nature that were all part of the earlier concerns of an ascetic Christianity."[63] Biltekoff, Guthman, and other scholars made it clear that how contemporary Americans looked at food, obesity, and health could not be separated from middle-class cultural values.

The third key argument that Guthman and others made was that there was no clear proof people had increased their food intake; even if they had, there was no definitive evidence that increased obesity was *caused* by increased consumption in the late twentieth and early twenty-first centuries. Instead, she argued that much more attention should be paid to endocrine disruption, which resulted from a proliferation since 1940 of certain synthetic chemicals throughout American life, including pesticides, solvents, perfumes, surfactants, plastics, and others. Endocrine-disrupting chemicals could affect the expression of genes, having an epigenetic effect that might account for the sharp increase in obesity. In supporting this argument, Guthman pointed to the increase between 1980 and 2001 of overweight infants below the age of six months from 3.4 percent to 5.9 percent; since young infants only consumed milk and exercise was not a factor, the usual explanations for increasing obesity did not hold.[64]

The important contributions of Julie Guthman and Charlotte Biltekoff, as well as those of Warren Belasco, Nick Cullather, Jessica Mudry, and others to the discussion about obesity and food in the modern United States made clear how difficult it was to untangle the cultural, scientific, and political threads of this issue. They also laid bare some of the fault lines in the contemporary field of food studies and its shifting discourses. Nestle, of course, was an active voice in this evolving field and a bridge between academic debates and the popular understanding of them. In this role, Nestle's positions had also evolved, particularly in her acknowledgment that culture and environment might also be factors to consider along with the amount of food eaten. A reconsideration of what Nestle had to say about obesity reveals some of this evolution as well as nuance beyond the formulation of "calories in/calories out."

Nestle began her consideration of obesity with the observation that throughout the twentieth century there was an abundance—an overabundance—of available food in the United States. Large food companies had not only adapted to this abundance but also built a business model predicated on the goal of always getting people to "eat more" in order to earn a profit. Nestle had spent the bulk of her career exposing the market manipulations of Big Food at the expense of citizens' health. Obesity, then, was one more consequence of the relentless pressure to eat more. She and Nesheim laid out a struggle of individuals against these behemoths: "We try to provide an appreciation of what you are up against if you want to control your body weight in today's 'toxic,' obesity-promoting—or as we like to call it, 'eat more'—food marketing environment."[65] In *Why Calories Count* and in other (especially later) books, Nestle sought to arm her readers with information about food and nutrition and inspire them to take action. Readers were encouraged to "Get organized. Eat less. Eat better. Move more. Get political," and to "Vote with your fork."[66] It was not unreasonable to view Nestle's message as a confirmation of neoliberal assumptions that individuals were responsible for their food and their fate; yet, it was also clear in this book and others that the object of Nestle's ire was—and always had been—food companies, *not* individuals subject to constant pressure from those companies. In a 2004 special issue of *Time* on obesity in the United States, Nestle cowrote a response to a scholar from the Cato Institute who asserted that people were responsible for their own weight. Nestle countered: "Governments collude with industry when they shift attention from conditions promoting poor diets to the individuals who consume them."[67] For Nestle, individuals were neither helpless victims nor completely in charge of their food choices. In *Slow Cooked*, she emphasized that individuals had agency, but that systemic changes were best achieved through political action: "Personal choices can certainly encourage food-system improvements, but policies make a bigger difference."[68]

Regardless of an individual's control over food choices, Nestle argued in *Why Calories Count*, as in earlier writing, that there was no disputing that food consumption overall had increased. She relied on the measurable increase in per-capita calories available in the late twentieth and early twenty-first century, and studies that had shown increased availability led to increased consumption to conclude that caloric intake had indeed gone up. She argued that these pieces of information were more reliable than self-reporting studies by individuals about what they ate and how much; such reporting was notably unreliable with estimates that people underreported caloric intake by about 30 percent (as well as overestimating their level of physical activity). In addition, Nestle and Nesheim observed that food consumption had been encouraged by the increase of snacking throughout the day and the number of places where it had become acceptable to eat.[69]

If we assume some (though not unanimous) consensus on the question of increased caloric consumption, the question of physical activity levels seemed more confused. Nestle and Nesheim argued that the relentless "eat more" environment caused obesity, not a decline in exercise, which was a favorite defense of companies such as Coca-Cola and PepsiCo. In *Soda Politics,* for example, Nestle detailed how the industry supported research that made such arguments which Nestle labeled "the 'physical activity diversion.'"[70] Nestle and Nesheim observed that, although there were anecdotal observations of less physical activity, hard evidence was scant.[71] Julie Guthman, meanwhile, noted that lessening physical activity was unlikely to be the cause of obesity since those who did more physical work had higher average weight, and that the big increase in office (i.e., sedentary) work *preceded* rather than coincided with the significant increases in BMI.[72] A clear measure of physical activity in the population and its correlation with obesity remained elusive.

There was another question in the obesity discussion that called out for more research: biological barriers to weight loss. Nestle and Nesheim noted that losing weight was not easy because "there are physiological defenses against weight loss," such as slower metabolism as food consumption went down.[73] Nevertheless, the authors' discussion of such barriers was cursory as compared with the much greater emphasis they put on the simple "calories in/calories out" equation of determining weight. Another area of ongoing biological research was the impact of endocrine disruptors on obesity and the great increase of certain refined food products (such as fructose) in the American diet. For Guthman and others, this was a serious and urgent issue; based on preliminary studies, Guthman argued, "Much of this upward trajectory in BMI values appears to be a consequence of exposures to a set of barely regulated chemicals and food substances."[74] Nestle placed little importance on the *source* of calories when it came to weight gain. This was illustrated in her discussion in *Soda Politics* of the changing types of sugar used in soda, and affirmed by Nestle and Nesheim in *Why Calories Count:* "The sources of the calories may make a small difference in weight maintenance or loss, but it appears to me much less important than the ability to resist pressures to overeat calories in general."[75]

While Nestle did not close the door on the idea that calories in various types of foods (i.e., different types of sugars) might impact weight gain differently, she seemed to have less interest in further research of endocrine disruptors. In her 2006 book *What to Eat,* Nestle concluded: "Whether nanogram amounts of endocrine disruptors really are responsible for health problems seems unlikely, but it is a question that cannot be easily investigated," since plasticizers (she gave the example) had leeched into many foods.[76] Fourteen years later, in *Let's Ask Marion,* Nestle remained open to the idea that several factors might influence weight gain, though she made no mention of chemicals such as endocrine disruptors: "Some overeaters gain more weight more quickly than others, perhaps because of genetics, the foods the calories come from, or even the microbiome. But everyone who overeats gains weight."[77] Thus, Nestle asserted clearly that the overconsumption of calories remained the key issue, even if there were other complicating factors.

One complicating factor was excessive consumption of *sugar* calories. As noted above, Nestle agreed with Gary Taubes's assertion that overconsumption of carbohydrates represented a serious health risk in American society. In *Why Calories Count,* she and Nesheim laid out Taubes's discussion of how carbohydrates induced the pancreas to secrete more insulin, changing how food was metabolized and how appetite was sated; thus, there was a clear line from eating carbohydrates and sugar to obesity, diabetes, and other diseases. Nestle praised aspects of Taubes's argument and detailed collection of information, but agreed with critics who found his theory reductionist.[78] Taubes may have focused on the effects of carbohydrates, but his 450-plus-page book, *Good Calories, Bad Calories: Fats, Carbs, and the Controversial Science of Diet and Health,* was less a reductionist argument than a challenge to a key tenet of mainstream nutritional advice about *fat.* A brief review of how most nutritionists viewed dietary fat tells us much about evolving nutritional guidelines—as well as Nestle's recommendations. Since the mid-twentieth century, an increasing number of nutritionists—including Marion Nestle—came to believe that the most serious threat to modern American health was the overconsumption of fat—especially animal fat—which led to high cholesterol, strokes, heart disease, obesity, and related conditions. And most of those nutritionists (Nestle included) held fast to that belief, despite mounting evidence to the contrary.

The earliest and best-known voices warning about the dangers of dietary fat were Ancel and Margaret Keys, who wrote in 1959 a book entitled *Eat Well & Stay Well.*[79] The book began with the acknowledgment that "an almost endless supply of all kinds of foods encourages us to eat more." Moving beyond the concern of overabundance, the authors offered familiar recommendations for good health, including eating fresh vegetables and fruits, avoiding too much salt and sugar, and getting plenty of exercise. Their primary set of recommendations, though, was to reduce fat intake, especially meat, dairy, and other saturated fats, and to control calorie intake. The book contained various menus, recipes, and calorie/nutrient tables to accomplish these goals.[80] The Keyses' anti-fat message was soon widespread. By the beginning of 1961, *Time* magazine published an article recommending that Americans cut their fat intake from an average of 40 percent of calories to 15 percent, and saturated fats from an average of 40 percent of all fats consumed to 27 percent. The radical suggestion elicited a note of caution from the administrator of the USDA's Agricultural Research Service, B. T. Shaw, who asserted that "The role of fat in human nutrition is complex and much further research is needed to clarify this role."[81]

The caution expressed by Shaw was soon eclipsed. Most nutritionists in the late twentieth century absorbed the lessons laid out by the Keys, as illustrated in the "consensus" exemplified by the USDA's 1977 *Dietary Goals.* As Nestle correctly observed, these goals were a turning point for nutritionists to shift collectively from an "eat more" view to an "eat less" one. Yet, as discussed above, this shift was not just in the amount of food consumed, but in the type of foods, limiting animal and saturated fats. Gary Taubes, then, presented a challenge to the nutritionist orthodoxy represented by Keys.

Taubes began *Good Calories, Bad Calories* by tracing the work of Ancel Keys and its widespread acceptance.[82] Taubes described how different parts of Keys's theory were not supported by evidence and that there was confusion, for example, between dietary cholesterol and blood cholesterol; nevertheless, the *Time* cover story on Keys's views in 1961 and other press articles omitted such details. "The press," Taubes concluded, "played a critical role in shaping the evolution of the dietary-fat controversy by consistently siding with proponents of those who saw dietary fat as an unnecessary evil." The support for Keys's thesis, then, culminated in the 1977 *Dietary Goals,* which Taubes argued "sparked a chain reaction of dietary advice from government agencies and the press that reverberates still." As an illustration of Taubes's point, Jane Brody observed in 1981 in the *New York Times:* "The Dietary Goals are beginning to reshape the nutritional philosophy of America, if not yet the eating habits of most Americans." Such was the power of the anti-fat consensus that it sometimes led to unintended confusions among people. For example, chef Michael Ruhlman wrote about observing a woman in the grocery store selecting "fat free half and half." He asked what she thought was in the product, since the very name and reason to buy half and half was for its fat content; the woman explained that fat should be avoided—and did not realize that the fat in the product had been replaced with corn syrup.[83] Although many of the scientific questions about the importance of a low-fat diet remained unanswered, the anti-fat consensus was strong as was the assumption that no harm could come from reducing dietary fat. Similar to other nutritional recommendations from the federal government, the 1988 *Surgeon General's Report on Nutrition and Public Health*, edited by Marion Nestle, also urged Americans to cut consumption of fatty foods.

Such was the power of Keys's thesis and the generation of recommendations it spawned that "By the early 1970s," Taubes observed, "all potential causes of heart disease, or potentially any chronic disease, had to be capable of coexisting with the belief that dietary fat was the primary cause of coronary heart disease." More than three decades later, Taubes challenged Keys's hypothesis with one of his own: he argued that obesity, diabetes, and many chronic diseases were "caused by the singular hormonal effects of a diet rich in refined and easily digestible carbohydrates." Taubes asserted that the quantity of calories consumed was less important than the quality of calories, particularly those that stimulated an overproduction of insulin.[84]

A decade after his first book, Gary Taubes narrowed his focus from all refined carbohydrates to sugar in particular. In *The Case against Sugar*, he laid out a damning case that linked sugar to obesity, diabetes, and cancer—all widespread in the early twenty-first century United States. As in his earlier book, Taubes made it clear that the quantity of sugar was not the main issue, but its properties: "unique physiological, metabolic, and endocrinological (i.e. hormonal) effects in the human body that directly triggers these disorders." Taubes argued that medical researchers understood this link by the late 1980s, even though it was not popularly known: "The medical research community came to recognize that insulin resistance and a condition now known as 'metabolic syndrome' is a major, if not *the* major, risk factor for heart disease and diabetes."[85]

While some medical researchers may have fully understood the health significance of insulin resistance, such knowledge had not permeated the public culture by the early twenty-first century. Meanwhile, other critics raised different questions about the orthodoxy of USDA nutritional assumptions. For example, Walter Willett, in *Eat, Drink, and Be Healthy*, wrote that the USDA had ignored much new nutritional research since its 1977 *Dietary Goals* and its 1992 pyramid: "The USDA never renovated the Pyramid but left it to crumble under the weight of new scientific evidence." Willett had even more scorn for the 2005 updated USDA "MyPyramid," which he pronounced "wishy-washy, [with] scientifically unfounded advice."[86] Nestle also did not mince words regarding MyPyramid, describing it as "a disaster . . . [that] lacks any notion of a hierarchical ranking . . . of nutritional desirability."[87] At the center of his book, Willetts presented his own "Healthy Eating Pyramid." Willett's guidelines differed from the USDA ones in several ways, including a recommendation for plant oils, an increase in whole grains, vegetables and fruits, and a shift of red meat, white rice, white bread, white pasta, and potatoes to the top-of-the-pyramid category of foods that should only be eaten "sparingly."[88] Jessica Mudry observed that his most important departure from the USDA guidelines was asserting that not all fats were bad and that eating fats did not equate to becoming fat.[89] Thus, his call to incorporate plant oils and the HDL cholesterol ("good cholesterol," as opposed to "bad" LDL cholesterol) they contained.

Aspects of Willett's recommendations became fairly mainstream. Respected nutritionists, such as Marion Nestle, in academia and in the USDA and other federal agencies, had shifted some of their recommendations to emphasize more the value of whole grains, vegetables, and fruits and the harm of added sugars and ultraprocessed foods, but they continued to urge caution when it came to saturated fats. For example, in her 2006 book *What to Eat,* Nestle explained her dilemma regarding cheese, since the best-tasting cheeses were high in fat; she revealed that her solution was to "save up" for the fat and calories of a small amount of a good cheese, rather than settle for a not very good low-fat cheese.[90] Thus, Nestle, along with most other nutritionists, held to many of the diet recommendations put forward in the 1977 *Dietary Goals.* This approach to food advice pointed back to another underlying theme of *Food Politics* and much of what Nestle wrote subsequently. With the notable exception of advising people about the myriad dangers of fat, particularly saturated fat, Nestle and most mainstream nutritionists shied away from advice that condemned entire groups of foods or that embraced particular foods as having magical properties. In later years, Nestle backed away from some of her prescriptions about fat. In 2022, she commented upon the emphasis on fat in the 1988 *Surgeon's General Report,* which she had edited: "The focus on fat, a nutrient rather than a food, still makes me wince"; she stood by the dietary recommendations of the report overall, "aside from the emphasis on fat."[91]

Nestle's disdain for "magical" or "super" foods was reflected in the last part of *Food Politics,* "Inventing Techno-Foods." Nestle began with a description of enrichment and fortification practices over the course of the twentieth century to improve health. There were different motivations for adding specific nutrients to foods, some more benign than others. With commercial milling of the grains used in flours, pasta, and bread, some vitamins and minerals were lost, such as thiamin, niacin, and riboflavin. During World War II, the Food and Drug Administration created standards to enrich flours and thus restore the lost nutrients. By the 1950s, food producers fortified some food products, adding more nutrients than might have been in original ingredients.[92] By 1969, experts meeting at the White House Conference on Nutrition recommended an expansion of fortification in foods such as breakfast cereals to improve nutrition especially among poorer citizens without variety in their diets. Widespread support for fortification continued, though this sometimes had unintended consequences in the rush to improve foods and general nutrition. For example, Nestle explained that the addition of folic acid/folate to many grain products in order to lessen the chances of spina bifida and related birth defects in roughly 4,000 children a year interfered with the diagnosis of B-12 deficiencies, especially in the elderly. Thus, Nestle argued that this decision to "improve" foods was mainly to benefit child-bearing women, but harmed some elderly as a consequence. Rather than trying to fortify foods, Nestle believed the better course would have been to advise eating more fruits and vegetables.[93]

Nestle was not only critical of the unintended consequences of manipulating foods, but also the commercial motivation to do so: with "a substantial price incentive, manufacturers began to expand voluntary fortification of food products."[94] Nestle used breakfast cereals as an example to argue that "fortification permits manufacturers to market foods of dubious nutritional quality as health foods." While food producers might have pointed to some fortifications as very successful, eliminating diseases such as rickets, goiter, and pellagra, Nestle cautioned that the cause and effect was not always clear. She noted, for example, that pellagra had already been declining before niacin was added to many foods and that there were changes in food availabilities, habits, income, and other factors that might have accounted for a reduction in certain conditions. Beyond enrichment and fortification, Nestle reserved particular scorn for efforts to create "functional" foods and marketing special benefits to consumers from foods, such as fiber, soy, oats, or "cholesterol-blocking" margarine. Nestle ended this discussion in *Food Politics* with a critique of the "ultimate techno-food: Olestra." Olestra was an ill-fated artificial fat-substitute that added no calories to processed foods because it was *indigestible*, but thereby resulted in unpleasant side effects, such as cramping and loose stools.

Throughout her career, Nestle remained wary of marketers who championed single foods or ingredients. She condemned both laboratory creations, such as Olestra, as well as naturally occurring foods said to have near-medicinal properties, or "superfoods." Nestle was fairly consistent on both points. For example, more than twenty years after the marketing push for Olestra, Nestle expressed skepticism of laboratory-made meats, including Impossible Burger and Beyond Burger. Although Nestle agreed that Americans, and other Westerners generally, ate too much meat, which was bad for their health as well as the environment and that the mass production of meat often abused animals and treated them cruelly, she questioned the efforts to create plant-based meat substitutes: "I consider them the poster children for twenty-first century food capitalism."[95] While neither product contained saturated fat nor killed animals, they were "ultraprocessed" foods with ingredients not found in ordinary kitchens. Thus, she saw no good reason to opt for the fake-meat products: "They raise the question of whether a better-for-you option is necessarily a *good* choice."[96] Similarly, she remained convinced in 2020 that "super-foods" (as well as a variety of supplements) were unnecessary, since "Eating a wide variety of relatively unprocessed foods usually takes care of nutrient needs and keeps the nutrients in balance."[97] Finally, Nestle made clear that such foods, similar to various laboratory creations, were more about boosting sales than about improving health: "Supplements, fortified foods, and "superfoods" are about marketing, not science."[98] Or, as she had told *Time* magazine in 2006, "Food is food. Medicine is medicine. Health claims are a slippery slope. . . . And food companies pay for these endorsements."[99]

While dismissive of superfood boosterism, Nestle was occasionally inconsistent in this regard. As noted above, Nestle and most nutritionists continued to adhere to the precepts laid down by Keys about the dangers of dietary cholesterol. Nestle advised people to limit items in their diets, such as too much red meat, high fat cheese, and eggs. In 2006, she followed the American Heart Association recommendation not to have more than one egg a day and, at the same time, to limit other foods with eggs on any day she had an egg. She told readers that if they chose to eat eggs, they should eat small ones, which contained less cholesterol than large ones. She also put forward two options to lessen cholesterol further. She was not a personal fan of liquid egg substitutes, since they were highly processed and had many ingredients, but wrote that they would help one to avoid cholesterol. She also described recent research about how omega-3 fats could lessen cholesterol and how some enterprising scientists had added omega-3s to eggs. Thus, in one sentence, Nestle scorned all sorts of "designer eggs," which had ingredients such as omega-3s and a higher price tag, and in another explained that these were the eggs she bought.[100] Elsewhere, Nestle also recommended that people eat fish because it was rich in omega-3s.[101]

A brief tangent is in order to explain why Nestle might have made an exception to her injunction against "techno-foods" when it came to omega-3s. Nestle was not alone in her attention to omega-3s. Science writer Susan Allport in *The Queen of Fats* described why these fats were unique and necessary.[102] Equal parts critique of the industrial food system and superfood boosterism, Allport's book explained that pervasive processing and the diet that resulted favored omega-6s (found more in grains) over omega-3s (found more in greens) to the detriment of human health. While most Americans had subscribed to Keys's mid-century indictment of dietary fat, they had misunderstood the importance and necessity of some types of fat, especially omega-3s. Many nutritionists and medical writers, such as Walter Willett, agreed with Allport on the importance of omega-3s; Willett, for example, emphasized them in his Healthy Eating Pyramid.[103] Allport provided various suggestions to increase the amount of omega-3s one ate, including the suggestion made by Nestle to buy omega-3 enriched eggs. Both Allport and Nestle came to their embrace of this techno-food due to studies of nutritional science, rather than marketing slogans.

Nestle's common-sense approach to dispensing broad nutritional advice to ordinary Americans was the organizing principle behind her 2006 book, *What to Eat.* Moving beyond the critiques of *Food Politics,* this book was a wide-ranging survey of foods in the American food system, offering advice about what to eat and why. It contained mainstream nutritional advice about all different foods and food groups, highlighted environmental impacts of food production, and provided numerous examples of how the food industry manipulated people to buy their products and "eat more." The book gave advice consistent with what Nestle had written about in *Food Politics* but added new topics, such as understanding organic foods and caffeine levels in coffee and tea. The book was clearly aimed at ordinary Americans deciding what to eat, not academics interested in critiques of the food industry; that intention was reflected in the book's organization; it was divided into the sections that corresponded to aisles of a modern supermarket. An article in *People* magazine caught the goal perfectly: "Nestle develops your cart smarts by tackling the conventional wisdom about healthy eating."[104] Thus, the book acknowledged that the primary way for Americans to interact with their food was as *consumers*; the book was titled *What to Eat,* but it was really about what to *buy.* The tone was one that might have been found in *Consumer Reports,* empowering people to make rational choices in the face of producer manipulations, but nevertheless accepting the dynamics of a consumer/producer paradigm and its role in determining what people ate. Nestle, of course, was never completely comfortable with those dynamics, since she believed that nutritional science should determine what people ate, while producers constantly tried to undermine science. This discomfort became clearer in Nestle's later writing and appearances, as her emphasis became less like that of *Consumer Reports* and more a champion of the new food movements.

Examples from *What to Eat* illustrate *both* its acceptance of a consumerist paradigm and its critique of the existing food system.[105] For instance, when

Nestle explained to readers the meaning of "local," "conventional," and "organic" labels on produce, she said that consumers could assume that local foods would be fresher and that certified organic produce would lessen pesticides in one's body, as well as in soil and water. Her preference for local and secondarily organic was clear, but the dominant comparison in the section was initially the price of each. Nevertheless, Nestle encouraged readers to "vote with their fork" (or pocketbook) for organic food and its environmental benefits and local food not only for environmental reasons (lack of transportation costs), but also to strengthen communities and have fresher food.

Nestle's discussion of the dairy and meat sections in a supermarket were occasions to revisit some of her advice about avoiding too much saturated fat (such as "a good butter is a wonderful treat," so one should use only a little and store it in the freezer to make it last), but nevertheless to avoid highly processed substitutes, such as margarine, which lacked saturated fat, but contained transfats, or nondairy creamers ("the less said about them the better"). Nestle detailed the high environmental costs of factory-farmed meat and ridiculed producers' advertisements touting their meat as an important source of protein ("Americans are anything but protein deficient"). More importantly, she argued that the health science was clear no matter what the advertisements said: "If you do not eat beef, pork, lamb, or even chicken, your risk of heart disease and certain cancers is likely to be lower than that of the average meat-eating American."[106]

Nestle's attempt to educate Americans about what food to buy sought to empower people to resist manipulations by producers as well as sellers. The book began with a discussion of supermarkets as a business. She offered a detailed critique of how space was used, why particular products were located in particular places, and how all aspects of the supermarket experience were intended to encourage people to *buy more.*[107] While it would be difficult for most Americans to avoid supermarkets completely, Nestle did not even suggest alternatives to her readers. Equipping people to understand the industrial food system, rather than go outside of it, was the expectation. For example, Nestle discussed how to prevent salmonella contamination of eggs, describing how producers should immediately refrigerate eggs and do sample laboratory testing for the bacteria. Small farms with free-range chickens would have had difficulty with immediate refrigeration and might not have had the same risk of salmonella contamination. Understandably, Nestle wanted to reach the majority of Americans who might not have known of any choice outside of industrial eggs.

Nestle's section on egg contamination and safety harkened back to her earlier book, *Safe Food,* which was somewhat outside of the topics she usually focused upon.[108] Originally, Nestle had planned for the material in *Safe Food* to be incorporated into *Food Politics*, but split it off at the request of her publisher. Appearing just two years after *Food Politics*, Nestle explained at the start of this book that it was based on some of the same themes of the first book: the overproduction and overabundance of food led to a relentless "eat more" approach from industry; industry pressure on government regulators; the manipulation of science for marketing purposes; a clash between consumer, government, and industry interests; and the inescapable conclusion that "food is political." While the book followed predictable paths Nestle had laid out earlier critiquing the manipulations of the food industry, she began with a discussion about the meaning of food "safety" since "Safety is relative . . . we can define a safe food as one that does not exceed an acceptable level of risk. Decisions about acceptability involve perceptions, opinions, and values, as well as science. When such decisions have implications for commercial or self-interested motives, food safety enters the realm of politics." Nestle explained that people decided what was an "acceptable level of risk" based in part on whether that risk was involuntary, unfamiliar, inequitable, and disputed among experts. Even if people might disagree about the meaning of safety, Nestle expressed her preference for a food system in which foods and ingredients had to be *proven* safe before they could be sold—an approach to safety known as the "precautionary principle." Although such a principle was not in effect in the United States, Nestle observed that most people assumed, sometimes erroneously, that if the government and industry allowed a product to be sold, it was certifiably safe.

Nestle divided the threats to safe food into two categories: first, food-borne pathogens and contamination; second, biotechnology. In the first, the main culprit discussed was the failure of meat and dairy industries to institute rational, proven safety systems based on biology, simple steps, and checklists. Failures to implement such basic systems stemmed from a confusing government regulatory structure with diffuse responsibilities and a lack of enforcement and from industry failing to prioritize safety systems over efficiency and profits. Meanwhile, much of the biotechnology risk discussed included genetically modified organisms (GMOs), the widespread adoption of which failed to take account of allergenicity, antibiotic resistance, and potential environmental harm. The book ended with simple steps that industry, government, and the public should take to improve consumer safety. For the public, Nestle proposed the type of activist steps that would become more common in her later books: advocating for domestic and international programs on safety, joining a consumer group on the issue, and electing people who cared about food safety.[109]

Activism may have been more overt in some of Nestle's books than in others, but it reflected a consistent underlying approach to food and diet. Over the years, Nestle presented healthy eating as a matter of common sense, a *rational* process based on basic knowledge about health. Problems with food choice arose when industry and government interfered in science-based research and common sense. Nestle seemed convinced that when people were presented with the facts and not manipulated by self-interested entities they would make the right choices. Thus, Nestle's attention to nutrition education over many years and the particulars of government guidelines mattered deeply. Nestle felt she was answering a need, as she explained at the start of *What to Eat,* saying that people frequently *asked her* what to eat, confused about the advice they heard in the public culture. She was also determined to present information in an accessible way, talking about food more than about its components; too often she felt that advice took "nutrients out of their dietary context. People don't eat nutrients. They eat lots of different foods."[110] Other nutrition writers agreed with Nestle that the public needed help in the face of marketing manipulations; Jane Brody's review of *Unsavory Truth,* for example, began: "Confused about what to eat and drink to protect your health? I'm not surprised."[111]

One might speculate that the increasingly activist tone in Nestle's writing and her embrace of new food movements was due to continual frustration at trying to reign in Big Food and improve American eating habits through rational education and government dietary guidelines. The shift could also be due to Nestle's notoriety as a fearless critic of food corporations so people sought her support, or to the variety of new food movements emerging around her, or to the urgency of food-related environmental problems and inequalities, or to the evolution of a scholar looking at the connections among disparate topics. It is reasonable to assume that a variety of factors were at work. The new food movements were several—and will be discussed in greater detail in the next chapter—but can be broadly described as challenges to the existing industrialized food system for reasons of health, environmental crisis, social justice, political ideology, and changing cultural narratives about food. As a long-time critic of Big Food, it was not surprising that Nestle embraced these new directions to one degree or another. Here are some examples.

Nestle had long used the phrase "vote with your fork," reflecting that food was political and that ordinary people had agency in their relationship to it. While some critics worried that putting too much responsibility on individuals for their food choices encouraged a neoliberal framework and consumerist view of food, many more people increasingly embraced such rhetoric and the goal of empowering people against the existing system. While consumers were arguably to blame, at least in part, for their poor food choices, Nestle never equivocated that Big Food held more power and therefore more responsibility for what Americans ate. With the spread of new food movements, she was increasingly in good company amid calls for individual empowerment, making it clear that "voting with your fork" was the action of being a citizen, not just a consumer. In *Unsavory Truth*, Nestle wrote of the obligation of "citizens" to speak out against dishonest corporate practices because they endangered democracy; she concluded: "The public—and this means all of us—has a big influence on what food companies make and do. . . . Hold food companies accountable."[112] As far back as 2006, she had made the point that voting with one's fork had an impact beyond the food system: "[it affected] not only the food you want to eat, but what kind of world you want to live in."[113]

Nestle's entreaties for citizen action led her to support broader political critiques, as reflected, for example, in the foreword she contributed to Eric Holt-Giménez's 2017 book, *A Foodie's Guide to Capitalism.*[114] Nestle framed the book with the assertion that the sole goal of food companies was to make money, creating a system in which "profits take precedence over any other human value." This critique of capitalism was accompanied by the observation that government policies had further supported overproduction and cheap food, resulting in obesity.[115] Although Nestle did not write much about labor issues in food production, she clearly agreed with many political aspects of Holt-Giménez's argument, including: "When voting with our fork, we should remember that the freedom to buy food according to our values does not in and of itself change the power of commodities in our food system. If we want to change the power of commodities in the food system, we will have to change the way we value the labor in our food as well."[116] As Nestle made clear in *Let's Ask Marion* three years later, she agreed with Holt-Giménez's broad political critique: "Capitalism converts food—a substance essential for life—into a commodity to be bought and sold like any other widget."[117]

Another part of the new food movements that Nestle embraced was advocating for eating and supporting local and organic food, even if she had not always had that view. In an article solicited for the 2005 *World Economic Forum*, Nestle wrote, "Despite being a long-time analyst of the politics of nutrition, I must confess to a rather late interest in organic foods." Nevertheless, she strongly endorsed organic food even if there was not definitive scientific evidence that organic foods were more nutritious (although she assumed that research might eventually prove that to be so): "Are foods better if they are organic? Of course they are, but not primarily because of nutrition," whereupon she cited more safety for farmworkers and less environmental contamination.[118] As noted above, in *What to Eat*, Nestle praised the virtues of organic food and local food, the latter especially because it was fresher. And for fresher food, she also noted the virtues of seasonality—though this was not a frequent topic in her writing. She also supported the local and do-it-yourself messages of others. For example, she was interviewed in the 2011 film *Truck Farm* about the possibilities of growing food in the back of a pickup truck in the middle of a city. The documentary by director Ian Cheney was intended to encourage the spread of such micro-urban farms to increase access to fresh vegetables and to change attitudes about food production. Nestle appeared on camera sampling the greens out of a truck, praising their taste, and offering some observations about the desirability of fresh food accessible to all.[119] Nevertheless, reflecting her pragmatic outlook, Nestle was not an absolutist when it came to seasonality, locality, or organics; as she said in an interview a few years earlier, "I'm not a purist, and I don't expect other people to be either."[120]

Another motivation for activists in the new food movements was the environmental crisis. Although Nestle had often used the term "environment" in discussions of the "food environment" created by Big Food that encouraged poor food choices, over time, she became more concerned with the environmental impact of food production.[121] By the time she wrote *Soda Politics* in 2015, she recommended to readers that one of the strategies they could use in local campaigns against soda was to focus on the environmental impact of millions of plastic bottles as well as the energy needed to transport them. She also suggested that anti-soda campaigns could be tied to local bottle bans and deposit laws.[122]

In her 2020 book, *Let's Ask Marion*, Nestle discussed the serious greenhouse gas emissions of food production (although noting that people disagreed on the exact figures), and she encouraged the embrace of regenerative agriculture to conserve water, capture and retain carbon in soil, and increase biodiversity, summarizing that it seemed to her like these practices were in accord with the original intent of organic farming: "Preserve soil resources and put back what you take out."[123] By the time she wrote her memoir in 2022, Nestle observed that, although she had been slow to understand that the quality of food depended on how it was grown, she now wholeheartedly believed that "what we eat cannot be understood without knowing how food is produced."[124]

Arguments in support of the new food movements were not only environmental, political, or economic; they were also cultural, aimed at changing attitudes toward food, including finding new pleasures in food. Early in her career, the scientist Nestle was skeptical about understanding food through culture, especially in academic fields, assuming that writing about food culture was not scholarly.[125] Yet, these doubts were less in evidence over time, as Nestle's focus broadened, and she embraced the new food movements. Still, her ever-present rational arguments and frequent references to science and politics made this observation in *What to Eat* surprising: "For me, food is one of life's great pleasures, and I have been teaching, writing, and talking about the joys of eating as well as the more cultural and scientific aspects of food for nearly thirty years."[126] More than a decade later, she included a similar passage in the introduction to *Let's Ask Marion,* adding that pleasure "underlies all of my thinking about food and food issues. Food is delicious as well as nourishing and is one of the supreme joys of human culture."[127] There was no reason to doubt Nestle's sincerity, but such reveling in food pleasure was certainly not a prominent aspect of her writing and speaking, even if it was paramount in her own mind. Perhaps, it was not just that Nestle had changed, but that the culture around her had also changed. Early in her career, a (female) nutritionist discussing pleasure might have led some to dismiss her as emotional and not scientific or serious. By the second decade of the twenty-first century, many gendered double standards had been weakened and references to personal pleasure had become more common in food discourse—as the following chapter will discuss further.

As much as Nestle embraced cultural messages and other priorities of the new food movements, she did not jettison beliefs that had been foundational for her work. Nestle never gave up the expectation that scientific research provided the information necessary to make the right food choices and support good health; choosing what to eat—she believed—was a rational process. Nevertheless, in *Slow Cooked,* Nestle observed that scientific facts could lose out to personal opinions: "beliefs are stronger influences on human behavior than scientific facts—a good lesson to learn."[128] Nestle never stopped believing that the government had an important role to play in disseminating nutritional science through education and public policy. In 2020, Nestle asserted that food and nutrition policies should be reorganized and better coordinated; responding to an interview question about whether that might entail appointing a "National Food Policy Advisor," Nestle responded: "I want that job!"[129] Similarly, assuming that food choice should be based on scientific consensus, Nestle never found occasion to reject some of the bedrock nutritional paradigms of the late twentieth century, such as an emphasis on lowering fat intake. Rational choice also meant dealing with the system as it currently existed. Although

Nestle supported nonindustrial and do-it-yourself alternatives in the new food movements, she made it clear that the central focus needed to remain empowering people to make the right choices in a consumer-based system. Generally, Nestle's writing was more in the vein of *Consumer Reports* than radical manifestos. Finally, although Nestle remained highly critical of Big Food, as she argued in *Unsavory Truth,* nutritionists had to continue to engage with the industry and accept its money, despite the dangers that might lurk. In *Let's Ask Marion,* Nestle acknowledged: "It is human nature to think that other people are biased, but never ourselves." Yet, she also argued that well-trained scientists "go out of our way to control for our conscious and unconscious biases." In the end, she reasoned, "It's not that all industry-funded research is biased: it's just that most of it appears to be."[130]

In her decades-long critique of how Big Food manipulated what Americans ate, Marion Nestle was telling a story about power imbalances. She argued that Americans did not really make their food choices freely in large part because corporations—motivated solely by profit seeking—worked to obscure the science of health and nutrition. Thus, Nestle spent her career shining a light on the impact of politics and marketing within the existing food system. The next chapter discusses how Alice Waters proposed alternatives to that system by making connections between production, environment, and food choice.

6

Alice Waters and a Reimagined Food System

"Food," Alice Waters wrote in her first book, "must be experienced." Although adamant, she recognized the irony of attempting to convey an understanding of *experience* through her words. As she put it: "I worry that writing about it may not make the sense I want it to!"[1] Nevertheless, here and in subsequent writing and interviews, she used language to describe her experience of food, inviting others to partake in what she would later call a "delicious revolution." Importantly, Waters made it clear that the only way to participate in the revolution, to experience food, was through one's *senses.* Food, thus, was a sensuous experience.

This observation might appear obvious and ordinary; after all, the first association many people have with evaluating food is taste. Moreover, others, such as Julia Child, encouraged Americans to celebrate the taste of delicious food. For Waters, though, "delicious food" was defined by much more than its taste. Experiencing delicious food meant challenging the industrial food system, recognizing the connection between food and the natural world, and reinvigorating community. A revolution indeed.

The following chapter will discuss Waters's ambitions and impact, why she was referred to as one of the most famous American chefs in the early twenty-first century and was credited with creating—or at least personifying—the California Food Revolution and what became various iterations of a New Food Movement.

Alice Waters became famous as the founder of the restaurant Chez Panisse in Berkeley, California. The restaurant opened in 1971 as an unassuming, local establishment, became nationally known with a 1975 review in *Gourmet* magazine, and earned the title best restaurant in America by 2001.[2] As its fame grew, Chez Panisse hosted dinners for luminaries in the food world (such as Richard Olney and Marion Cunningham), the cultural world (such as Mikhail Barishnikov and Peter Sellers), and in the political and international world (such as the Dalai Lama and President Bill Clinton).[3] For observers of American food culture in the late twentieth century, it is hard to overstate the impact of Chez Panisse. For example, in his biography of Waters and her restaurant, writer Thomas McNamee asserted that Chez Panisse was more than a restaurant: "It is a standard-bearer for a system of moral values. It is the leader of a style of cooking, of a social movement, and of a comprehensive philosophy of doing good and living well. It is also a work of art—the work of many, the masterpiece of one."[4] While McNamee's tone might sound hyperbolic, his observations about the restaurant's impact were not. Chef and food writer Ruth Reichl made a similar point more briefly in 1989: Chez Panisse "changed the way America eats."[5] Reichl's conclusion indicated that Chez Panisse's impact went beyond its cultural legacy. As will be discussed below, the restaurant also had an important environmental legacy. It challenged how food was produced and how it connected people to the natural world.

Before thinking about the varied impacts of Chez Panisse on cultural and environmental history, it makes sense to go back to its origins and Waters's motivation in creating it. Parts of this story have been told often in the world of food culture—and might sound somewhat familiar to those who know the well-trod tale of how Julia Child became a chef. Julia Child fell in love with French food from her first lunch of *sole meunière* when she and her husband arrived in France in 1948. Similarly, Alice Waters, with no background in food or cooking, fell in love with French food when she went to live in France for a junior year abroad in 1965. She, too, described a revelatory lunch, hers of cured ham and melon, whole trout with slivered almonds, and a raspberry tart the memory of which remained indelible: "It was one of those perfect little meals. Years later when I opened Chez Panisse, I looked back on that experience as a blueprint."[6] Child and Waters were not the only postwar Americans to fall in love with French cuisine. As discussed earlier, this was a common theme in middle-class American food culture. Most enjoyed French food vicariously, by experimenting at home or going to French restaurants; meanwhile, chefs and food writers beyond Julia Child, such as James Beard, M. F. K. Fisher, and Richard Olney, made pilgrimages to France to immerse themselves in its cuisine. Waters recognized her own debt to Child in particular, writing that she was inspired by her and that "Julia Child's [television] show allowed Chez Panisse to flourish . . . if Julia hadn't prepared people for French cooking, our little French restaurant never would have worked."[7]

Waters sought to recreate all that she had absorbed about French food and French food culture from her time in France.[8] She and her traveling companion had spent more time going to restaurants and cafés in France than to classes at the university. Waters particularly embraced "la cuisine du marché," or market cooking, simple fare determined by what fresh ingredients were found in the market. In addition to the taste of the dishes she ate, Waters enjoyed how much the French celebrated and planned their meals; she recalled being surprised how much time people took to decide where they would dine. In addition, Waters embraced the atmosphere of restaurants that were warm and casual, yet crisp and exacting in their food standards. She hoped to recreate the whole aesthetic of dining in France at Chez Panisse. The name of the restaurant also reflected her love of French culture. Honoré Panisse was the name of a character in a trilogy of Marcel Pagnol films (*Marius, Fanny,* and *César*) who spent much of his time socializing in a café. When Chez Panisse started, the prix fixe menu of French dishes changed daily, and was written out (by hand) in French. (It was not until 1977 that the menu was written in English, excepting untranslatable French words.) Waters made trips to France during the 1970s to find new inspirations for the menu. She also had other role models for her French restaurant. Waters wrote how much she admired Elizabeth David's *French Country Cooking,* including its aesthetics, as shown in the book's photographs. She also studied the cooking techniques of Richard Olney, whose career focused on French cuisine. Much of what Waters initially embraced in French cuisine continued to shape all that she did later, even as her culinary approach and philosophy evolved after the 1970s.

The origins of Alice Waters's food revolution and the new food movements that followed lay not just in the wonders of French cuisine. Most histories of this transformation also discussed how Waters and the new food movements were spawned by "the counterculture." This connection was sometimes vague, alluding to the idea that Waters sought to change the food status quo in the way that the counterculture had transformed the United States and that she had opened her restaurant in the temporal and geographic center of the counterculture, Berkeley, California, in 1971. Others who sought a change in the established food system around the same time, such as Frances Moore Lappé, were also described as coming out of the counterculture. There was no denying that Lappé's and Waters's ideas about food were shaped by the counterculture, but the nature of that connection was more interesting and specific than many assumed. Waters was *not* an heir of late 1960s vegetarian hippies who spurned old world aesthetics; her sensibilities grew out of the early 1960s search for meaning, authenticity, and individuality. In particular, Waters was inspired by one of the leaders of the Free Speech Movement, Mario Savio.

Savio was a graduate student in philosophy at the University of California, Berkeley, in 1964; he inspired fellow students in the Free Speech Movement by articulating connections between the civil rights movement and the student movement, both of which fought for democracy and due process of law.[9] More specifically, he argued that the Free Speech Movement confronted "what may emerge as the greatest problem of our nation—depersonalized, unresponsive bureaucracy."[10] In addition, he said that the dangers were magnified because bureaucracies were self-perpetuating, and administrators within them labored under the false belief that history had ended and the ideal society had already been achieved. In contrast, students wanted the freedom to articulate the problems around them and strive to improve society. Yet, many students felt the relentless pressure to conform to the "system," to "compromise those principles which were most dear to them... [and] suppress the most creative impulses that they have."[11] Savio concluded that in the sterile "consumer's paradise," the only flashes of meaning were found in the "movements to change America" by a "minority of men and women" who would "die rather than be standardized, replaceable, and irrelevant."[12]

Alice Waters's identification with Savio's arguments was lasting and revealed much about her goals in founding Chez Panisse. Years later, she described how, when she transferred from the University of California, Santa Barbara, to Berkeley, she felt at home on the campus that was more diverse and more political. In particular, she identified the Free Speech Movement and Savio as formative in her life. In the multi-authored *40 Years of Chez Panisse,* Waters quoted from Savio's most famous speech that "America is becoming ever more the utopia of sterilized, automated contentment" and asserted that "hearing this would later help give me the courage to search for a contentment that was unsterilized and fertile and handmade, a contentment that I would find a few years later in the kitchen, a contentment that would last my entire life."[13] Greil Marcus, a historian, member of the Chez Panisse board, and another contributor to the book, concluded: "More than anything else, it was Mario Savio's words that convinced Alice that she, in her own way, had to change the world."[14] Six years after the publication of *40 Years of Chez Panisse,* in her memoir, *Coming to My Senses,* Waters returned to the importance of the Free Speech Movement on her own trajectory and pointedly dedicated the book to Mario Savio.[15]

It's also important to note that Waters's passion for the Free Speech Movement was shared by many of her Berkeley friends, including her live-in boyfriend, artist and printer David Goines. Waters and Goines met in Berkeley in 1966; Waters was volunteering on a congressional campaign for which Goines did some of the printing. Shortly thereafter, the two became a couple and remained so through the founding of Chez Panisse. Goines was a leader in the Free Speech Movement and was expelled from UC Berkeley for his role in it.[16]

It might seem a long way from Mario Savio's call for creative individuals to improve society in the face of a sterile bureaucracy to the establishment of a Berkeley restaurant, but the connection was always clear to Waters. Chez Panisse was a restaurant built not only with the goal of producing delicious French food that would excite the senses, but also on the idea that responding to one's senses, recognizing that "food is alive and that we have to follow that intuition," revealed more profound truths about community and values. In short, Waters, like Savio, sought to create a more authentic, better experience of the world.[17] Such values continued to motivate Waters later in her career as well. The subtitle of her memoir was instructive: *The Making of a Counterculture Cook*. Waters concluded: "the counterculture opened us up to the possibility that we *could* do things differently, if we saw a better path."[18]

Since the counterculture meant forging new pathways, it also meant that there was no single counterculture. Waters's path was different from that of other counterculture cooks of the 1960s and 1970s, many of whom found their ingredients in health food stores and food co-ops. Some were vegetarians inspired by *Diet for a Small Planet*; others sought whole, unrefined grains, rejecting plastic packages of processed foods; Eastern philosophies, religions, and diets influenced other people; and some environmentalists wanted organic foods grown without pesticides. Waters had a dim view of such cuisines and stores. Late in her career, for example, in her book *My Pantry*, she confessed that she had long held prejudices against whole grains (due to the dense loaves of health-food bread in the 1970s) and brown rice ("a grain I associated with the over-cooked globs that underlay so many undistinguished vegetarian curries during my college days in Berkeley").[19] She praised the fact that the 1970s co-op near her house carried organic food, but she found the place unappetizing overall: "The produce always felt overgrown and wilted, piled haphazardly in a dusty bin, with no presentation like you'd find in a French shop. It didn't excite me to cook with those vegetables: tired lettuce, limp carrots. And the store smelled bad, sort of like vitamin powder and bad incense."[20]

For Waters, it was not just that the provisions and stores of the 1970s fell short. She also rejected the whole approach to cooking and eating that they represented. She explained that she agreed with countercultural values when it came to such issues as the Vietnam War, corrupt politics, and sexual liberation, but parted company with what she described as an anti-intellectualism of the hippies who were more interested in smoking dope and dropping out, in contrast to the beatnik side of the counterculture. She described herself as "more in the beat place, in the intellectual place": "I thought the way to change was by engaging with society." Such philosophical differences were also reflected in how Waters viewed food: "I believed in formality and beauty and deliberation. My friends and I valued a European aesthetic that was at odds with the Summer of Love aesthetic." She rejected how hippies ate in "an indiscriminate way . . . cross-legged on couches or on the ground with none of the formality of the table. . . . I thought their approach was absolutely uncivilized, unrefined."[21]

Waters may have rejected hippie foodways, but she did embrace the communalism of the counterculture from the earliest days of Chez Panisse and over many years thereafter. Her goal was to create a collaborative, extended family among the staff and neighborhood patrons. The restaurant was communal in structure, not just in its ideals. It was founded by Waters and six friends, and in its early days Waters was not always prominent in press coverage about the restaurant. For example, in a 1979 article in the *Chicago Tribune* on Chez Panisse's annual garlic festival, Waters was not even mentioned.[22] Waters often described how part of her goal in starting the restaurant was to cook for and gather with friends. She and her partners made many of the early decisions together, including choosing the name of the restaurant and its design. In writing about Chez Panisse, Waters frequently used the collective "we" to describe goals and policies.[23] The restaurant had formal directors who intended to run it as both a community and a family.[24] Neighborhood diners were also counted in the community. Many locals came to Chez Panisse early on, but as its fame grew—and the cost of dining there rose—some of them were crowded out or priced out. Addressing this situation was one of the reasons that the more moderately priced café was opened upstairs from the restaurant in 1980.[25]

A brief survey of the workings of Chez Panisse illustrated Waters's communalism, when it succeeded and when it did not.[26] Waters worked with friends in 1971 to plan out the restaurant, with the goal of creating an informal, warm atmosphere, with outstanding food. There would be one prix fixe menu, changing each night, as if one were having dinner at a friend's house. Many of the original partners remained involved in the restaurant (or Waters's personal life) for many years thereafter.[27] Beyond her partners, Waters hired staff based on how well she thought they would mesh with the community and their attitude toward food, rather than their restaurant experience or expertise. In fact, the first chef she hired was a graduate student at Berkeley who was able to cook but had no restaurant experience whatsoever. Waters explained that the staff may have been inexperienced, "But they were smart and talented and believed in the vision." New dishes and menu changes grew from brainstorming among the kitchen staff—though final decisions were made by Waters. Staff rotated jobs in the restaurant when they were hired, so that everyone would have an understanding of the whole operation; overall, the organization minimized hierarchy. The lack of hierarchy, in particular, benefited women, who had traditionally been marginalized in restaurant roles. The communal spirit was also reflected in regular after-hours socializing in the restaurant among staff, as well as frequent and fluid liaisons among them. Waters wanted to spend most of her time in the front of the house overseeing everything, though she nevertheless worked in the kitchen roughly from 1976 to 1983. Within the first year, Thomas McNamee concluded that "Alice had created a little world and peopled it with like-hearted creatures." McNamee and others also observed that this little world might have been populated by like-minded people, but certainly not by businesspeople. Financial operations of Chez Panisse were often precarious and haphazard; the structure was streamlined more by the mid-1980s, when Waters's father helped to restructure the budget and other procedures and introduced computerization.

Similar to any organization, even one with less communal ideals, Chez Panisse had its highs and lows of morale. Lows came when staff were burned out or stale, or when not everyone was working toward the same vision. The best-known example of a rough patch for Chez Panisse was the period marked by tensions that eventually led to the departure of chef Jeremiah Tower. Tower was chef from 1973 to 1976; he was a creative artist, ambitious to make a name for the restaurant and himself. But with his goals of making ever-more elaborate French dishes, he began to chafe under Waters's vision of an informal, neighborhood restaurant that prized community and fresh food. Waters later described the period in this way: "We were trying to live a fantasy. But the truth is, we were losing our balance a bit."[28] Tower's culinary explorations also alienated some of the regular clientele, who had stopped coming to the restaurant. McNamee wrote, "His food struck many of them as fussy, overbearing, and excessively formal"; moreover, with the fame of the restaurant by the end of his tenure, "The jovial egalitarianism, the camaraderie between staff and clientele that had defined Chez Panisse as much as its exquisite food, had deteriorated badly, and the mood of the staff was darkening."[29] Tower decided to leave the restaurant after it became clear that he and Waters wanted different things. The final straw came when Tower returned from a trip to France with a plan to revamp the structure of Chez Panisse and increase the number of daily menus to four, jettisoning part of the restaurant's identity. Despite their different visions, the two parted on amicable terms.[30] Waters stepped into the role of chef and began redirecting the restaurant back to her original vision. Chez Panisse's reputation continued to grow, while it also recaptured some of its communal atmosphere.[31]

The difficulty of building a successful communal enterprise was illustrated by the contemporary restaurant, Moosewood, in Ithaca, New York, which was also still thriving in the second decade of the twenty-first century. Moosewood was another effort to realize the communal and food values of the counterculture. It opened in 1973, just two years after Chez Panisse, and was also based in a bustling college town. Similar to Chez Panisse, it, too, was founded by a collective (seven people), had one member who became more famous than all the others (Mollie Katzen), and challenged established food culture by serving alternative fare (vegetarian dishes, whole grains, and other unfamiliar ingredients). Moosewood also earned a place in American food history: it was named as one of the thirteen most influential restaurants of the twentieth century by *Bon Appetit*.[32] Beyond these similarities, there are many ways in which the paths of Chez Panisse and Moosewood diverged.

Moosewood's early history illustrated the difficulty of holding a collective together when fame and success beckoned. Mollie Katzen, a member of the original collective and an art student, collated, illustrated, hand lettered, and locally published a spiral-bound cookbook of the restaurant's recipes in 1974. Katzen left the collective in 1976 and published under her own name a version of it, *The Moosewood Cookbook*, with Ten Speed Press in California in 1977. There followed a decade of legal fights over who had the rights to the Moosewood name, animated by the growing fame of the 1977 book, which soon became known as pathbreaking, inspiring generations of vegetarian and alternative food cooking.[33] It, too, earned accolades from *Bon Appetit*, the James Beard Foundation, and the International Association of Culinary Professionals. It became one of the best-selling cookbooks ever and was viewed as formative for many home and professional cooks learning alternative foodways.[34] It is worth noting that the alternative foodways presented in the early *Moosewood Cookbook* did not propose going outside of the industrial food system. Similar to Julia Child's intention in *Mastering the Art of French Cooking*, in Mollie Katzen's book, author Jonathan Kauffman observed, "most of the recipes could be assembled from a grocery-store trip, no matter where you lived."[35]

The legal fight between Katzen and the restaurant collective was finally settled in 1987 with an agreement that the name "Moosewood Restaurant" could only be used in publications from the Moosewood Collective, which owned the restaurant and oversaw its publishing; Katzen's book would continue with the name *Moosewood Cookbook*, but not refer to the restaurant, and all of her subsequent books would not use the name Moosewood. The acrimonious split between Katzen and the collective could have derailed both, but each went on to great success. Katzen's book became a classic. She published many other cookbooks, and her permanent impact on American foodways had been established.[36]

Meanwhile, the restaurant and collective flourished. The original founders of the restaurant left in 1977, not long after Katzen did, and sold it to a group of workers who formed the Moosewood Collective.[37] The collective members were apparently determined not to risk another legal wrangle with a breakaway member and also wanted to protect their communal ideals.[38] Publication of future cookbooks was carefully controlled by partnership agreements, and some members of the collective were hired by the corporation to prepare the cookbook on behalf of the collective. In addition to details of legal ownership and responsibilities, the Moosewood policies codified its communal, countercultural values.[39] For example, members of the collective could apply for short-term, interest-free loans and no one would be *forced* to do the once-a-month thorough after-hours clean up—although they were encouraged to do so for extra pay. The handbook also took note of proscribing certain countercultural aesthetics when dealing with restaurant patrons, specifying dress and hygiene practices.[40]

Moosewood stayed a collective even if its countercultural aspect might have faded. Its fame spread outside of the alternative food community to the broader public culture.[41] Nevertheless, it is worth noting that Moosewood's reputation rested more on its cultural influence than upon the excellence of its cuisine. By 2005, the Moosewood Collective was mainstream and a large business that included not only the restaurant and cookbooks, but also frozen foods and merchandise with the logo.[42] Thus, Moosewood which began as a countercultural restaurant, challenging mainstream American cuisine and the capitalist system that produced it, was successful in both realms. Similarly, Chez Panisse had started as a countercultural, communal restaurant to challenge established foodways. It was also successful as a business, and instead of presenting a mere counterculture, it helped to establish a *new* food culture far beyond the doors of the restaurant. Before exploring how Waters and Chez Panisse accomplished this, it makes sense to go back and consider characteristics of the industrial food system that it challenged.

The preceding chapters have laid out some of the highlights of industrial agriculture and the food system it spawned. The early success of industrial farming in the nineteenth century rested on several foundations.[43] First was the Western expansion of the nation, facilitated by a growing railroad network, which helped certain regions to specialize in particular commodities, such as wheat in Minnesota and the Dakotas, corn and pork in the Midwest, and dairy in Wisconsin and Iowa. It was not long before large corporations built a growing industry to exploit the increasing quantities of commodities that were available for falling prices. Historian Harvey Levenstein described just how quickly this new industry was created, writing that, by 1900, 20 percent of the nation's manufacturing was in food processing.[44] The growth of agricultural capacity and output leapt forward with the demands created by World War I, leaving a glut in capacity and a depressed farm economy after the war. Abundance of output, nevertheless, continued, even if its benefits were not evenly distributed, especially during the Great Depression. Indisputable abundance encouraged Hazel Stiebeling and other USDA nutritionists to design diet plans for citizens, soldiers, and schoolchildren for optimal nutritional balance.

More dramatic change in food production followed World War II. As in many areas of the American economy, the two decades after the war were often viewed as a golden age—at least for industrial agriculture. Building on the technological and business innovations of the early twentieth century, agriculture was transformed with the civilian adoption of synthetic, petroleum-based pesticides, such as DDT, which had been developed for military use. Soon after the war, DDT became ubiquitous in American agriculture; it was used, for example, on grains, fruits, cotton, and in barns for insect control and led to the creation of new and more powerful pesticides. More than just reflecting the advances of modern chemistry, the explosion of pesticide use (which increased tenfold from 1945 to 1972) demonstrated the unquestioned conviction that the environmental landscape could be manipulated and shaped to satisfy human desires.[45] A cursory look at the transformation of postwar farming bolstered faith in human ingenuity and the new technologies (mechanical and chemical), as grain, dairy, and animal production on farms skyrocketed.[46] The new age of abundance was widely acknowledged and celebrated. For example, newspaper and magazine articles and advertisements in the 1940s and 1950s lauded the ballooning output and the technologies that brought it. Along with praise for the techniques of modern agriculture, newspapers and magazines also celebrated the processed and prepared foods that transformed raw materials into modern foodstuffs.

The day-to-day experiences of many Americans were shaped by the new realities of industrial food abundance. Food was relatively inexpensive, available in great variety, and unlimited by season. New suburban supermarkets had large, colorful aisles filled with produce and packaged products. This bounty inspired cooks, such as Poppy Cannon, who encouraged women to be creative with processed foods. Other cookbooks followed in this vein, with recipes for elaborate, brightly colored dishes of what one critic called "spirited artifice" that were subject to ridicule by modern-day sensibilities.[47] With a very different approach to cooking, Julia Child nevertheless tailored French cooking to the ingredients available in a modern American supermarket. Soon, though, others, such as Frances Moore Lappé and Marion Nestle, instead of celebrating the wonders of the industrial food system, criticized its environmental, political, and health consequences. It is in this context that we return to Alice Waters and what she sought to accomplish with Chez Panisse. More than just creating a restaurant reflecting the counterculture, Waters sought to build an intentional alternative to the modern food system. Her model was the one she had experienced as a college student in France: fresh food bought from local markets, selected for taste and appearance, and the assumption that each meal should be treated as a special occasion.

Waters began Chez Panisse by emulating French foodways but remained focused on the *quality* of ingredients throughout her career. In her first book in 1982, she wrote, "My one unbreakable rule has always been to use only the freshest and finest ingredients available."[48] In the 1980s, Ruth Reichl summed up Waters's distinction between French and fresh food: "Waters had an inspiration: what was good about French food wasn't the cooking—it was the food itself."[49] Whether or not Chez Panisse was a countercultural statement or an homage to French cuisine, Waters always made it clear that she was motivated by sensual exploration, not abstract goals. Writing about what she termed a "Delicious Revolution" in 2007, she asserted, "I was searching for flavor, not philosophy."[50] Further, in encouraging people to take up cooking, she told her readers to "Enjoy cooking as a sensory pleasure: touch, listen, watch, smell, and, above all, taste," since "It's the many dimensions of sensual experience that make cooking so satisfying."[51] In many of her recipe and other books, Waters emphasized the importance of how food tasted more than anything else, and the importance of the ingredients used: "What I really want is a restaurant where you just give people good bread and good wine and good olive oil and then you lead them to a wonderful garden and say 'There it is help yourself.'"[52] Taste guided Chez Panisse from its earliest days, as chef Jeremiah Tower said in 1975, "If you know the taste that you are trying to achieve, you can get there one way or another."[53] Waters's search for taste was unifying for all the staff at Chez Panisse. Chef Joyce Goldstein, who worked with Waters in the 1980s, observed that Waters "is not a chef and doesn't claim to be one, but rather works closely on menu concepts with the chefs she hires. She has an impeccable palate, and if you pay attention when she critiques your cooking, you will learn about balance and flavor."[54]

Waters's focus on the taste of quality ingredients encapsulated one of her fundamental values: simplicity in cooking. She often preached the value of simplicity and argued that it was a mistaken idea to assume that good cooking had to be complicated.[55] She described how simplicity was important in Chez Panisse menus and detailed how this value could be realized for the home cook in books such as *The Art of Simple Food: Notes, Lessons, and Recipes from a Delicious Revolution*, and *My Pantry: Homemade Ingredients That Make Simple Meals Your Own* in which she told readers, "Just remember, sometimes the best dishes are the simplest." In her book *In the Green Kitchen*, Waters also laid out how to provision one's own pantry with good, simple ingredients, since "An organic pantry is an essential resource."[56]

Waters's evaluation of food was based in taste and all the senses, particularly in what she judged to be "beautiful." Although she believed that some thought beauty to be unimportant ("It is easy to dismiss beauty"), she was convinced that the yearning for beauty was inborn: "Beauty is in our biological makeup. . . . Finding the beauty in food can change your life."[57] References to "beauty" were peppered throughout Waters's writing and interviews as a way to evaluate food. Waters encouraged people to select food at the market based on its appearance. Waters wanted to remind diners at Chez Panisse about the beauty of food through displays of fruits and vegetables at the entrance to the dining room: "our way of sharing our pleasure in the colors and textures of the raw materials we use in our cooking."[58] Waters also described her attention to the rest of the décor in the restaurant and café—including dishes, flowers, and light—to create a beautiful and welcoming space. Her collaboration with David Goines on the early menus and posters was also a reflection of how beauty was comprehensive and impacted the experience of the food and meal as a whole: "When something is well printed and designed, even a menu, people take it more seriously. It has a presence and reflects on what they're about to eat."[59]

More directly, she observed, "Calligraphy and cooking resemble one another in important ways. In both, something essential and necessary—either food or words—is made beautiful through craft and creativity."[60]

Waters's pursuit of beauty was also manifest in her perfectionism. Her partner David Goines observed that Waters was exacting as she was developing expertise as a cook. He recalled that if she curdled a béarnaise sauce, "she didn't even try to save it, just threw it right in the garbage. I was shocked. She was very demanding, very exacting. Everything had to be, within reasonable limits, perfect, or she wouldn't serve it." Once the restaurant was open, her perfectionism was also found in her search for beautiful and delicious ingredients, similar to ones she had had in France. Waters recounted that her determination to find haricot verts (nearly impossible in the United States at the time) led her to buy cases of Kentucky Wonder beans (more flavorful than ordinary green beans) and just take the little ones out of the bottom of the cases, throwing the rest on the compost pile. Later, Waters grew far more concerned about the issue of waste, but at the time, finding the right tasting ingredient was paramount. Waters understood her own nature well: "I am uncompromising," she observed. "And I am a purist. . . . I think you're always trying to make things better. Always trying to make things right." Waters did not apologize for her perfectionism: "I think people have criticized me for being uncompromising, and I don't regret it for one single second."[61]

More than mere appearance, "beauty" for Waters was inextricably connected to the experience of pleasure: "Food is the easiest way for all of us to engage with beauty in our everyday lives. Any meal has the potential to crack us open to pleasure and connection and joy."[62] Waters encouraged people to "delight" in food. Her conviction that beauty and pleasure were inseparable made her emphasis on experiencing food through the senses understandable. She also emphasized that the beauty of one's surroundings gave similar pleasure. For example, in describing the importance of creating a beautiful workspace she observed: "It shouldn't be an afterthought. The right environment around you can make whatever job you're doing pleasurable, no matter how small the task."[63] Thus, the juxtaposition of pleasure and purpose in her call for a "delicious revolution" became logical.

The link between pleasure and beauty experienced through the senses was also reflected in Waters's language. She often described food in a *sensuous* way—but also in a *sensual* way, at times using the words interchangeably, despite their different connotations, the latter being more sexualized. Waters's language was sometimes more direct, sometimes less so. For example, in describing her response to beauty, Waters wrote: "If I'm in a rapture of beauty, it's perfect to me."[64] She lamented that not everyone experienced such rapture: "I am sad for those who cannot see a lovely, unblemished apple just picked from the tree as voluptuous, or a beautifully perfect pear as sensuous." She contrasted such fruit with overgrown or wilted produce found in the supermarket, which she judged to be "offensive."[65] Waters often reminded readers that beauty was not just visual or aural, but discerned through all the senses, arguing even that "smell, touch, and taste are more intimate."[66] Going one step further, she asserted that "All the good cooks I know are sensualists who take great pleasure in the beauty, smell, taste, and feel of all the ingredients. They cook with their hands. Touch conveys so much about freshness, ripeness, condition, and texture."[67] It was hard to ignore the sensuality in Waters's approach to food. Asked directly by an interviewer whether she believed there was a connection between sex and food, Waters answered emphatically: "Of course I do. . . . Food and sex and love—it's something very precious, and it is about intimacy."[68]

Waters's call for the sensuous experience of food and delight in its sensual pleasures resonated with many. This celebratory and epicurean approach became one of the hallmarks of the new food movements—but also a source of criticism. For some, treating food as a sensual pleasure smacked of hedonism, shallow indulgence, and elite insensitivity. Many people—even in the midst of modern American food abundance—worried about affording sufficient quality food for their families. Moreover, in the context of American food culture, quantity and nutritional components were the more familiar (and preferred) way to evaluate food and diet. Thus, the embrace or rejection of Waters and the new food movements reflected a broader discussion about food production and food choice. Should the system be judged by its efficiency and quantities available or by the quality of food and the pleasure it afforded? The tension between these two poles was inescapable and—as the discussion in previous chapters indicates—fundamental. This issue will be dealt with in more detail below, but first we will turn to other values espoused by Waters and the new food movements.

Waters's primary concern at the founding of Chez Panisse was in using beautiful, quality ingredients to create pleasurable meals. But she was also interested in and supportive of producing food organically. Similar to many in the counterculture, she and her friends had read in Rachel Carson's *Silent Spring* about the ubiquitous use of pesticides and thus shopped in her local Berkeley food co-op, happy that they carried organic food—even if she was unhappy with its lack of fresh produce and its unattractive interior. Organic food for the restaurant was important, but less important than finding good, fresh food. Waters's early experience of lackluster organic produce made her slow to embrace organic food as a value. One organic farmer supplying Chez Panisse, Warren Weber in Marin County, said that Waters was reluctant to use the word "organic" on the menu early on, since it meant health food, not quality food.[69] Speaking to farmers such as Weber and others, Waters's views of organic food shifted, and the environmental issues organic foods raised became more important. Luckily for Waters, working with small local farmers and gardeners and foraging ingredients usually resulted in acquiring organic food. Thus, Waters came to organic food on a different path than did the average organic consumer; yet, she increasingly diverged from the organic *industry* as it grew in size and influence. This presents a logical question: why would someone such as Waters pull away from the organic industry just as more and more Americans embraced it?

Long before Rachel Carson's 1962 exposé on pesticides, some observers had been criticizing the industrialization of agriculture.[70] Particularly influential was Sir Albert Howard in England, who wrote about the importance of building healthy soils with organic matter, mature manure, and compost instead of synthetic fertilizers. His 1940 *An Agricultural Testament* influenced many American thinkers as well, especially J. I. Rodale, who launched the magazine *Organic Farming and Gardening* (soon renamed *Organic Gardening*) in 1942. By the end of the decade, subscribers reached 90,000 and then remained relatively stable until a jump in the 1970s. For Americans interested in organic food, the magazine and Rodale Press—publishing a variety of magazines and books on health and organics—was influential until its dissolution in 2017.

For the majority of Americans, though, the ideas espoused by Rodale and *Organic Gardening* were unknown or otherwise considered fringe. Even by the time of *Silent Spring*'s publication, Carson's supporters made sure that her argument about the overuse of pesticides *not* be confused with the "cultists and faddists," such as "organic gardening fanatics." Carson herself was careful in interviews to make it clear that she was not an organic food advocate.[71] Other establishment voices continued to ridicule those who advocated organic agriculture. For example, the secretary of agriculture during the Nixon administration, Earl Butz, condemned small organic farms as a Luddite "fantasy," and Harvard nutritionist Frederick Stare and his co-author Elizabeth Whelan wrote about health food "mania" and the organic "hoax."[72] Nevertheless, in the late 1960s and into the 1970s, the environmentalism espoused by Carson and the organic values championed by Rodale were taken up by members of the counterculture as part of a broader challenge to the status quo.

The coalescence of the counterculture, environmentalism, and organic food was demonstrated at opposite ends of the country among farmers in Maine and California who formed the Maine Organic Farmers and Gardeners Association (MOFGA) in 1972 and the California Certified Organic Farmers (CCOF) in 1973. Both organizations used standards set by Rodale to judge organic practices and then offered third-party certification of farms; this process was important not only at the time, but also in providing a model of certification according to set criteria. In California, the process went further in state law, first with a legal definition of "organic" set by the legislature in 1979 and then with the passage of the California Organic Foods Act in 1990. The 1990 law established state registration for organic farms, prohibited the use of chemical pesticides and fertilizers for at least one year before organic registration, and became the model for a federal organic law. Following this direction, the 1990 Organic Foods Production Act authorized the USDA to establish a National Organic Program as well as a National Organic Standards Board, but it would take until 2000 for a federal set of standards and regulations to be announced for producing and selling organic foods, with full implementation set for 2002. This protracted process reflected important characteristics of the system that emerged. First, there was opportunity for input from many different constituencies—perhaps giving the new system a better chance of support and success. But, second, the influence of food-industry representatives, large farmers, and government bureaucrats in the process did not inspire confidence that organic values, such as whole foods and diverse, small farms, would be part of the new organic sector.

Judged by one set of standards, the organic food sector by the early twenty-first century was a dramatic success. Certified organic cropland for grains, fruits, and vegetables more than doubled from 1992 to 1997, and then doubled again from 1997 to 2003. In the early 2000s, sale of organic food was rising faster than was the sale of conventionally produced food, and many big supermarket chains had growing sections for organic produce and processed foods. In addition, the number of farm markets in the United States—which usually sold much organic produce—doubled from 1994 to 2004, reaching 3,700, while the number of Community Supported Agriculture (CSA) subscription farms (usually organic) tripled in this period. By 2015, the number of CSAs had reached more than 7,300. The growth in organic farming and CSAs coincided with an overall increase in the number of farmers, going from 1,800 in 1994 to more than 8,000 in 2013. Even many land-grant universities, the research engines of conventional industrial agriculture, started sustainable agriculture programs.[73]

It should be noted that, despite the rapid growth of organic acres and sales, the overall sector remained a fraction of the US food system. In 2008, 1 percent of US farmland was organic and 3 percent of food purchases were organic ; by 2012, organic food comprised 4 percent of the market.[74]

For those in the food industry, though, as well as officials at the USDA and farmers, there was a more important measure of success than total organic acres or sales: organic farming was experiencing a rapid growth rate and had a large profit margin. Organic foods sold for more money than did conventional foods, and the organic business was a new, undeveloped economic sector. For farmers facing decades of consolidation and downward pressure on food prices, the higher profit margin of organic food was a life saver. Scholar Julie Guthman concluded that some small farmers saw the organic niche as the only way to survive.[75] Meanwhile, for food producers, organic food was an opportunity. Articles in the mainstream press took note of this new industry. One 2002 *Newsweek* article, for example, noted that sales of organic food had been going up 15 to 20 percent per year for the previous decade, five times faster than food sales overall. The 20 percent growth rate was still being cited in 2005, when a survey also observed that more than 25 percent of Americans ate fresh organic produce at least once a week, and an article in 2009 called the twenty-three-billion-dollar-a-year organic business "the fastest growing segment of the food industry." Specialty stores and new chains benefited from the organic market. Whole Foods, in particular, was the symbol of organic success and growth, increasing market share, sales, and earnings per share in the first decade of the century. In comparison with traditional supermarket chains, Whole Foods continued to have operating margins of 4.75 percent, 3 percent higher than its competitors. Supermarket chains capitalized on the trend by stocking organic products and creating their own, less-expensive store-brand organic lines, while major food manufacturers had been acquiring organic brands since the USDA regulations had been put in effect.[76]

Despite these measures of success, if the organic food sector of the early twenty-first century was judged by a different set of standards, it fell short of many expectations and hopes. As corporate farmers, processors, and supermarket chains celebrated the growth of a new industry, others bemoaned the watering down and corruption of the term "organic." For some involved in organic food—as farmers, sellers, producers, or consumers—this choice and the threat to the philosophical values of "organic" was wrenching. Many producers who went the corporate route, such as the chairman of Stonyfield Farms, Gary Hirshberg, argued that the increased sale of organic food—even if mass produced—was an absolute good, since it lessened the amount of pesticides released into the environment. For most in the mainstream media, the victory of Big Organic was clear, in both market share and in the government imprimatur represented in the 1990 Organic Food and Production Act and its subsequent implementation through the National Organic Standards Board. The board elicited strong opposition from some with its list of additives (such as ascorbic acid and xanthan gum) that were permitted in processed organic foods.[77] Nutritionist Joan Gussow criticized the evolution of industrial organic foods in her essay "Can an Organic Twinkie™ Be Certified?" She concluded with disgust that given federal law and the debates within the USDA, it was hard to imagine that such a certification could be denied.[78] Thus, there was a yawning gap between industrial organic and what some framed as original, pure, or authentic organic.

The debate about the meaning of organic was widespread and ongoing.[79] It took place among many involved in alternative food production and in the extended debates over federal regulations, but burst into the broader public culture with the publication of Michael Pollan's widely popular 2006 book, *The Omnivore's Dilemma*.[80] In his descriptions of food systems in modern America, Pollan sketched out the differences between what he labeled the oxymoronic "industrial organic" and the local producers who held fast to earlier organic models. Pollan helped readers understand that some of the success of industrial organic lay in the ways in which it seamlessly fit into the existing industrial structure and established business model, but also in its appeal to the sentiment of consumers eager to connect with the country's agricultural heritage. Pollan described the romanticization of small family farms realized in labeling: "Thus is a venerable ideal hollowed out, reduced to a sentimental conceit printed on the side of a milk carton: Supermarket Pastoral."[81] Pollan laid out different sides of the organic debate, but it was clear where his sympathies lay: local, small, diversified farms were superior in the food they produced, their economic impact, and their sustainability. The industrial model remained inherently flawed, since it relied "on monoculture, the original sin from which almost every other problem in our food system flows."[82] To illustrate the superiority of a local, diversified farm, Pollan presented a detailed portrait of libertarian farmer Joel Salatin, owner of Polyface Farms in Virginia, who described his methods as "beyond organic." Salatin disdained the government food rules and certifications and engaged in intensive rotations of animals on his farm to produce meat, fertilize the land, and minimize outside inputs. Salatin became a folk hero of the alternative farming movement and culture following Pollan's book, appearing in documentaries, giving lectures, and publishing books.

Michael Pollan's fame also skyrocketed. He and his book were frequently cited in discussions about alternative food systems, both in terms of how food was produced and what people chose to eat. Aside from the particular appeal of *Omnivore's Dilemma*, Pollan was widely cited because his arguments resonated with many criticisms of the American food system—the conventional one as well its various alternatives. Pollan highlighted, for instance, the hidden inefficiencies of monocrop agriculture that Frances Moore Lappé had focused upon and the inhumane practices of raising meat in factory farms. He critiqued the profit motive of food corporations and the dominance of unhealthy food that Marion Nestle criticized. Meanwhile, his critique of industrial organic also reflected a broader discussion about whether there were genuine alternatives in the American food system.

The economic success of organic food was not just reflected in the growth of Whole Foods and the introduction of organic sections in other supermarkets. It meant that large portions of organic sales shifted to conventional stores, including big box stores like Costco, Sams's Club, and BJ's Wholesale. In addition, organic companies, such as Stonyfield and Organic Valley, grew dramatically, while others were soon acquired by established food corporations. For example, Heinz joined with the alternative food company Hain in 1998, while Hain combined with Celestial Seasonings two years later. By 2010, the Hain Celestial Group owned many other natural or organic brands: Arrowhead Mills, Celestial Seasonings, Walnut Acres Organic, Earth's Best Organic, Garden of Eatin', Healthy Valley, Spectrum Naturals, Imagine Foods, Soy Dream, Rice Dream, DeBoles, MaraNatha, Sunspire, Avalon Organics, and JĀSÖN. Historian Robin O'Sullivan observed: "Even astute organic consumers often do not realize that many of their favorite brands actually all belong to the same owner."[83] The Hain example illustrated the consolidation and corporatization trend of the sector as a whole. For instance, in 2004, the thirty-eight largest organic businesses were owned by just eight food corporations.[84]

Before the processors and sellers ventured in, the industrialization of organics started with agriculture. Pollan discussed in detail the scale of such monocrop production on immense farms, such as those growing corn. Along with grain production in the Midwest, the other largest area of corporate agricultural output was California. Scholar Julie Guthman observed that California had been the number-one agricultural state in the United States for half a century and was sixth in the world if it was counted as its own country.[85] Guthman's examination of the "paradox" of organic agriculture in California found that the exponential growth of organic acres in California at the end of the twentieth century not only betrayed small family farm organic methods in favor of industrial monocropping, but also perpetuated economic gaps between large landowners/producers and small-scale farms and farmworkers. Organic agriculture was clearly industrialized; half of all organic agricultural sales came from just twenty-seven large farms in California. Organic agriculture in California, then, was no panacea for economic and political inequality and was often comprised of large corporate entities, not diversified family farms.[86] The industrialization of organic agriculture overall was reflected in the consumer market. Although farm sales direct to consumers (including farmers markets and CSAs) doubled from 1997 to 2007, they grew more slowly up until 2015 and then flattened out after that.[87]

Did the average consumer care whether or not production fulfilled the original organic ideals? Some did, but Americans bought organic food for a variety of reasons. Many people—in addition to those in the counterculture—were interested in organic food long before the implementation of the 2000 federal standards. One key turning point between organic food as a niche trend and a movement with broader interest came in 1989 with news stories about pesticide residues on food, particularly Chilean grapes (with cyanide) and American-grown apples (with alar).[88] Michael Pollan observed years later that with the panic over alar "Middle America suddenly discovered organic."[89] Predictably, defenders of the industrial food status quo attempted to tamp down the alarm with various arguments. For example, the secretary of agriculture at the time, Clayton Yeutter, told the National Newspaper Association that the publicity about these dangers were unnecessarily frightening people and risking financial harm to both grape and apple production. The bulk of his argument, though, rested on the idea that risk was unavoidable and should be considered dispassionately. He noted that everyone consumed some carcinogens every day, but that "there is a difference between having cancer and consuming carcinogens." He mused that banning all pesticides might lead us to "stop eating entirely" and that "when the Good Lord put us on this earth, he did not intend to give us a lifetime that would be risk-free."[90] His calculations might sound jarring to the modern ear, but most Americans in 1989 were not ready to give up industrially raised food. Some, though, increasingly sought out organic foods even after the 1989 furor died down, motivated by the perceived risks of ingesting foods raised with pesticides.

Others were not just choosing food based on the personal risk they faced from pesticides. For instance, a 2006 global survey listed other reasons reported by organic consumers: environment, taste, animal welfare, minimal processing, novelty, and fashion (or what historian Robin O'Sullivan referred to as "a certain self-image").[91] In addition, it is worth considering the behavior of the average organic consumer. A 2005 study from the trade group Natural Marketing Institute found that about 90 percent of all organic spending came from 27 percent of those who purchased organic foods. In other words, a small segment of the market was more devoted to organic food than was the majority, or as O'Sullivan concluded: "Very few people buy organic food in every instance. Most natural and organic consumers also add a mishmash of nonorganic products to their carts."

Alice Waters was not the average organic consumer. Indeed, as has already been made clear, she did not relate to food as an industrial consumer. Rather than go to a supermarket to buy food (whether organic or not), Waters found fresh ingredients from, at first, friends and neighbors who brought garden bounty or foraged locally. As the number of farmers markets grew, and Chez Panisse became established, Waters and the staff relied on these local markets as well as on direct relationships with farmers. Supplying produce for Chez Panisse was clearly in the interest of local farmers for the predictability it brought, as well as other unforeseen benefits. For example, organic farmer Warren Weber recalled that one of the chefs at Chez Panisse, Sibella Kraus, visited his farm asking about "baby lettuce." He was happy to discover that what she sought was lettuce plants five to six weeks old—when he usually sold lettuce that was ten to sixteen weeks old; his contract to supply lettuce to Chez Panisse three times a week doubled his income from the usual sales.[92]

Waters's quest for fresh baby lettuce revealed more than her commitment to organic food and her relationship with local farmers. It tells us something about her sensibilities and the foods that she prized. Indeed, her simple salad of baby lettuce and other greens became an iconic dish at Chez Panisse and of the California Food Revolution. When Waters had visited France, she fell in love with the salads of fresh greens, in a mixture known as mesclun. Waters explained in *We Are What We Eat* that mesclun originated in southern France and consisted of seven young greens (arugula, dandelion, chervil, frisée, and various lettuces), and that she was so enamored with the discovery that she brought back seeds from France and turned her back yard into garden beds to supply Chez Panisse in the early days.[93] Waters sought to recreate the French salad of her memory and upend the prevalent American idea of bland salad, often featuring iceberg lettuce. Chez Panisse's salad became well known, popular, and helped to redefine what many called "salad." It also expressed Water's values. Historian Samuel Fromartz summarized, "For Waters, baby lettuce wasn't just a dish, but an expression of an approach to good food simply prepared."[94]

Waters displayed this conviction in the late 1970s, when Chez Panisse was named by *Playboy* magazine as one of the top twenty-five restaurants in the United States. After the publication of the list, *Playboy* invited chefs and owners to a special dinner in New York where they were asked to prepare a dish from their restaurant. Waters chose to serve her signature salad of fresh greens with herbs. Surrounded by chefs serving elaborate dishes, she was at first embarrassed but reported that the positive reception to her salad reinforced her confidence in the sensibilities of Chez Panisse: "I . . . felt a kind of pride in the simplicity of what we were doing at the restaurant."[95] With the opening of the Chez Panisse Café upstairs from the restaurant in 1980, Waters further refined her signature salad to create another iconic, previously unknown dish: greens with warm goat cheese on top, what author Thomas McNamee called "a classic of California cuisine."[96] Waters well understood her role in the wide adoption of mesclun, writing: "There are not many things I feel like I can take credit for, but I do believe the word *mesclun* came into the American vocabulary in part because of that mixture of lettuces we served at Chez Panisse." She noted what this change signified: "if there's one thing I'm responsible for in this country, something that I can take a little credit for, it's the propagation of real salad in the United States."[97]

To create her salads and everything else, Waters recalled that Chez Panisse built a patchwork of fruit and vegetable suppliers within a limited radius of Berkeley (except for the Chino Family Farm near San Diego, with which Chez Panisse maintained a relationship over decades). By the early 1980s, Waters sought a steadier relationship with one organic farm as the dominant supplier—a partner—within ninety minutes of Berkeley. Following an application process run by her parents, Waters began an ongoing partnership with Bob Cannard, who had a diverse thirty-five-acre organic farm in Sonoma County. Waters observed, "Our relationship with him makes it possible for us to cook almost as if we had a garden right outside the kitchen door."[98] The relationship between Chez Panisse and Cannard's farm was symbiotic in another way: kitchen scraps were collected from the restaurant and sent back to the farm for compost.

Waters came to prize the relationship with Bob Cannard and with others who raised or produced food. Throughout her career, she expressed this value as one of the foundations of a healthy food system and delicious food: "I believe that 90 percent of taste comes from an understanding of what seed should be planted in what place, how to care for the plant, when to pick it, and how quickly to eat it."[99] For instance, the *Chez Panisse Café Cookbook* included descriptions of the farmers, fisherman, and other purveyors on whom the café relied to encourage readers to seek out such "dedicated" stewards of the land in their own areas. Waters recognized the environmental impact of such stewards, who engaged in "the sustainable, ecologically sound harvest of nature's bounty."[100] For Waters, the importance of high-quality, fresh ingredients was closely connected to the people who provided them. Michael Pollan noted this confluence in Chez Panisse's offering of fresh fruit for dessert: "Since it first appeared on the menu in 1991, the fruit bowl has been Alice Waters's wordless way of saying that the true genius behind her food resides in the farmers who grew it; the chef merely celebrates that genius by seizing on the moments and setting it off between the quotation marks of a dish. . . . Rightly seen, rightly tasted, the fruit bowl reminds us, the commonplace becomes miraculous."[101]

Celebrating the purveyors of food was not just important for Waters and Chez Panisse. This became a central value for many chefs in the late twentieth and early twenty-first centuries, and a defining characteristic of the California Food Revolution, closely related to various iterations of the new food movements, including the local food movement and the farm-to-table movement and its subsequent restaurants. Along with Waters, other restauranteurs established mutually beneficial relationships with farmers. Chef Tom Colicchio recalled that early in his career he collaborated with farmers who would grow the specific seeds he requested.[102] Similarly, chef Dan Barber also asserted that it was essential for chefs to work with farmers to choose seeds—as well as be involved in the soil of a farm, in the methods used, and in decisions about when vegetables were picked. In addition, Barber built cooperative relationships with at least one farmer not only by buying produce, but also by having the farmer work on and improve Barber family land in western Massachusetts. Barber asserted that while Americans celebrated the "brilliance" of business entrepreneurs, such as Bill Gates and Steve Jobs, most failed to recognize that a farmer who transferred the energy of the sun to plants and then animals, used companion planting to build healthy soils, and produced delicious food was "a very brilliant person."[103]

Such an ethos of collaboration between farmer and chef was embraced widely beyond Barber, Colicchio, and Waters. It was, of course, economically significant for small farmers trying to compete in a market dominated by corporate suppliers. This was also true for small fisherman and was illustrated by the example of Ingrid Bengis-Palei, a writer and scholar of literature, who founded a seafood company in Stonington, Maine, in 1985 and was soon supplying fresh seafood to top chefs, including Jean-Georges Vongerichten, Wolfgang Puck, and Thomas Keller. She worked with the same fishermen over many years and made sure the restaurants she supplied were respectful of the food as well as those who labored to produce it.[104] Many restaurants began to identify on their menus food purveyors and what they provided for a dish. The practice sometimes used elaborate prose that eventually became the source of parody by critics who skewered the descriptions as pretentious. Celebrating food purveyors in brief biographies began at Chez Panisse, spread to other restaurants, and moved to the aisles of Whole Foods, which posted lists of those who supplied their food, sometimes including detailed portraits of the farmers. Mass produced by a grocery chain, such descriptions were akin to the nostalgic pictures printed on the side of organic milk cartons (what Michael Pollan dubbed "supermarket pastoral") and were also criticized in some quarters.[105] Thus, the sincere goal of many chefs and organic sellers to remake the values of the American food system, to celebrate the work of producers—Kim Severson observed, "People mock it now, but it was radical then"—was ripe for ridicule and exploitation as it became corporatized and a tool for marketing.[106]

This exploitation was successful to the extent that it tapped into the desire of ordinary consumers to feel connected to farmers, a yearning for connection that reflected deeply held cultural ideals in the United States. Many Americans looked back to a simpler age when small family farmers had dominated the country. Far from being just an expression of modern dissatisfaction, the agrarian ideal had had a powerful hold on the nation's identity since its founding. Thomas Jefferson's dictum that those who worked on the land were the chosen people of God remained a bedrock of American culture long after the vast majority of citizens left the land for other types of employment.[107] Such powerful ideals could be co-opted for commercial ends and tapped into the nostalgia that seemed to permeate the new food movement.

We need to pause here to lay out the contours of this movement—or what some have dubbed a revolution. As is already clear, if Waters was considered a godmother of the movement, it reflected many of her values, including using fresh, seasonal ingredients (such as Waters's cuisine du marché), prepared in new and less elaborate ways (e.g., mesclun and warm goat cheese), incorporating various cuisines from different countries (France, Italy, and others), and emphasizing the creative freedom of individual chefs (Waters, Barber, and many others). The new food movements were the broad successors to the California food revolution, which had been spurred on by the diverse climate and abundant produce available in the state; it also incorporated a more casual approach to restaurant dining than previously (for instance, open kitchens. such as was built in Chez Panisse in the 1990s, became more common).[108] Chef Joyce

Goldstein observed that "California cuisine originated in restaurants" (not homes), but that its impact was broad and long-lasting. Goldstein (who worked for three years at Chez Panisse) declared: "By the late 1990s, California cuisine had begun to influence every aspect of the food universe: home as well as restaurant cooking, what was grown, how it was grown, how fresh it had to be, and where it could be purchased." Cultural scholar Benjamin Wurgaft observed that a singular definition of California cuisine remained elusive even into the twenty-first century: "Ask three chefs to define California cuisine and explain its origins and you will get four slightly different answers, most of which will involve the local character of ingredients, the expenditure of effort, and the relationship between a given plate of food and a very specific network of regional farmers and gleaners."[109]

Thus, the new food movements or revolution were broad, both in their origins and in their impact. They were widely embraced by many on the left, and included chefs, writers, and agricultural, environmental, and social activists.[110] All three of the women profiled in this book who criticized the late-twentieth-century food system were part of these movements: Frances Moore Lappé, Marion Nestle, and Alice Waters. The movements stemmed from a fundamental dissatisfaction with the industrial food system, aiming for less-processed, fresher foods, produced without pesticides or other chemicals.[111] Attempting to turn back the clock on the globalization of food, which shipped commodities thousands of miles, the movements celebrated local foods and relationships with producers, which anchored foods in particular places and seasons. Local, seasonal food was desirable not only for environmental reasons, but because it tasted better. Waters was pivotal in bringing these multiple goals of the new food movements together. Goldstein concluded: "[Waters] drove the train of the ingredient revolution. I cannot tell you how many times her name came up while I was interviewing farmers, artisans, and chefs who she supported and pushed to do more and better."[112]

There were, indeed, numerous examples of Waters's lasting influence on the "ingredient revolution" and its implications. One can be found in Chef Tom Colicchio's Craft restaurants—first opened in 2001—which emphasized the simple pleasures of quality ingredients; Colicchio asserted that he wanted to focus on food as "craft" not "artistry," and simply highlight great, unadulterated foods.[113] Chef Dan Barber who founded the Michelin-starred Blue Hill restaurant further asserted that the quality of good ingredients was key—for its own sake and for its environmental implications. "A true primal taste," according to Barber, would indicate that food was grown in the right, ecologically sound way.

In addition, for Barber—similar to Waters—taste, production, and pleasure were intimately connected: "Pleasure is affected by more than the food's taste. When you connect people with where food comes from, it tastes better. People who love food care about the story of people who are producing it." So the pleasure of taste would lead one to a healthy environment and a healthy body: "My point is that you don't have to be an environmentalist, you don't have to be a nutritionist, you don't have to be anything other than somebody who just seeks good tastes."[114] Waters was also convinced that "taste was what won people over" and that it had "led me to the doorsteps of . . . organic farmers."[115]

As did Waters, Barber asserted that rebuilding traditional systems of food production working in harmony with nature was practical as well as desirable. He sought to demonstrate this not only in his New York City restaurant, but also in its sister restaurant located at Stone Barns, which was a multipurpose restaurant, farm, and education center in upstate New York. Barber's descriptions of his endeavor were suffused with nostalgia as well as how he changed his understanding of the food system. In his book *The Third Plate,* he told lovingly of his grandmother's farm where he spent childhood summers and then wrote about the skepticism with which he greeted one farmer's practice of planting corn, beans, and squash in a mutually nourishing patch, using the "Seven Sisters" strategy of Native Americans. He judged the farmer's idea quaint, yet wrote, "I had nothing against honoring agricultural traditions, but I didn't need a sisterhood of beneficial relationships. I need a polenta with phenomenal flavor." Come harvest time, "It was an awakening," as his senses were overcome by the flavor of a particular corn: "It was polenta I hadn't imagined possible, so *corny* that breathing out after swallowing the first bite brought another rich shot of corn flavor."[116] As did Waters, Barber happily embraced nostalgia and taste as mutually supportive, not competing goals in the food revolution. Moreover, Barber continued to celebrate taste as the best way to evaluate environmental and human health: "Taste is a soothsayer, a truth teller. And it can be a guide in reimagining our food system, and our diets, from the ground up."[117]

If the new food movement of California and then the rest of the nation began in restaurants with famous chefs such as Waters, Barber, and others looking for exceptional taste by obtaining fresh ingredients directly from farmers they knew, it also tapped into a simultaneous agricultural movement. As indicated above, the explosive growth in organic agriculture found an outlet in the growth of farmers markets in which—ideally—people bought directly from farmers, eliminating middlemen. Creating a direct relationship with farmers went one step further with the spread of CSAs, or community supported agriculture, in which people paid a particular fee upfront and received a weekly share of farm produce or credit for their investment. CSAs gave farmers predictable income and seed money (literally) and strengthened the commitment of customers to the success of a particular farm. Estimates of the numbers of such farms reached several thousand by 2015.[118]

Waters's cooking philosophy was based on fresh food from local farmers, so she encouraged people to seek out ingredients from local markets before deciding what to cook; she frequently mentioned the benefits of going to farmers markets or joining a CSA. Waters believed once people had tasted delicious food from local purveyors and understood food production, they would inevitably choose what was best for themselves, the community, and for the environment: "if we can educate the senses, and break down the wall of ignorance between farmers and eaters, I am convinced—because I have seen it with my own eyes time and again—people will inevitably choose the sustainable way."[119]

Outside the walls of her famous restaurant, Waters sought to "educate the senses" of children through what they ate at school. By the late twentieth century, school lunches represented the epitome of processed meals from industrial food production, nominally based on meeting nutritionist guidelines for consumption. Even if nutritional checkmarks had determined what Stiebeling and other USDA staffers had recommended decades before, ambitions for the school lunch were often broader. For instance, at a 1957 government conference on school lunches, one speaker declared that food service at school "should shift from being a gastronomical filling station to that of being an important educational experience." He observed that the education of a school lunch program sometimes had "more significance in the lives of children than the actual nutritional benefit." He went on to give examples of how school lunches could be integrated into all aspects of the curriculum, including science (the chemistry of food preservation and preparation), math (the costs of food production), social studies (sources of food and cultural customs), and art (table decorations).[120] This speaker's vision of how lunch programs could play a role in all aspects of the curriculum foreshadowed what Alice Waters would establish four decades later in the Edible Schoolyard Project.

The project began in 1995 after the principal of Martin Luther King Jr. Middle School located near Chez Panisse in Berkeley contacted Waters about planting a garden out front to beautify the school.[121] Waters responded to the principal with a counter proposal to build a garden with the participation of the children and to grow food for lunches that children would prepare and share together. Waters had long been convinced that food could transform lives and had been inspired by a successful garden project run by Catherine Sneed at a men's prison that had improved the quality of life of the men housed there. In addition, Waters was convinced that if American food culture were to change, that change needed to start when people were young. The project drew heavily on Waters's training as a Montessori teacher after college. Montessori philosophy emphasized educating the whole child by encouraging them to learn by doing and by using all senses. Waters sought to integrate the growing, preparing, and eating of food into the curriculum of the school, fostering better health among the children, greater respect for food, and a connection to the natural world. The project embodied many of Waters's values—filtered through a Montessori sensibility. For example, Waters wrote: "At the Edible Schoolyard Project, we often say, 'Beauty is the language of care.'" She reported that the kitchen was kept orderly so that children could easily work there and that the beauty of the space often led students to come there to do homework after school. Lunches at the school were served family style, emphasizing that enjoying food together was a social act; Waters noted that an added benefit was that this arrangement taught children portion control and consideration for others. Fundamentally, of course, the project was to teach children the joys and rewards of raising and preparing their own food, grown from the earth, not made in a factory.

Waters built the project step-by-step, collaborating with the school; she invited teachers and area principals to a meal at Chez Panisse to explain the goals of the project and show that she valued their input. Waters began raising money for building the garden and hired a garden manager to help run it. As the garden was prepared, built, and planted, its broad scope was realized, including refurbishing a boarded up small building on the campus for the children to work and eat in. Waters hired a manager for the kitchen and established the Chez Panisse Foundation to provide financial support and stability for the project.[122] More than a decade after its start, Waters reported that it had an intrinsic appeal as "hopeful and uplifting," strengthening the school and neighborhood community and attracting volunteers. She and others in the project designed a structure that could be replicated at other schools and in other communities, leading to affiliate gardens in other American schools. In addition, many other garden projects not directly affiliated with the foundation opened in scores of schools in the United States and around the world in subsequent years; by 2020, there were more than 7,000 similar programs across the globe. The Edible Schoolyard also attracted visitors from many countries (there were more than a thousand visits a year in the 2000s), including from Africa and Prince Charles from England. At the end of her book *Edible Schoolyard*, Waters summarized her idealistic ambition that the "integration of a school garden and kitchen and cafeteria into the very core of the teaching mission" could reverse dire problems, including "runaway obesity and diabetes," "the disintegration of the American family," and "harm we've done to the natural environment."[123]

Waters directed some of this ambition toward the White House. In 1993, President Bill Clinton had eaten at Chez Panisse, and Waters had had an initial, cursory conversation with the president about a White House garden. In 1995, Waters wrote to Clinton with the proposal that the Edible Schoolyard could be a model to rethink school lunches throughout the country and again suggested a White House Garden. She received no commitments from Clinton on either initiative, though she tried one more time, unsuccessfully, at the start of his second term.[124]

In the Obama White House, Waters's ideas found more resonance with Michelle Obama's organic garden, begun in 2009. Although Waters was not directly involved in Obama's White House garden, the Edible Schoolyard project—well-established and well-known—was an obvious inspiration. Food journalist Kim Severson observed: "[Michelle Obama] didn't credit Alice directly, but I promise you the garden is there in good part because of her."[125] As in the Edible Schoolyard, an important characteristic of the White House garden was to have local schoolchildren visit and work in the garden, learning the lessons of growing organic vegetables and changing their eating patterns. A number of press stories covered the venture and Obama's efforts to involve Washington, DC, children in the planting and harvesting—as well as eating from—the garden.[126] The garden was one response to Michelle Obama's concern about childhood obesity—which was at an all-time high. She wanted to encourage children to eat more fresh, whole foods, as well as offer the possibility of growing food in cities, especially in neighborhoods where access to fresh food was limited (so-called food deserts). Obama's garden and discussion about diet were also linked with her Let's Move! exercise campaign to lessen childhood obesity. In *We Are What We Eat,* Waters praised the importance of the Obama garden: "It sends a huge message about stewardship, community involvement, and childhood nutrition."[127]

Many might have been inspired by the Obama garden, just as some might have been by the Edible Schoolyard project. Both projects, though, were preceded by a rich cultural discourse that celebrated agriculture as one of the foundations of American identity: the agrarian ideal described above. This discourse had also been manifested in concrete examples of home food gardens—even in the age of industrialization and urbanization, most famously in Victory Gardens established during World War I, the Great Depression, and especially World War II, when the scale of the gardens loomed largest. These successful, widespread efforts reflected cooperation among the Department of Agriculture, the Office of War Information, the Office of Civil Defense, and the (private) National Victory Garden Institute. In 1943, the peak year of such gardens, twenty million households were growing food, amounting to more than 40 percent of all the vegetables eaten in the United States, as well as 4.1 billion jars of canned food produced. The government agencies charged with overseeing the program were motivated not only by the pounds of food that might be produced, but also by the opportunity to boost civilian morale by encouraging a patriotic but enjoyable recreational activity.[128] The success of the gardens left a warm glow of nostalgia around the wartime program, which in turn inspired many modern gardeners outside of projects such as Edible Schoolyards.

The renaissance in urban gardening in the early twenty-first century built on the historical legacy of Jefferson's agrarian ideal and Victory Gardens and challenged the idea that people should be mere consumers of food. The ethos of urban gardening, instead, called on people to be producers as well and to understand that the benefits of such production went beyond the food grown; they could strengthen the civic order, communal bonds, and individual feelings of satisfaction and accomplishment. Positive press stories about urban gardening reflected this discourse, beginning with references to the Victory Gardens of an earlier age. One article in *Organic Gardening,* "Victory Gardens 2.0," for example, described a campaign in San Francisco named Victory Gardens, "building on the historic model, while redefining victory for modern cities."[129] Similarly, profiles of community gardens in New York and Chicago also explicitly argued that the modern-day projects were modeled on the successful ones of World War II.[130]

Along with historical models, many modern urban gardeners also situated themselves as activists in the new food movements, challenging mainstream ideas about consumption. They spread the word through a genre of books on alternatives to the modern food system, especially emphasizing *local* food. In particular, urban gardeners were not only calling for local food but for do-it-yourself food. They were inspired by Waters's *The Art of Simple Food* and Michael Pollan's *The Omnivore's Dilemma* and others who followed in their footsteps.[131] Barbara Kingsolver and Alisa Smith and J. B. MacKinnon also wrote popular first-person accounts about eating local.[132] Other authors wrote various handbooks for the "locavore" movement—a subset of the new food movements. Environmentalists emphasized the importance of eating local; for example, the Sierra Club film *The True Cost of Food* (2005) praised organic farms, but it noted that agriculture could not be sustainable if food was shipped great distances. There were different manifestations of the locavore movement, such as the more than one thousand people who made a formal pledge in 2005 to eat food that was grown only within one hundred miles of home and share stories about their efforts on locavore.com.[133]

It was then not a far leap to write about eating local from *within* cities. The Canadian author Lorraine Johnson wrote about being a "city farmer," while the bestselling American author Novella Carpenter wrote about a "Farm City."[134] Another example of a first-person account hoping to spread the gospel of urban farming—and more widely than in the white middle-class community—came from MacArthur Grant winner Will Allen, founder of the community gardening organization "Growing Power."[135] These accessible narratives argued that urban gardening was important for many reasons, including health, justice, and community, and that it was one part of a broader food revolution. Within a few years, the genre of first-person accounts of urban gardening experiences and activism also made its way into documentary film. *Truck Farm*, about growing food in a truck bed, was released in 2010, and produced by the same filmmakers of the popular *King Corn*, and, three years later, another pair of filmmakers released *Growing Cities: A Film About Urban Farming in America*, with a similar message.[136]

For those inspired to grow vegetables in the middle of a modern city, there was a veritable explosion of how-to books on urban gardening in the early twenty-first century, especially after 2009.[137] Meanwhile, predating this renaissance in urban food gardening, there had been a prior increase in grassroots gardening in the 1970s and 1980s. These earlier gardeners were more motivated to re-energize and beautify blighted city lots and strengthen community groups as opposed to providing food.[138] A survey of mainstream press articles on urban gardening from 1980 to 2000 reflected that building *community* remained the most important goal of community gardens in these years.[139] After 2000, media attention to urban gardening remained steady, and some of the same themes were emphasized as in the earlier stories; building community remained the most important motivation behind the gardens.[140]

There was a subtle, but nevertheless clear shift in the views about urban gardening after 2005 and especially after 2009 and Michelle Obama's launch of the White House garden. Part of this shift reflected the growth of such projects throughout the nation. In 2009, there were one million community gardens, and by 2011 thirty million households had vegetable gardens (an increase of

20 percent over the previous five years, while at the same time flower gardening had dropped 10.5 percent).[141] Many articles repeated that this was a growing "trend" and that many people were gardening vegetables.[142] Increasingly, then, the cultural attention to urban gardening—and presumably the motivation to engage in it—was to encourage people to become producers not just consumers of food, and to find satisfaction in that role. A number of articles continued to discuss how urban gardens strengthened "communities" as in the earlier period, but more emphasis was placed on the purpose of growing fresh, local food in urban areas, where residents had few options outside of convenience stores. Some stories bemoaned the "food deserts" of poor neighborhoods, and explicitly linked food deserts to poor nutrition and, thus, poor health. Decreasing obesity, diabetes, and heart disease were discussed as motivations to start vegetable gardening.[143]

Along with the recognition that urban gardening had become widespread, there were a number of related articles about not just gardening, but "homesteading." Profiles of homesteaders described various DIY efforts of food preservation and raising animals in addition to growing vegetables. The motivation of these urban homesteaders was not only to provide themselves with good, local, economical food, but also to challenge "food politics" and "industrial food."[144] On many levels, the urban gardeners of the early twenty-first century set out to reimagine food production and consumption as a do-it-yourself enterprise that tied one to the natural world—even if that natural world was a patch of soil surrounded by asphalt and tall buildings. Urban gardening, then, was one manifestation of the new food movements that Alice Waters championed and had participated in with her own lettuce crop in her Berkeley backyard. In her first book, Waters advised readers that "The best way to find high-quality fruits and vegetables with a genuine intensity of flavor is to grow your own. The cultivation of a small plot of ground, or containers on an apartment porch, or even a few clay pots has become a virtual necessity for good cooking."[145] Over the years, Waters wrote often about the value of growing one's own food in addition to buying it from a local farmer, even linking the activity back to the experience of food: "A garden can help to make the kitchen the sensual center of your house."[146]

For Waters, growing one's own food or buying it from local farmers also reinforced an important value: eating seasonally. Fresh food was seasonal food. In one of her earliest books, *Chez Panisse Vegetables,* Waters made this explicit by listing each vegetable's season and ideal climate. Waters recalled that although she always knew the importance of seasonality, it was not the main focus of early menus at Chez Panisse. This attitude changed over time as the restaurant's relationship with Bob Cannard's farm grew and when "At a certain point, instead of feeling limited by seasonality, we started to embrace it." In criticizing one of the hallmarks of the industrial food system—that food availability could be unlimited by season or geography—Waters charged that such a system led to "mediocrity" instead of enjoying fruit and vegetables at the peak of ripeness. For Waters, paying attention to what was ripe was intimately connected to her primary goal of finding pleasure in food: "If you feed your appetite with second-best foodstuffs for most of the year, you will miss the joyous experience of savoring the tomato during its peak season. . . . It is pleasurable not only to the senses, but it allows you to give proper consideration and attention to the other produce *only* when it is good." She noted that individuals could capture seasonality with preservation methods, such as pickling, curing, canning, drying, and freezing, as an alternative to the offerings of the global food system. Lest anyone be confused that preservation was the same as the industrial offerings, she clarified: "Preserving fruits and vegetables is about carrying the brightness and bounty of one season into those that follow. Good preserves don't mimic the flavor of a fresh ingredient so much as they offer variations on it." She pushed back against the idea that eating seasonally was not possible in regions of the country with shorter growing seasons. In addition to preservation, Waters called for the formation of networks of small and medium-sized farms as an alternative to long-distance global shipping. She also found examples of alternative farmers who found creative solutions to farming in different seasons, highlighting Eliot Coleman's use of greenhouses in wintertime Maine and urban farmer Will Allen using composted byproducts of local Milwaukee breweries to heat his greenhouses.[147]

Waters's embrace of urban gardening and seasonal eating—along with many other values of the new food movements—were reflected in a contemporary global food initiative: slow food. The movement was founded by Italian journalist and activist Carlo Petrini following a protest he organized in 1986 against the building of a McDonald's at the Spanish Steps in Rome. Similar protests followed, and within three years participants from fifteen countries met and pledged "to preserve the diversity of the world's foods."[148] The movement was an answer to the deadening sameness of industrial food, eaten with little care or intentionality. Petrini likened the impersonal, fluorescently lit McDonald's to a "protein filling station" rather than a restaurant.[149] As slow food grew, chapters were established in many different countries, sometimes with members numbering in the thousands. The international movement began publishing a quarterly journal, and periodic gatherings brought together traditional and local food producers to share their bounty and knowledge. Petrini argued that "the education of taste is the Slow way to resist McDonaldization" and that it was important to embark on this education beginning with children. Following such advice, local chapters of Slow Food USA established edible schoolyard projects around the country.[150]

It was little wonder that Alice Waters embraced the slow food movement: she developed a close relationship with Petrini; joined the organization's board; became vice president of Slow Food International in 2003; and integrated Petrini's philosophy with her own.[151] Long before she met Petrini in 1988, it was clear that Waters and Chez Panisse expressed slow food values. In Water's first book, she observed: "I strongly believe that much of what has gone wrong with American food has been the result of mechanization and the alienation that comes with it."[152] Similarly, Waters believed that people should have an active role in providing food: "Cooking and shopping for our food brings rhythm and meaning to our lives."[153] In addition, Petrini and Waters both shared a belief that taste and pleasure were the most important values in food culture and food systems. For Petrini, pleasure in food was not sought for its own sake, but was a reflection of life itself: "Alimentation is an essential part of life and that quality of life is therefore linked to the pleasure of eating in healthy, varied, and flavorful ways."[154] Petrini was well aware of the dangers of celebrating pleasure: "Pleasure was, and is, a thorny subject: moralistic people feel itchy at the sound of the word; if you are involved in any sort of social cause or movement, your fellows will rebuke you for mentioning it . . . and anyone will regard an interest in pleasure as a sign of superficiality." Counter to the idea that pleasure was "purely hedonistic and a political retreat," Petrini argued that pleasure in food was part of living a harmonious life and, increasingly, helped to address environmental crises wrought by industrial food production.[155] And, in answering the charge that pleasure seeking in food was elitist, Petrini asserted that "Pleasure is a universal right and [in food and drink] . . . a world necessity."[156]

Waters's 2021 book *We Are What We Eat: A Slow Food Manifesto* offered the clearest example of how well her views coincided with Petrini's slow food values. The book was dedicated to Petrini and divided into two parts, "Fast Food Culture" and "Slow Food Culture." Each part was then further divided into chapters naming the values of each culture. Waters summarized fast food culture as based on convenience, uniformity, availability, trust in advertising, cheapness, more is better, and speed; meanwhile, she described the values of slow food as beauty, biodiversity, seasonality, stewardship, pleasure in work, simplicity, and interconnectedness. The book was instructive not only for what it told about fast/slow food cultures, but also for how it illustrated both the fundamental consistency of Waters's values and at the same time the evolution of how she articulated those values. In this book, many strands of Waters's career came together, including the reasons she started Chez Panisse, her social activism, her love of food, and the importance of educating children (such as in the Edible Schoolyard using Montessori methods), "before they were indoctrinated by the pervasive fast food world around them."[157] Understanding foodways was essential ("How we eat is how we live. This is the guiding philosophy of my life."), but Waters made it clear that fast food culture went beyond industrially produced, processed food to reflect culture more broadly: "Culture is the invisible moral structure underneath us, guiding us all subconsciously and shaping everything we do. Fast food culture has become the dominant culture in the United States, and it's becoming the dominant culture in the world."[158] To demonstrate the pervasiveness and power of this culture, Waters offered a critique in each chapter of the values that had been absorbed in our subconscious, e.g., that "everything should be available to us, all the time," that "more is better," or that "food should look and taste the same, no matter the season." Waters was careful to make links between food culture and general values; for instance, her discussion of convenience foods led her to conclude, "Convenience leads to passivity and ignorance in all areas of our lives."[159]

One of the distinctions Waters made between fast and slow food values was that the former treated everything as a consumer good—even food. As she had throughout her career, Waters explained the value of procuring food from local producers or growing it oneself. Moreover, she argued that many people were seduced by the illusion of choice in a consumerist system—even if many of those choices were mediocre and came from the same large corporations not different producers. Waters argued that the illusion of choice led to excess and food waste (30–40 percent of food is thrown away per year in the United States), and serious environmental consequences. In this book, Waters discussed not only the environmental harm of the industrial food system, but also how methods of food production determined its "authenticity" and its appeal: "Food cannot be divorced from nature. If I learn that food has come from an industrial farm, it's no longer beautiful to me, no matter how it's shined up or how cleverly it's presented."[160] Others agreed, and that was partly why Chez Panisse was so successful. Food writer Kim Severson wrote, "The more you know about where the food comes from, the greater the pleasure. . . . There is a purity of flavor, a truth, to the food at Chez Panisse."[161] Waters's holistic understanding of food choices was clear. Desirable food was food that was beautiful and authentic, and food could only be beautiful if it was raised in an environmentally sound way with slow food values. Moreover, food that was healthy for the environment was also healthy for humans. Everything was connected.

It was not only important *where* one procured food, but *how* one prepared it. One of the values of the slow food and new food movements more generally was to encourage people to cook and prepare food in their own homes. Waters and others encouraged people to eschew readymade processed foods and to take the time to cook from scratch, not only in order to make better tasting meals, but also to feel connected to food and the earth. This sensibility grew out of the counterculture and the goal of reclaiming authentic experiences erased by industrialization. The call by some in the counterculture to go "back to the land" and raise their own food went hand in hand with the call to go back to the kitchen to cook. Rediscovering authenticity, though, could come at a cost, often times for women, who many assumed would take up a greater share of household and cooking duties.[162] Nostalgia, explained writer Betty Fussell, sometimes led people to forget the problems of the preindustrial food system: "When we yearn for that Edenic world in which grapes fall from the vines into the vat and cream from the cow into the custard, we forget the flies in the buttermilk, the ants in the ointment, the maggots in the ham. We forget how unremitting and exhausting was the practice of rural and domestic economy."[163] Food historian Rachel Laudan had sharper criticism for slow food and the new food movement, or what she dubbed "culinary luddism." Writing as if people like Petrini and Waters rejected *all* types of processing (including grinding and fermenting) and "culinary modernism" overall, she argued that many industrial food products (such as fine soy sauce, good chocolate, and canned tomatoes) improved cuisine.[164] Such criticisms distorted the arguments of slow food, which called for shifting the balance in the food system and bringing local foods back into the picture. Waters, for example, noted that she endorsed Petrini's (unfortunately named) "virtuous globalization": "buying coffee, tea, spices, chocolate, and other nonperishable goods from people in other countries who are using best farming and labor practices."[165]

The connection among food, pleasure, and the environment brings us back to the most serious and complex charge against Waters, Petrini, and others in the new food and slow food movements: *elitism.* If the appeals to pleasure as well as social and environmental activism coexisted, they were undeniably in tension. Placing too much value on food pleasure could devolve into hedonism for elites, many charged. Critic Rebecca Solnit laid out these relationships with food as a zero-sum equation. “Food,” Solnit wrote, “has become both an upscale fetish . . . and a poor people’s radical agenda.” In a related observation about one DIY aspect of the new food movements, she argued that urban gardening was used by some individuals to escape from the political activism actually needed to challenge the industrial food system; urban gardening can “too easily slide over into disengagement or the belief that your activism can stop with the demonstration of your own purity and lack of culpability.”[166] Did this mean that growing food for oneself was inherently a selfish pursuit if one did nothing more to challenge the status quo of unequal food access?

Solnit’s comments also gestured to the power of the food status quo. An unintentional example from the feel-good urban gardening documentary *Truck Farm* made a corollary point about the danger of letting individual consumption choices drive food production. For most of the film, the success of the filmmakers growing vegetables in the back of a pick-up truck left the audience convinced that urban gardening could replace industrial agriculture. The filmmakers then interviewed a well-meaning chef at a fancy Greenwich Village restaurant, Dan Barber of Blue Hill, who judged their fresh herbs quite *nice*, but swiftly pointed out the impracticality of relying on such a system for actual food needs, since he would be unable to get all of the ingredients he desired when he desired them. Instead of challenging the idea that his restaurant’s particular desires should drive production, the film cut to a montage of children visiting the truck farm and learning how to grow seedlings in paper cups. Unintentionally, then, the film presented a binary proposition: ineffectually try to smash the system with impractical truck gardens and children planting seedlings *or* accept the necessity of large-scale agriculture to get the food needed.

This anecdote illustrated the danger of evaluating urban gardening and other local food movements according to existing consumption standards of abundance, affordability, and year-round choice. Judging food production only by volume and price reduced it to a mere industrial commodity. But there was also no denying that a system based around individual food desires could become impractical or elitist. Food was not either an object of desire *or* a commodity. Food, of course, was many things all at once: a commodity, a biological necessity, a source of pleasure, a source of health, a connection to the natural world, and a repository of culture. Thus, in this complexity lay the difficulty of carrying out a food revolution that fulfilled multiple goals and that benefited people equitably.

Dan Barber’s contribution to the new food movements illustrated both elitism and sincere environmental and social activism. According to Barber, a diner at Blue Hill at Stone Barns (located on the old Rockefeller estate in Pocantico

Hills, New York) had "a conversation with the captain and your waiter, and the conversation is something along the lines of what do you like to eat, . . . why you've come to the farm and why you've come to the restaurant and all of that."[167] Barber unselfconsciously used the much derided language of Reagan-era politics to explain that the food revolution "trickles down" from white table restaurants to bistros to everyday food culture.[168] Nevertheless, Barber's commitment to the environment and food justice was also clear. For instance, he pointed out that industrial food was not really inexpensive, since it relied on heavily subsidized petroleum at all stages of its production.[169] Subsidized petroleum, as others had pointed out along with Barber, was just one example of how many of the costs—economic, political, health, environmental—of industrialized agriculture were externalized and hidden. Thus, Barber and others asserted that the pursuit of flavor and environmental responsibility were not in opposition to "cheapness" but a different metric.

Waters and others agreed that when the costs of industrial food were externalized, people mistakenly believed that food was cheap. Waters, moreover, argued that this mistake was deliberately perpetuated by those who benefited from it: "I cannot compromise when it comes to wholesomeness. Our health begins in the ground. Period. The health of the soil is the most important thing right now for our health and for the climate. I cannot accept any excuses, because I don't believe they're true. They're myths promoted by the fast food industry: 'It's too expensive to eat organic, regenerative food.' It is not. If you know how to cook and you don't eat huge amounts of meat and cheese, it is not more expensive. It doesn't take more time. We can do it. That is what I am trying to help people understand."[170]

Waters directly criticized government subsidies that bolstered the industry "smokescreen" about hidden costs: "Organic foods seem elitist only because industrial food is artificially cheap, with its real costs being charged to the public purse, the public health and the environment." In addition, Waters argued that the myth of elitism fed off the expectation (shared by rich and poor alike) that food *should* be cheap, as well as the failure to value people who raised the food: "the language of cheapness is inescapable." She observed that "even the rich, who pay a tinier fraction of their incomes for food than has ever been paid before in human history, grumble at the price of an organic peach—a peach grown for flavor and picked, perfectly ripe, by a local farmer who is taking care of the land and paying his workers a fair wage!"[171]

Waters never ceased trying to convey these lessons and to respond to criticism that her restaurant and what she advocated was elitist. Even back in 1979, one newspaper article briefly observed that Chez Panisse was "patronized by the Berkeley, California elite."[172] Not wanting to compromise on the quality of the restaurant, Waters tried to address the issue of access by opening the more affordable café, upstairs from the main restaurant. Affordability, though, was relative, and the café still might have been rarified to some. In her books and interviews, Waters talked about judging simple food by quality ingredients available to all: "One of my favorite things is grilled bread with mashed fava beans. Wholesome good food should be an entitlement of all Americans, not just the rich."[173] Waters lived these values in her work on food access, not only through the Edible Schoolyard, but also working with the Food First Institute, which studied world hunger, and Share Our Strength and Daily Bread Project, which coordinated restaurant leftovers for the poor. Her friend food writer Ruth Reichl asserted: "Alice is the least elitist person I know." Another writer who also knew Waters, Kim Severson, added that Waters understood that she was "a privileged white woman" and that her restaurant was expensive, but "she works hard to broaden her perspective. She thinks quite a bit about how to get good food to people without the means to eat at places like Chez Panisse."[174]

Another dimension to the elitism discussion was the idea that criticism of consumerism within the industrial food system was class coded. Critic Daniel Harris noted that discussions about consumerism were often "contemptuous appraisals of the ugliness and vulgarity of capitalism [that] are in fact simply covert attacks on the bad taste of the lower classes."[175] An example was discussed by political scientist Aaron Bobrow-Strain, who looked at evolving attitudes toward store-bought white bread, such as Wonder Bread, the quintessential American processed food product. He observed that negative attitudes toward such foods grew out of the counterculture, but morphed into moral judgments about good and bad bread, with unspoken assumptions that poor and working-class Americans enjoyed highly processed food products rather than fresh, whole foods.[176] Ironically, another criticism of the new food movements among academics was that, rather than challenging the power of a modern consumerist, industrial food system, its DIY ideals actually reinforced pervasive neoliberal values. For instance, historian Charlotte Biltekoff wrote that involvement in food production was presented as "a social responsibility, moral duty, and a means of self-fulfillment." She had a similar criticism of the Edible Schoolyard, which "reinforced the neoliberal notion that good citizenship was practiced through responsible consumption."[177]

The class coding of food was discernible by its appearance, not just its substance. The unnaturally white Wonder Bread or brightly colored processed foods broadcast to all that they were products of a factory, cheap in price, and the antithesis of local, whole food. Appearances, though, might be deceiving. In her playful celebration of aesthetically pleasing foods (at least from her perspective), blogger Adeline Waugh illustrated that beautiful food was in the eye of the beholder and not necessarily related to the substance of a given food. Waugh was one of the originators of a minor fad called "unicorn food," characterized by rainbow colors, intermittent sparkles, and a fanciful sensibility, akin to that of the mythical creature for which it was named. An essential part of unicorn food included documenting and sharing the image of the item in question over Instagram and other platforms. Even Starbucks made its contribution to the fad with its sugary Unicorn Frappuccino, available for just five days in April 2017.[178]

On first glance, unicorn food appeared to be a parody of industrialized food, encouraging selfish pleasure seeking and the consumption of food products (such as brightly colored cupcakes) loaded with empty calories. Or, if not a parody, an extreme example of consuming what Michael Pollan labeled "foodlike substances."[179] But, upon second glance, the story became more complicated. Aside from posting images of her unicorn creations, Waugh was a food stylist who also blogged about health and wellness. She had been experimenting with natural food dyes—such as beets, chlorophyll, and blueberries—to make her food pictures more colorful, and the trend began to spread after her first posting. Her foods were all made from natural ingredients—unlike many sprinkle and marshmallow bedecked items later created by Starbucks and others—and were intended to make nutritious foods more aesthetically appealing and fun. For Waugh, then, beauty and enjoyment were not guilty or shallow pleasures, and they were not incompatible with healthy food.[180] Moreover, Waugh's creations harkened back to the highly processed industrial foods of the 1950s.[181] But Waugh challenged the industrial food system on different terms. Her playful take on healthy food rejected artificial chemicals and encouraged people to eat wholesome foods that nourished their bodies. At the same time, she was challenging the assumptions of health food purists and new food adherents who were appalled by rainbow-colored foods that looked artificial even if they were not. (Waugh faced an angry backlash after some of her Instagram postings appeared.) Waugh, then, was playfully pushing the aesthetic boundaries of wholesome food, while at the same time indulging—and upending—nostalgia for industrial food.

Waters and others in the new food movement, though, had no nostalgia for industrial foods. They sought to re-educate people's tastes away from such products. Despite the sincerity of Waters and others in the new food movements, it was still hard to escape the charge that "foodies" and those in search of responsible consumption and culinary adventures were elitist because they had the luxury to think about pleasure, not just survival. One answer to this charge was articulated by the writer and agricultural activist Wendell Berry. In his 1989 essay "The Pleasures of Eating," Berry asserted that taking pleasure in food was neither elitist nor selfish but necessary. He asserted that food should be pleasurable—for everyone: "The pleasure of eating should be an *extensive* pleasure, not that of the mere gourmet. People who know the garden in which their vegetables have grown and know that the garden is healthy will remember the beauty of the growing plants, perhaps in the dewy first light of morning when gardens are at their best. Such a memory involved itself with the food and is one of the pleasures of eating."[182] Thus, Berry found pleasure in local food and knowledge about the land from which it grew. His view was similar to that of Waters when she asserted that for her industrial food could not be beautiful. In his call to find pleasure in the relationship between the land and food, Berry also challenged another aspect of the industrial food system. He rejected the idea that the relationship to food was merely about "consumption," arguing that the food industry wanted people to be "mere consumers—passive, uncritical, and dependent." As consumers, people were unlikely to realize that "the overriding concerns [of the food industry] are not quality and health, but volume and price."[183] Michael Pollan joined this view and asserted that pleasure should not be reserved only for the privileged: "Why shouldn't pleasure figure in the politics of the food movement? Good food is potentially one of the most democratic pleasures a society can offer, is one of those subjects, like sports, that people can talk about across lines of class, ethnicity, and race." Going even further in his argument that the food movement was not elitist, Pollan argued that the rise of fast food culture was both a reflection and a cause of economic inequality. He observed that fast food was only cheap because it was produced by low-wage workers and that over-worked, low-wage workers had little time to cook from scratch: "The advent of fast food (and cheap food in general) has, in effect, subsidized the decline of family incomes in America."[184]

Even if one accepted the link that Pollan and others made between fast food culture and economic inequality, there were other charges that the new food movements were not only elitist but also impractical. One of the great successes of the industrial food system was the abundance that it created. Many people took it for granted that the measure of any food system going forward would be the quantity of food produced, since providing food for a growing world population was most often discussed as a looming, inescapable crisis. For example, *National Geographic* in May 2014 had a lengthy section, "A Five-Step Plan to Feed the World."[185] The article detailed all different aspects of the global industrial food system, including the extent to which it contributed to global warming. The conclusion offered was that industrial agriculture might have many downsides, but no one could afford to be a purist since maximum food production was needed; instead, the world needed both industrial *and* local, organic agriculture.

Alice Waters had a different answer to the problem of providing sufficient food. She argued that local food production, as well as networks of small and medium-sized farms, would raise enough food and better food than the industrial system was currently doing. Such a change, of course, meant shifting expectations. For instance, availability of unlimited amounts of all foods despite the season would not be possible nor would the continuation of seemingly cheap food with externalized costs. To illustrate, Waters summarized: "Meat is an inherently expensive ingredient, but it is made cheap by the way the animals are raised."[186] Furthermore, Waters asserted that the assumption that massive production models were necessary made people blind to endemic waste in the system and unwilling to consider any alternatives. She saw this firsthand when she tried to convince people to endorse the Edible Schoolyard and other models to provide school food. She was frequently asked: "How do we scale up in order to feed all of our school children organic food? My immediate response was: We don't need to scale up . . . the idea is ingrained in us that we *have* to supersize farming and distribution in order to feed the millions of students in the public school system. . . . I believe it's the reverse: we need to decentralize and localize and support as many different small and medium-size organic farms and ranches as we can." Waters directly rejected the assumption that if something did not scale up it was "not practical . . . not financially feasible."[187]

Charges that the new food movements were impractical or elitist were inescapably complex. People argued over the meaning of "beauty" and its value, the importance of "taste" as compared with price and efficiency, and the long-term healthfulness of eating industrial food versus short-term nutritional needs. Undeniably, Marion Nestle's call to "vote with your fork" and Alice Waters's encouragement to embrace the "delicious revolution" offered advice to people with the means to make those choices. Nevertheless, does that mean that those with less means should not also be offered or encouraged to make such choices? One of the problems of the debates about elitism was that it often became a distraction from the enormity of the task: changing the food status quo was not an either/or proposition of individuals embracing new values *or* being limited to the existing industrial model.

Perhaps, though, there was a way to escape from the circular nature of this argument. Journalist Tom Philpott summarized the problem with market solutions in the early twenty-firstst century: "We have reached the limits of 'market-as-movement' to transform the food system. In an economy marked by severe inequality, wage stagnation, and persistently high levels of poverty, the market approach excludes the population that can't afford to pay the higher prices of organic, local food or devote time to cooking from scratch." He agreed that people who could vote with their forks *should* do just that, but making such a choice by itself would not be enough to change the industrial food system.[188] On this, critics and new food adherents agreed: systemic changes (in both government policy and production models) and individual actions were both necessary and desirable.

Over the course of her career, Alice Waters participated in many of the debates over the new food movements, discussing what made a food system practical or not, elitist or accessible. Regardless of the particular issues or arguments, Waters remained consistent in her own goal. As former colleague and Chez Panisse chef Joyce Goldstein observed: "Her genius is that she inspires people to help her realize her dreams, and those dreams are big ones. Underneath a whispery voice and flirty manner lies a will of steel. She has stayed on message for forty years, driven not by money but by an unflagging commitment to make better food available to all."[189]

Conclusion

By the early twenty-first century, counterculture activists were not the only critics of the industrial food system and food culture. The criticism was mainstream. First Lady Michelle Obama's organic garden at the White House coupled with her Let's Move! campaign against child obesity challenged common views about conventional agriculture, food processing, and the American diet. Obama followed the example set by Alice Waters, bringing schoolchildren to tour the garden and feel connected to their food through the soil. She embraced the lessons of Marion Nestle, calling on food processors to "entirely rethink the products that you're offering . . . and how you market those products to our children."[1] Obama's garden and campaign were highly visible and judged by many to have been successful; her work prompted discussion of alternative food systems, encouraged changes in school lunch programs, and led some people to start growing food in their backyards.

Leadership from the White House may have been an important symbol, but its impact was nevertheless limited. For example, the Healthy Hunger-Free Kids Act of 2010, which Michelle Obama supported, set nutrition standards for all food in schools, including that in vending machines. But as Marion Nestle pointed out, counter lobbying by the food industry weakened the legislation, resulting in a law dependent on local policies and staff in schools who oversaw food programs.[2] Thus, as this example illustrates—and as the preceding pages have argued—the industrial food system and food culture were solidly entrenched, hindering substantive change. Scholar Julie Guthman observed that Obama's work was celebrated—especially in the alternative food movement—but did little to bring *systemic* changes in the agriculture and food industries since it relied on educating people to change what they ate: "Obama's garden . . . throws into sharp relief the limitations of alternative food as a change strategy."[3]

Guthman's observation highlighted one of the ongoing debates about the American diet. Who or what is responsible for what people eat: individuals and their (assumed) freedom of choice *or* economic and political systems beyond their control? Surveying cultural attitudes toward food and diet over several decades, the preceding pages have highlighted individual agency. Nevertheless, individuals, as made clear above, are constrained by the systems around them, and those systems—economic, political, agricultural, and cultural—resist challenge. Responsibility for the American food system and what people eat is, thus, less clear-cut than many people assume.

As the preceding pages have argued, no factor is more important in understanding the American food system and what people eat than abundance. Abundance has been a clear blessing—but also a paradoxical curse with environmental, health, economic, and political consequences. Government policymakers sometimes referred to abundance as *the* agricultural problem of the twentieth century, leading to decades of price supports and long-term storage of commodities, as well as efforts to find uses for surpluses, such as the school lunch program and various foreign aid programs. Historian Bryan McDonald argued that the problem of surplus food at home became an essential tool in twentieth-century foreign policy: "The governing vision for the postwar food system [was] the strategic deployment of American abundance."[4]

Abundance also shaped domestic policy, leading government officials to encourage Americans to eat more. For example, the secretary of agriculture under Dwight Eisenhower, Ezra Taft Benson, told Iowa farmers in 1957 that, while Americans had been increasing their consumption of meat, poultry, and dairy products, they were still "behind" Australians, New Zealanders, and Argentinians: "We can go farther in shifting consumption to milk, eggs, and other highly nutritious livestock products."[5] Benson gave similar advice to the National Restaurant Association ("our market for food in this country is far from saturated, if we price food realistically and merchandise it effectively") and the National Wholesale Grocers' Association ("there is not much wrong with farm prices and income that markets won't cure") to increase food consumption through marketing.[6] Despite such interventions from the federal government to increase food consumption for the economic benefit of farmers, grocers, restauranteurs, and processors, Benson eschewed responsibility for the health consequences of such advice; instead, he encouraged industry representatives to offer dietary advice: "Our doctors are becoming increasingly concerned about obesity. In many cases, this means that some people are eating too much of the wrong kinds of food. There's an educational job to be done—and who is in a better position to do it than the food marketer?"[7]

Marketing that was driven by agricultural abundance had a broad impact on many aspects of the American diet—and what people chose to eat. Historian James McWilliams, for example, observed that the increasing size of pecan crops in the 1940s and 1950s led to a "pecan-dessert craze": "With astonishing abruptness, pecans were transformed into a ubiquitous dessert addendum as production increased and prices dropped." McWilliams noted that the trend was not merely the result of spontaneous actions by farmers but was spurred by "federal promotion efforts." The marketing push to eat pecans, McWilliams concluded, continued through the end of the century, "to keep American consumers wedded to their native nut." He also likened the efforts by marketers to find new uses for the pecan to industry efforts to incorporate other surplus commodities into processed foods, especially corn and soy.[8] The story he told, then, was a common one, illustrating the fluid relationship between abundance, marketing, and food culture.

Related to the abundance of so many foods is another factor that shapes what people eat: low prices, which hide the true costs of food production. Most Americans have celebrated cheap food and have come to expect it. The industrial food system is uniquely structured to provide cheap food not only through economies of scale, but also through agricultural subsidies, labor policy, and lax environmental regulations. A clear reflection of low cost was the decreasing percentage of income spent on food in the United States through the twentieth century and into the twenty-first century. According to the USDA, the average percentage of income spent on food by 1960 was 17 percent, falling to 10.1 percent by 1998, and just 9.5 percent of income in 2019. Compared to other countries, the United States was unusual in this regard. For example, in the 2010s, the average spending on food in France was 13.5 percent of income, in China 25.5 percent, and in Nigeria more than 56 percent. But cheap food for the *average* American did not mean that everyone benefited equally. As the per capita cost of food continued to fall in the late twentieth and early twenty-first centuries, the income and wealth gap in the United States went in the opposite direction. Thus, households in the lowest quintile in 2019 spent an average of 36 percent of their income on food, and the second lowest quintile still spent almost 20 percent of their income on food. Meanwhile, households in the highest income quintile spent 8 percent of their income on food.[9]

There were still other benefits of abundance besides low cost and widespread access, notwithstanding the undeniable inequalities. Many people have enjoyed not only a year-round variety of raw foods, but unprecedented new convenience foods, ranging from ultraprocessed products to what became staples of modern pantries, such as mayonnaise and ketchup. For many critics, some of these products (such as frozen meals with multiple chemical ingredients) symbolized all that was wrong with the industrial food system; meanwhile, other convenience foods (including canned tomatoes, salad dressings, tamari sauce, and pasta) were deemed acceptable. Historian Rachel Laudan argued that there was a certain willful blindness among critics ("Culinary Luddites") of the industrial food system who nevertheless benefited from "Culinary Modernism." One benefit was not only access to labor-saving ingredients and a varied diet, but also more egalitarianism with ingredients "available more or less equally to all."[10] Access to convenience foods has been part of what historians Gary Cross and Robert Proctor have described as the "packaged pleasure revolution," which they agree has been accessible to all: "The revolution is . . . about the democratization of consumption: the poor can now have goods once available only to the rich."[11]

Thus, one of the attractions of the industrial food system—flowing from abundance, low cost, and convenience—is the promise embedded in most aspects of consumerism: to transcend class through the acquisition of goods and services. Yet, such appeals to classlessness are often illusory, as illustrated by the relative cost of food for the rich and for the poor, noted above. Moreover, the classist divisions of the food system overlap with its gendered expectations, as sociologist Shelley Koch has argued: "Poor women may be perceived as bad mothers or failed women if they are not able to cook the 'right' meals or provide 'healthy' food for their families."[12] As discussed in the preceding chapters, the definitions of what was right and healthy was defined by a middle-class mainstream, institutional culture. Historian Jennifer Price summarized what has been observed by many: "In the United States, the middle class often has had the upper hand on social authority."[13] When it came to food, the social authority rested mainly with middle-class white women, from the codification of home economics in the early twentieth century to the new food movements of the twenty-first century. It was assumed that women would be the primary grocery shoppers and cooks, even among those who eventually called for an "alternative" food system. For instance, in the mid-twentieth century, cookbooks instructed women that food was the best way to "catch" a man, advertisements appealed to women specifically with slogans such as "Nothing says lovin' like something from the oven," and women's magazines such as *McCall's* instructed women on their domestic responsibilities (including food shopping and cooking).[14] These gendered and class assumptions have been challenged by Guthman, Koch, and others.

Beyond gender and class identities, the American food system has also rested on ever-expanding global trade. As Frances Moore Lappé argued more than fifty years ago, the globalization of the industrial food system, spearheaded by the United States, was unsustainable for multiple reasons. Pressure on farmers abroad to fulfill the orders of multinational corporations led to local food shortages, environmental devastation, the impoverishment of small farmers, and the loss of food diversity. Recent production of and demand for meat worldwide has accelerated all of these trends.[15] The global economic system, which has benefited large food companies and consumers in wealthy countries most, functions within the US domestic market in a similar way: it has reduced the number of farmers in favor of large corporate producers, relied on exploited, low-paid labor, and sent an ever-smaller percentage of the food dollar directly to individual farmers.[16] Integration into the global food system has also resulted in some unexpected ironies. For instance, although the United States produces abundant amounts of food, by 2017, the nation was importing more than half of its fruit and one-third of its vegetables.[17]

The discussion in the preceding chapters has highlighted not only uneven benefits of the global food system, but also the uneven benefits of abundance at home. The women discussed in this book have illustrated these contradictions, both celebrating and challenging the American food system and food choices. They were all influential and successful in an arena, food, often ceded to women's authority. Hazel Stiebeling, Poppy Cannon, and Julia Child all wanted to improve the American diet and food culture but found little to criticize in the system that produced food in great abundance and variety. Stiebeling followed in the footsteps of early-twentieth-century home economists and nutritionists, encouraging Americans to take advantage of the industrial food system and to eat a variety of food groups with sufficient nutrients in economical meals. She spent a career demonstrating that the experts in the US government had an important role in guiding nutritional choices and providing balanced meals to school children.

USDA nutrition guidelines and school lunches tell us something about the influence of Hazel Stiebeling—as well as the assumptions behind her work and the government approach to food choices. Both the guidelines and the lunches were shaped by a paradigm that reduced food to its nutritional components (an approach known as "nutritionism") regardless of quality, culture, or its impact on the environment. One of the great ironies of these two government efforts to shape the American diet was that they did little to make Americans healthier. Despite a century of nutritional guidelines from the USDA, many Americans nevertheless suffered from chronic conditions tied to diet.[18] And, school lunches, far from transmitting sound nutritional guidelines to succeeding generations, became the epitome of poor eating habits, while also reinforcing class and racial segregation. Beyond these social and health consequences, the programs helped to reinforce industrial agriculture and the modern food industry. Because of their good intentions, school lunches helped to mask the fact that commodity and agricultural surpluses were at best an unintended consequence of industrialized agriculture and at worst a destructive, environmental absurdity. Wendell Berry observed that food surpluses, far from being good, were used by "apologists" to "disguise the damage by which [they] were produced."[19]

Stiebeling and her fellow nutritionists did not share Berry's concerns. They were focused on making sure Americans ate the right quantity of nutrients, not the quality of the food that contained those nutrients or how it was produced. In sum, Stiebeling was a chemist who viewed food from a scientific perspective as a collection of nutrients. She and her colleagues were guided by a dispassionate pragmatism that failed to see food as something greater than the sum of its nutrients.[20]

To improve the American diets, Stiebeling and USDA nutritionists believed that people could be taught to *choose* the right foods among the abundant supply available to ensure proper nutrition and thereby good health. Stiebeling's work and career, then, was built on faith in science and a practical approach to food. For example, in the first chapter to the USDA's annual agricultural yearbook in 1959, she wrote: "Modern science shows that all of us, regardless of purse, can add years to our life and life to our years, if we follow today's nutritional advice."[21]

Poppy Cannon and Julia Child were less utilitarian in their approach to the American diet, hoping instead to inspire American women through their best-selling cookbooks to be creative in their meal preparations.[22] Cannon's recipes were based on a manipulation of processed foods, producing the façade of a gourmet meal presented with panache—glamorizing hot dogs, for instance, or tapping the magic properties of Kitchen Bouquet Browning & Seasoning Sauce. To the modern reader, her recipes appear simplistic, even farcical, but most of the women who followed those recipes embraced the idea that they *were* being creative. Nevertheless, some criticized her approach to cooking at the time, and others continued to do so in the years that followed. For example, one writer condemned Cannon's "no-holds-barred sellout to the processed foods industry."[23] Others, such as Laura Shapiro, have been more nuanced in their assessment; she observed that Poppy Cannon was "at the crossroads of commerce and cuisine, and there she flourished."[24]

Cannon was not alone in her embrace of food products. She was a cultural touchstone, reflecting an age of abundance, new industrial processes, changing expectations for cuisine, and an enhanced domestic role for women. Like many of her contemporaries, she celebrated the large corporations that transformed the food system and gave little thought to the connection between food and nature, instead helping to normalize the use of processed ingredients into everyday cooking. Cannon was also like her contemporaries in her gendered assumptions about who was most responsible for procuring, preparing, and serving food. Her books were addressed to women and specifically to white, middle-class women, aspiring to a modern and cosmopolitan lifestyle.

It would be a mistake, though, to dismiss Poppy Cannon as a caricature of bygone sensibilities, encouraging odd combinations of packaged foods and acting as a cheerleader for large corporations. Cannon was a more complicated figure and left an important legacy. She enjoyed food and was interested in learning about foods from different cultures—although her letters indicate that she cared more about personal and social relationships and her career than she cared about food per se. Her encouragement of creativity in the kitchen and pleasure in meals reflected and reinforced the increased financial resources and leisure of middle-class Americans. Yet, her celebration of canned and other processed goods was not frivolous and not merely for enjoyment or dramatic spectacle. She also spoke about making life easier for working women who might be too busy to make meals from scratch. Her books reinforced gender food roles, while also challenging some of their underlying assumptions.

Julia Child similarly encouraged women to be creative in the kitchen, although she cared more about taste, authenticity, and traditional cooking practices than the mere illusion of gourmet cooking. Like Cannon, Child assumed that women had the latitude to be creative, since easy access to sufficient food was never in doubt. Child's legacy, though, went far beyond the precepts in her best-selling books. An exact replica of Child's kitchen from her house in Cambridge was put on display at the Smithsonian Museum of American History in Washington, DC, in 2001. The exhibit was intended to be temporary, but its great popularity led to permanent installation in the museum. Historian Megan Elias observed that it "has become a kind of shrine to which people . . . make pilgrimages of tribute."[25] Such adulation demonstrated a rare level of celebrity. More importantly, it was a recognition of the profound impact that Child had on American culture and foodways.

Child had spent her career leading American audiences on a quest for delicious food. But the pursuit of taste took effort, learning proper techniques, and using creativity. Child encouraged cooks to believe that anyone could learn to blend techniques and creativity: "A natural rightness rather than a pedantic correctness is my goal in cooking."[26] Good cooking was, Child told Americans, both an art and a science the reward of which was not only delicious meals, but the fun of achieving them, as she wrote in 1972, "Cooking [was] one of the happiest and most immediately rewarding of the creative arts."[27]

Child encouraged Americans to enjoy food and to respect cuisine as a discipline. She understood some of the limitations of the modern food system that allowed Americans to enjoy food as never before, even though ingredients in the supermarket might not always be prime. For example, in her 1978 book, *Julia Child and Company*, she discussed the poor quality of some supermarket tomatoes, since many tomatoes did not ship well and were picked too early. But instead of concluding that recipes should be altered or that one should cook with tomatoes only when local ones were available, Child concluded, "Perfect or not, the market tomato is an indispensable item."[28] Thus, Child's understanding of taste did not lead her to question the modern food system or to acknowledge that food was very much tied to how and where it was grown. From the start of her career, although inspired by living and eating in France, she was nevertheless convinced that the terroir was immaterial. She believed that the food she ate in France could be reproduced anywhere.

New generations of authors and chefs parted company with Child's views in this regard. Starting in the 1970s and beyond, Frances Moore Lappé, Marion Nestle, and Alice Waters spoke for many people who found much to criticize in the American food system despite its sufficiency. Lappé criticized the global and political implications of dietary choices, arguing against overreliance on meat and international distribution networks. Her impact on the debates over these issues was great, as noted in the introduction to a 2019 *New York Times Magazine* interview: Lappé was "one of the few people who can credibly be said to have changed the way we eat, and one of an even smaller group to have done so for the better."[29]

Frances Moore Lappé established her fame and credibility with the publication of *Diet for a Small Planet*, an association that remained over many decades. Lappé became for many the godmother of vegetarianism, providing inspiration and practical advice in the popular culture for a new approach to diet.[30] As observed above, Lappé's lengthy discussion of protein needs and replacing meat led reasonable people to conclude that her most important argument was to call for widespread vegetarianism. Many readers embraced this society-wide mission in a personal way.[31] Meanwhile, the book inspired other readers to focus on their personal diets, rather than the improvement of society. Writer Mary

Drake McFeely placed Lappé in a broader cultural shift in the 1970s: "The language of the whole earth gave way to that of self-help and self-interest."[32]

While some of her readers may have turned inward, exploring their own food choices, Lappé spent the next five decades trying to broaden and refine her arguments, working to expose the unavoidable connections between what people ate and the quality of their political and economic life. She was a relentless critic of the global industrial food system as wasteful and inefficient, producing great quantities of food but still ensuring that millions of people lacked access to affordable food and had little control over what they ate. Her highest goal was to foster true democracy, or "living democracy." "Participating in democracy," Lappé concluded, "is the essence of a good life."[33] From Lappé's perspective, food was a tool for a political end. Reimagining people's diets and the food system was a way to expand democracy. Yet, Lappé's concerns were even broader than the expansion of democracy. She argued that the limitations of the industrial food system were environmental as well as economic and political, and she was not alone in these views. Increasingly in the 1970s and after, food writers and scholars made it clear that decisions about food systems were unavoidably environmental decisions.

Marion Nestle agreed with many of the critiques offered by Lappé, but she focused more on the health consequences of the industrial food system than on its environmental and political impacts. Nestle's influence on the debates about diet and health rested on her solid reputation in the public culture; she was a trusted authority for journalists, who often consulted her. Before *Food Politics* made Nestle well-known outside of scholarly circles, she was already familiar in the nonacademic press. For example, in the magazine *Health*, Nestle was profiled in summer 2001 with the introduction: "If anyone deserves the title of America's Nutritionist, it's Marion Nestle, PhD, chair of the department of nutrition and food studies at New York University." Meanwhile, *Walking: The Magazine of Smart Health and Fitness* had referred to her a year earlier as "one of the nation's most esteemed and outspoken nutritionists."[34] The marketing and reception of *Food Politics* in 2002 broadened and strengthened Nestle's reputation. For example, the publisher approached Julia Child for a cover blurb, which Child enthusiastically provided: "Marion Nestle has presented us with a courageous and masterful exposé [of the food industry]." Soon after the book's publication, Nestle's authority grew.[35] Within a couple of years, Nestle was discussed in a *Time* magazine article "The Obesity Warriors" as one of several scientists who "have stepped out of the ivory tower of academe to challenge communities, industry, and government to do more to fight obesity."[36] Thus, many journalists sought out Nestle for numerous press stories, and she also began a regular column for the *San Francisco Chronicle.*

Almost twenty years after the publication of *Food Politics,* Nestle remained the go-to authority for basic nutritional advice and, especially, an interpreter of marketing manipulations and government euphemisms. Nestle's priority remained using *science* for this decoding process, to help ordinary people and improve their health. For example, when the USDA released its updated "Dietary Guidelines for Americans" in December 2020 (a process that happened every five years), an outraged Nestle criticized the final product in the *New York Times,* explaining, "I'm stunned by the whole thing . . . they ignored the scientific committee which they appointed, which I thought was astounding."[37] A key reason for government failing to listen to scientists, Nestle believed in 2020—as she had decades earlier—was the influence and power of Big Food. Back in 2000, Nestle summarized her advice to ordinary citizens: "If you recognize that you are being sold food as a commodity, and that every product has a lobbying organization whose job it is to encourage you to eat more of that food, I think it's easier to be discriminating."[38] Nestle, a scientific truth-teller, was determined to help people do just that.

Alice Waters had much in common with Frances Moore Lappé and Marion Nestle, and their criticisms of the American food system and diet. Meanwhile, Waters was more a descendant of Poppy Cannon and Julia Child than of Hazel Stiebeling. Waters embraced creativity, beauty, and taste, and the idea that food was foremost an expression of culture as well as a political statement. Thus, the new food movements—of which she was a part—offered alternatives to the existing food system and diet from multiple perspectives. Alice Waters's impact on food culture was (and remains) visible everywhere, from the mesclun mix in the produce aisles of supermarkets to urban gardens to the explosion of farm-to-table restaurants with seasonal menus. Many recognized Waters's unique contribution, including policymakers in Washington, DC, who awarded her the National Humanities Medal in 2014. The citation highlighted her work as a chef, activist, and educator and praised her for "celebrating the bond between the ethical and the edible" as well as "champion[ing] a holistic approach to eating and health."[39] Such achievements were well beyond Waters's ambitions when she started Chez Panisse in 1971. The restaurant and what it represented started as a rejection of the status quo in American food culture but grew into a challenge of the industrial food system that reverberated far beyond the restaurant's doors.

Waters began Chez Panisse based on certain principles: her love of French foodways; her embrace of the counterculture; and her identification with the

Free Speech Movement, particularly the way in which it asserted the interconnectedness of life. These principles were a reaction against a modern society in which many of the connections among individuals and communities had been severed, including an atomized food system seemingly divorced from the earth, environment, culture, and community. Throughout her career, Waters worked to re-establish these connections, and to view systems in a holistic way. Irrespective of these principles, Chez Panisse's success as a gourmet institution was secured early on, allowing Waters to focus more broadly on challenging the social and environmental aspects of food consumption and becoming a leading voice of the California and then new food movements as reflected in her writing and launch of the Edible Schoolyard project. Meanwhile, the restaurant itself was widely imitated; Calvin Trillin noted that, by the first decade of the twenty-first century, "Every middle-size American city has a couple of restaurants that are modeled, in one way or another, on Chez Panisse."[40]

We can push back on Trillin's observation somewhat. Were so many restaurants imitating Chez Panisse, or was Waters's restaurant representative of several movements that would have existed without her? The answer is both. Alice Waters was a leader and an inspiration to many chefs, but she was also a cultural touchstone of converging trends. She presented an appealing example of how the counterculture could make an alternative food system. She demonstrated that there are clear links among health, food, and the environment and that food should not just be evaluated on its quantity but on its quality. She articulated for American audiences the numerous problems of industrial food and fast food culture, as well as the appeal of a reimagined slow food culture. She demonstrated that individuals could play a role in constructing an alternative food culture based on whether they raised their own food, where they bought their food, how they cooked their food, and what they chose to eat. Such expectations were compatible with neoliberal ideas of individual action and self-improvement, but also led critics to charge that they were selfish pursuits of frivolous pleasure for elites at the expense of social and political change that would benefit all. Herein lay the most serious criticism of Waters and the new food movements, although Waters consistently rejected these charges as reductionist, presenting a false dichotomy between the continuation of an abundant, superficially cheap food supply and a precious, impractical alternative.

Almost half a century of challenges to the modern industrial food system and the dominant American diet—such as those from Alice Waters, Marion Nestle, and Frances Moore Lappé—have yielded mixed results. One observation is that the industrial food system and the characteristic American diet remain firmly entrenched despite the many "alternatives" offered. Food remains abundant, even if access to inexpensive, quality fresh food remains elusive for many Americans. Abundance has meant the steady increase in available calories per person as well as the amount of food turned into products (i.e., processed food) and restaurant meals beckoning people to abandon cooking and eat out. Writer Mark Bittman observed that 50 percent of food was eaten outside of the home by the early twenty-first century, while a lot of what was eaten at home was hyper-processed. In addition, as historian Elaine McIntosh and others have observed, people adapted their eating habits to fast foods, increasing the amount of snacking, grazing, and ad-hoc meals. The fast food industry benefited most from these trends: with one-third of Americans eating fast food daily by 2021.[41]

Many observers have made the connection between the rise of available calories and processed foods and the deterioration of American health. The increase in diet-related health conditions, including diabetes, obesity, and hypertension, has not lessened despite decades of government health advice, countless self-help books, media attention, and encouragement from new food activists. Michelle Obama was so alarmed that she planted her garden and launched the Let's Move! campaign. But such efforts have been inadequate, for reasons that are complex. One is the long-standing failure of Americans to follow abstract nutritional advice. This was true when Hazel Stiebeling was crafting her recommendations, as well as years later when the USDA introduced (and then updated) its ubiquitous food pyramids. USDA surveys from 1970 to 2005, for instance, showed that fewer than 5 percent of American adults ate the recommended daily amounts of fruits and vegetables.[42] Historian Paul Freedman noted that health recommendations alone made little sense because "people are not swayed by science as much as by emotions, resentments, experience, and other strong but nonmaterial factors." Freedman added that "in a grossly unequal society, you have to be affluent in order to fuss about food and health."[43] Moreover, no matter what the desires or poverty of individuals, systemic barriers to food choice and access remained. Thus, many observers have decried the neoliberal tendency to focus on individual actions and responsibility—in other words, the power of consumerism—for improving diet, health, and even the entire food system. Bittman made clear that while such intentions were reasonable, they were simplistic: "Admonitions to 'get up and move' or even to 'eat a wide variety of foods' aren't *wrong*, but unless they're accompanied by changes in supply and policy, they'll do little to challenge the status quo."[44]

The failure to change diets or increase consumption of less-processed foods is also a result of class dynamics and identity, not just wealth and the power of Big Food. Historian Shelley Koch explained: "Food practices and knowledge are a language for signaling one's social class. For middle and upper-middle class individuals and households, this manifests as a disdain for convenience and industrial foods in favor of organic and natural food, 'authentic' food and home-cooked meals, and a cultural omnivorousness. The ability to purchase and enact food knowledge is a resource that separates 'foodie' women from those in lower classes, who often value tradition and frugality over novelty or exotic food choices."[45]

These identities not only discourage collaborations across class lines, but also undermine support for the new food movements. Some critics dismiss "foodies" and their concerns as indulgent and frivolous, failing to focus on the exploitation and inequalities of a global food system that relies on externalizing the true costs of food. Some discussions of the new food movements have challenged these binaries, assuming the health, environmental, and cultural challenges to the food status quo were as substantive as the inequality issues raised by the alternatives. Nevertheless, affordability of food in a reimagined food system resists simple prescriptions.

Some challenges to the food system and mainstream diets have had an impact, both in the number of supermarkets carrying organic foods (ranging from Walmart to Whole Foods) and in the spread of "farm-to-table" restaurants. Upon closer examination, though, those examples might reflect the appearance of change, rather than actual, systemic change. As discussed above, organic food accounted for just 4 percent of the American market, and the organic products (some highly processed) found in most supermarkets fit seamlessly into the industrial system rather than challenge it. As for farm-to-table establishments, chef Joyce Goldstein has noted that looks can be deceiving. A restaurant may, for example, have three items from local farmers listed on its menu and then get the rest of its food from industrial suppliers.[46] Buying organic yogurt from Walmart or getting lunch in a farm-to-table restaurant might seem like an alternative, but in reality it might just reinforce conventional production and distribution systems. In addition, it is striking how the movements for organic and local foods—as they became more "successful" and widespread—became less about a mission to lessen the environmental impact of the conventional food system. These were instead mainly *consumer* movements, to benefit an individual's health, satisfy their taste, or telegraph social identity. As journalist Jonathan Kauffman observed, "It may have become harder to be a food revolutionary, but it has become a hell of a lot easier to shop like one"[47]

Similarly, Americans who prided themselves on having more sophisticated and eclectic tastes than their grandmother's bland meat-and-potato dinners or casseroles made with condensed mushroom soup, were partially right, although that did not mean that the industrial food system had been threatened, much less weakened. Rather, the system adapted to evolving consumer tastes. Adaptions within the industrial food system were illustrated in the absorption of ethnic foods into mainstream products and restaurants. For example, historian Donna Gabaccia has written about the American penchant to mix and match their own ethnic foodways with those of their neighbors, changing culture along the way; thus: "Eating habits both symbolize and mark the boundaries of cultures." Meanwhile, Paul Freedman argued that foods from new immigrant groups were changed at the outset: "Ethnic restaurants prospered in the United States because of their inexpensive exoticism and the accommodations the proprietors made to American tastes, leaving out dishes popular at home such as tripe that would not appeal to American patrons, moderating the spice content or making dishes sweeter."[48] One other recent example of the absorption of ethnic foods into the American diet was the spread of sushi. Writer Priscilla Parkhurst Ferguson observed that the popularity of the food should not surprise: "[W]hat is sushi but 'fast fish'? It fits surprisingly well with American consumption habits that emphasize snacks, food eaten with one's hands and on the go, and informality of consumption."[49]

In the second decade of the twenty-first century, then, the American food system and the American diet was in some ways very different from that of a century before. Various ethnic foods were woven into the diets of many Americans, no matter their own ethnicities. Organic foods had become big business, while at the same time local foods were celebrated for their authenticity. New ideas about taste had been ushered in by the California Food Revolution and knowledge of vegetarianism had spread. Thus, people such as Frances Moore Lappé, Marion Nestle, and Alice Waters had helped to shift the discourse, raising important questions about the modern food system. But the assumptions of Hazel Stiebeling, Poppy Cannon, and Julia Child—that food was and would remain cheap, abundant, and unaffected by the season—had prevailed. The power of Big Food and the dominance of industrial production, distribution networks, and marketing were strong. Food was just one more industrial product with only a tangential relationship to the natural world. Consumption of food per capita had increased, and people routinely ignored nutritional advice from government and medical authorities. For most Americans, the true costs of abundant food—economic, social, medical, and environmental—remained hidden.

Acknowledgments

As most authors know, a book is not an individual achievement, but the result of collaboration with and support from colleagues and institutions. I have been fortunate to have benefited from the wisdom of many colleagues and the material support of institutions.

In the course of researching this book, I have presented work in progress at meetings of the American Society for Environmental History, the World Congress of Environmental History, the European Society for Environmental History, the Agricultural History Society, and the Israeli Conference on Environmental History. I have also presented work from this project at the University of Leipzig, Agder University, the Berlin-Brandenburg Colloquium, Ludwig-Maximillans-Universität München, Rheinishe Fredrich-Wilhelms-Universität Bonn, and Universität zu Köln. On each of these occasions, generous colleagues offered helpful feedback that improved future iterations of the material. I was also fortunate to have workshopped material from the book at the Center for the History of Global Development at Shanghai University, Renmin University, the University of Bologna, and the Rachel Carson Center for Environment and Society; the interactive work in these meetings strengthened the later book.

Many individuals at these meetings and workshops offered useful comments. In particular, I am grateful for the feedback of Scout Blum, Iris Borowy, Fritz Davis, Matthias Heymann, Nina Mackert, Dan Phillipon, Adam Rome, and Anna Zeide. I would also like to thank anonymous reviewers for *Global Environment* and *Weber: The Contemporary West* for comments on related article drafts.

Research for this project was aided by helpful archivists and staff at the following: Beinecke Library and Manuscripts Collections, Yale University; Cornell University Archives; Fales Library and Special Collections, New York University; National Agricultural Library, US Department of Agriculture; National

Records and Archives Administration II; New York Public Library and Manuscripts Division; and, Schlesinger Library, Radcliffe Institute for Advanced Study, Harvard University.

I am happy that this book found a home at the University of Alabama Press in the NEXUS: New Histories in Science, Technology, the Environment, Agriculture & Medicine series. I am grateful that the series editors—Alan Marcus, Mark Hersey, and Alexandre Hui—chose the book for inclusion; Mark Hersey's comments and observations have been particularly helpful. Anonymous reviewers for the press provided incisive feedback that helped me to improve the final manuscript. Acquisitions editor Kristen Hop was most helpful in navigating the publication process.

I am also fortunate to have had financial and professional support from Penn State University in the form of research grants, travel funds, and a sabbatical leave to work on the project.

My professional and personal acknowledgments overlap in recognizing the assistance of David Walker. David reviewed the entire manuscript and provided insightful comments throughout, greatly improving the final book. Other family members, especially Hannah and Tobias, provided good excuses to turn my attention to pursuits beyond the doors of my study. Over the course of several years, I discussed the emerging project with my mother to whom the book is dedicated; I regret that she did not live to see its completion.

Notes

Introduction

1. For discussion of how the industrial food system grew before World War II—as well as how the war era was "an intensification" of it, see Benjamin Cohen, Michael Kideckel, and Anna Zeide, eds., *Acquired Tastes: Stories about the Origins of Modern Food* (Cambridge, MA: MIT Press, 2021), 2, 5.

2. Cohen, Kideckel, and Zeide, eds., *Acquired Tastes*, 7.

3. Diner noted the impact on immigrants was especially great: "Food was available at a price and in quantities which staggered the imagination of women and men who had been hungry." Hasia Diner, *Hungering for America: Italian, Irish, and Jewish Foodways in the Age of Migration* (Cambridge, MA: Harvard University Press, 2001), 16, 229.

4. Warren Belasco, *Meals to Come: A History of the Future of Food* (Berkeley: University of California Press, 2006), 48.

5. Donna Gabaccia, *We Are What We Eat: Ethnic Food and the Making of Americans* (Cambridge, MA: Harvard University Press, 1998), 226.

6. Shelley Koch, *Gender and Food: A Critical Look at the Food System* (Lanham, MD: Rowman & Littlefield, 2019), 59.

7. For example, see discussion of particular food traditions brought by immigrants to the United States in Diner, *Hungering for America*, and how ethnic food has permeated American cuisine in Gabaccia, *We Are What We Eat*. Also see the discussion of evolving African American foodways absorbing both southern and African traditions in Jennifer Jensen Wallach, *Getting What We Need Ourselves: How Food Has Shaped African American Life* (Lanham, MD: Rowman & Littlefield, 2019).

Chapter 1

1. Unknown, "Top Administrators in USDA during World War II (Including Hazel K. Stiebeling)," undated photograph, Special Collections, National Agricultural Library (hereinafter abbreviated NAL), United States Department of Agriculture (hereinafter abbreviated USDA). Photo available on NAL website; accessed Nov. 8, 2019.

2. Gyorgy Scrinis, *Nutritionism: The Science and Politics of Dietary Advice* (New York: Columbia University Press, 2013).

3. Background information about Stiebeling here and below from Alfred Harper, "Contributions of Women Scientists in the U.S. to the Development of Recommended Dietary Allowances," *Journal of Nutrition* 133 (2003): 3698–3702; loose leaf notebooks (also with press clippings), Selected Papers and Pictures, Dr. Hazel Katherine Stiebeling, 1896–1989;

finding aid, Hazel Katherine Stiebeling Papers, NAL; "Apron Strings and Kitchen Sinks: The USDA Bureau of Home Economics, A National Agricultural Library Digital Exhibition," accessed 2019; folder "Home Economics Research: Chronology of Organizational Changes," Box 1, General Records Concerning the History and Philosophy of Home Economics and Nutrition Research, 1932–1970, RG 310 Agricultural Research Service, National Archives and Record Administration (hereinafter abbreviated NARA) II. See also Edna Yost, *American Women of Science* (Philadelphia: Frederick A. Stokes, 1943).

4. Sherman worked in the intersection of nutrition and chemistry and was described by a writer in 1943 as "one of the world's foremost authorities on chemistry of food and nutrition." Yost, *American Women*, 164.

5. Harper, "Contributions of Women Scientists," 3699; Yost, *American Women*, 175.

6. Interestingly, Stiebeling's graduate school mentor and authority on food chemistry and nutrition, Dr. Henry Sherman, became chief of the reorganized Bureau of Human Nutrition and Home Economics in 1943, while she was named assistant chief of bureau, until her promotion in 1944.

7. Historian Megan Elias observed that this reorganization at the USDA, in essence dissolving the Bureau of Human Nutrition and Home Economics as a stand-alone unit to one subsumed under ARS and its male director, reflected a trend of devaluing the woman-led field of home economics in these postwar years. Megan Elias, *Stir It Up: Home Economics in American Culture* (Philadelphia: University of Pennsylvania Press, 2008), 129.

8. The honorary degrees were from Iowa State College, Skidmore College, Bowling Green State University, and Carnegie Institute of Technology. Elinor Lee, "Dr. Stiebeling is First So Honored: Woman Wins Ike Award," *Washington Post and Times Herald*, Jan. 29, 1959. One of the other four recipients of the President's Award with Stiebeling was Werner von Braun, an acclaimed and controversial rocket engineer who was a member of the Nazi Party during World War II.

9. Yost, *American Women*, 164, 171.

10. About the USDA on agency website, accessed 2023; Marion Nestle, *Food Politics: How the Food Industry Influences Nutrition and Health* (Berkeley: University of California Press, 2002, 2007), 33.

11. "Nation's Surveys of Food Consumption," three-page report, and "USDA Family Food Plans and Costs," three-page report, Nutrition Publications from Sandy Facinoli (Facinoli Papers, unprocessed), NAL. For more on Atwater's career, see Jessica Mudry, *Measured Meals: Nutrition in America* (Albany: State University of New York Press, 2009), 24–53.

12. Mudry, *Measured Meals*, 40.

13. "Nation's Surveys of Food Consumption" and "USDA Family Food Plans and Costs," Facinoli Papers, NAL.

14. Nestle, *Food Politics*, 34–35. See also Harvey Levenstein, *Revolution at the Table: The Transformation of the American Diet* (Berkeley: University of California Press, 2003), and Mudry, *Measured Meals*, 47–51.

15. Levenstein, *Revolution at the Table*, 109. For a discussion of these intersecting political and social imperatives as they related to food, see Helen Zoe Veit, *Modern Food, Moral Food: Self-Control, Science, and the Rise of Modern American Eating in the Early Twentieth Century* (Chapel Hill: University of North Carolina Press, 2013), and Levenstein, *Revolution at the Table*.

16. For an overview of the field's history, see Danielle Dreilinger, *The Secret History of*

Home Economics: How Trailblazing Women Harnessed the Power of Home and Changed the Way We Live (New York: Norton, 2021).

17. Scrinis, *Nutritionism.* See also an example in the popular literature: Michael Pollan, *In Defense of Food: An Eater's Manifesto* (New York: Penguin, 2008), 8–11.

18. Scrinis, *Nutritionism*, 6.

19. Beyond *quantifying* nutrients, Scrinis wrote that the second period, starting in the mid-1960s, focused on identifying which nutrients were good and which were bad and telling people what *not* to eat. And, finally, he discussed the present period of "functional nutritionism," when foods have been embraced as tools to enhance normal, bodily functions—or to "optimize" them. Scrinis, *Nutritionism*, 11–13.

20. Information about the field and its evolution here are taken from Elias, *Stir It Up* and Dreilinger, *Secret History.*

21. Elias, *Stir It Up*, 4.

22. Dreilinger, *Secret History*, x.

23. Dreilinger, *Secret History*, 62.

24. Elias, *Stir It Up*, 25, 27–28, 31.

25. "Nation's Surveys of Food Consumption," Facinoli Papers, NAL.

26. Charlotte Biltekoff, *Eating Right in America: The Cultural Politics of Food and Health* (Durham, NC: Duke University Press, 2013), 50.

27. Mudry, *Measured Meals*, 55–58; Hazel Stiebeling, "Proper Diet Can Lengthen Your Span of Life," *Everybody's Weekly in Philadelphia Inquirer*, Dec. 10, 1944; clipping, no title, *Journal of Home Economics*, Oct. 1944, unlabeled scrapbook; "Hazel K. Stiebeling, 93, Dies; Was USDA Research Official," (no publication), May 20, 1989, Stiebeling Papers, NAL.

28. Yost, *American Women*, 170.

29. For example, "Did You Happen to See—Dr. Hazel Stiebeling?" *Washington-Times Herald*, Nov. 18, 1943, and Hazel Stiebeling, "Proper Diet Can Lengthen Your Span of Life," *Philadelphia Enquirer*, Dec. 10, 1944.

30. Yost, *American Women*, 169, 173.

31. Genevieve Forbes Herrick, no title, *Country Gentleman*, Dec. 1939, in unlabeled binder, Stiebeling Papers, Box 1, NAL.

32. "Did You Happen to See—Dr. Hazel K. Stiebeling?"

33. No title, *Journal of Home Economics*, Oct. 1944; see also "Proper Diet Can Lengthen Your Span of Life."

34. Vylla Poe Wilson, "Chief Homemaker of the Nation," *Promenade*, Mar. 1961, 11, Stiebeling Papers, NAL.

35. Elias, *Stir It Up*, 90.

36. Dreilinger, *Secret History*, 91.

37. Harper, "Contributions of Women Scientists in the U.S.," 3699–3700; Yost, *American Women*, 170; "Did You Happen to See—Dr. Hazel K. Stiebeling?"; "What's New in Home Economics," Oct. 1946, unlabeled binder, Selected Papers and Pictures, Box 1, Stiebeling Papers, NAL.

38. "USDA Family Food Plans and Costs," Facinoli Papers, NAL.

39. Harper, "Contributions of Women Scientists in the U.S.," 3699.

40. Stiebeling, "Proper Diet Can Lengthen Your Span of Life."

41. Dreilinger, *Secret History*, 109–10.

42. Dreilinger, *Secret History*, 112.

43. Harper, "Contributions of Women Scientists," 3700; Mudry, *Measured Meals*, 61–66.

44. Mudry, *Measured Meals*, 63. Harper notes that in her research in the process of developing the RDAs, it is hard to discern the exact contribution of Stiebeling as opposed to others on the committee and the FNB. But it is clear that Stiebeling is the only one of the three on the subcommittee who had worked with dietary allowances and that the first RDAs closely resembled the earlier values that had been put forward by Stiebeling and her colleague Esther Phipard. See Harper, "Contributions of Women Scientists," 3701. At the end of the twentieth century, other measures of nutrition were introduced based on RDAs: the Dietary Reference Intake (DRI) and Reference Daily Intake (RDI); food labels in the United States and Canada also began using Daily Value (DV) and (%DV) to detail nutrients.

45. Biltekoff, *Eating Right*, 45–52; Nestle, *Food Politics*, 35; "Family Food Plans and Costs" and "Food Selection Guides," three-page report, Facinoli Papers, NAL.

46. "Food Selection Guides," Facinoli Papers, NAL.

47. "Eat the Right Foods to Help Keep You Fit" (May 1941), Leaflets for Good Nutrition, Bureau of Human Nutrition Information Service Records (unprocessed), NAL.

48. "When You Eat Out, Food for Freedom" (Aug. 1942), "Family Food Plans for Good Nutrition" (Dec. 1943), "Food for Two" (June 1945), Leaflets for Good Nutrition, Bureau of Human Nutrition Information Service Records (unprocessed), NAL.

49. "Food Selection Guides," Facinoli Papers, NAL.

50. Dreilinger, *Secret History*, 113.

51. Dreilinger, *Secret History*, 117.

52. Biltekoff, *Eating Right*, 54, 59; Nestle, *Food Politics*, 36.

53. Examples of government wartime leaflets can be found in notes 47 and 48 above.

54. For example, Jane Holt, "News of Food: Well-Balanced Diet Makes Use Each Day of One Item from Each of 7 Basic Groups," *New York Times*, Feb. 5, 1944, 11.

55. Along with the food guides addressed to ordinary citizens that seemed to minimize fears of food shortages, there were other government campaigns directed at farmers to maximize their production. One, for example, in cooperation with the private company Ralston Purina, was called "Food for Victory Crusade." Farmers were admonished, "Producing food is now the number one battle on the home front. Be sure that your farm is operating at peak wartime efficiency." "Progress Report: Food for Victory Crusade," Nov. 30, 1943, folder 2, Food for Victory Crusade (Ralston), NAL. In addition to this Ralston campaign, there were a number of other companies that worked with the Office of War Information to combine their ads with those of the government in support of war aims. This collaboration was beneficial to both the companies and the government. Amy Bentley, *Eating for Victory: Food Rationing and the Politics of Domesticity* (Urbana: University of Illinois Press, 1998), 33–58. Lizzie Collingham also discusses the generous food rations for US soldiers, which represented an important dietary improvement for many. Lizzie Collingham, *The Taste of War: World War II and the Battle for Food* (New York: Penguin, 2012), 434–36.

56. Bentley, *Eating for Victory*, 4–5, 35–36.

57. Bentley, *Eating for Victory*, 61–62; see also Collingham, *Taste of War*, 430–31.

58. These twin motivations—not to mention the actual food produced—has left a warm glow of nostalgia around the program, which is cited by many recent urban gardeners to help explain the value of their activity. Bentley, *Eating for Victory*, 114; Laura J. Lawson, *City*

Bountiful: A Century of Community Gardening in America (Berkeley: University of California Press, 2005), 172–202; Elias, *Stir It Up*, 67. See also Collingham, *Taste of War*, 415–64.

59. "National Food Guide, Eat this Way Every Day" (Aug. 1946), Bureau of Human Nutrition Information Service Records, NAL.

60. Confidential Memo Office of Foreign Agricultural Relations to Cabinet Committee on World Food Programs, "The World Food Situation," Jan. 1, 1947, folder 2B, Box 1, Abstracts of Meetings of the Cabinet Committee on World Food Problems, 1946–1948, RG 16 Office of the Secretary, NARA II.

61. Collection of Citizens Food Committee Program (1947), including poster boxes Blue Box I and II 173 C493P, and documents Boxes 2, 5, 6, 7, 8, 9, NAL.

62. Bentley, *Eating for Victory*, 142–65. Following this period, there were many US government initiatives to use food aid for humanitarian purposes and to stabilize political and economic situations; Public Law (PL) 480 had a lasting impact with the establishment of the Food for Peace Program in 1954, which remained in place even as it evolved in subsequent administrations; American aid programs began—and remained—a way to provide a market for agricultural surpluses. This will be discussed more in subsequent chapters.

63. Press Release, Gaynor Maddox, "NEA's Food Editor Reviews 'Best Seller' Cookbook," no date, unlabeled binder, Stiebeling Papers, Box 1, NAL.

64. Jane Nickerson, "News of Food: Booklet of Department of Agriculture Offers 150 Money Saving Dishes," *New York Times*, Apr. 22, 1948, 32; Jane Nickerson, "News of Food: US Interviewers Go Into City's Kitchens to Find What's Cooking for the Families," *New York Times*, May 25, 1948, 30. See also Jane Nickerson, "New Program for Consumers," *New York Times*, May 16, 1948, 42.

65. One leaflet to publicize this was "National Food Guide, Eat this Way Everyday" (Aug. 1946), Leaflets for Good Nutrition, Bureau of Human Nutrition Information Service Records, unprocessed, NAL. See also Bentley, *Eating for Victory*, 68–72.

66. Bureau of Agricultural Economics, Report "Homemakers' Acceptance of Nutrition Information in an Urban Community," Feb. 1948, Box 25, Records Relating to the School Lunch Program, 1940–1973, Food and Nutrition Service, Child Nutrition Division, RG 462, Records of the Food and Consumer Services, NARA II.

67. Mary Meade, "Five Point Plan to Help Stretch Food Dollars," *Chicago Tribune*, May 4, 1948, 20; "A Pin-Up Chart of Food Favorites," *Seventeen*, Dec. 1946, 207.

68. "Nation's Surveys of Food Consumption," Facinoli Papers, NAL. For more on the conclusions of these surveys, see T. C. Byerly, Assistant Director, Science and Education to N. P. Ralston, Deputy Director of Science and Education, Apr. 30, 1969, folder Jan. 1–Apr. 31, 1969, Box 5064, General Correspondence 1906–1976, RG 16, NARA II.

69. It's interesting to note that the memos here indicate that Stiebeling was very formal in her address and tone toward the secretary, while the secretary's response two months later praised Stiebeling's work but was perfunctory. Memo, Stiebeling to Secretary of Agriculture Nov. 10, 1950, and Bannan to Stiebeling, Jan. 16, 1951, folder Nutrition, Box 2008, General Correspondence 1906–1976, RG 16, NARA II.

70. Memo, Stiebeling to N. R. Clark, Office of the Secretary, June 8, 1954, folder nutrition, Box 2462, General Correspondence 1906–1976, RG 16, NARA II.

71. Statement by Stiebeling in press release, June 21, 1948, re the twenty-fifth anniversary of the BHNHE, folder Home Economics Research in USDA, Box 2, General Records Concerning History and Philosophy of Home Economics and Nutrition Research, 1932–1970,

RG 310, NARA II. Nutritional guidelines were steady in their issuance and most of their recommendations; they were revised slightly to meet particular concerns at a given time. For example, in the 1960s, there was increasing concern about making sure that poor Americans were getting proper nutrition, and one "best-selling" leaflet, "Family Meals at Low Cost," reflected this. Folder Information Public Relations FY 1965, Box 2, Records of the Food and Nutrition Service Program Planning and Development Files, 1959–1966, RG 462, NARA II.

72. B. T. Shaw, Administrator, to E. L. Peterson, Assistant Secretary, May 10, 1956, folder Food, Box 2770. The urgency behind encouraging diets that led to optimum fitness grew when the Kennedy administration came into office, reflecting the president's concern with "vigor" and "toughness." Memo, B. T. Shaw, Administrator to Secretary of Agriculture, Mar. 31, 1961, folder Food, Box 3597. General Correspondence 1906–1976, RG 16, NARA II.

73. E. L. Peterson, Assistant Secretary, to Senator Joseph Clark, Mar. 25, 1958, folder Nutrition, Box 3175, General Correspondence 1906–1976, RG 16, NARA II. By the late 1960s, USDA officials remained concerned about those Americans whose diets were still considered to be "poor." In fact, consumption surveys revealed that the percentage of Americans with poor diets *rose* from 15 percent in 1955 to 21 percent in 1965. Report to the Committee on Agriculture, US House of Representatives, Apr. 1968, folder Nutritive Quality of Diets, USA, Box 4, General Records Concerning the History and Philosophy of Home Economics and Nutrition Research, 1932–1970, RG 310, NARA II.

74. Mudry, *Measured Meals*, 68–70.

75. "Food for Fitness, A Daily Food Guide," Mar. 1958, slight revisions Sept. 1977, Bureau of Human Nutrition Information Service Records, unprocessed, NAL.

76. For example, T. R. Van Dellen, MD, "How to Keep Well: Basic Food Groups," *Chicago Daily Tribune*, Mar. 31, 1960, 12, and Mary Meade, "Better Meals: Grouping Aids Diet Balance," *Chicago Daily Tribune*, Sept. 13, 1960, A2.

77. Cynthia Kellogg, "U.S. Home Bureau Marks 30th Year," *New York Times*, July 1, 1953, 32; "What's Cooking in Washington?" *Chicago Daily Tribune*, Feb. 24, 1957, F35.

78. "Hazel Stiebeling," *Cosmopolitan*, Aug. 1961, 75.

79. "Did you Happen to See—Dr. Hazel K. Stiebeling?"; Vylla Poe Wilson, "Chief Homemaker of the Nation," *Promenade*, Mar. 1961, 11. Other examples: Stiebeling, "Proper Diet Can Lengthen Your Span of Life"; Mary W. Farrell, "Better Nutrition for All Peoples," *What's New in Home Economics*, Feb. 1947, 48–49; "Food Nutrition Expert Knows Her Garden Beans as Well as Vitamins," *Pudding County Republican*, Sept. 30, 1948. All articles from unlabeled binder/scrapbook, Stiebeling Papers, NAL.

80. "Mrs. Truman Entertains at White House Luncheon," *Washington Post*, Nov. 15, 1946, loose-leaf notebook, Stiebeling, unprocessed box, Stiebeling Papers, NAL.

81. Dreilinger, *Secret History*, 130, 191–92.

82. Jessie Fant Evans, "New U.S. Bureau Nutrition Chief Wins Fame at Home and Abroad," (Washington, DC) *Sunday Star*, May 28, 1944; Marilyn Gardner, "World's Homemakers Are Her Concern," *Milwaukee Journal*, June 26, 1959, 2; sidebar to Stiebeling, "Proper Diet Can Lengthen Your Span of Life."

83. For example, see Cyrene Dear, "Author Questions Pesticide Programs," (Elizabeth City, NC) *Advance*, Feb. 18, 1963, folder 1129, Box 64; other examples are "Critic of Pesticides: Rachel Louise Carson," *New York Times*, June 5, 1963, folder 1291, Box 73, and

Frances Lewine, "Rachel Carson, 'No Crusader,'" (Charlotte, NC) *Observer*, June 6, 1963, folder 1290, Box 73, Series I, Rachel Carson Papers, Beinecke Library.

84. Large drawing/portrait of Stiebeling with biographical paragraph underneath, (Washington, DC) *Sunday Star*, Dec. 29, 1946.

85. Farrell, "Better Nutrition for All Peoples," 48–49, 183; "Food Nutrition Expert."

86. Edwin Lahey, "She'd Rate with St. Peter," *Chicago Daily News*, Jan. 24, 1959.

87. Farrell, "Better Nutrition for All Peoples," 48–49, 183.

88. Yost, *American Women*, 174, 175.

89. Hazel Stiebeling, "What Price Adequate Diets," in unlabeled binder, Stiebeling Papers, Box 1, NAL.

90. Mudry, *Measured Meals*, 74; James Lileks, *The Gallery of Regrettable Food: Highlights from Classic American Recipe Books* (New York: Crown, 2001), 142.

91. Farrell, "Better Nutrition for All Peoples."

92. Megan Elias, *Food in the United States, 1890–1945* (Santa Barbara, CA: ABC Clio, 2009), 77–81.

93. Yearbook Separate #3004, reprint from 1959 Yearbook of Agriculture, USDA, School Lunches, Nutrition Publications, Facinoli Papers (unprocessed), NAL; Susan Levine, *School Lunch Politics: The Surprising History of America's Favorite Welfare Program* (Princeton, NJ: Princeton University Press, 2008), 71. Other important studies of the school lunch program include Janet Poppendieck, *Free for All: Fixing School Food in America* (Berkeley: University of California Press, 2010), and A. R. Ruis, *Eating to Learn, Learning to Eat: The Origins of School Lunch in the United States* (New Brunswick, NJ: Rutgers University Press, 2017).

94. Collingham, *Taste of War*, 426–28.

95. Levine, *School Lunch Politics*, 39; Ruis, *Eating to Learn*, 10.

96. Kendra Smith-Howard, *Pure and Modern Milk: An Environmental History since 1900* (New York: Oxford University Press, 2014), 80.

97. Undersecretary True Morse to F. Bruce Baldwin, President Milk Distributors Association, July 14, 1954, and Secretary Benson to Dr. E. Allen Bateman, Superintendent, Department of Public Instruction, July 8, 1954, file BA-BM, Box 1, Correspondence of Secretary of Agriculture and Assistant Secretary of Agriculture Relating to the AMS, 1954, RG 136, Records of the Agricultural Marketing Service, NARA II. Draft Memo, Freeman to President, folder Secretary Jan.–June 1964, Council of Economic Advisors, 1961-Intra-Bank, 1966, Records of John Schnittker, Box 9, RG 16, NARA II.

98. Agricultural Marketing Service, "The National School Lunch Program: Fifteen Years of Progress, 1947–1961," Dec. 1961. See also "Planning Type A School Lunches," Apr. 1954, Box 24, Records Relating to the School Lunch Program, 1940–1973, Food and Nutrition Service, Child Nutrition Division, RG 462, NARA II.

99. Levine, *School Lunch Politics*, 60, 64–66.

100. Other reimbursements to schools came from state and local governments, which meant that in its first decades, some poorer school districts decided that they could not participate if there were not sufficient local funds. Scrapbook, Oct. 10–16, 1965, 10th Anniversary of National School Lunch Week, Box 1, National School Lunch Week Collection, MS Coll 112, NAL. USDA Production and Marketing Administration, June 1952, "The National School Lunch Program: A Progress Report," Box 33, Records Relating to the School Lunch Program, 1940–1973, Food and Nutrition Service, Child Nutrition Division, RG 462, NARA II.

101. The recipes (usually for 100 servings) were for every category of food—from cheese to turkey to nonfat dry milk to potatoes to dried fruit and more—apparently to answer questions for all available foods and to encourage varied menus. Booklets and recipe cards, folder National School Lunch Program, Historical Recipe File, Box 1, Records Relating to the School Lunch Program, 1940–1973, Food and Nutrition Service, Child Nutrition Division, RG 462; also booklets and planning guides, "A Menu Planning Guide for Type A School Lunches," 1966, and "Planning Type A School Lunches," 1955, folder Type A, History Nutrient Standard, 1953–1962, Box 1, Records of the Food and Nutrition Service School Programs Division, School Lunch Program Subject Files, 1943–1977, Records of the Food and Nutrition Service and Food, Nutrition, and Consumer Services, 1969–1994, RG 462, NARA II.

102. This sort of nutritional advice was even a concern of the secretary of agriculture in 1949, who requested from his deputy a full report on nutritional advice publicized by the USDA. Memo, B. T. Shaw, Deputy Administrator to the Secretary, Dec. 9, 1949, Memo, Hazel Stiebeling, Chief of BHNHE, to B. T. Shaw, Deputy Administrator ARA, Dec. 9, 1949, folder Nutrition, Box 1750, General Correspondence 1906–1976, RG 16, NARA II.

103. Collingham, *Taste of War*, 428.

104. E. Allen Bateman, "The Place and Purpose of School Food Services in the Total Educational Program in Elementary and Secondary Schools," National Conference on School Lunch and Direct Distribution Programs, Aug. 27, 1957, folder Speeches and Articles, 1943–1958, Box 1, Records of the Food and Nutrition Service School Programs Division School Lunch Program Subject Files, 1943–1977, RG 462, NARA II.

105. Levine, *School Lunch Politics*, 89. For more on the logistical difficulties of using food surpluses for school lunches during World War II, see Collingham, *Taste of War*, 426–27.

106. "School Lunch, Milk Program Is Largest Ever," *Chicago Daily Tribune*, Oct. 31, 1957, W5; "15 Years Later, School Lunch Is Big Business," *Chicago Daily Tribune*, Oct. 2, 1961, C6; "U.S. Aids Lunch Program," *Pittsburgh Courier*, Oct. 20, 1962, 3; "School Lunch Program Is Larger Than Ever," *Chicago Daily Defender*, Oct. 29, 1962.

107. Levine, *School Lunch Politics*, 95–99, 113, 166, 179.

108. Nestle, *Food Politics*, 175–220; Levine, *School Lunch Politics*, 182.

109. Speech, Assistant Secretary of Agriculture George Mehren at Annual Meeting of the American School Food Service Association, Oct. 31, 1963, folder speeches and articles, 1959–1963, Box 1, Records of the Food and Nutrition Service School Programs Division School Lunch Program Subject Files, 1943–1977, RG 462, NARA II.

110. Scrapbook, 1956, 10th Anniversary of National School Lunch Week, Box 1, National School Lunch Week Collection, MS Coll 112, NAL.

111. Scrapbook, 1956, 10th Anniversary of National School Lunch Week.

112. Poppendieck, *Free for All*, 53. USDA Production and Marketing Administration, June 1952, "The National School Lunch Program: A Progress Report," Box 33, Records Relating to the School Lunch Program, 1940–1973, Food and Nutrition Service, Child Nutrition Division, RG 462, NARA II. (Statistics of participation differ slightly in these sources.)

113. Information National School Lunch Week, Oct. 11–17, 1964, Scrapbook 1964, Box 2, and Scrapbook, Oct. 10–16, 1965, 10th Anniversary of National School Lunch Week, Box 1, National School Lunch Week Collection, MS Coll 112, NAL.

114. Scrapbook 1966, National School Lunch, Oct. 9–15, 1966, Box 3, National School Lunch Week Collection, MS Coll 112, NAL.

115. "Federal Official Credits School Lunches with Helping Improve Nutrition of Families," *New York Times*, Nov. 18, 1949, 27; Van Dellen, "How to Keep Well," 10; "School Children Eating Better Than Ever Now," *New Journal and Guide*, Feb. 10, 1962, C6.

116. See examples from press clippings in scrapbooks in Boxes 1, 2, and 3, National School Lunch Week Collection, MS Coll 112, NAL.

117. Informational materials were put out by groups such as the American School Food Service Association (ASFSA), the Dairy Council of California, the National Peanut Council, and the Wheat Flour Institute, and in publications such as the *Arizona Grocer*, and *Canning Trade*. See examples of industry materials and clippings in scrapbooks in Boxes 1, 2, and 3, National School Lunch Week Collection, MS Coll 112, NAL.

118. "Lunch at School Serves the Nation: 20 Years of Progress in the National School Lunch Program," Consumer Marketing Service, USDA, National School Lunch, Oct. 9–15, 1966, Box 3, National School Lunch Week Collection, MS Coll 112, NAL.

119. Examples: USDA Employee Newsletter; Carol Murphy, "Teens Get Real Bargain—School Lunch," *Atlanta Constitution*; 10th Anniversary National School Lunches Week. See also Bertha Gehrke, "Turning Out 35 Cent School Lunches Is Her Job," *Chicago Daily Tribune*, Feb. 14, 1958, B3.

120. Murray Miles, "News and Views," Tennessee Farm Bureau Federation; 10th Anniversary National School Lunches Week, Box 1, and USDA Publication/AMS September 1964, Box 2, National School Lunch Week Collection, MS Coll 112, NAL.

121. "Lunch at School Serves the Nation."

122. Van Dellen, "How to Keep Well," 14. See also "Poor Nutrition Found Among Nation's Teenagers," *Chicago Defender*, Feb. 27, 1960, 20.

123. Gladys Denny Shultz, "Our Underfed Children," *Ladies Home Journal*, Mar. 1951, 44–45ff.; Ann Usher and Donald Cooley, "Should You Be Ashamed of Your Youngster's Diet?" *Better Homes and Gardens*, Oct. 1958, 115ff.

124. Gardner, "World's Homemakers are Her Concern," 2.

125. Letter, Freeman to Leroy Sipes, Sipes Food Stores, Aug. 31, 1961, folder Food, Box 3597, General Correspondence 1906–1976, RG 16, NARA II.

126. Address, Secretary of Agriculture Orville Freeman, March 26, 1963, folder, speeches and articles, 1959–1963, Box 1, Records of the Food and Nutrition Service School Programs Division, School Lunch Program Subject Files, 1943–1977, RG 462, NARA II.

127. Speech, Orville Freeman, May 20, 1963, Box 3, Statements and Speeches of the Secretary of Agriculture, 1959–1968, Office of Information, RG 16, NARA II.

128. Address, Assistant Secretary of Agriculture George Mehren, Oct. 31, 1963, folder, speeches and articles, 1959–1963, Box 1, Records of the Food and Nutrition Service School Programs Division, School Lunch Program Subject Files, 1943–1977, RG 462, NARA II.

129. There is an extensive literature about US foreign aid programs after World War II. PL 480 was passed in 1954 as the Food for Peace program and continued in many guises. For discussion of US aid programs and how they worked with domestic agricultural programs, see Bryan L. McDonald, *Food Power: The Rise and Fall of the Postwar American Food System* (New York: Oxford University Press, 2017). Further context for the program and its implementation is found in Papers of Raymond Andrew Ioanes, administrator of the Foreign Agricultural Service in the Kennedy, Johnson, and Nixon administrations. Unprocessed, one box, NAL. From the Kennedy administration, Secretary of Agriculture Orville Freeman celebrated Food for Peace as "one of the great human humanitarian efforts of all time." Freeman

to Food for Peace Council Meeting, 30 September 1963, Box 3, Statements and Speeches of the Secretary of Agriculture, 1959–1968, Office of Information, RG 16, NARA II.

Chapter 2

1. Poppy Cannon, *The Can-Opener Cookbook* (New York: Thomas Y. Crowell, 1951, 1952), 4. Italics in the original.

2. The magazines Cannon wrote for were part of a genre directed at women and intended to instruct women, observed historian Nancy Walker, in "appearance, duties, and values." For an overview on how the magazines served as instruction manuals for women's roles, including their responsibility for cooking, see Nancy Walker, ed., *Women's Magazines, 1940–1960: Gender Roles and the Popular Press* (Boston: Bedford/St. Martin's, 1998), 5; the quotation is from her introduction to that volume For more on the changing landscape of women's magazines from the late nineteenth through the late twentieth century, see Kathleen Endres and Therese Lueck, *Women's Periodicals in the United States: Consumer Magazines* (Westport, CT: Greenwood Press, 1995).

3. Lawrence Van Gelder, "Poppy Cannon, 69, Dead; Writer Was Authority on Food," *New York Times*, Apr. 2, 1975.

4. In addition to the *New York Times* obituary, information about Cannon's background also comes from her early 1950s résumé, n.d., found in folder 382, Box 37, Walter White and Poppy Cannon Papers, Beinecke Library, Yale University; hereinafter White and Cannon Papers, Beinicke. See also Laura Shapiro, *Something from the Oven: Reinventing Dinner in 1950s America* (New York: Viking Penguin, 2004), 92–94.

A note on Cannon's papers: the papers are a joint collection for Walter White and Poppy Cannon, 1910–1956. They are dominated by White's papers and issues concerning their lives together; and the collection ends nineteen years before Cannon's death. Thus, many aspects of her life, and especially work, are only hinted at here.

5. Cannon résumé.

6. For example, in folders 349 and 351, Box 33, White and Cannon Papers, Beinecke.

7. In some respects, of course, the overarching importance of White in Cannon's life was due to the huge political and social impact of the NAACP leader over several decades. White interacted with politicians and activists, presidents and world leaders, and was a key voice in civil rights work against lynching, segregation, and other forms of oppression. The impact of his work, as well as his broad social connections is reflected in his papers, beginning with his correspondence while alive, and the volume of condolence letters and telegrams sent to Cannon upon his death in 1955. Condolences sent to Cannon (Mrs. Walter White) can be found in Boxes 13 and 14, Series I: Correspondence, White and Cannon Papers, Beinecke. The range of White's relationships is illustrated by the example of correspondence with literary lights, such as James Weldon Johnson, and politicians, such as Chester Bowles. For example, folder 260, Box 38, Series I Correspondence, James Weldon Johnson and Grace Nial John Papers, Beinecke, and folder 461, Box 147 and folder 705, Box 162, Chester Bowles Papers, Beinecke. During their marriage, White and Cannon became well-known as a couple. See for example, a segment on Edward R. Murrow's *Person to Person*, profiling the two at home. See script, Oct. 1, 1954, folder 67, Box 10, White and Cannon Papers, Beinecke.

8. Samples of this sentiment can be seen in her self-deprecating letter to Dwight Eisenhower to accompany her gift of *The Can Opener Cookbook* and White's last book before his death. Cannon to Eisenhower, Oct. 24, 1955, folder 23, Box 9, White and Cannon Papers,

Beinecke. Earlier that month, in another letter to the president, Cannon affirmed (as she did elsewhere) that she was a "life-long Republican," even if she wished the party changed some of its positions: "I wish that our stand on Civil Rights were a great deal stronger." Cannon to Eisenhower, Oct. 2, 1956, folder 23, Box 9, Cannon and White Papers, Beinecke. Cannon's Republicanism predated her marriage, and it seemed that she and White engaged in some good-natured political debate. For example, in 1947, she wrote to White commenting on one of his newspaper columns in which she felt he unfairly engaged in stereotypes of all people in big business as being against civil rights. Cannon to White, Jan. 24, 1947, folder 109, Box 9, White and Cannon Papers, Beinecke.

9. Observations from manuscript drafts found in Boxes 30 and 31, Series II: Major Works, White and Cannon Papers, and Poppy Cannon, *A Gentle Knight: My Husband, Walter White* (New York: Rinehart, 1956), esp. 3–9, 10, 38–39. Contrary to Cannon's implications, historian Laura Shapiro made a clear determination that their affair started in 1944, continuing until their marriage in 1949. Shapiro, *Something from the Oven*, 99–101.

Cannon alluded to some of the controversy about their marriage in the book, but she was indirect. For instance, she noted that White went on a one-year leave from the NAACP at the time of the marriage and honeymoon, and she referred to some criticism that White faced from within the NAACP for his marriage. Cannon's obituary, though, noted that the controversy was short lived. That the controversy even erupted, of course, reflected the persistence and peculiarities of America racism. White was blond and blue-eyed, though still considered a "Negro" since he was "five thirty-seconds" Negro according to his obituary. White deliberately chose his Black identity and spent a lifetime of activism fighting injustice on behalf of the NAACP. Van Gelder, "Poppy Cannon, 69, Dead," and "Walter White, 61, Dies in Home Here," *New York Times*, Mar. 22, 1955. Not surprisingly, others judged White's work to be more valuable than Cannon's—even her own son. Cannon's son from her second marriage (Alf Landon) referred to *A Gentle Knight* as his mother's "first real book," in comparison with her earlier cookbooks. Alf to Cannon, n.d., folder 322 Major Works, Box 31, White and Cannon Papers, Beinecke.

10. For samples of Cannon's letters to White, see folders 226–28, Box 7, and folders 229–44, Box 8; for samples of White's letters to Cannon, see folders 108–19, Box 12, Series I, Correspondence, White and Cannon Papers, Beinecke. A number of the letters, especially from 1947 to 1949, concern the difficulty Cannon has in negotiating for a divorce from her third husband, Claude Philippe, who was maitre d'hotel of the Waldorf Astoria.

11. Cannon, *Can-Opener Cookbook*, 1. Other Cannon works based on the same premise were *The New, New Can-Opener Cookbook* (New York: Thomas Y. Crowell, 1968) and *The Electric Epicure's Cookbook* (New York: Thomas Y. Crowell, 1961). Cannon's books also included *The Bride's Cookbook* (New York: Henry Holt, 1954); *Unforbidden Sweets: Delicious Desserts of 100 Calories or Less* (New York: Thomas Y. Crowell, 1958); *Eating European: Abroad and at Home* (Garden City, NY: Doubleday, 1961); *The Frozen-Foods Cookbook* (New York: Thomas Y. Crowell, 1964); with Patricia Brooks, *The Presidents' Cookbook: Practical Recipes from George Washington to the Present* (New York: Funk & Wagnalls, 1968); *Poppy Cannon's All-Time, No-Time, Any-Time Cookbook* (New York: Thomas Y. Crowell, 1974); *Italian Cooking* (New York: Grosset & Dunlap, 1975). Also important as discussed below were *A Gentle Knight* and Alice B. Toklas, *Aromas and Flavors of Past and Present* (New York: Harper, 1958), for which she wrote an introduction and commentary.

12. Cannon, *Bride's Cookbook*.

13. Cannon, *Can-Opener Cookbook*, 3.

14. Cannon, *Can Opener Cookbook*, 41–44.

15. Cannon, *Can Opener Cookbook*, 47, 50, 54–56.

16. Cannon, *Can Opener Cookbook*, 92–93, 72, 79, 82, 83.

17. Cannon, *Bride's Cookbook*, 19, and Cannon, *New, New Can-Opener*, 26.

18. Cannon, *Frozen Foods*, 44.

19. Cannon, *Bride's Cookbook*, 13, and Cannon, *New, New Can-Opener*, 116, 220.

20. Clementine Paddleford, "Today's Living: Food for Happiness: Brides School Text," Mar. 21, 1951, and Clementine Paddleford, "Poppy Cannon Serves up Gourmet Food in a Jiffy," May 28, 1951, *New York Herald Tribune*. Press Release, from ABC WJZ-TV, n.d., "Meet WJZ-TV's Poppy Cannon, Orchids on Her Apron Strings!" Also, Clementine Paddleford, "New Hors d'Oeurves," *New York Herald Tribune*, Mar. 24, 1952. All in folder 144, Box 14, White and Cannon Papers, Beinecke.

21. Mary Drake McFeely, *Can She Bake a Cherry Pie? American Women and the Kitchen in the Twentieth Century* (Amherst: University of Massachusetts Press, 2000), 98.

22. James Lileks, *The Gallery of Regrettable Food: Highlights from Classic American Recipe Books* (New York: Crown, 2001), 32–36, 42–48, 128. Lileks's book and other samples of magazines and cookbooks from the era were also notable for garish, poor-quality photographs. The photos themselves—especially in comparison to the quality of modern food photography—were almost a self-parody and probably contributed to the late-century judgments about earlier American cuisine.

23. Cannon, *Can Opener Cookbook*, 137.

24. Cannon, *Bride's Cookbook*, 43–53, 65–78, 95.

25. "Poppy Cannon's Guide to the Bride on Buying Food," folder 325, Box 32, White and Cannon Papers, Beinecke.

26. Or the acceptability of using an ingredient in a particular way changed. For example, Cannon's recipe for "Puree of Peas de Luxe" was a dish based on doctored "strained peas for babies"; such a use of what we would call "baby food" today would not be countenanced. Cannon, *New, New Can Opener Cookbook*, 169.

27. Cannon, *Can-Opener Cookbook*, 126. Her observations about what poultry was available in stores and its changing costs reflected a huge shift in this market in the United States through the course of the twentieth century, making what had been a special occasion or Sunday dinner meal the most widely consumed meat by the end of the twentieth century. For more on the changing place of chicken, see Roger Horowitz, *Putting Meat on the American Table: Taste, Technology, Transformation* (Baltimore: Johns Hopkins University Press, 2006).

28. Anna Zeide, *US History in 15 Foods* (London: Bloomsbury, 2023), 141, 150–51. Anna Zeide also examined the evolution and earlier spread of canned foods in modern America, and how these products illustrated both confidence and distrust in the industrial food system. See her *Canned: The Rise and Fall of Consumer Confidence in the American Food Industry* (Oakland: University of California Press, 2018).

29. McFeely, *Can She Bake a Cherry Pie*, 57.

30. Benjamin Cohen, *Pure Adulteration: Cheating on Nature in the Age of Manufactured Food* (Chicago: University of Chicago Press, 2019).

31. Paul Freedman, *American Cuisine and How It Got This Way* (New York: Liveright, 2019), 157.

32. Laura Shapiro, "Do Women Like to Cook?" in Molly O'Neill, ed., *American Food Writings: An Anthology with Classic Recipes* (New York: Library of America, 2007), 597–98.

33. Freedman, *American Cuisine and How It Got This Way*, 137–38; Harvey Levenstein, *Paradox of Plenty: A Social History of Eating in Modern America*, rev. ed. (Berkeley: University of California Press, 2003), 101.

34. Levenstein, *Paradox of Plenty*, 109–10. Many critics have turned their lens on the extremes of twentieth-century processed foods that are more akin to laboratory creations than to food. Coca-Cola and Twinkies, among other products, elicit such analysis. See, for example, Steve Ettlinger, *Twinkie, Deconstructed: My Journey to Discover How the Ingredients Found in Processed Foods are Grown, Mined (yes, Mined), and Manipulated into What America Eats* (New York: Hudson Street, 2007).

35. In a related statistic, 30 percent of housewives went into the labor force by the early 1950s. Levenstein, *Paradox of Plenty*, 105. See also Freedman, *American Cuisine and How It Got This Way*, 194–200.

36. For instance, the market share of corporate chains was 35 percent in 1948 and 50 percent in 1963. Michael Ruhlman, *Grocery: The Buying and Selling of Food in America* (New York: Abrams, 2017), 52–53.

37. Shane Hamilton, *Supermarket USA: Food and Power in the Cold War Farms Race* (New Haven, CT: Yale University Press, 2018).

38. Lizabeth Cohen, *A Consumers' Republic: The Politics of Mass Consumption in Postwar America* (New York: Knopf, 2003).

39. Veronica Volpe, "1954 Food Supplies Plentiful," *Pittsburgh Post-Gazette*, Feb. 24, 1954, 7.

40. Gary Cross and Robert Proctor, *Packaged Pleasures: How Technology and Marketing Revolutionized Desire* (Chicago: University of Chicago Press, 2014), 19.

41. Quoted in Sherrie Inness, *Dinner Roles: American Women and Culinary Culture* (Iowa City: University of Iowa Press, 2001), 160.

42. Mary McCarthy, *The Group* (San Diego, CA: Harcourt Brace, 1954, 1982), 81.

43. Jessamyn Neuhaus, *Manly Meals and Mom's Home Cooking: Cookbooks and Gender in Modern America* (Baltimore: Johns Hopkins University Press, 2003), is very helpful in its survey of many different publications and what messages they conveyed about gender. Also important is Megan Elias, *Food on the Page Cookbooks and American Culture* (Philadelphia: University of Pennsylvania Press, 2017). Anne Mendelson, *Stand Facing the Stove: The Story of the Women Who Gave America* The Joy of Cooking (New York: Henry Holt, 1996) focuses more specifically on one book. Other cookbooks were manuscript or communal endeavors, outside of commercial publishing. Such works told something about women's lives and the communities in which they lived. Sociologist Janet Theophano observed of this genre: "cookbooks have thus served as meditations, memoirs, diaries, journals scrapbooks, and guides." Janet Theophano, *Eat My Words: Reading Women's Lives Through the Cookbooks They Wrote* (London: Palgrave Macmillian, 2002), 6. Maria McGrath observed of cookbooks that they "often showcase a period's cultural-culinary gestalt." *Food for Dissent: Natural Foods and the Consumer Counterculture Since the 1960s* (Amherst MA: University of Massachusetts Press, 2019), 56.

44. Quoted in McFeely, *Can She Bake a Cherry Pie*, 58.

45. Cannon, *Electric Epicure's Cookbook*, 1.

46. Cannon, *Electric Epicure's Cookbook*, 196, 19, 220, 3–4, 35–37.

47. Cannon *Electric Epicure's Cookbook*, 2, 44–46, 133–38.

48. Cannon, *Can Opener Cookbook*, 83.

49. Cannon, *Can Opener Cookbook*, 85.

50. Cannon, *Electric Epicure's Cookbook*, 173, 169–70.

51. Cannon, *Can Opener Cookbook*, 31.

52. Cannon, *New, New Can-Opener Cookbook*, 246–47.

53. Cannon, *Can Opener Cookbook*, 237, 231, 225, 212, 132; Cannon, *Electric Epicure's Cookbook*, 138.

54. Cannon, *New, New Can Opener Cookbook*, 51.

55. Lovegren, *Fashionable Food*, 220.

56. Cannon, *Can Opener Cookbook*, 7.

57. Cannon, *Bride's Cookbook*, 83.

58. Cannon to Elizabeth Gordon, July 17, 1953, folder 31, Box 10, White and Cannon Papers, Beinecke.

59. Cannon, *Electric Epicure's Cookbook*, 217.

60. Shapiro, *Something from the Oven*, 107. Justin Spring also observes how the move to *House Beautiful* in 1953 led Cannon to assume that her readers had more spacious, well-appointed kitchens. Justin Spring, *The Gourmands' Way: Six Americans in Paris and the Birth of the New Gastronomy* (New York: Farrar, Straus and Giroux, 2017), 223.

61. Cannon, *Can Opener Cookbook*, 187, 79.

62. Cannon, *Can Opener Cookbook*, 39.

63. Cannon, *Bride's Cookbook*, 167.

64. Cannon, *Bride's Cookbook*, 249.

65. Cannon, *Bride's Cookbook*, 323, 321.

66. Cannon's decision to highlight the elegant possibilities of frozen foods was apt; historian Shane Hamilton explained that the market for frozen foods had exploded in the 1950s, and by the 1960s marketers advertised specialty and gourmet frozen ingredients. Shane Hamilton, "The Economies and Conveniences of Modern-Day Living: Frozen Foods and Mass Marketing, 1945–1965," *Business History Review* 77 (1) (Spring 2003): 33–60.

67. Cannon, *Can Opener Cookbook*, 1.

68. Cannon, *Bride's Cookbook*, 371.

69. Cannon, *Can Opener Cookbook*, 173.

70. Many historians and scholars have studied the complex relationship of women and food in American life in the twentieth century. For a sample of this literature, see Shapiro, *Something from the Oven*; Elias, *Food on the Page*; McFeely, *Can She Bake a Cherry Pie*; Inness, *Dinner Roles*. See also Ruth Schwartz Cowan, *More Work for Mother; The Ironies of Household Technology from the Open Hearth to the Microwave* (New York: Basic Books, 1983).

71. Cannon, *Bride's Cookbook*, ix.

72. Cannon, *Bride's Cookbook*, 234.

73. Cannon, *Bride's Cookbook*, 219, 169.

74. Press Release, "Meet WJZ-TV's Poppy Cannon, Orchids on her Apron Strings!" n.d., folder 144, Box 14, White and Cannon Papers, Beinecke.

75. Cowan also indicates that the increased domestic burden on women continued to escalate through the postwar period as the number of middle-class women working outside the home grew. Cowan, *More Work for Mother*, 192–201. See also discussion of this irony in Shapiro, *Something from the Oven*, and McFeely, *Can She Bake a Cherry Pie*.

76. Inness, *Dinner Roles*, 149.

77. Shapiro, *Something from the Oven*, discusses the issue, 76–80, as does McFeely, *Can She Bake a Cherry Pie*, 100; many other scholars also discuss what has become a well-known question about women's roles and manufactured foods.

78. For example, Shapiro, *Something from the Oven*, highlights women's continued enjoyment of home cooking with unprocessed ingredients and resistance to manufactured foods, whereas Elias, *Food on the Page*, writes of women's more ready adoption of such foods.

79. Cannon, *Bride's Cookbook*, 191.

80. Inness, *Dinner Roles*, 26.

81. Cannon, *Can Opener Cookbook*, 178.

82. Sylvia Lovegren, *Fashionable Food: Seven Decades of Food Fads* (Chicago: University of Chicago Press, 1995, 2005), 173.

83. Inness, *Dinner Roles*, 23.

84. Inness, *Dinner Roles*, 27.

85. McFeely, *Can She Bake a Cherry Pie*, 103; Inness, *Dinner Roles*, 28.

86. Elias, *Food on the Page*, 100; see also Inness, *Dinner Roles*, 31.

87. McCarthy, *The Group*, 79–80, 96.

88. Elias, *Food on the Page*, 90.

89. Elias, *Food on the Page*, 91, 97.

90. Cannon, *New, New Can-Opener Cookbook*, for example, 25, 30–31, 46, 153, 158–59.

91. Cannon, *New, New Can-Opener Cookbook*, 53.

92. Cannon, *New, New Can-Opener Cookbook*, 65–66, 114, 240.

93. Cannon, *Can Opener Cookbook*, 50.

94. Cannon, *Eating European*, xii–xiii, xvi.

95. Cannon, *Italian Cooking*, 15.

96. Cannon, *Unforbidden Sweets*, 10, 12.

97. Alice B. Toklas, *The Alice B. Toklas Cook Book* (New York: Harper, 1954).

98. Toklas, *Aromas and Flavors of the Past and Present*, xxv, xxvi.

99. Spring, *Gourmands' Way*, 221.

100. Linda Simon, *The Biography of Alice B. Toklas* (Garden City, NY: Doubleday, 1977), 236.

101. Spring, *Gourmands' Way*, 219, 235–36, 241.

102. Simon, *Biography of Alice B. Toklas*, 219.

103. Toklas, *Aromas and Flavors*, 1, 138.

104. Toklas, *Aromas and Flavors*, 34.

105. Toklas, *Aromas and Flavors*, 75.

106. Toklas, *Aromas and Flavors*, 137.

107. Toklas, *Aromas and Flavors*, 84.

108. Toklas, *Aromas and Flavors*, 8, 95.

109. Toklas, *Aromas and Flavors*, 2, 27–28.

110. Toklas, *Aromas and Flavors*, 118.

111. Cannon, introduction, *Aromas and Flavors*, vii, viii, xiii, xiii-xvi, xx–xxii.

112. Toklas, *Aromas and Flavors*, xix, 29.

113. Cannon, introduction, *Aromas and Flavors*, xviii.

114. Cannon, introduction, *Aromas and Flavors*, ix–x.

115. Cannon, *Gentle Knight*, 169. Cannon's assertion that women's roles were more varied

than sometimes assumed in the media would be taken up years later by revisionist feminist scholars writing about diversity among women in postwar America. See Joanne Meyerowitz, "Beyond the Feminine Mystique: A Reassessment of Postwar Mass Culture, 1946–1958" in Meyerowitz, ed., *Not June Cleaver: Women and Gender in Postwar America, 1945–1960* (Philadelphia: Temple University Press, 1994).

116. Shapiro, *Something from the Oven*, 122–23.

117. Cannon, *All-Time, No-Time, Any-Time*, x.

118. Cannon, *All-Time, No-Time, Any-Time*, xv

119. Cannon, *All-Time, No-Time, Any-Time*, 190–91, 3, 1–2.

120. Cannon, *All-Time, No-Time, Any-Time*, 73, 82.

Chapter 3

1. Beck, Simone, Louisette Bertholle, Julia Child, *Mastering the Art of French Cooking* (New York: Knopf, 1961), vii, viii.

2. This practice has even found its way into scholarly works that usually adhere to a greater formality. See, for example, Laura Shapiro, *Julia Child* (New York: Viking, 2007).

3. Figure cited in Shapiro, *Julia Child*, 92. By 1974, the book had sold 1.3 million copies. In the first decade of the twenty-first century, it was still selling 18,000 copies a year.

4. Biographical stories about Julia Child are numerous. The following have been helpful here: Joan Reardon, *M. F. K. Fisher, Julia Child, and Alice Waters: Celebrating the Pleasures of the Table* (New York: Harmon Books, 1994); Shapiro, *Julia Child*; Betty Fussell, *Masters of American Cookery: M. F. K. Fisher, James Andrews Beard, Raymond Craig Claiborne, Julia McWilliams Child* (New York: Times Books, 1983); Shapiro, *Something from the Oven*; Spring, *Gourmands' Way*. The fictional film, *Julie & Julia* (2011), based on a memoir by Julia Powell and a posthumously published coauthored autobiography by Julia Child, enjoyably dramatizes Child's years in France.

5. Spring, *Gourmands' Way*, 92. Reardon, *M. F. K. Fisher, Julia Child, and Alice Waters*, 14. Paul and Julia Child had met during World War II in Sri Lanka when both worked for the Office of Strategic Services. Not long after their marriage in 1946, the couple moved to Paris in 1948 for Paul's job with the United States Information Agency. Over the next dozen years, Child was posted to three other cities (Marseilles, Bonn, and Oslo), after which he retired from the foreign service. He and Julia returned to the United States in 1961.

6. Spring, *Gourmands' Way*, 89–91, 98–99.

7. For example, folder 4, Journal, 1974, Box 1, Series I, Biographical, Julia Child Papers, Schlesinger Library.

8. Child to Beard, Dec. 12, 1962, folder 128, Box 10, Series II, Correspondence, Child Papers, Schlesinger Library.

9. Child to Beard, Dec. 18, 1966, folder 129, Box 10, Series II, Correspondence, Child Papers, Schlesinger Library.

10. Beck, Bertholle, Child, *Mastering the Art.*

11. Shapiro, *Julia Child*, 69.

12. Shapiro, *Julia Child*, 112. Another example of this common observation: Robert MacKenzie, "Review: Julia Child and Company," *TV Guide*, Feb. 17, 1979, folder 264, Box 20, Series II, Correspondence, Child Papers, Schlesinger Library.

13. Philip Nobile, "Uncommon Conversations: Julia Child: The Fairest Chef of All," Nov. 12, 1972, folder 282, Box 22, Series II, Correspondence, Child Papers, Schlesinger Library.

14. Reardon, *M. F. K. Fisher, Julia Child, and Alice Waters*, 15.

15. Beck, Bertholle, Child, *Mastering the Art*, viii.

16. David Strauss, *Setting the Table for Julia Child: Gourmet Dining in America, 1934–1961* (Baltimore: Johns Hopkins University Press, 2011), 225–26, 235–38. On Child and Beck's collaboration, see also Reardon, *M. F. K. Fisher, Julia Child, and Alice Waters*, 141.

17. Beck, Bertholle, Child, *Mastering the Art*, 1–31.

18. Beck, Bertholle, Child, *Mastering the Art*, 54.

19. Beck, Bertholle, Child, *Mastering the Art*, vii.

20. Freedman, *American Cuisine and How It Got This Way*, 228.

21. Beck, Bertholle, Child, *Mastering the Art*, 54.

22. Beck, Bertholle, Child, *Mastering the Art*, 94.

23. Beck, Bertholle, Child, *Mastering the Art*, 239.

24. Beck, Bertholle, Child, *Mastering the Art*, 288.

25. Beck, Bertholle, Child, *Mastering the Art*, 81, 79–86.

26. Beck, Bertholle, Child, *Mastering the Art*, 175.

27. Beck, Bertholle, Child, *Mastering the Art*, 37.

28. Beck, Bertholle, Child, *Mastering the Art*, 187.

29. Julia Child, in collaboration with E. S. Yntema, *Julia Child and Company* (New York: Ballantine Books, 1978), 16.

30. Beck, Bertholle, Child, *Mastering the Art*, 66.

31. Beck, Bertholle, Child, *Mastering the Art*, 167.

32. The recipe involved boning, stuffing, and re-forming a duck, then trussing the bird and baking inside of a pastry. Child offered two options before it was brought to the table, both of which included carefully removing the pastry top without damaging it, removing the duck from the shell, and snipping off its trussing; the duck was then returned to the shell, the top replaced, and the dish served at the table. Beck, Bertholle, Child, *Mastering the Art*, 569–75.

33. Beck, Bertholle, Child, *Mastering the Art*, 613.

34. Beck, Bertholle, Child, *Mastering the Art*, 643.

35. Child to Beard, Jan. 22, 1968, folder 130, Box 10, Series II, Correspondence, Child Papers, Schlesinger Library.

36. Beck, Bertholle, Child, *Mastering the Art*, vii.

37. Beck, Bertholle, Child, *Mastering the Art*, 57.

38. Beck, Bertholle, Child, *Mastering the Art*, 115.

39. Beck, Bertholle, Child, *Mastering the Art*, 422.

40. Beck, Bertholle, Child, *Mastering the Art*, 442.

41. Beck, Bertholle, Child, *Mastering the Art*, 439.

42. Beck, Bertholle, Child, *Mastering the Art*, 475.

43. Beck, Bertholle, Child, *Mastering the Art*, 467, 484, 517.

44. Later in the book, Child made another rare mention of a processed ingredient only to condemn it: "store-bought ladyfingers are usually so dreadful in taste and texture that they cannot be used in good cooking, [and] it is useful to know how to make your own." Beck, Bertholle, Child, *Mastering the Art*, 534–35, 665.

45. Beck, Bertholle, Child, *Mastering the Art*, 16.

46. Beck, Bertholle, Child, *Mastering the Art*, 45–46.

47. Beck, Bertholle, Child, *Mastering the Art*, 94, 399.

48. Beck, Bertholle, Child, *Mastering the Art*, 421.

49. Beck, Bertholle, Child, *Mastering the Art*, x.

50. Beck, Bertholle, Child, *Mastering the Art*, 126.

51. Beck, Bertholle, Child, *Mastering the Art*, 158.

52. A number of writers have commented on this experimental aspect to preparing the book. For example, see Strauss, *Setting the Table*, 230–31.

53. Its last issue was in November 2009. Ruth Reichl, its final editor from 1999 to 2009, recounts what was a frantic search for more advertising dollars in the early twenty-first century in her memoir, *Save Me the Plums: My* Gourmet *Memoir* (New York: Random House 2019). See also Andrew Smith, *Eating History: 30 Turning Points in the Making of American Cuisine* (New York: Columbia University Press, 2009), 185–91.

54. This section is drawn from a discussion on *Gourmet* found in Strauss, *Setting the Table*, 70–71, 189–90, and Megan Elias, *Food on the Page: Cookbooks and American Culture* (Philadelphia: University of Pennsylvania Press, 2017), 73–75, 89–90, 97.

55. Strauss, *Setting the Table*, 70–71, 190.

56. Lovegren, *Fashionable Food*, 158.

57. Reichl writes of the excitement such recipes elicited in her as a girl leafing through the magazines in 1960. Reichl, *Save Me the Plums*, 256.

58. Elias, *Food on the Page*, 82.

59. Levenstein, *Paradox of Plenty*, 137–40.

60. Clarence Miller Assistant Secretary to Senator Leverett Saltonstall, May 1, 1959, folder—Food, Box 3301, 1959 Finance—Food Products 2, General Correspondence, 1906–1976, RG 16, NARA II.

61. Betty Fussell, *My Kitchen Wars* (New York: North Point Press/Farrar, Straus and Giroux, 1999), 127, 153.

62. Nora Ephron, "The Food Establishment: Life in the Land of the Rising Soufflé (Or Is It the Rising Meringue?)" in O'Neill, ed., *American Food Writing*, 411–12.

63. Strauss, *Setting the Table*, 1.

64. Child to Beard, Jan. 22, 1968, folder 130, Box 10, Series II, Correspondence, Child Papers, Schlesinger Library.

65. Child to Beard, Jan. 22, 1968.

66. Child to Beard, June 5, 1973, folder 131, Box 11, Series II, Correspondence, Child Papers, Schlesinger Library.

67. Child to Fisher, May 11, 1972, folder 224, Box 18, Series II, Correspondence, Child Papers, Schlesinger Library.

68. McFeely, *Can She Bake a Cherry Pie*, 120.

69. Philip Nobile, "Uncommon Conversations: Julia Child: The Fairest Chef of All," folder 283, Box 22, Series II, Correspondence, Child Papers, Schlesinger Library.

70. Fussell, *My Kitchen Wars*, 154.

71. Beck, Bertholle, Child, *Mastering the Art*, vii.

72. Fussell, *My Kitchen Wars*, 158–59.

73. Fussell, *My Kitchen Wars*, 155.

74. Spring, *Gourmands' Way*, 87.

75. Spring, *Gourmands' Way*, 146–48. Strauss, *Setting the Table*, 224–25.

76. Spring, *Gourmands' Way*, 153.

77. Strauss, *Setting the Table*, 230.

78. Fussell's memoir of cooking in the postwar period and her discovery of French food read as a sexual awakening for her and her friends. She was explicit that French food was not only sensual, it was also sexual: "Foods we had known as American but now cooked French revealed a world of innuendo we had missed in our own language. Asparagus that might have gone limp in a steamer stayed stiff with a quick dip in boiling water. Artichokes that had seemed tedious to unleave took on vulvate meaning when the tops of the leaves were cut off and the pith removed and the center made wet with vinaigrette, so that each leaf brought the mouth a step closer to consuming the heart. The canned peach halves that were a staple of my father's table didn't at all resemble the glossy operatic breasts of *pêches melbe*, cushioned on velvet ice cream and rosied by raspberry *coulis*." Fussell, *Masters of American Cookery*, 3, 128.

79. Shapiro, *Julia Child*, xvi.

80. Betty Friedan, *The Feminine Mystique* (New York: Norton, 1963).

81. McFeely, *Can She Bake a Cherry Pie*, 124.

82. Shapiro, *Something from the Oven*, 224; Shapiro, *Julia Child*, 90–92.

83. For example, Reardon, *M. F. K. Fisher, Julia Child, and Alice Waters*, 95; Elias, *Food on the Page*, 84; Strauss, *Setting the Table*, 221.

84. Ephron, "The Food Establishment," in O'Neill, ed., *American Food Writing*, 412.

85. Spring, *Gourmands' Way*, 277.

86. Lovegren, *Fashionable Food*, 227.

87. While Sheraton noted that there was an increase in the availability of specialty ingredients, she also observed that those who sought such items did not care about *fresh* foods as cooks would later do. She described elite restaurants in the 1950s and 1960s that served canned vegetables as long as they were imported; for example, owners of the 21 Club in New York, defended themselves against her criticism that they served canned peas by explaining that they were "petit pois" from France. Mimi Sheraton, oral history, July 20, 2009, Fales Library and Special Collections, New York University.

88. Elias, *Food on the Page*, 107.

89. Irma S. Rombauer and Marion Rombauer Becker, *Joy of Cooking* (Indianapolis: Bobbs-Merrill, 1936). *Better Homes and Gardens New Cook Book* (New York: Meredith, 1953). *Betty Crocker's Picture Cookbook* (New York: Wiley, 1950). All three had multiple printings thereafter.

90. Kim Severson, "Does the World Need Another 'Joy'? Do You?" *New York Times*, Nov. 1, 2006.

91. Lovegren, *Fashionable Food*, 221.

92. Following what many felt to be a disastrous revision in 1997, much of what people liked best about the earlier editions was restored for a seventy-fifthth anniversary edition in 2006 and the most recent in 2019. Severson, "Does the World Need Another Joy."

93. McFeely, *Can She Bake a Cherry Pie*, 200.

94. Rombauer and Becker, *Joy of Cooking*, 526, 542, 512.

95. A few of the allusions to "freshness" indicate a different period of time than modern urban readers might encounter; for example, Rombauer and Becker advise that "Poultry cooks and tastes best if used within 8 to 24 hours after slaughter." One can safely assume that many readers who lived in cities were not eating chickens slaughtered within the previous eight hours. Rombauer and Becker, *Joy of Cooking*, 460.

96. Rombauer and Becker, *Joy of Cooking*, 63.

97. Lovegren, *Fashionable Food*, 122, 139.

98. Rombauer and Becker, *Joy of Cooking*, 1, 9.

99. Rombauer and Becker, *Joy of Cooking*, 553, 619, 250, 88.

100. *Better Homes and Gardens.*

101. *Better Homes and Gardens*, 61.

102. McFeely, *Can She Bake a Cherry Pie*, 91; Shapiro, *Something from the Oven*, 177–79.

103. Elias, *Food on the Page*, 108.

104. Elias, *Food on the Page*, 111–13.

105. Inness, *Dinner Roles*, 141–42.

106. The influence of the book has been written about widely. It is discussed in Laura Shapiro, *Perfection Salad: Women and Cooking at the Turn of the Century* (New York: Modern Library, 1986, 2001). A brief overview of Fannie Farmer's significance is found in Julia Moskin, "Fannie Farmer: Modern Cookery's Pioneer," *New York Times*, June 13, 2018.

107. Moskin, "Fannie Farmer." For the themes and impact of *The Fannie Farmer Cookbook*, see also Elias, *Food in the United States*, 11.

108. *The Fannie Farmer Cookbook*, 12th rev ed., Marion Cunningham with Jeri Laber (New York: Knopf, 1979, 1987). Reviews of the Cunningham revision include William Rice, "The Updated, Revised, But Otherwise Original *Fannie Farmer Cookbook*," *Washington Post*, Sept. 27, 1979, and Craig Claiborne, "New Life, New Spice for Classic Cookbook," *New York Times*, Sept. 12, 1979.

109. Letters between Child and Cunningham were often very affectionate and familiar. and included several discussions of the revision process; Child's husband, Paul, is also included in the correspondence. Another topic of the letters was their mutual friendship with James Beard, with whom Cunningham used to work. The correspondence includes the following: Cunningham to Child and Child, Dec. 30, 1975; Child to Cunningham, Feb. 29, 1976; Child to Cunningham, Jan. 20, 1977; Child to Cunningham, June 8, 1977; Cunningham to Child and Child, May 23, 1977; Cunningham to Child and Child Mar. 15, 1978, folder 206, Box 17, Series II, Correspondence, Child Papers, Schlesinger Library.

110. McFeely, *Can She Bake a Cherry Pie*, 99. Others have observed that convenience foods in the 1960s were not only used because they were quick, but because they were modern. Syliva Lovegren observed that this connotation made them a fad in the 1960s: "The Sixties were the high point of instant food, quick food, space age food. In that age of astronauts and plastic go-go boots it was not only practical to eat instant food. It was chic." Lovegren, *Fashionable Food*, 217.

111. Elias, *Food on the Page*, 119.

112. Elias, *Food on the Page*, 108.

113. Later in the 1960s, another example of this ethos was similarly direct: Lynn Dallin's 1968 *The Stay Out of the Kitchen Cook Book*. Elias, *Food on the Page*, 120; Shapiro, *Something from the Oven*, 162–64.

114. Fussell, *Masters of American Cookery*, 16, 9. Claiborne was an influential restaurant critic and book author.

115. Elias, *Food on the Page*, 76–77. See Joan Reardon, *Poet of the Appetites: The Lives and Loves of M. F. K. Fisher* (New York: North Point, 2004), esp. 332–46. Informative overviews of Fisher's impact can also be found in James Villas, "Exclusive Interview: A Country Lunch with M. F. K. Fisher," *Bon Appetit*, Nov. 1978, folder 226, and Elizabeth Hawes, "M. F. K. Fisher: A Profile," *Gourmet*, Nov. 1983, folder 229, Box 18, Series II, Correspondence, Child Papers, Schlesinger Library. For a sample of Fisher's writing, especially regarding local food

in France, see "Two Kitchens in Provence," in M. F. K. Fisher, *As They Were* (New York: Vintage Books, 1983).

116. Correspondence between Child and Fisher can be found in folders 222–30, Box 18, Series II, Correspondence, Child Papers, Schlesinger Library. And for more on their friendship, see Reardon, *M. F. K. Fisher, Julia Child, and Alice Waters*, 69–101. There is a strange footnote to the later years of their friendship: a public rift from January to March 1987 over the formation of the James Beard Foundation to hold seminars, foster discussion, and encourage excellence in American cuisine. While Child was one of the driving forces behind the creation of the foundation designed to honor her friend and ennoble cooking, Fisher criticized that effort in an interview with *Time* magazine, leading Child to send her own biting letter to the editor (a toned-down version of which was printed one month later). The two exchanged letters after this public argument that seemed to indicate all had been repaired. See Mimi Sheraton, "With Bold Pen and Fork," *Time*, Jan. 26, 1987; Child to Editor (cc to Fisher), *Time*, Feb. 5, 1987; Child letter in *Time*, Mar. 2, 1987; all in folder 132, Box 11, Series II, Correspondence, Child Papers, Schlesinger Library. See also Child letters to Fisher, folder 230, Box 18, Series II, Correspondence, Child Papers, Schlesinger Library.

117. For more on Fisher's views of France, see Hawes, "M. F. K. Fisher."

118. Strauss, *Setting the Table*, 249; Shapiro, *Something from the Oven*, 3. In a 2009 oral history, Hilary Baum discussed the collaboration between her father, Joseph Baum, founder of The Four Seasons, and James Beard, on that restaurant, as well as other theme restaurant projects. Hilary Baum, oral history, Sept. 22, 2009, Fales Library.

119. Like Child throughout her career, Beard also encouraged cooks to avoid food fads. Elias, *Food on the Page*, 115–16.

120. Judith Jones, oral history, May 7, 2009, Fales Library.

121. The following observations come from a survey of correspondence: folders 128, 129, 130, Box 10; folders 131, 132, Box 11, Series II, Correspondence, Child Papers, Schlesinger Library.

122. Child to Beard, Jan. 28, 1976, folder 132, Box 11, Series II, Correspondence, Child Papers, Schlesinger Library.

123. McFeely, *Can She Bake a Cherry Pie*, 21; Shapiro, *Something from the Oven*, 226; Shapiro, *Julia Child*, 110–11.

124. Fussell, *Masters of American Cookery*, 47.

125. Reardon, *M. F. K. Fisher, Julia Child, and Alice Waters*, 156.

126. Fussell, *Masters of American Cookery*, 51.

127. McFeely, *Can She Bake a Cherry Pie*, 123–24.

128. Child's long television career can be found in snippets on the internet. This episode, written about elsewhere, was found in 2020 on Youtube. Over the years, *The French Chef* and other Child programs were rebroadcast or sold as sets for home viewers.

129. Elias, *Food on the Page*, 104; Shapiro, *Something from the Oven*, 230.

130. Robert MacKenzie, "Review: Julia Child and Company," *TV Guide*, Feb. 17, 1979, folder 264, Box 20, Series II, Child Papers, Schlesinger Library.

131. Charles Gandee, "Gandee at Large: Julia Child—Still Cooking at 76," clipping, folder 248, Box 19, Series II, Correspondence, Child Papers, Schlesinger Library.

In the *Saturday Night Live* skit, Akroyd was dressed as Child, with her characteristic blouse, necklace, and haircut. He spoke in a falsetto voice, liberally used French terms, and acted in a nonchalant manner when he injured himself with a knife, hemorrhaging all over the countertop. The skit could be found on Youtube in 2020.

132. Child remained unflappable, even as Letterman threw food to the audience and made fun of some of her recipes; she traded barbs with the comedian, including running jokes about her appearances on the rival network's *Good Morning America*, giving cooking mistakes to her husband, and eating seals. All of the appearances were accessible on Youtube in 2020.

133. Shapiro, *Julia Child*, 111.

134. Reardon, *M. F. K. Fisher, Julia Child, and Alice Waters*, 165, 167.

135. Fussell, oral history, Mar. 24, 2009, Fales Library; David Letterman, *Late Night with David Letterman*, Oct. 25, 1994, available on Youtube.

136. Reardon, *M. F. K. Fisher, Julia Child, and Alice Waters*, 184–85, 188.

137. Reardon, *M. F. K. Fisher, Julia Child, and Alice Waters*, 190, 192.

138. Judith Jones, oral history, May 7, 2009, Fales Library.

139. Quoted in Reardon, *M. F. K. Fisher, Julia Child, and Alice Waters*, 73. Similarly, she observed that the French were often content to work in kitchens that were inferior to American ones. She wrote to James Beard in 1966 about needed kitchen renovations at her house in southern France: "Really, the Froggies are 40–50 or more years behind mechanically, and one just has to get used to it . . . but I love them." Child to Beard, Jan. 3, 1966, folder 129, Box 10, Series II, Correspondence, Child Papers, Schlesinger Library.

140. Child to Narcisse Chamberlain, June 18, 1963; see also letter Chamberlain to Child, June 6, 1963, folder 181, Box 15, Series II, Correspondence, Child Papers, Schlesinger Library.

141. Reardon, *M. F. K. Fisher, Julia Child, and Alice Waters*, 162, 168, 177.

142. Reardon, *M. F. K. Fisher, Julia Child, and Alice Waters*, 169.

143. Fussell, *Masters of American Cookery*, 48–49.

144. Child to Fisher, May 25, 1982, folder 229, Box 18, Series II, Correspondence, Child Papers, Schlesinger Library; also, Reardon, *M.F.K. Fisher, Julia Child, and Alice Waters*, 179–80.

145. Spring, *Gourmands' Way*, 364.

146. Quoted in Shapiro, *Julia Child*, 93.

147. Child to Beard, Jan. 28, 1973, folder 131, Box 11, Series II, Correspondence, Child Papers, Schlesinger Papers.

148. Child to Beard, June 5, 1973, folder 131, Box 11, Series II, Correspondence, Child Papers, Schlesinger Papers.

149. Reardon, *M. F. K. Fisher, Julia Child, and Alice Waters*, 188–89.

150. Child, *Julia Child and Company*, vi.

151. A number of commentators have written about this food movement; here are two contemporary examples: Raymond Sokolov, "In French Culinary Art—The Beginnings of a Subtle Revolution," *New York Times*, Mar. 30, 1972, folder 349, and Mimi Sheraton, "The Non-So-Nouvelle Cuisine" *New York Times*, Sept. 5, 1979, folder 351, Box 26, Series II, Correspondence, Child Papers, Schlesinger Library.

152. Child to the Editor, *Newsweek*, Aug. 15, 1975, folder 282, Box 22, Series II, Correspondence, Child Papers, Schlesinger Library.

153. Child to William Rice, Aug. 18, 1975, folder 303, Box 22, Series II, Correspondence, Child Papers, Schlesinger Library.

154. Fussell, *Masters of American Cookery*, 52.

155. Child, *Julia Child and Company*, 88.

156. Child, *Julia Child and Company*, 30–35.

157. Child to Fisher, Sept. 1977, folder 226, Box 18, Series II, Correspondence, Child Papers, Schlesinger Library.

158. Child to Fisher, Mar. 14, 1987, folder 230, Box 18, Series II, Correspondence, Child Papers, Schlesinger Library.

159. Child to Fisher, May 29, 1988, folder 230, Box 18, Series II, Correspondence, Child Papers, Schlesinger Library.

160. See range of correspondence (with specific examples cited) in folder 121, Box 10, Series II, Correspondence, Child Papers, Schlesinger Library.

161. Shapiro, *Julia Child*, 159–60.

162. Shapiro, *Julia Child*, 165.

163. Shapiro, *Julia Child*, 79.

164. Marion Nestle, *Slow Cooked: An Unexpected Life in Food Politics* (Oakland: University of California Press, 2022), 136.

165. Child to Fisher, Sept. 3, 1977, folder 226, Box 18, Series II, Correspondence, Child Papers, Schlesinger Library; Child, *Julia Child and Company*, 51, 53.

166. Child letter to the editor, *Time*, Mar. 2, 1987, folder 132, Box 11, Series II, Correspondence, Child Papers, Schlesinger Library. On her July 1990 appearance on *The Late Night Show with David Letterman*, she reiterated the idea that gastronomy was a real discipline and that people should be able to get degrees in just like any other course of study; she made this assertion as she explained to Letterman why she was a founding member of the American Institute for Food and Wine. Letterman appearances available on Youtube in 2020.

Chapter 4

1. Frances Moore Lappé, *Diet for a Small Planet*, rev. ed., illustrated by Kathleen Zimmerman and Ralph Iwamoto (New York: Ballantine Books, 1975), 16. Most of Lappé's books have concerned food in some respect, but not all. Other single authored books by Lappé include the following: *Daring Democracy: Igniting Power, Meaning, and Connection for the America We Want* (Boston: Beacon Press, 2017); *Democracy's Edge: Choosing to Save Our Country by Bringing Democracy to Life* (San Francisco: Wiley, 2006); *EcoMind: Changing the Way We Think, to Create the World We Want* (New York: Nation Books, 2011); *Getting a Grip^2 Clarity, Creativity and Courage for the World We Really Want*, rev. ed. (Cambridge, MA: Small Planet Media, 2010); *Liberation Ecology: Reframing Six Disempowering Ideas That Keep Us From Aligning with Nature—Even Our Own* (Cambridge, MA: Small Planet Media, 2009); *Rediscovering America's Values: A Dialogue That Explores Our Fundamental Beliefs and How They Offer Hope for America's Future* (New York: Ballantine Books, 1989); *What to Do After You Turn Off the TV: Fresh Ideas for Enjoying Family Time* (New York: Ballantine Books, 1985). Her Coauthored books are the following: Lappé, Joseph Collins, and David Kinley, *Aid As Obstacle: Twenty Questions About Our Foreign Aid and the Hungry* (Oakland, CA: Institute for Food and Development Policy, 1980); Lappé, Rachel Shurman, and Kevin Danaher, *Betraying the National Interest* (New York: Grove Press, A Food First Books, 1987); Lappé and Joseph Collins, with Cary Fowler, *Food First: Beyond the Myth of Scarcity*, rev. ed. (New York: Ballantine Books, 1978); Lappé and Ellen Buchman Ewald, *Great Meatless Meals* (New York: Ballantine Books, 1974); Lappé and Anna Lappé, *Hope's Edge: The Next*

Diet for a Small Planet (New York: Penguin Putnam, Inc., 2002); Lappé and Adele Beccar-Varela, *Mozambique and Tanzania: Asking the Big Question* (Oakland, CA: Institute for Food and Development Policy, 1982); Lappé, Joseph Collins, and Paul Rice, *Nicaragua: What Difference Could a Revolution Make?* (New York: Grove Press, 1986); Lappé and Joseph Collins, *Now We Can Speak: A Journey Through the New Nicaragua* (Oakland. CA: Food First Books, 1982); Lappé and Paul Martin Du Bois, *The Quickening of America: Rebuilding Our Nation, Remaking Our Lives,* (San Francisco: Jossey-Bass, 1994); Lappé and Rachel Schurman, *Taking Population Seriously* (published first as *Food First Development Report 4, September 1988: The Missing Piece in the Population Puzzle*) (San Francisco: A Food First Book, The Institute for Food and Policy Development, 1988, 1990); Lappé, Joseph Collins, Peter Rosset, with Luis Esparza, *World Hunger: Twelve Myths,*. 2nd ed. (New York: Grove Press, 1998); Lappé and Jeffrey Perkins, *You Have the Power: Choosing Courage in a Culture of Fear* (New York: TarcherPerigee, 2005).

2. For overviews of these nineteenth and twentieth century developments, see Steven Stoll, *Larding the Lean Earth: Soil and Society in Nineteenth-Century America* (New York: Hill and Wang, 2003); Bruce Gardner, *American Agriculture in the Twentieth Century: How It Flourished and What It Cost* (Cambridge, MA: Harvard University Press, 2002); Deborah Fitzgerald, *Every Farm a Factory: The Industrial Ideal in American Agriculture* (New Haven, CT: Yale University Press, 2003).

3. McDonald, *Food Power*, 23.

4. For a discussion of how these structural weaknesses in plains agriculture contributed to the Depression, see Donald Worster, *Dust Bowl: The Southern Plains in the 1930s*, 25th anniversary edition (New York: Oxford University Press, 2004).

5. For an overview of these issues and background on this statistic, see Levenstein, *Paradox of Plenty*, chapter 4.

6. In addition to the specific notes that follow, information from this section comes from Amy Bentley, *Eating for Victory: Food Rationing and the Politics of Domesticity* (Urbana: University of Illinois Press, 1998), 92–115; Levenstein, *Paradox of Plenty*, 81–93; McDonald, *Food Power*, 25–28.

7. Levenstein also wrote that most of the meat given to soldiers was beef; daily rations were 10 ounces of beef, 4 ounces of pork, 2 ounces of chicken, and 2 ounces of bacon. Levenstein, *Paradox of Plenty*, 89, 93.

8. Bentley, *Eating for Victory*, 92–93; McDonald, *Food Power*, 26.

9. Levenstein, *Paradox of Plenty*, 96.

10. McDonald, *Food Power*, 26.

11. Bentley, *Eating for Victory*, 152.

12. Bentley, *Eating for Victory*, 164; Levenstein, *Paradox of Plenty*, 96.

13. Sample posters and planning for the campaign are found in Blue Boxes I and II, and other posters, radio scripts, and campaign plans, are in Boxes 2, 5–9, Citizens Food Committee Program (1947), NAL.

14. Poster, Box 5, Citizens Food Committee Program (1947), NAL.

15. McDonald, *Food Power*, 12.

16. Nick Cullather, *The Hungry World: America's Cold War Battle against Poverty in Asia* (Cambridge, MA: Harvard University Press, 2010), 103; Gardner, *American Agriculture*, 51; Marty Strange, *Family Farming: A New Economic Vision* (Lincoln: University of Nebraska Press, 1988), 2.

17. Bill Winders, *The Politics of Food Supply: U.S. Agricultural Policy in the World Economy* (New Haven, CT: Yale University Press, 2009), 9.

18. Cullather, *Hungry World,* 5; Sarah Phillips, "The Price of Plenty: Getting Farm Policy Right in the 1960s," *Journal of American History* 109 (3) (Dec. 2022): 597.

19. Raymond Moley, "The Tyranny of Plenty," *Newsweek,* Aug. 30, 1954, 80; "The Golden Glut," *Time,* Aug. 10, 1953, 20.

20. Phillips, "Price of Plenty," 597.

21. For more detail on the Bannan Plan and the reasons for its failure, see Winders, *Politics of Food Supply,* 83–84. For discussions on agricultural policy debates more generally, see McDonald, *Food Power,* 81–161, and specific citations below.

22. Levenstein, *Paradox of Plenty,* 144, 148. Despite the expansion of food programs in the 1960s, hunger has remained a serious issue in the United States through the first decades of the twenty-first century, when the problem was exacerbated by growing inequality. For further discussion of continuing hunger and food insecurity, see Joel Berg, *All You Can Eat: How Hungry Is America?* (New York: Seven Stories Press, 2008).

23. McDonald, *Food Power,* 135; also, 138–41.

24. Winders, *Politics of Food Supply,* 8.

25. McDonald, *Food Power,* 96–97; see also Levenstein, *Paradox of Plenty,* 145.

26. McDonald, *Food Power,* 143–44, 152–53; Levenstein, *Paradox of Plenty,* 145.

27. Hamilton, *Supermarket USA.*

28. The Green Revolution has been written about by a number of historians, as well as by observers who have criticized its social and economic impact in Third World countries. For an introduction to the topic and a sample of criticism, see Cullather, *Hungry World*; David Kinkela, *DDT & the American Century: Global Health, Environmental Politics, and the Pesticide That Changed the World* (Chapel Hill: University of North Carolina Press, 2011); Vandana Shiva, *The Violence of the Green Revolution: Third World Agriculture, Ecology and Politics* (London and New Jersey: Zed Books, Ltd. And Penang, Malaysia: Third World Network, 1991); John H. Perkins, *Geopolitics and the Green Revolution; Wheat, Genes, and the Cold War* (New York: Oxford University Press, 1997); Marci Baranski, *The Globalization of Wheat: A Critical History of the Green Revolution* (Pittsburgh: University of Pittsburgh Press, 2022); and Charles Mann, *The Wizard and the Prophet: Two Remarkable Scientists and Their Dueling Visions to Shape Tomorrow's World* (New York: Knopf, 2018).

29. For example, Charles Mann observed that, in the 1970s, the UN Research Institute for Social Development completed fifteen analyses of the Green Revolution, all of which were strongly negative; meanwhile, from 1970 to 1989, there were more than three hundred academic studies of the Green Revolution, four out of five of which were negative. *Wizard and the Prophet,* 437.

30. Baranski, *Globalization of Wheat,* 10.

31. Enrique Ochoa, "Political Histories of Food," in Jeffrey Pilcher, ed., *The Oxford Handbook of Food History* (New York: Oxford University Press, 2012), 30.

32. For a discussion of the impact on one Florida community of producing "cheap" food, see Dale Finley Slongwhite, *Fed Up: The High Costs of Cheap Food* (Gainesville: University Press of Florida, 2014).

33. Vandana Shiva, *Who Really Feeds the World? The Failures of Agribusiness and the Promise of Agroecology* (Berkeley: North Atlantic Books, 2016), 87.

34. McDonald, *Food Power,* 51–54.

35. Cohen, *A Consumers' Republic*, 367–68.

36. Memo Freeman to President, Oct. 29, 1965, folder Food Aug 7-Nov 4, 1965, Box 4299, 1965, General Correspondence, 1906–1976, RG 16, NARA II.

37. Memo, Harold Lewis, Director of Information USDA, to Secretary, George Mehren, Rod Leonard, Jan. 27, 1965, folder Food Jan 1–Mar. 18, 1965, Box 4299 1965; Memo, George Mehren, Assistant Secretary to Secretary and Under Secretary, July 6, 1964, Folder Food Jan. 1–June 20, 1964, Box 4124 1964; see also Memo Trienah Meyers, Deputy Assistant Secretary to Secretary, Nov. 19, 1964, Folder Food Jan.–June 20, 1964, Box 4124 1964, General Correspondence, 1906–1976, RG 16, NARA II.

38. Freeman to Kathryn Faller, Feb. 20, 1962, Folder Food, Box 3768 1962, General Correspondence, 1906–1976, RG 16, NARA II.

39. Paul and Anne Ehrlich, *The Population Bomb* (Berkeley, CA: Sierra Club, 1968). The book went into several printings and subsequent editions. This controversial book was often criticized for its thesis that population alone was responsible for so many problems. It also became central to the debate about the impact of humans on the earth's mineral and other resources, not just food. Ehrlich founded the group Zero Population Growth to advocate for a radical reversal in current trends. In contrast to his views, others argued that humans could adopt technological solutions to accommodate and pay for the needs of a growing population. For an example of this debate between Ehrlich and an economist and business professor, see Paul Sabin, *The Bet: Paul Ehrlich, Julian Simon, and Our Gamble over Earth's Future* (New Haven, CT: Yale University Press, 2013).

40. Memo, Administrator ARS to N.C. Brady, Director of Science and Education, May 11, 1965, Folder Nutrition, Box 4344 1965, General Correspondence, 1906–1976, RG 16, NARA II.

41. Lappé, *Diet for a Small Planet*, 8, 10.

42. Lappé, *Diet for a Small Planet*, 16.

43. Lappé was part of a global conversation about world hunger and the increase of meat consumption, especially with the book she co-authored in 1977: Lappé and Collins, with Fowler, *Food First*. See Charles Hardin, "Feeding the World: Conflicting Views on Policy, Review Essay," *Agricultural History* (Oct. 1979): 787–95. See also the discussion of the world food issue in the *New York Times*, Ann Crittenden, "World Hunger Is Exacting High Human Toll," Aug. 17, 1981, and "Consumption of Meat Rising in the Developing Countries," Aug. 25, 1981.

44. Lappé, *Diet for a Small Planet*, see examples on 78, 128–29, 135.

45. Lappé, *Diet for a Small Planet*, 142.

46. Lappé, *Diet for a Small Planet*, 153, 154–55.

47. Freedman lumped Lappé in with others who advocated for health foods in the 1970s, arguing that they "eschewed pleasure in favor of a restricted and unattractive list of approved foods." Freedman, *American Cuisine and How It Got This Way*, 314. Jonathan Kauffman labeled the recipes in *Diet for a Small Planet* "sturdy fare." Kauffman also discussed the evolution of the book and Lappé's collaboration with Ellen Buchman Ewald to quickly create recipes that were vegetarian and "protein-boosted." *Hippie Food: How Back-to-the-Landers, Longhairs, and Revolutionaries Changed the Way We Eat* (New York: William Morrow, 2018), 136–41.

48. Lappé, *Diet for a Small Planet*, 298.

49. All from *Cosmopolitan:* Jane Wilson, "Cosmo Girl's Guide to Vegetarianism," Sept.

1972, 200–203ff.; Maya Pines, "What Vegetarianism Can Do for You!" Nov. 1975, 178–82ff.; Ellen Roddick, "Dieter's Notebook," May 1977, 92–93; Gary Selden, "The Virtues of Vegetarianism," May 1980, 136ff.

50. Wilson, "Cosmo Girl's Guide," 202; Pines, "What Vegetarianism Can Do," 180; Roddick, "Dieter's Notebook," 93; Paula Heil, "How to Be Frugal Without Being Cheap," *Cosmopolitan*, Nov. 1980, 102.

51. Selden, "Virtues of Vegetarianism," 138.

52. Pines, "What Vegetarianism Can Do," 180.

53. Peggy Hutchinson, "In My Opinion: Eating Vegetarian is Better!" *Seventeen*, Dec. 1975, 52.

54. Eliza Dinwiddie-Boyd, "Raising Vegetarians: Vegetarian Meals are the Smart Choice for Families Concerned with Health and Well-Being," *Essence*, May 1992, 146, 148.

55. For example, "What You Should Know About Protein," *Chatelaine*, Jan. 1982, 26, 28; Rowena Eloise, "Protein Deficiency and the Essential Amino Acid Connection," *Natural Life*, July/Aug. 1998.

56. Raymond Sokolov, "Tofu or Not Tofu," *Natural History*, Dec. 1985, 86. See also Margaret Sheridan, "Soy Talk with Father Tofu," *Los Angeles Times*, Sept. 26, 1996, 10. And in other contexts, references to Lappé as the vegetarian authority can be found, for example, Christina McCarroll, *The Christian Science Monitor*, Jan. 2, 2002, 20; Cindy France, "Vegetarian," *Camping Magazine*, May/June 1997, 26–28; Kit Paraventi, "Unsung Heroes: Hillary Morris," *The Animals' Agenda*, Mar./Apr. 1998, 18.

57. Mary Fisher, *Midwifery Today*, Dec. 31, 1999, 30.

58. Wayne Roberts, "Green Eggs and Ham: The Often Embraced Environmental Arguments against Meat Has More Holes than Swiss Cheese," *Alternatives Journal* (Spring 2002): 13–14; and Jim Motavalli, "Across the Great Divide: Do Real Greens Eat Meat," 34–39, and "Case Against," 26–32, *Environmental Magazine*, Jan./Feb. 2002.

59. Adam Shprintzen, *The Vegetarian Crusade: The Rise of an American Reform Movement, 1817–1921* (Chapel Hill: University of North Carolina Press, 2013).

60. Shprintzen, *Vegetarian Crusade*, 6.

61. Shprintzen, *Vegetarian Crusade*, 5–8, 208, 210, 211.

62. Horowitz, *Putting Meat on the American Table*, 152.

63. Horowitz, *Putting Meat on the Table*, 13–44, see also 44–69 for the changing place of pork. For more on the changing place of pork and efforts to adapt pork to a changing marketplace, see J. L. Anderson, "Lard to Lean: Making the Meat-Type Hog in Post-World War II America," in *Food Chains: From Farmyard to Shopping Cart*, ed. Warren Belasco and Roger Horowitz (Philadelphia: University of Pennsylvania Press, 2009), 29–46.

64. Anderson observed that pork suffered from the trend away from animal fats, such as lard and tallow, for cooking and the increased publicity regarding the health effects of eating too much animal fat. Pork producers attempted a memorable ad campaign beginning in 1987, the "other white meat," to highlight how pork compared with chicken. The advertising campaign notwithstanding, a number of critics judged that the lower-fat pork did not always taste as good as the earlier breeds. Anderson, "Lard to Lean," 32, 41–44.

65. Horowitz, *Putting Meat on the Table*, 18. Historian Joshua Specht examined the creation of the modern industrialized beef market, based in part on the unique desirability of this particular meat. *Red Meat Republic: A Hoof-to-Table History of How Beef Changed America* (Princeton, NJ: Princeton University Press, 2019).

66. Belasco, *Meals to Come*, 3.

67. Jonathan Safran Foer, *Eating Animals* (New York: Little Brown, 2009), 137; Horowitz, *Putting Meat on the Table*, 152. For more on the rise of chicken eating and the rise of the chicken industry in the United States, see Steve Striffler, *Chicken: The Dangerous Transformation of America's Favorite Food* (New Haven, CT: Yale University Press, 2005), and Maryn McKenna, *Big Chicken: The Incredible Story of How Antibiotics Created Modern Agriculture and Changed the Way the World Eats* (Washington, DC: National Geographic, 2017).

68. Of such activists, Sylvia Lovegren wrote: "as long as the food they were eating was prepared with 'natural' ingredients and was full of nutrients, what it tasted like didn't really matter." Lovegren, *Fashionable Food*, 260. Mollie Katzen, *The Moosewood Cookbook* (Berkeley, CA: Ten Speed, 1977). We will return to a more in-depth discussion of food and the countercultural movement in the chapter on Alice Waters.

69. The world food crisis has been discussed by many historians. A good summary is found in McDonald, *Food Power*, 162–84, and Joel Solkoff, *The Politics of Food: The Decline of Agriculture and the Rise of Agribusiness in America* (San Francisco: Sierra Club Books, 1985, 40–73).

70. Cohen, *A Consumers' Republic*, 369, and Solkoff, *Politics of Food*, 57. A year before these price increases, Secretary of Agriculture Earl Butz bragged that the percentage of income that Americans spent on food would fall below 16 percent that year, possibly to 15.6 percent, an all-time low. Robert Choate to Richard Lying, Assistant Secretary of Agriculture, Feb. 18, 1972, folder Food, Jan 1 to Dec 31, 1972, Box 5566, General Correspondence, RG 16, NARA II.

71. Solkoff, *Politics of Food*, 40–41.

72. Solkoff, *Politics of Food*, 73.

73. Winders, *Politics of Food Supply*, 136, 155.

74. Lappé and Collins with Fowler, *Food First*, for this paragraph, see esp. 8, 9, 13, 112–14, 42–43, 225, 240, 152, 156–57, 171, 271.

75. Lappé, *Rediscovering America's Values*, xvi.

76. Lappé, *EcoMind*, 110.

77. A sample of articles include the following: from *Sojourners*, with Paul Martin Du Bois, "The Renewal of Citizen Politics," Oct. 1990, 17–18; "Democracy's Lifeblood," Nov./Dec. 1995, 40–44; "The Shortage Isn't Food, It's Democracy," July 2005, 16–18; from *Mother Earth News*, with Anna Moore Lappé, "The Genius of Wangari Maathai," Apr./May 2005, 20–21; from *Tikkun*, with Peter Rosset and Joseph Collins, "Lessons from the Green Revolution," 15, (2): 52–56; "Heart-Centered Realism," Jan./Feb. 2008, 26–31.

78. "Fantasies of Famine: The Case for Modest Optimism about a Man-Made Disaster," *Harper's*, Feb. 2003, 51–54ff.; "Farming for a Small Planet: Agroecology Now," *Development*, Dec. 2016, 299–307.

79. For example, Dorothy Friesen, "Food First: Creating Scarcity Out of Plenty," *Sojourners*, July 1978, 35–37; "Real Food Revival," *Mother Earth News*, June/July 2002, 1; Nancy Jo Hoy, "We All Need a Public Life: An Interview with Frances Moore Lappé," *The Literary Review*, Sept. 2004, 92–98; David Marchese, "Talk: She Changed the Way We Eat; She Wants to Fix Our Democracy, Too," *New York Times Magazine*, Dec. 22, 2019, 13–15.

80. Hoy, "We All Need a Public Life," 92.

81. Peter Singer, *Animal Liberation: A New Ethics for Our Treatment of Animals* (New York: Avon Books, 1975). Singer and a coauthor followed this up five years later with Jim Mason and Peter Singer, *Animal Factories* (New York: Crown, 1980).

82. Singer, *Animal Liberation*, 183.

83. Singer, *Animal Liberation*, 170.

84. In subsequent years, other authors and animal-rights activists would also publish graphic evidence of the cruelty of factory farms. See, for example, a book with extensive photos and text, Daniel Imhoff, ed., *CAFO (Concentrated Animal Feeding Operation): The Tragedy of Industrial Animal Factories* (San Rafael, CA: Earth Aware, 2010).

85. Mason and Singer, *Animal Factories*, 116–17.

86. Mason and Singer, *Animal Factories*, 133.

87. Peter Singer and Jim Mason, *The Way We Eat: Why Our Food Choices Matter* (Emmaus, PA: Rodale, 2006); for this paragraph, see esp. 15, 83, 90, 101–10, 116, 133, 187–90, 248, 250, 271, 275, 276, 278.

88. Singer and Mason, *The Way We Eat*, 3.

89. James McWilliams, *The Modern Savage: Our Unthinking Decision to Eat Animals* (New York: St. Martin's, 2015); for this paragraph, see esp. 1, 14–15, 41, 53.

90. Imhoff is the author of several books, including *CAFO.* Dan Imhoff, oral history, Apr. 14, 2011, Fales Library.

91. Foer, *Eating Animals*, and *We Are the Weather: Saving the Planet Begins at Breakfast* (New York: Farrar, Straus and Giroux, 2019). Foer also wrote various essays in the press summarizing some of his arguments, including ones that made the issues more urgent during the COVID pandemic, which began in 2020; see, for example, Jonathan Safran Foer, "The End of Meat Is Here," *New York Times*, May 21, 2020.

92. Foer, *Eating Animals*, 263.

93. Foer, *Eating Animals*, 196; see also 194–95.

94. Foer, *Eating Animals*, 258, 261.

95. Foer, *Eating Animals*, 55. An example of a different view is found in Sandor Katz, who wrote about the importance of striving for "humane meat." Sandor Ellix Katz, *The Revolution Will Not Be Microwaved: Inside America's Underground Food Movements* (White River Junction, VT: Chelsea Green, 2006), 255–56.

96. Foer, *We Are the Weather*, 71.

97. Foer, *We Are the Weather*, 65, 71.

98. Jillian Kubala, "What is the Impossible Burger, and Is It Healthy?" May 4, 2020, healthline.com; Tiffany Hopkins, "The Best Plant-Based Burgers You Can Buy at the Store," Jan. 8, 2020, Epicurious.com; Bee Wilson, "Are You Ready to Eat Meat Grown in a Lab?" Review of *Billion Dollar Burger: Inside Big Tech's Race for the Future of Food* by Chase Purdy, *New York Times*, June 16, 2020. For a consideration of older efforts to "create meat," see Warren Belasco, "Algae Burgers for a Hungry World? The Rise and Fall of Chlorella Cuisine," *Technology and Culture*, July 1997, 608–34.

99. "Impossible Burger has 89% Smaller Carbon Footprint than Beef," Future VU: Sustainability, Mar. 29, 2019, Vanderbilt University, Vanderbilt.edu.

100. Emma Newburger, "As the Lab-Grown Meat Industry Grows, Scientists Debate If It Could Exacerbate Climate Change," Oct. 19, 2019, cnbc.com. For more on the philosophical and other debates around "cultured meat," see Benjamin Aldes Wurgaft, *Meat Planet: Artificial Flesh and the Future of Food* (Oakland: University of California Press, 2019).

Chapter 5

1. Julie Creswell, "The Question of Authority: Chewing Out the Food Industry," *Fortune*,

Feb. 25, 2002, folder 2, Articles in Magazines (4 of 5), 2002–2004, Box 51, Series VII, Subseries A, Marion Nestle Papers, 1970–2017, Fales Library.

2. Email Ellen J. Fried to Nestle 11 May 2011, folder 4, Box 75; Danny Meyer to Nestle, 16 January 2011, folder 4, Box 75; anecdote about NYC initiative, folder 7, Box 74. For other examples, see correspondence folders in Boxes 72–75, Series VII, Subseries E, Nestle Papers, Fales Library.

3. Marion Nestle, *What to Eat* (New York: North Point, 2006), 8.

4. Nestle's detailed curriculum vitae can be found at foodpolitics.com, along with Nestle's active, almost daily blog and other information about her writing, work, and background. Many details about Nestle's personal background and professional career are also summarized in her memoir, *Slow Cooked.*

5. "Word of Mouth," *Cooking Light: The Magazine of Food and Fitness*, May 1999, 94–95, folder 1, Articles in Magazines [3 of 5], Box 51, Series VII, Subseries A, Nestle Papers, Fales Library.

6. Nestle, *Slow Cooked*, 231.

7. Marion Nestle, *Food Politics: How the Food Industry Influences Nutrition and Health* (Berkeley: University of California Press, 2002). New editions of this book appeared in 2007 and 2013.

8. *Safe Food: Bacteria, Biotechnology, and Bioterrorism* (Berkeley: University of California Press, 2003); *What to Eat; Pet Food Politics: The Chihuahua in the Coal Mine* (Berkeley: University of California Press, 2008); with Malden Nesheim, *Feed Your Pet Right* (New York: Free Press/Simon and Schuster, 2010); with Malden Nesheim, *Why Calories Count: From Science to Politics* (Berkeley: University of California Press, 2012); *Eat, Drink, Vote: An Illustrated Guide to Food Politics* (Emmaus, PA: Rodale Books, 2013); *Soda Politics: Taking on Big Soda (and Winning)* (New York: Oxford University Press, 2015); *Unsavory Truth: How Food Companies Skew the Science of What We Eat* (New York: Basic Books, 2018); with Kerry Trueman, *Let's Ask Marion: What You Need to Know About the Politics of Food, Nutrition, and Health* (Oakland: University of California Press, 2020); *Slow Cooked.* Other publications include the following: *Nutrition in Clinical Practice* (Greenbrae, CA: Jones Medical Publications, 1985); as managing editor, *The Surgeon General's Report on Nutrition and Health* (Washington, DC: Department of Health and Human Services, 1988); coeditor, with l. Beth Dixon, *Taking Sides: Controversial Issues in Food and Nutrition* (New York: McGraw Hill, 2004); coeditor, with Simon N. Williams, *Big Food: Critical Perspectives on the Global Growth of the Food and Beverage Industry* (New York: Routledge, 2016).

9. The dense and lengthy *Surgeon General's Report* was more than seven hundred pages long, divided into nineteen chapters, and covered many topics ranging from heart disease to cancer to infections and immunity to aging. The advisors, editors, contributors, and reviewers of the report ran twenty-three pages, with Marion Nestle in the Office of Disease Prevention and Health Promotion in the Department of Human Services as the managing editor. The report amassed evidence in support of the existing Dietary Guidelines for Americans as jointly put forward by the Departments of Health and Human Services and Agriculture. The conclusions of the report were a familiar restatement of long-standing nutritional advice: "The recommendations in this Report promote a dietary pattern that emphasizes consumption of vegetables, fruits, and whole grain products—foods that are rich in complex carbohydrates and fiber and relatively low in calories—and of fish, poultry prepared without skin, lean meats, and low-fat dairy products selected to minimize

consumption of total fat, saturated fat, and cholesterol." *The Surgeon General's Report on Nutrition and Health*, 9.

10. Nestle to Kathleen O'Malley, Oct. 28, 1991, folder 2, Correspondence, Box 72, Series VII, Subseries E, Nestle Papers, Fales Library.

11. Nutritionists were one branch of the broader home economics field dominated by women in the twentieth century. For an overview of the field's evolution, see Elias, *Stir It Up*.

12. Nestle, *Food Politics*, 33–34; Nestle and Nesheim, *Why Calories Count*, 26–36.

13. Nestle and Nesheim, *Why Calories Count*, 27.

14. Nestle, *Food Politics*, 34–35.

15. McDonald, *Food Power*, 58–59.

16. For discussion of this shift, see Cohen, *A Consumers' Republic*.

17. Cross and Proctor, *Packaged Pleasures*, 242, 243, 249.

18. Cross and Proctor, *Packaged Pleasures*, 272.

19. Others also critiqued the consumerist approach to food that predominated from the mid-twentieth century onward. For example, see Ruhlman, *Grocery*.

20. Nestle, *Food Politics*, for the quotations that follow in this paragraph, see esp. 12, 9, 1, 3.

21. Nestle, *Slow Cooked*, 1.

22. For this discussion, see Nestle, *Food Politics*, 40–42.

23. See, for example, discussion in Mudry, *Measured Meals*, 77–78.

24. Nestle, *Food Politics*, 43.

25. The various departments of the USDA translated reports into accessible guidelines, including ones meant to teach Americans how to make affordable meal plans. For example, in the file Food Plans, 1970–1975, the following was included: "Your Money's Worth in Foods, January 1974," "Family Food Budgeting for Good Meals and Nutrition, 1964, 1971," in Food Plans 1976–1978, "Food for Thrifty Families, 1978," "Your Money's Worth in Foods, 1977," folder Food Plans 1970-1975, folder Food Plans 1975-1976, folder Food Plans 1976-1978, Box 1. There were also several reports indicating that USDA nutritionists were particularly concerned about low-income families getting adequate nutrition. See "Recommended Dietary Allowances as Standards for Diets of the Low-Income Population," folder Dietary Guidelines 1980–1981, and "Recommended Dietary Allowances as Standards for Family Food Plans" in folder Dietary Guidelines 1982–1983, Box 4, Records Relating to Family Food Plans, Nutrition Education Division, RG 310, NARA II.

26. Mudry, *Measured Meals*, 77.

27. Secretary of Agriculture Edward Madigan was defensive about the revisions from an earlier version of the pyramid to the final one, indicating that this department was driven by science. See Statement, Madigan on the Food Guide Pyramid, Apr. 28, 1992, folder 2, Box 1, Speeches and Statements of Agriculture Secretary Edward Madigan, 1991–1993, Office of the Secretary, RG 16, NARA II.

28. Nestle, *Food Politics*, 67, 91; see also 51–91.

29. For samples of government guidelines and booklets, see "Nutrition and Health, Dietary Guidelines for Americans" (Feb. 1980) and 3rd ed., Nov. 1990, Leaflets for Good Nutrition; for a report on changing USDA nutritional advice, see Susan Welsh, Carole Davis, Frances Cronin, Nutrition Education Division, Human Nutrition Service, USDA, "Background Paper on the Dietary Guidelines for Americans—USDA Perspective," 1988, Bureau of Human Nutrition Information Service Records, unprocessed, NAL. In addition to

pamphlets, the US government conveyed nutritional guidance in posters that addressed a variety of topics, including infant nutrition, exercise and nutrition, and budgeting and nutrition. See files, Posters to Promote Healthful Eating (1980–1990), Posters Providing Food and Nutrition Guidelines (1996–2006), Eat Smart, Play Hard (2001–2004), Team Nutrition Posters (1995–2005), RG 462, NARA II.

30. Interview with Marion Nestle, *Eating Well: The Magazine of Food and Health*, Summer 2000, 17, folder 10, Articles in Magazines, Box 50, Series VII, Subseries A, Nestle Papers, Fales Library.

31. Nestle comment in Steinhardt School of Education (NYU) Newsletter, n.d. (probably early 2005), folder 3 Correspondence, Box 73, Series VII, Subseries E, Nestle Papers, Fales Library.

32. Nestle, *Food Politics*, 111.

33. Nestle, *Unsavory Truth*, for this paragraph, see esp. 11, 81, 85–87, 71, 147–48, 31–32.

34. Levenstein, *Paradox of Plenty*, 188–89. Stare was well known as a nutritional authority in the public culture, giving interviews and answering questions in newspapers. For a sample, see Frederick Stare and Mary B McCann, "Nutritional Quiz on Protein, Iron, and Wheat Germ," *Philadelphia Inquirer*, Nov. 10, 1960, 16.

35. Nestle, *Unsavory Truth*, 111–12, 193–95.

36. Nestle, *Unsavory Truth*, 205.

37. Nestle, *Unsavory Truth*, 9.

38. Nestle, *Slow Cooked*, 134.

39. Nestle, *Unsavory Truth*, 6, 132.

40. Nestle, *Slow Cooked*, 228.

41. Nestle, *Food Politics*, 200. Other scholars provided more in-depth studies on the nutritional inadequacies of school lunch programs, how they were implemented, and how they changed from the Type A meal recommended by Hazel Stiebeling to fast food dominated, a la carte offerings. See Poppendieck, *Free for All.*

42. Nestle, *Soda Politics*, for this paragraph, see esp. 103, 13, 37, 77, 253, also 64–82.

43. Sidney Mintz, *Sweetness and Power: The Place of Sugar in Modern History* (New York: Penguin, 1985), esp. 208–9.

44. Gary Taubes, *The Case against Sugar* (New York: Knopf, 2016), 153; also, Gary Taubes, *Good Calories, Bad Calories: Fats, Carbs, and the Controversial Science of Diet and Health* (New York: Anchor Books, 2007, 2008).

45. Nestle, *Soda Politics*, for this paragraph, see esp. 54–57, 170, 211–21, 343–45, 362–69.

46. Statistics on obesity can be found in many sources. These are taken from Warren Belasco, *Food: The Key Concepts* (New York: Oxford University Press, 2008), 88–89; slightly different figures are cited by Marion Nestle, and the ones from 2007–8 cited above are taken from her: Marion Nestle, *Why Calories Count*, 141–42.

47. Levenstein, *Paradox of Plenty*, 202–3.

48. Nestle, *Slow Cooked*, 17–18.

49. Nestle and Nesheim, *Why Calories Count*, for this paragraph, see esp. 1, 17, 27.

50. See Cullather, *Hungry World*, and Mudry, *Measured Meals.*

51. Mudry, *Measured Meals*, 3.

52. Nestle and Nesheim, *Why Calories Count*, 28–29, 3, 79.

53. Nestle and Nesheim, *Why Calories Count*, for this paragraph, see esp. 121, 139–42, 183–84, 154, 220.

54. In *Food Politics*, Nestle summarized the increase of available calories for Americans from 3,200 per capita per day in 1970 to 3,900 in the late 1990s. Nestle, *Food Politics*, 8.

55. Nestle, *What to Eat*, 285.

56. A sample article summarizing the common media discussion is Joseph P. Williams, "The Great Body-Acceptance Debate: A Battle Over the Perils of Obesity Is Playing Out in Pop Culture and the Medical Community," *U.S. News and World Report*, Feb. 3, 2020.

57. Veit, *Modern Food, Moral Food*, esp. 158–76. Harvey Levenstein also summarizes the changing standards for female beauty in the early twentieth century in *Revolution at the Table*, 165–66.

58. One summary of these ideals is in Belasco, *Food*, 91–93.

59. Weight Watchers International, Inc., begun in 1963, illustrated this phenomenon over many decades. See Smith, *Eating History*, 245–54.

60. Julie Guthman, *Weighing In: Obesity, Food Justice, and the Limits of Capitalism* (Berkeley: University of California Press, 2011), esp. 188.

61. Guthman, *Weighing In*, 18, see also 17–22, 128. This ideological imperative for individuals to achieve good health through their own behaviors Guthman dubbed "healthism" (47, 191, 194).

62. Guthman and others furthermore argued that the dividing lines between categories of overweight and obese became consequential in health discourse, even if only separated by one digit, and that the changing mean BMI numbers might mask a skewed distribution of weight, thus overdramatizing a national epidemic. Guthman, *Weighing In*, 28, see also 27–31, 98.

63. Charlotte Biltekoff, "Critical Nutrition Studies," in Pilcher ed., *Oxford Handbook of Food History*, 173–74, see also 184. See also Biltekoff, *Eating Right*.

64. Guthman, *Weighing In*, 92, 100–112, 99.

65. Nestle and Nesheim, *Why Calories Count*, 2.

66. Nestle and Nesheim, *Why Calories Count*, 218, 226.

67. Marion Nestle and Kelly Brownell, con position in "Are You Responsible for Your Own Weight," in cover story "Overcoming Obesity in America," *Time*, June 7, 2004, folder 10 Articles in Magazines, Box 50, Series VII, Subseries A, Nestle Papers, Fales Library.

68. Nestle, *Slow Cooked*, 164.

69. Nestle and Nesheim, *Why Calories Count*, 6–7, 183. See also Nestle, *Food Politics*, 9. For more on the cultural evolution of the "meal" in the United States, as well as changes in snacking in the late twentieth century, see Abigail Carroll, *Three Squares: The Invention of the American Meal* (New York: Basic Books, 2013).

70. Nestle, *Soda Politics*, 108.

71. Nestle and Nesheim, *Why Calories Count*, 178–79.

72. Guthman, *Weighing In*, 94.

73. Nestle and Nesheim, *Why Calories Count*, 138, 154.

74. Guthman, *Weighing In*, 111.

75. Nestle, *Soda Politics*, 11–16; Nestle and Nesheim, *Why Calories Count*, 172.

76. Nestle, *What to Eat*, 414–15.

77. Nestle and Trueman, *Let's Ask Marion*, 73.

78. Nestle and Nesheim, *Why Calories Count*, 161–62.

79. Ancel Keys and Margaret Keys, foreword by Paul Dudley White, MD, *Eat Well & Stay Well* (Garden City, NY: Doubleday, 1959).

80. Keys and Keys, *Eat Well & Stay Well*, 14–15, 17–18, 40, 53, 60. Less familiar to

modern ears was such advice as "Be sensible about cigarettes, alcohol, excitement, business strain." While the Keys focused on dietary fat and its health consequences, there were other nutritionists who were focusing more broadly on the connection between diet and long-term health. Adelle Davis, for example, who worked as a dietician in New York City, wrote several books including *Let's Keep Right to Keep Fit* (1954), which told readers to focus on the quality of food in a balanced diet and became known on television and radio presenting the outlines of a good diet. Levenstein, *Paradox of Plenty*, 164–65.

81. Memo, B. T. Shaw to F. J. Welsh, Assistant Secretary, Jan. 27, 1961, folder Nutrition, Box 3634, National Defense 6 Emergency Stockpiling, General Correspondence 1906–1976, RG 16, NARA II.

82. Taubes wrote that Keys "deserves the lion's share of credit for convincing us that cholesterol levels predict heart disease and that dietary fat is a killer." Taubes, *Good Calories, Bad Calories*, for this paragraph, see esp. 16, 9, 19, 21, 24, 44–45, 46, 58, 60, 66.

83. Ruhlman, *Grocery*, 79, 85.

84. Taubes, *Good Calories, Bad Calories*, 124, 224–25, 393.

85. Taubes, *Case against Sugar*, 16–17, 199–200.

86. Walter Willett, MD, with Patrick Skerrett, *Eat, Drink, and Be Healthy: The Harvard Medical School Guide to Healthy Eating* (New York: Free Press, 2001), 11, 12.

87. Marion Nestle, "Eating Made Simple," *Scientific American*, Sept. 2007, folder 8 Articles, "What to Eat" 2007, Box 51, Series VII, Subseries A, Nestle Papers, Fales Library.

88. Willett, *Eat, Drink, and Be Healthy*, 13.

89. Mudry, *Measured Meals*, 117–19.

90. Nestle, *What to Eat*, 95–96.

91. Nestle, *Slow Cooked*, 100, 102.

92. One lasting example of a popular enrichment recipe to create a healthier bread was from nutritionist Clive McCay, who taught at Cornell University. His "Cornell Bread," or as he called it, "Golden Triple Rich Bread," included soy flour, dry milk, and Vitafed flour. He wrote about his experimentation to produce a better-tasting, more nutritious bread, and he gave the recipe to the food co-op in Ithaca, New York, and other venues and even made the formula public for all to use. The bread was endorsed by the Connecticut Department of Health, the Council of Social Agencies, other agencies, and many home bakers. *Co-Op Bulletin*, June 1, 1950, Clive McCay, "The Quest for Better Bread," n.d., *Co-Op Bulletin: Cooperative Consumers of New Haven Inc.*, Feb. 15, 1951, Memo, Robert Meigs, Cornell University, n.d., file Bread, Analysis, formula, discussions, and file Meigs, Bread, Box 1, Clive McCay Papers, 1920–1967, Cornell University.

93. Nestle also pointed out that, by the time this unnecessary fortification took place, the incidence of spina bifida was already declining. Nestle, *Food Politics*, 301–4.

94. Nestle, *Food Politics*, for this paragraph, see esp. 305, 308, 311, 319, 321, 338.

95. Nestle and Trueman, *Let's Ask Marion*, 46.

96. Nestle and Trueman, *Let's Ask Marion*, 50.

97. Nestle and Trueman, *Let's Ask Marion*, 55.

98. Nestle and Trueman, *Let's Ask Marion*, 59.

99. "Eating Smart: Decoding the Grocery Store," *Time* June 12, 2006, folder 5 Magazine Articles [1 of 3] 2006, Box 51, Series VII, Subseries A, Nestle Papers, Fales Library.

100. Nestle, *What to Eat*, 248–51, 257, 272.

101. Nestle, *What to Eat*, 183.

102. Susan Allport, *The Queen of Fats: Why Omega-3s Were Removed from the Western Diet and What We Can Do to Replace Them* (Berkeley: University of California Press, 2006), see 2, 45–51, 68, 107–8, 139–45.

103. Willett, *Eat, Drink, and Be Healthy*, 67–68, 85–93.

104. Ericka Souter, "Eat, Drink, Be Wary," *People*, May 22, 2006, 155ff., folder 7 Magazine Articles [3 of 3] 2006, Box 51, Series VII, Subseries A, Nestle Papers, Fales Library.

105. Nestle, *What to Eat*, see esp. 32–35, 42, 45, 66.

106. Nestle, *What to Eat*, 126, 125, 108–13, 142, 146.

107. Nestle, *What to Eat*, 18–23, see also 268.

108. Nestle, *Safe Food*; for this paragraph, see esp. x, 16, 21, 23–27.

109. Nestle, *Safe Food*, 172, 273.

110. "The Rules for Eating Smarter," *BusinessWeek*, May 22, 2006, folder 6 Magazine Articles [2 of 3] 2006, Box 51, Series VII, Subseries A, Nestle Papers, Fales Library.

111. Jane Brody, "Confused by Nutrition Research?" *New York Times*, Oct. 29, 2018.

112. Nestle, *Unsavory Truth*, 229.

113. "My Dinner with Marion," *Oprah Magazine*, Apr. 2006, folder 5 Magazine Articles [1 of 3] 2006. Another example of her understanding of the impact of such actions was in a 2009 article: "I am proud to be part of this food revolution, which holds so much promise for making our world a better place as well as improving what we eat for dinner." Marion Nestle, "Reading the Food Social Movement," *World Literature Today Magazine: The Food Issue*, Jan./Feb. 2009, folder 9 Reading the Food Social Movement, Jan/Feb 2009. Both are in Box 51, Series VII, Subseries A, Nestle Papers, Fales Library.

114. Eric Holt-Giménez, *A Foodie's Guide to Capitalism: Understanding the Political Economy of What We Eat*, with a foreword by Marion Nestle (New York: Monthly Review Press and Food First Books, 2017).

115. Nestle in Holt-Giménez, *Foodie's Guide*, 10–11.

116. Holt-Giménez, *Foodie's Guide*, 73.

117. Nestle and Trueman, *Let's Ask Marion*, 124.

118. Marion Nestle, "In Praise of the Organic Movement," *World Economic Forum*, 2005, 218–19, folder 11, folder 10 Articles in Magazines [1 of 5], Box 50, Series VII, Subseries A, Nestle Papers, Fales Library.

119. *Truck Farm*, A Wicked Delicate Film, directed by Ian Cheney, produced by Ian Cheney and Curt Ellis, written by Ian Cheney and Simon Beins, 2010, 48 minutes.

120. "My Dinner with Marion," 160.

121. For example, Q and A with Nestle in *University of California Public Health Magazine*, spring 2004, folder 10 Articles in Magazines [1 of 5], Box 50, Series VII, Subseries A, Nestle Papers, Fales Library.

122. Nestle, *Soda Politics*, 279–89.

123. She also brought this discussion of the environmental impact of food production back to nutrition, referring to new research that found food grown in high-carbon atmospheres had reduced nutrients. Nestle and Trueman, *Let's Ask Marion*, 134–36.

124. Nestle, *Slow Cooked*, 159.

125. Nestle to Kathleen O'Malley, Oct. 28, 1991, folder 2 Correspondence, Box 72, Series VII, Subseries E, Nestle Papers, Fales Library.

126. Nestle, *What to Eat*, 3.

127. Nestle and Trueman, *Let's Ask Marion*, 6.

128. Nestle, *Slow Cooked*, 51.

129. Nestle and Trueman, *Let's Ask Marion*, 104, 109.

130. Nestle and Trueman, *Let's Ask Marion*, 25–26.

Chapter 6

1. Alice Waters, *The Chez Panisse Menu Cookbook* (New York: Random House, 1982), ix. Alice Waters has written (alone and with others) numerous other books, some directly tied to her restaurant Chez Panisse and others not. They include (in chronological order): with Patricia Curtan and Martine Labro, *Chez Panisse Pasta, Pizza & Calzone* (New York: Random House, 1984); *Chez Panisse Vegetables* (New York: Harper Collins, 1996); *Fanny at Chez Panisse: A Child's Restaurant Adventures with 46 Recipes* (New York: William Morrow Cookbooks, 1997); *Chez Panisse Café Cookbook* (New York: Harper Collins, 1999); *Chez Panisse Fruit* (New York: William Morrow Cookbooks, 2002); *The Art of Simple Food* (New York: Clarkson Potter, 2007); with Daniel Duane, photographs by Davie Littschwager, *Edible Schoolyard, A Universal Idea* (San Francisco: Chronicle Books, 2008); *In the Green Kitchen: Techniques to Learn by Heart* (New York: Clarkson Potter, 2010); Waters and Friends, *40 Years of Chez Panisse: The Power of Gathering* (New York: Clarkson Potter, 2011); *The Art of Simple Food, II* (New York: Clarkson Potter, 2013); with Fanny Singer, *My Pantry: Homemade Ingredients That Make Simple Meals Your Own: A Cookbook* (New York: Clarkson Potter, 2015); with Bob Carrau, illustrations by Ann Arnold, *Fanny in France* (New York: Viking Books for Young Readers, 2016); *Coming to My Senses: The Making of a Counterculture Cook* (New York: Clarkson Potter, 2017); *We Are What We Eat: A Slow Food Manifesto* (New York: Penguin, 2021).

2. Thomas McNamee, *Alice Waters & Chez Panisse: The Romantic, Impractical, often Eccentric, Ultimately Brilliant Making of a Food Revolution* (New York: Penguin, 2007), 5, 111.

3. Waters and Friends, *40 Years of Chez Panisse*, 146, 156, 164, 168, 212, 215.

4. McNamee, *Alice Waters & Chez Panisse*, 6.

5. Ruth Reichl, "The '80s, A Special Report Tastemakers," *Los Angeles Times*, Dec. 24, 1989, 11.

6. Waters, *Coming to My Senses*, 111.

7. Waters, *Coming to My Senses*, 122.

8. Observations in this paragraph are taken from several sources: Waters, *Chez Panisse Menu Cookbook*, ix–x; Waters and Friends, *40 Years of Chez Panisse*, 32–42; Andrea Barnet, *Visionary Women: How Rachel Carson, Jane Jacobs, Jane Goodall, and Alice Waters Changed Our World* (New York: Ecco, 2018), 333–34, 343–45, 358; McNamee, *Alice Waters & Chez Panisse*, 15–18, 31, 124, 134, 145.

9. A sample of Savio's views are found in his famous November 1964 "End to History" speech, found in Van Gosse, *The Movements of the New Left 1950–1975: A Brief History with Documents* (Boston: Bedford/St. Martin's, 2005), 87–90.

10. Savio, "End to History," 87.

11. Savio, "End to History," 90.

12. Savio, "End to History," 90.

13. Waters and Friends, *40 Years of Chez Panisse*, 15.

14. Waters and Friends, *40 Years of Chez Panisse*, 16.

15. Waters, *Coming to My Senses*, 84–94, and dedication page.

16. Almost three decades later, Goines wrote a nearly eight-hundred-page book detailing

the four months of events he took part in at Berkeley in 1964. David Lance Goines, *The Free Speech Movement: Coming of Age in the 1960s* (Berkeley, CA: Ten Speed, 1993).

17. Waters, *Coming to My Senses*, ix.

18. Waters, *Coming to My Senses*, 302. There were many other examples of ethical entrepreneurs who had come of age during the counterculture and held on to their principles of valuing community and creating an alternative to the existing economic models. For example, activist for local and ethical businesses Judy Wicks started the White Dog Café in Philadelphia in 1983. She gained national fame and by the time she wrote a memoir thirty years later, and her book was endorsed by other food and environmental activists, including Alice Waters, Frances Moore Lappé, and Bill McKibben. Judy Wicks, *Good Morning, Beautiful Business: The Unexpected Journey of an Activist Entrepreneur and Local Economy Pioneer* (White River Junction, VT: Chelsea Green Publishing, 2013).

19. Waters with Singer, *My Pantry*, 66, 74. For a discussion of how countercultural food evolved, including its political implications and present-day manifestations, see Kauffman, *Hippie Food*, and McGrath, *Food for Dissent.*

20. Waters, *Coming to My Senses*, 147.

21. Waters, *Coming to My Senses*, 148–49.

22. Mark Blackburn, "Sign of the Times: Berkeley Switches from LSD to Garlic," *Chicago Tribune*, June 30, 1979. For another example of its communal spirit, see James Beard, "Ready for Baked Heads of Garlic?" *Philadelphia Inquirer*, Apr. 18, 1978.

23. Among many examples, see Waters, *We Are What We Eat*, 100–101.

24. Waters and Friends, *40 Years of Chez Panisse*, 24–27, 44–46.

25. Waters, *Chez Panisse Café Cookbook*, xv–xvi.

26. Sources here include the following: McNamee, *Alice Waters & Chez Panisse*, 40–49, 47, 65, 199–203; Waters, *Coming to My Senses*, 16, 283, 302; Waters and Friends, *40 Years of Chez Panisse*, 24–35; David Marchese, "Talk: Interview with Alice Waters," *New York Times Magazine*, May 23, 2021, 17; Barnet, *Visionary Women*, 361–408; Joyce Goldstein with Dore Brown, *Inside the California Food Revolution: Thirty Years That Changed Our Culinary Consciousness* (Berkeley: University of California Press, 2013), 66–67, 98. Former Chez Panisse chef Joyce Goldstein noted that Waters's decision to hire staff with some education and broader exposure to history and culture had another unintended consequence outside of Chez Panisse: "the kitchen became a very stimulating place to be. I think it reinforced the notion that this is an exciting profession and a profession of prestige" (67).

27. For example, Waters's boyfriend when Chez Panisse opened was David Goines, an artist and printer who designed the menu and other written materials for the restaurant, including a striking poster to celebrate its opening. Long after Waters and Goines had split as a couple, he continued to make annual posters for Chez Panisse for more than forty years, as well as other posters for special occasions and themed dinners. Waters said of his work that it "was not quite Art Nouveau, not quite Art Deco. It was expressive . . . and it became a fundamental part of the restaurant's style." David Lance Goines, foreword by Alice Waters, *The Poster Art of David Lance Goines: A 40-Year Retrospective* (Mineola, NY: Dover, 2010).

28. Waters and Friends, *40 Years of Chez Panisse*, 50, see also 48–50. See also McNamee, *Alice Waters & Chez Panisse*, 79–81, 114–21.

29. McNamee, *Alice Waters & Chez Panisse*, 121.

30. Barnet, *Visionary Women*, 387. For more on the relationship with Tower, see 379–91, 395.

31. Tower opened his own restaurant in San Francisco, Stars, which closed in the 1990s, after which he had a variety of short-term positions, and moved to Mexico. His relationship with Waters soured as her fame grew, his diminished, and he felt that he did not receive credit for helping to create the new American food movement. Dana Goodyear, "Jeremiah Tower, A Forgotten Father of the American Food Revolution," *The New Yorker*, May 1, 2017.

32. This title has been reprinted in many places, including the restaurant's website, moosewoodcooks.com.

33. The cookbook was revised and reprinted over the years; a comparison of two of the editions illustrates how the collective splintered. The title page of the original hardcover edition from 1977 includes this tagline "Recipes from Moosewood Restaurant, Ithaca, New York" and a qualified authorship: "Compiled, Edited, Illustrated and Hand-Lettered by Mollie Katzen." The following page lists thirty-seven names, followed by this statement: "The Moosewood People, who have created the Moosewood Restaurant in Ithaca, New York, from which this book has sprung." This was then followed by three more pages about the restaurant, including photos of it and Mollie Katzen in front of it. The paperback new revised edition had scrubbed any mention of the restaurant from the title page and eliminated the page listing the people at the Moosewood Restaurant, as well as the three pages about the restaurant. Katzen instead added a five-page essay, "A Personal History of This Book," which was more about Katzen than about the restaurant. See Mollie Katzen, *Moosewood Cookbook*. The revised new edition appeared in 1992.

34. Leah Mennies, "Moosewood, the Restaurant that Taught Americans to Eat Healthy-ish, Has a New Cookbook," *Bon Appetit*, Sept. 26, 2017.

35. Kauffman, *Hippie Food*, 234.

36. For example, see "Mollie Katzen's *Vegetable Kingdom*," *People*, Nov. 24, 1997, 35; "Moosewood Revisited," *New Age Journal*, Oct. 1992; "Marvelous Mollie Katzen: Still Life After Moosewood," *East West*, Sept. 1988, 69–77.

37. Mitch Broder, "The (Whole Wheat) Toast of the '80s: With No Meat, No Regular Menu, No Boss, Moosewood Restaurant Packs in Patrons from All Over," (Rochester, NY) *Democrat and Chronicle*, July 19, 1987, file—Articles, Reviews, Publicity 1988–2005, Box 2, Moosewood Collective Records, 1973–2000, Cornell University Manuscript Library.

38. Each member of the collective owned shares in a corporation, the Vegetable Kingdom, the bylaws of which detailed officers, directors, ownership, and rights of all shareholders and members of the collective. Details here are from several policy documents and legal agreements found in file Moosewood Policy Notebook, mid-1980s, illus. by Maureen Vivino, 1–34, inc. By Laws of the Vegetable Kingdom and Partnership Agreement, Box 1, Moosewood Collective Records, 1973–2000, Cornell University Manuscript Library.

39. For example, the handbook specified that bicycles were not allowed in the locker room because there was not enough room, but asked members for their agreement: "Please secure them downstairs, OK?" The collective subsidized childcare for members, outlined the terms under which children could work alongside parents during some shifts, and what foods children of workers were allowed to eat for free.

40. Workers were asked to limit the wildness, skimpiness, and messiness of their clothes, to monitor the neatness of their hair, and to monitor the odors of their armpits and breath; standards of decorum, though, remained a suggestion in the mid-1980s, not a requirement: "Cleanliness and good taste are highly recommended." Staff minutes from 1983 observed that "unflattering apparel and offensive odors *have* been noted." The solution offered was

collective: "Use the buddy system: ask a buddy if you smell." File Moosewood Policy Notebook, Box 1, Moosewood Collective Records, 1973–2000, Cornell University Manuscript Library.

41. A sample of some of the publicity about the restaurant is found in file—Articles, Reviews, Publicity, 1988–2005, Box 2, Moosewood Collective Records, 1973–2000, Cornell University Manuscript Library; "Meatless and Marvelous," *Family Circle*, Mar. 15, 1988; Madeleine Brand, NPR transcript, Oct. 26, 2005; Deborah Krasner, "Happy 30th, Moosewood," *Vegetarian Times*, Apr. 2003; Jim Morrison, "Of Ideals and Vegetables," *American Way* (American Airlines), Aug. 1991; Susan Weitz, "Green Worlds," *Ithaca Times*, Nov. 1996, 21–27; Nancy Harmon Jenkins, "A 70s Restaurant of Ideas and Ideals," *New York Times*, October 24, 1990.

42. In a 2005 story on Moosewood, NPR reporter Madeleine Brand observed: "for some foodies, Moosewood is so unthreatening it's downright boring." She went on to quote cookbook author Jeff Morgan, who observed that the Moosewood books paid little attention to finesse in dishes, subtle use of herbs, and other culinary qualities. Brand concluded that mainstream business success had been unexpected to the collective: "They became canny businesspeople who understand the power of branding. Hard to believe, but that scruffy moose in the restaurant window symbolizes a brand that's worth a lot of money now, as what was once considered fringy is solidly mainstream." NPR transcript Oct. 26, 2005, file—Articles, Reviews, Publicity, 1988–2005, Box 2, Moosewood Collective Records, 1973–2000, Cornell University Manuscript Library.

43. The growth of industrial agriculture and food in this period has been chronicled in several places. For a discussion of these transformations as they affected the food industry, see Levenstein, *Revolution at the Table*, 30–41. For discussion of how industrial expectations came to permeate agriculture in this period, see Fitzgerald, *Every Farm a Factory.*

44. Levenstein, *Revolution at the Table*, 37.

45. For further discussion of the cultural assumptions behind the postwar spread of synthetic pesticides, see Michelle Mart, *Pesticides, A Love Story: America's Enduring Embrace of Dangerous Chemicals* (Lawrence: University Press of Kansas, 2015). There was a long history of pesticide use in the United States before the age of synthetics; for a discussion of pest control in the pre-1945 period, see James McWilliams, *American Pests: The Losing War on Insects from Colonial Times to DDT* (New York: Columbia University Press, 2008), and James Whorton, *Before Silent Spring: Pesticides and Public Health in Pre-DDT America* (Princeton, NJ: Princeton University Press, 1974).

46. Gardner, *American Agriculture*, 14, 24, 147–48. From 1930–1950, mechanical harvesters use had increased ninefold. Peter Pringle, *Food, Inc.: Mendel to Monsanto—The Promises and Perils of the Biotech Harvest* (New York: Simon and Schuster, 2003), 47.

47. For examples of ridicule, see Tamar Adler, photographs Maurizio Cattelan and Pierpaolo Ferrari, "Joy of Looking: The Absurd, Repulsive, Gorgeous Creations of the Betty Crocker Recipe Card Library," *New York Times Magazine*, Nov. 1, 2015, 53–59 (quote on 54); see also Lileks, *The Gallery of Regrettable Food.* For discussion of the appeal of brightly dyed food in the United States, see Joe Pinsker, "Americans' Bizarre Relationship with the Color of Their Food," *The Atlantic*, May 8, 2017; and for background on the dye industry that created such foods, see Carolyn Cobbold, *A Rainbow Palate: How Chemical Dyes Changed the West's Relationship with Food* (Chicago: University of Chicago Press, 2020).

48. Waters, *Chez Panisse Menu Cookbook*, x.

49. Reichl, "The '80s," 11.

50. Waters, *Art of Simple Food*, 3.

51. Waters, *Art of Simple Food*, 6–7, 4.

52. Quoted in Reichl, "The '80s," 11.

53. Lisa Bercovici, "For Them, Haute Cuisine Beats Higher Learning," *New York Times*, Nov. 12, 1975, 56.

54. Goldstein, *Inside the California Food Revolution*, 42.

55. For example, see Waters, *Chez Panisse Menu Cookbook*, 161–65.

56. Waters with Singer, *My Pantry*, 12; Waters, *In the Green Kitchen*, 3.

57. Waters, *We Are What We Eat*, 97.

58. Waters, *Chez Panisse Café Cookbook*, 2.

59. Waters, *Coming to My Senses*, 131.

60. Waters, *The Poster Art of David Lance Goines*, foreword.

61. Barnet, *Visionary Women*, 352, 364, 369; see also Kim Severson, *Spoon Fed: How Eight Cooks Saved My Life* (New York: Riverhead Books, 2010), 22–23.

62. Waters, *We Are What We Eat*, 105.

63. Waters, *Coming to My Senses*, 49.

64. Waters, *Coming to My Senses*, 160.

65. Waters, *Chez Panisse Menu Cookbook*, 3.

66. Waters, *We Are What We Eat*, 98. Diane Ackerman observed that people experienced food through the senses, but that these were not just personal experiences. "Taste is largely social . . ." she wrote, "If an event is meant to matter emotionally, symbolically, or mystically, food will be close at hand to sanctify and bind it." Ackerman, *A Natural History of the Senses* (New York: Vintage Books, 1990), 127. For a broader discussion of taste in different historical contexts, see Mark M. Smith, *Sensing the Past: Seeing, Hearing, Smelling, Tasting, and Touching History* (Berkeley: University of California Press, 2007).

67. Waters, *In the Green Kitchen*, 2.

68. Marchese, "Talk," 16.

69. Samuel Fromartz, *Organic, Inc.: Natural Foods and How They Grew* (Orlando, FL: Harcourt, 2006), 120–21.

70. The following discussion draws on a discussion of spectrum of attitudes toward organic food in Mart, *Pesticides, A Love Story*, 204–16. For an overview of organic food, see Robin O'Sullivan, *American Organic: A Cultural History of Farming, Gardening, Shopping, and Eating* (Lawrence: University Press of Kansas, 2015). For more details on the impact of J. I. Rodale and the organic industry, see, Andrew N. Case, *The Organic Profit: Rodale and the Making of Marketplace Environmentalism* (Seattle: University of Washington Press, 2018). In particular, Case highlights how Rodale's market success illustrates the entanglement of environmental values and commerce in modern organics. For a discussion of some of the contradictions of the organic industry as it grew, see Julie Guthman, *Agrarian Dreams: The Paradox of Organic Farming in California*, 2nd ed. (Oakland: University of California Press, 2014), and Fromartz, *Organic, Inc.*

71. Quote from Interior Department staffer Charles Stoddard in Mart, *Pesticides, A Love Story*, 69, see also 73.

72. O'Sullivan, *American Organic*, 110, 112, 119.

73. The organic farms, CSAs, farmers markets, and food coops tended to be concentrated in the politically liberal areas of the Northeast, Pacific coast, and upper Midwest. Mart, *Pesticides, A Love Story*, 204. Tom Philpott, *Perilous Bounty: The Looming Collapse of American*

Farming and How We Can Prevent It (New York: Bloomsbury, 2020), 176. For more on the involvement of young people in the new wave of organic farming, see Laura Sayre and Sean Clark, eds., *Fields of Learning: The Student Farm Movement in North America* (Lexington: University Press of Kentucky, 2011).

74. Mart, *Pesticides, A Love Story*, 210; O'Sullivan, *American Organic*, 178.

75. Guthman, *Agrarian Dreams*, 33–34.

76. Mart, *Pesticides, A Love Story*, 210–11.

77. Mart, *Pesticides, A Love Story*, 211.

78. Joan Dye Gussow, "Can an Organic Twinkie™ Be Certified?" in *For ALL Generations: Making World Agriculture More Sustainable*, ed. J. Patrick Madden and Scott G. Chaplowe (Glendale, CA: OM Publishing and World Sustainable Agriculture Association, 1997), 143–53.

79. Scholars, food writers, and activists all participated in the debate over organic and its manifestations. A scholarly sample includes the following: Guthman, *Agrarian Dreams*; Fromartz, *Organic, Inc*; O'Sullivan, *American Organic*; James McWilliams, *Just Food: Where Locavores Get It Wrong and How We Can Truly Eat Responsibly* (New York: Little, Brown, 2009). A sample from food writers and activists related to organic debates includes the following: Katz, *The Revolution Will Not Be Microwaved*; Barbara Kingsolver, with Steven Hopp and Camille Kingsolver, *Animal, Vegetable, Miracle: A Year of Food Life* (New York: Harper Perennial, 2007); and Dan Barber, *The Third Plate: Field Notes on the Future of Food* (New York: Penguin, 2014).

80. In an age of industrial abundance and lacking strong food traditions and culture, Pollan argued that Americans were not compelled to eat any particular type of food but had to choose among competing diets. Michael Pollan, *The Omnivore's Dilemma: A Natural History of Four Meals* (New York: Penguin Books, 2006). For a sample of commentary on Pollan's influence (and as it intertwined with Waters's impact) see Biltekoff, *Eating Right in America*, 85–106.

81. Pollan, *Omnivore's Dilemma*, 158.

82. Pollan, *Omnivore's Dilemma*, 258.

83. O'Sullivan, *American Organic*, 196, see also 194–95.

84. Fromartz, *Organic Inc.*, 188.

85. Guthman, *Agrarian Dreams*, 13. A more recent discussion of corporate consolidation in agricultural production in both the Midwest and California is in Philpott, *Perilous Bounty*. For background on the creation of the California industry, see Steven Stoll, *The Fruits of Natural Advantage: Making the Industrial Countryside in California* (Berkeley: University of California Press, 1998); see also Lawrence Jelinek, *Harvest Empire: A History of California Agriculture*, 2nd ed. (San Francisco: Boyd and Fraser, 1982).

86. Guthman also argues that the romantic celebration of the family farm—given new life in the organic ideal—is unrealistic in an era of low food prices, high land values, and an entrenched industrial agricultural system. Guthman, *Agrarian Dreams*, chaps. 8 and 9. See also Fromartz, *Organic Inc.*, 188.

87. Philpott, *Perilous Bounty*, 177. For more on the rise of CSAs, organic agriculture, and industrial organic, see David E. Goodman, Melanie DuPuis, and Michael K. Goodman, *Alternative Food Networks: Knowledge, Practice, and Politics* (London and New York: Routledge, 2012).

88. Kathleen Doheny, "Organic Produce: What It Means and How to Find It," *Los Angeles Times*, Mar. 14, 1989, 1; Robin Goldwyn Blumenthal, "Trade Group Seeks to End

Confusion Over What Exactly Is Organic Farming," *Wall Street Journal*, Aug. 1989, 1; Maria LaGranga, "Demand for Organics Wilting," *Los Angeles Times*, June 15, 1990, 1; Connie Chung, *NBC Evening News*, Mar. 14, 1989. When "organic" was not yet the standard terminology, one NBC News story used "natural farming" more as a contrast to "use of chemicals." Ann Rubenstein, *NBC News*, Dec. 7, 1989.

89. Pollan, *Omnivore's Dilemma*, 153.

90. Address Yuetter to National Newspaper Association, Mar. 17, 1989, folder Speeches and Statements of Clayton Yeutter, Box 1, Speeches and Statements of Agriculture Secretary Clayton Yeutter, 1989–1991, RG 16, NARA II.

91. O'Sullivan, *American Organic*, 232, 230. Information about both the 2005 and 2006 studies, and the quote in this paragraph can also be found here.

92. Fromartz, *Organic Inc.*, 120–21.

93. Waters, *We Are What We Eat*, 115–16; Waters, *Coming to My Senses*, 103.

94. Fromartz, *Organic Inc.*, 116.

95. Waters, *Coming to My Senses*, 104.

96. McNamee, *Alice Waters & Chez Panisse*, 159.

97. Waters, *We Are What We Eat*, 116; Waters, *Coming to My Senses*, 103.

98. Waters, *Chez Panisse Vegetables*, xviii.

99. Waters, *Coming to My Senses*, 251.

100. Waters, *Chez Panisse Café Cookbook*, xviii.

101. Pollan, afterword in Waters and Friends, *40 Years of Chez Panisse*, 295.

102. Oral history, Tom Colicchio (part II), and oral history, Dan Barber (part II), Voices from the Food Revolution: People Who Changed the Way Americans Eat, 2011, Fales Library.

103. Barber discussed his reasons for collaborating with farmers and details of these relationships in parts II and III of his oral history in Voices from the Food Revolution, Fales Library.

104. Bengis-Palei also started a local foundation in 2009 to provide support for those who made a living from raising food where she lived on Deer Isle, Maine. She died of cancer in 2017. Emily Burnham, "Writer Who Sold Famous Chefs on Maine Seafood Dies of Cancer," *Bangor Daily News*, July 28, 2017, C5.

105. The history of the remarkably successful Whole Foods grocery chain entered a new stage in summer 2017, when its growth had slowed and it was acquired by Amazon, which promptly announced new policies in August 2017. Nick Wingfield and Michael J. de la Merced, "Amazon to Buy Whole Foods for $13.4 Billion," *New York Times*, June 16, 2017; Nick Wingfield and David Gelles, "Amazon's Play to Rival Whole Foods Rivals: Cheaper Kale and Avocado," *New York Times*, Aug. 24, 2017.

106. Severson, *Spoon Fed*, 64.

107. A member of the new generation of organic farmers observed the irony of this connection as seen in the socialization of young children: "That agrarian ideal still exerts a powerful grip on the American imagination, even though our actual experience with it may extend no further than mouthing the words to 'Old McDonald had a Farm.'" Nicola Smith, with photographs by Geoff Hansen, *Harvest: A Year in the Life of an Organic Farm* (Guilford, CT: Lyons, 2004), 7. Smith also quotes from Jefferson's contemporary whose work is usually cited alongside as demonstration of our fundamental connection to the land. In his *Letters from an American Farmer*, J. Hector St. John de Crèvecoeur writes about the importance of

the land: "On it is founded our rank, our freedom, our power as citizens" (14).

108. Calvin Trillin observed that Chez Panisse "uncoupled good eating from fanciness." foreword to Waters and Friends, *40 Years of Chez Panisse*, 7.

109. Wurgaft, *Meat Planet*, 135.

110. The breadth of participants was illustrated by a special issue of *The Nation* magazine on Sept. 11, 2006, "Wake Up, America! Pay Attention to What You Eat! The Food Issue" which had more than nineteen contributors, constituting a Who's Who of the movement.

111. One dramatically visible challenge to processed foods, which are mainly collections of isolated chemical ingredients, was a book published in 2015 by a photographer who depicted processed foods in their component parts of chemical powders or dollops of liquids and gels—with little resemblance to an actual "food." Dwight Eschliman, text by Steve Ettlinger, *Ingredients: A Visual Exploration of 75 Additives & 25 Food Products* (New York: Regan Arts, 2015).

112. Goldstein, *Inside the California Food Revolution*, 3, 12, 43.

113. Oral history Collichio (part II), Voices from the Food Revolution, Fales Library.

114. Oral history Dan Barber (part II), Voices from the Food Revolution, Fales Library; quoted in Goldstein, *Inside the California Food Revolution*, 145.

115. Waters, *Coming to My Senses*, 251.

116. Barber, *Third Plate*, 1–7 (quotations from 6, 7).

117. Barber, *Third Plate*, 22.

118. There is no consensus on the exact number, and some controversy about the numbers gathered in 2007, 2012, and 2015. Data from websites: Community Supported Agriculture, National Agricultural Library (NAL), USDA and Community Supported Agriculture, *Local Harvest* (a nonprofit organization website); accessed 2024.

119. McNamee, *Alice Waters & Chez Panisse*, 346. Seven years later, she continued to emphasize the importance of this communal and environmental impact: "Our vision at Chez Panisse has always been a world where delicious food enriches the celebration of life and strengthens our connection to nature and culture." Waters and Friends, *40 Years at Chez Panisse*, 9.

120. E. Allen Bateman, "The Place and Purpose of School Food Services in Total Educational Programs in Elementary and Secondary Schools," at the National Conference on School Lunch and Distribution Programs, Washington, DC, Aug. 27, 1957, folder Speeches and Articles, 1943–1958, Box 1, Records of the Food and Nutrition Service School Programs Division School Lunch Program Subject Files, 1943–1977, RG 462, NARA II.

121. For a pictorial description and history of the project, see Waters et al, *Edible Schoolyard.* Other information about the project is found in Barnet, *Visionary Women*, 414–26, Waters, *We Are What We Eat*, 102–3, 159–60, 168–71, 185. Water's commitment to reaching children with her messages about transforming our relationship with food is also illustrated by her cooperation with (and Afterword to) the children's book, Jacqueline Briggs Martin, illustrated by Hayelin Choi, afterword by Alice Waters, *Alice Waters and the Trip to Delicious* (Bellevue, WA: Readers to Eaters, 2014), and Waters, *Fanny at Chez Panisse.*

122. Waters organized ongoing fundraising efforts to benefit the foundation and project. For example, her 2010 *In the Green Kitchen* enlisted the support of friends and cooks (some from Chez Panisse and some not, though famous names within the new food movement) to create a book of brief recipes and advice for home cooks, the proceeds of which all went to the foundation. A few years later, Waters launched a different sort of school project with

a residential college at Yale University, the Yale Sustainable Food Project, when her daughter Fanny started attending Yale; Waters worked to build an organic, sustainable food system for the college. Waters, *We Are What We Eat*, 69–70; McNamee, *Alice Waters & Chez Panisse*, 304–6, 328.

123. Whether or not the project fulfilled all of these ambitions, there was early evidence that it did improve the lives of children. A Harvard Medical School study of students from the original Edible Schoolyard in Berkeley found that after one year of participation, students had "improved behavior, fewer emotional problems, higher grade point averages and a better grasp of ecology." Anna Lappé, "Doing Lunch: Ann Cooper Serves Up a New Vision of School Food," in "Wake Up, America! Pay Attention to What You Eat! The Food Issue," *The Nation*, Sept. 11, 2006, 35–36.

124. Barnet, *Visionary Women*, 426; McNamee, *Alice Waters & Chez Panisse*, 256–57, 268–71.

125. Severson, *Spoon Fed*, 76.

126. For example, see Jennifer Lawson, "Teaching Healthy Eating Habits to Students Early in Life," *Philadelphia Tribune*, Oct. 4, 2009, T2; Jennifer Dignan, "A Growing Trend," *Scholastic Scope*, Oct. 19, 2009, 14; Barbara Mahany and Beth Botts, "And the Plot Thickens . . . " *Chicago Tribune*, Mar. 22, 2009, 7. Some were threatened by the White House garden. For example, the pesticide trade association CropLife wrote to Obama in 2009 applauding the garden plan, *but* encouraging the First Lady to be more practical and consider using some "crop protection technologies." O'Sullivan, *American Organic*, 157.

127. Waters, *We Are What We Eat*, 140.

128. Bentley, *Eating for Victory*, 114; Lawson, *City Bountiful*, 172–202. See also Collingham, *The Taste of War*, 415–64.

129. Beth Huxta, "Victory Gardens 2.0," *Organic Gardening*, Apr. 2009, 44.

130. Robert Channick, "Victorious Gardens," *Chicago Tribune*, Sept. 3, 2010, 4, and Genevieve Belmaker, "A Greener New York," *The Epoch Times*, Apr. 22, 2014, A10–11.

131. Pollan, *Omnivore's Dilemma*, and Alice Waters, *Art of Simple Food*.

132. Kingsolver, Hopp, and Kingsolver, *Animal, Vegetable, Miracle*, and Alisa Smith and J. B. MacKinnon, *The 100-Mile Diet: A Year of Local Eating* (Toronto: Vintage Canada, 2007).

133. Examples of books related to the locavore movement include the following: Doug Fine, *Farewell, My Subaru: An Epic Adventure in Local Living* (2008); Amy Cotler, *The Locavore Way: Discover and Enjoy the Pleasures of Locally Grown Food* (2009), Leda Meredith, *The Locavore's Handbook: The Busy Person's Guide to Eating Local on a Budget* (2010), and Katherine Gustafson, *Locavore USA: How a Local-Food Economy is Changing One Community* (2012). O'Sullivan, *American Organic*, 159–62. Local food, of course, did not necessarily fix all of the problems of the industrial food system. Margaret Gray wrote about the continued exploitation of farm labor at some small and medium-sized farms that marketed their produce locally. See *Labor and the Locavore: The Making of a Comprehensive Food Ethic* (Berkeley: University of California Press, 2014).

134. Lorraine Johnson, *City Farmer: Adventures in Urban Food Growing* (Vancouver: Greystone Books, 2010) and Novella Carpenter, *Farm City: The Education of an Urban Farmer* (New York: Penguin, 2009).

135. Will Allen, with Charles Wilson, foreword by Eric Schlosser, *The Good Food Revolution: Growing Healthy Food, People, and Communities* (New York: Avery, 2012).

136. *Truck Farm*, directed by Ian Cheney; *Growing Cities: A Film About Urban Farming in America*, First Run Features, directed by Dan Susman, produced by Dan Susman, Andrew Mombouquette, and Dana Altman, 2013; 93 minutes. Some urban gardeners were also inspired by the writings of Wendell Berry—even if they rejected his anti-urban message. Berry argued that the rise of industrial agriculture and the depopulation of rural America led not only to poor food, but also to "a calamitous disintegration and scattering-out of the various functions of character: workmanship, care, conscience, responsibility." Wendell Berry, *The Unsettling of America: Culture and Agriculture* (San Francisco: Sierra Club Books, 1986, 1997), 19, 137.

137. A sample of various how-to urban gardening books with similar themes and goals included the following: Alice Bowe, *High-Impact, Low-Carbon Gardening: 1001 Ways to Garden Sustainably* (Portland, OR: Timber, 2011); Maria Finn, illustrations by Eika Yokoyama, *A Little Piece of Earth: How to Grow Your Own Food in Small Spaces* (New York: Universe Publishing, 2010); H. C. Flores, foreword by Toby Hemenway, illustrations by Jackie Holmstrom, *Food Not Lawns: How to Turn Your Yard into a Garden and Your Neighborhood into a Community* (White River Junction, VT: Chelsea Green, 2006); Rachel Kaplan with K. Ruby Blume, *Urban Homesteading: Heirloom Skills for Sustainable Living* (New York: Skyhorse, 2011); Alex Mitchell, Photography by Sarah Cuttle, *The Edible Balcony: Growing Fresh Produce in Small Spaces* (New York: Rodale, 2011).

138. See discussion in Lawson, *City Bountiful*, esp. 206.

139. A sample of newspaper and magazine articles on urban gardening from these years includes the following: Tracie Rozhon, "Urban Farmers Develop Their own Market," *New York Times*, Sept. 6, 1981, CN2; Deirdre Carmody, "Urban Farmers Seek to Keep Garden Growing," *New York Times*, Apr. 30, 1983, 25; Douglas Dabney, "City Gardeners Make Philadelphia a Growing Concern," *Philadelphia Tribune*, Sept. 12, 1986, 2A; Nancy Maes, "Gardeners Staking Out Vacant Lots," *Chicago Tribune*, Mar. 3, 1989, NB51; Tim Golden, "Common Good in the Bronx: Will It Be Houses or Roses?" *New York Times*, June 6, 1990, B1; William Aldrich, "Plots of Gold: Small Back-yard Gardens Can Yield a Nutritious Bounty," *Chicago Tribune*, Oct. 7, 1990, 286; Nancy Crabb, "Urban Gardening Turns 21! Growing Veggies in the Middle of the City," *Philadelphia Tribune*, Mar. 27, 1998, 1; Joanna Poncavage, "Organic in Bayonne," *Organic Gardening*, May/June 1998, 48–51; Hugo Martin, "Concern Growing at Urban Garden," *Los Angeles Times*, Sept. 29, 1998, 1; Mark Harris, "Urban Edens: Community Gardens Help Neighborhoods Nourish the Body, heal the Spirit and Enrich the World," *Vegetarian Times*, Mar. 2000, 79ff.

140. A sample of articles from 2001 to 2005 include the following: David Jawanier, "Urban Gardening Plants Seeds for Food, Friendship," *Philadelphia Tribune*, Apr. 6, 2001, 4; Diane Cardwell, "No Red Barn, but That's a Farm in Red Hook," *New York Times*, Aug. 20, 2003, B1; Nina Koziol, "Space to Grow: Community Minded Gardeners Create Places Where Plants and People Thrive," *Chicago Tribune*, Jan. 4, 2004, 15; Nicole Lewis, "To Sow With Love," *Black Enterprise*, Apr. 2005, 63; Zazel Loven, "Community Gardening," *Organic Gardening*, Apr./May 2005, 26, 28–33; Beth Botts, "Sometimes It Takes a Village to Raise a Garden," *Chicago Tribune*, July 31, 2005, 15.

141. Dignan, "A Growing Trend"; see also Anne Marie Chaker, "Flower Bulbs Put on a Show to Get back into Gardeners' Beds," *Wall Street Journal*, Oct. 17, 2012, D1.

142. Other examples include the following: Mary MacVean, "Food by the Yard," *Los Angeles Times*, May 6, 2009, E5; Kimberly Stevens, "Let Good Manners Take Root," *Los Angeles*

Times, Aug. 23, 2014, E9; Kibibi Blount-Dorn, "Food Policies at Work in Detroit," *Michigan Citizen*, Apr. 6, 2014, A5.

143. A sample of articles include the following: Mary MacVean, "Eden's Garden," *Los Angeles Times*, Aug. 7, 2010, E1; Pete Reinwald, "A Garden in the 'Desert,'" *Chicago Tribune*, Aug. 11, 2010, 4; Starla Muhammad, "Food, Urban Farms and Our Very Survival," *Louisiana Weekly*, Dec. 27, 2010, 9; Ramon Gonzalez, "Where Gardeners and Plants Rub Elbows," *Chicago Tribune*, Feb. 26, 2012, 6; Doriane Miller, "Healthy Eating Means Returning to Our Roots," *Chicago Weekend*, May 9, 2012, 2; Amelia Pang, "East New York: An Unlikely Oasis for Superfoods," *Epoch Times*, June 20, 2013, D1–2; Jeff Spurrier, "They Have to Pull Up Roots," *Los Angeles Times*, Jan. 18, 2014, E13; Kevin Taylor, "Will an Apple a Day Keep the Food Desert Away?" *High Country News*, Jan. 20, 2014, 12–13; Brittney Walker, "Equal Access to Fresh Healthy Food Starts Here," *New York Amsterdam News*, Nov. 17, 2016, 36.

144. For examples, see Phoebe Connelly and Chelsea Ross, "Farming the Concrete Jungle," *In These Times*, Sept. 2007, 20–24; Veronique de Turenne, "Farmville Altadena," *Los Angeles Times*, Mar. 10, 2011, E1; Roger Doiron, "Subversive Plots: Use Your Garden to Disconnect from Industrial Food," *Mother Earth News*, Aug./Sept. 2012, 24–25; Rachal Kaplan, "Guide to Urban Homesteading," *Mother Earth News*, Apr./May 2014, 36–40; Rachel Lincoln Sarnoff, "The New DIY," *Natural Foods Merchandiser*, July 2015, 21–23. Urban homesteading in the early twenty-first century rekindled the niche countercultural movement of the 1970s to go "back to the land" outside of cities.

145. Waters, *Chez Panisse Menu Cookbook*, 296.

146. Waters, *Chez Panisse Café Cookbook*, xviii.

147. Waters, *We Are What We Eat*, 121–27 (quotations on 122 and 125); Waters, *Chez Panisse Menu Cookbook*, 51–56 (quotation from 53); Waters with Singer, *My Pantry*, quotation, 50.

148. Alice Waters, foreword in Carlo Petrini, translated by William McCuaig, *Slow Food: The Case for Taste* (New York: Columbia University Press, 2001), ix. For more on the slow food philosophy, see the collection of articles from the journal *Slow:* Carlo Petrini with Ben Watson and Slow Food, eds., *Slow Food: Collected Thoughts on Taste, Tradition, and the Honest Pleasures of Food* (White River Junction, VT: Chelsea Green, 2001).

149. Petrini with Watson, *Slow Food*, 32.

150. Petrini with Watson, *Slow Food*, 69, 72, 142.

151. McNamee, *Alice Waters & Chez Panisse*, 324, 328.

152. Waters, *Chez Panisse Men Cookbook*, 7.

153. Waters, *In the Green Kitchen*, 3.

154. Petrini with Watson, *Slow Food*, xvii.

155. Petrini with Watson, *Slow Food*, 20, 12, 16, 24.

156. Petrini with Watson, *Slow Food*, xxii.

157. Waters, *We Are What We Eat*, 4.

158. Waters, *We Are What We Eat*, 6, 11.

159. Waters, *We Are What We Eat*, 12, 22.

160. Waters, *We Are What We Eat*, 70, 73–77, 102.

161. Severson, *Spoon Fed*, 66.

162. Writer Ann Vileisis gave an overview of the evolution of industrial food and the reaction to return to cooking from scratch in *Kitchen Literacy: How We Lost Knowledge of*

Where Food Comes from and Why We Need to Get It Back (Washington, DC: Island Press/ Shearwater Books, 2008). This ideology was illustrated in Laurel Robertson, Carol Flinders, and Bronwen Godrey, *Laurel's Kitchen: A Handbook for Vegetarian Cookery and Nutrition*. The 1976 book was reprinted several times and had revised editions. Focusing more on liberation from consumerism, not gender inequality, historian Megan Elias observed that *Laurel's Kitchen* "celebrat[ed] the value of women's unpaid traditional work in the home." *Stir It Up*, 160, also 150–60.

163. Betty Fussell, *Food in Good Season* (New York: Knopf, 1988), 5.

164. Rachel Laudan, "A Plea for Culinary Modernism: Why We Should Love New, Fast, Processed Food," *Gastronomica*, Feb. 2001, 36–44.

165. These foodstuffs, of course, would better be described as *less* perishable. Waters, *We Are What We Eat*, 126.

166. Rebecca Solnit, "Revolutionary Plots: On Urban Gardening," in Rebecca Solnit, *The Encyclopedia of Trouble and Spaciousness* (San Antonio, TX: Trinity University Press, 2014), 289, 297.

167. Oral history, Dan Barber, Mar. 15, 2011, Voices in American Food, Fales Library.

168. Barber, *Third Plate*, 10.

169. Oral history, Dan Barber (part III), Voices from the Food Revolution, Fales Library.

170. Marchese, "Talk: Alice Waters," *New York Times Magazine*, May 23, 2021, 17.

171. Waters, "Slow Food Nation," *The Nation*, Sept. 11, 2006, 13. Waters, *We Are What We Eat*, 59, also 60–65. Waters, of course, was not the only writer who criticized how food had been reduced to a commodity, and its value measured by the price tag that consumers saw. For discussion of the rise of consumerism, see Cohen, *A Consumers' Republic*, and for how this was manifest in the food sector, see Ruhlman, *Grocery*. Ellen Ruppel Shell examined the corrosive effects of cheapness in consumer culture in *Cheap: The High Cost of Discount Culture* (New York: Penguin, 2009), and Bryant Simon detailed how factory-farmed meat hurt workers and communities: *The Hamlet Fire: A Tragic Story of Cheap Food, Cheap Government, and Cheap Lives* (New York: New Press, 2017). A consideration of how shopping can both hurt or help communities is found in Sharon Zukin, *Point of Purchase: How Shopping Changed American Culture* (New York: Routledge, 2004). The ubiquity of evaluating food according to its visible price tag was well-illustrated by publications such as *Consumer Reports*. For instance, three issues highlighting food ("How to Eat Clean and Live Healthy," May 2015; "How to Shop Smarter for Food Today," July 2017; "Your Smart Guide to Healthier Eating," Nov. 2017) discussed issues such as health and freshness and pesticides, but the most important source of comparison always came back to price. One article title clearly illustrated that *Consumer Reports* did not subscribe to Waters's slow food values: "Faster, Fresher, Cheaper," July 2017, 30ff. Finally, related to the critique that food had been reduced to a mere consumer item, many critics of modern agriculture (in addition to Waters) have argued that modern food is only cheap because many of its costs are externalized. See, for example, Strange, *Family Farming*, 85–107.

172. Blackburn, "Sign of the Times," E3.

173. Quoted in Barnet, *Visionary Women*, 410.

174. Barnet, *Visionary Women*, 415, 410–11. Severson, *Spoon Fed*, 69. Elitism—as with many values—can be relative. When Waters wrote about the expectations of constant food availability in modern America, she used the following to illustrate her point: "How many of us, when we get to a hotel room, go straight to the mini bar to see what's there? We expect to

find the same little packages of salted nuts, the same soft drinks and chocolate bars and potato chips . . . we're being forever tempted to eat the fast food that's right there in front of us." (Waters, *We Are What We Eat*, 43) High-end hotels routinely have well-stocked mini bars, but most hotels do not. Moreover, only hotel guests with no concern about the cost of overpriced mini bars (or desperate in the middle of the night for a snack) would raid the hotel room selections.

175. Daniel Harris, *Cute, Quaint, Hungry and Romantic: The Aesthetics of Consumerism* (Boston, MA: Da Capo, 2000), xv.

176. Aaron Bobrow-Strain, *White Bread: A Social History of the Store-Bought Loaf* (Boston: Beacon, 2012), esp. 163–88.

177. Biltekoff, *Eating Right in America*, 92–93, 98. For broader discussion framing the ubiquity of neoliberalism, Wendy Brown, *Undoing the Demos: Neoliberalism's Stealth Revolution* (New York: Zone Books, 2015).

178. Liam Stack, "Unicorn Food is Colorful, Sparkly, and Everywhere," *New York Times*, Apr. 19, 2017.

179. Michael Pollan, *In Defense of Food: An Eater's Manifesto* (New York: Penguin Books, 2008), 1–2.

180. Some critics also reclaimed pleasure in food as an answer to what they asserted was overblown anxiety over such issues, having led to a dysfunctional, guilt-laden food culture and an obsession with obesity. For such a framing of cultural discourses, see John Coveney, *Food Morals and Meaning: The Pleasure and Anxiety of Eating*, 2nd ed. (London and New York: Routledge, 2006).

181. For a thoughtful discussion of how many Americans both embraced and remade food ideals and practices in the 1950s, see Shapiro, *Something from the Oven*.

182. Wendell Berry, "The Pleasures of Eating," in Berry, *Bringing It to the Table: On Farming and Food* (Berkeley: Counterpoint, 2009), 233. The book contains an introduction by Michael Pollan.

183. Berry, "Pleasures of Eating," 228, 231.

184. Michael Pollan, "The Food Movement Rising," *New York Review of Books*, June 10, 2010.

185. Jonathan Foley, "A Five-Step Plan to Feed the World," *National Geographic*, May 2014, 27ff. There were several additional sidebars and photo spreads related to the article.

186. The idea that many people failed to understand that meat was inherently expensive was illustrated by writer Susan Allport's consideration of the prolific number of deer in Westchester, New York—what in other circumstances might be exploited as "convenient packets of protein and fat" for human consumption. Yet, they were often left undisturbed to feast on most of the edible plants around suburban houses. This was an example of blindness brought by abundance and cheap meat from factory farms. Susan Allport, *The Primal Feast: Food, Sex, Foraging, and Love* (New York: Harmony Books, 2000), 4, 18.

187. Waters, *We Are What We Eat*, 62, 78, 79. Historian James McWilliams was a critic of the industrial food status quo but also a critic of what he charged to be extreme positions in the new food movement, such as saying that organic and local food was always better. He argued that local food would not always be sufficient and that food producers *did* need to consider how to scale up food production and distribution. See McWilliams, *Just Food*.

188. Philpott, *Perilous Bounty*, 189.

189. Goldstein with Brown, *Inside the California Food Revolution*, 42.

Conclusion

1. Quoted in Nestle, *Soda Politics*, 133.

2. Nestle in conversation with Trueman, *Let's Ask Marion*, 80–82.

3. Guthman, *Weighing In*, 186.

4. McDonald, *Food Power*, 49.

5. Benson, Address to Iowa State Club, May 6, 1957, folder 1957–1958, Box 3, and Benson, Address to National Wholesale Grocers' Association, Mar. 6, 1956, Box 2, RG 16, NARA II.

6. Benson, Address to National Restaurant Association, May 14, 1953, folder 1953–4, Box 1, RG 16, NARA II.

7. Benson, Address to Co-Ordinating Committee of the Food Industries, Grange League Federation, Northeast Poultry Producers Council, and National Frozen Food Distributors Association, Feb. 24, 1954, folder 1953–1954, Box 1, RG 16, NARA II.

8. James McWilliams, *The Pecan: A History of America's Native Nut* (Austin: University of Texas Press, 2013), 115, 119, 120, 130.

9. Domestic statistics taken from the Economic Research Service of the USDA, from website page on Agriculture and Food Statistics, Food prices and spending (updated Dec. 16, 2020, accessed 2023). International statistics vary depending on specific year and are for food consumed at home, not total food and drink. See, for example, the USDA site listed above and Brad Plumer, "Map: Here's How Much Each Country Spends on Food," Aug. 19, 2015, *Vox*, and "Share of Consumer Expenditure Spent on Food," on Our World in Data non-profit website, using USDA/ERS data 2023 (accessed 2023).

10. Laudan, "A Plea for Culinary Modernism," 42. See also Rachel Laudan, *Cuisine and Empire: Cooking in World History* (Berkeley: University of California Press, 2013), 346–47.

11. Cross and Proctor, *Packaged Pleasures*, 271.

12. Koch, *Gender and Food*, 65, also 11, 14, 49, 63.

13. Jennifer Price, *Flight Maps: Adventures with Nature in Modern America* (New York: Basic Books, 1999), 122.

14. Tracey Deutsch, *Building a Housewife's Paradise: Gender, Politics, and American Grocery Stores in the Twentieth Century* (Chapel Hill: University of North Carolina Press, 2010), 196, also 183–84; Gail Collins, *When Everything Changed: The Amazing Journey of American Women from 1960 to the Present* (New York: Little, Brown, 2009), 50; and Stephanie Coontz, *A Strange Stirring: The Feminine Mystique and American Women at the Dawn of the 1960s* (New York: Basic Books, 2011), 65, 67.

15. For further discussion, see McDonald, *Food Security*. In addition to the pressures of the system for staple commodities, local cuisines also faced pressure when particular foodstuffs were "discovered" by consumers in the United States and other rich countries, became fads, and thus became unaffordable in their home countries. See Sidney Mintz, *Tasting Food, Tasting Freedom: Excursions into Eating, Culture, and the Past* (Boston: Beacon, 1996), 114–16; see also Claude Fischler, "The McDonaldization of Culture," in *Food: A Culinary History from Antiquity to the Present*, ed. Jean-Louis Flandrin and Massimo Montanari (New York: Columbia University Press, 1999), 543.

16. A summary of these trends is in Belasco, *Food*, 56.

17. For the fruits and vegetables grown in the United States, the majority came from California, where intensive agriculture exacerbated water shortages and soil salinization. Philpott, *Perilous Bounty*, 174–75.

18. The reasons for these failures are varied, including overconfidence in scientific knowledge about health and in industrial agriculture, the economic power of private interest groups, and the fundamental contradiction of trying to tell people what they should eat, while at the same time emphasizing that each individual's choice of what to eat remained paramount.

19. Berry, *Bringing It to the Table*, 5.

20. Examples of this perspective are found throughout USDA materials and reports on nutritional research within the department. Research was invariably focused upon measuring and evaluating nutrients, even if sometimes acknowledging that qualities such as palatability had to be addressed if only to entice people into ingesting the right nutrients; for example, one 1961 report on food and agriculture argued: "The attractiveness and palatability of the food as prepared for eating influence the amount and type of food eaten and ultimately the nutrient intake of the consumer." "Food and Agriculture, a Program of Research; Part 3 Unit 11 Human Nutrition," Sept. 27, 1961, Box 2, Research Progress Reports, RG 310, NARA II. Stiebeling understood that most people did not act in such rational ways when it came to food. For example, she observed in a 1953 letter that people selected foods rather than nutrients and that habits and cultural ideas about meals shaped those choices. Stiebeling's letter is cited here, though not available in the file: Callie Mae Coons, Assistant Chief to Harry Andrews, July 31, 1953, folder Nutrition, Box 2284, General Correspondence 1906–1976, RG 16, NARA II.

21. Quoted in Bernard Brenner, "Hard Fact: People are Fat Because They Eat Too Much," *New Journal and Guide*, Oct. 3, 1959, 9. To encourage such rational decision-making, USDA administrators briefly considered in 1958 whether it was practical to label nutritional content on specific fruits and vegetables. The suggestion was not carried out as the administrator realized that the nutrient specifications might not be exact, since they were affected by soil, climate, shipping, season, etc. E. L. Peterson, Acting Secretary to Representative Charles Teague Oct. 10, 1958, folder food, Box 3120, General Correspondence 1906–1976, RG 16, NARA II.

22. The influence of cookbooks in the mid-twentieth century was great. Historian Ken Abala has observed that cookbooks "reflect peoples' aspirations." Ken Abala, "Cookbooks as Historical Documents," in *Oxford Handbook of Food History*, ed. Pilcher, 229.

23. Spring, *Gourmands' Way*, 227.

24. Shapiro, *Something from the Oven*, 91.

25. Elias, *Food on the Page*, 142.

26. Child, *Julia Child and Company*, 89.

27. Julia Child, "Cooking with Children," *New York Times Book Review*, Nov. 5, 1972, folder 192, Box 16, Series II, Correspondence, Child Papers, Schlesinger Library.

28. Child, *Julia Child and Company*, 226.

29. David Marchese, "Talk: She Changed the Way We Eat; She Wants to Fix Our Democracy, Too," *New York Times Magazine*, Dec. 21, 2019, 14.

30. This narrow interpretation of Lappé's book predominated, including in the scholarly world, where, for instance, food historian Roger Horowitz used Lappé's emphasis on the importance of protein consumption as a justification for meat eating: "Even a critic such as Frances Moore Lappé conceded that 4 to 6 ounces of meat contains 100 percent of an adult's daily protein need." Horowitz, *Putting Meat on the Table*, 3.

31. For example, food writer and activist Dan Imhoff recalled that reading Lappé's *Diet for*

a Small Planet "changed me"; similar to some of his contemporaries, Imhoff became a vegetarian for a number of years and embarked on an exploration of diet and his relationship to the land. Imhoff, oral history, Fales Library.

32. McFeely, *Can She Bake a Cherry Pie*, 148.

33. Quoted in Marchese, "Talk," 14.

34. "Changing the Way America Eats," *Health*, July–Aug. 2001, folder 11 Articles in Magazines and Publications [2 of 5] 2001, 2005, Box 50, and Judtih Mandelbaum-Schmidt, "A Healthy Dose of Marion Nestle," *Walking: The Magazine of Smart Health and Fitness*, Oct. 2000, folder Articles in Magazines [3 of 5] 1999–2000, Box 51, Series VII, Subseries A, Nestle Papers, Fales Library.

35. For example, the magazine *Eating Well* published a lengthy interview and article on Nestle in 2002, referring to her as an "esteemed nutritionist." *Eating Well: The Magazine of Food and Health*, summer 2002, 16, folder 10 Articles in Magazines [1 of 5], Box 50, Series VII, Subseries A, Nestle Papers, Fales Library.

36. Claudia Wallis, "Obesity Warriors," *Time* June 7, 2004, folder 10 Articles in Magazines [1 of 5], Box 50, Series VII, Subseries A, Nestle Papers, Fales Library.

37. Roni Caryn Rabin, "U.S. Diet Guidelines Sidestep Scientific Advice to Cut Sugar and Alcohol," *New York Times*, Dec. 29, 2020.

38. Mandelbaum-Schmidt, "A Healthy Dose of Marion Nestle."

39. National Endowment for the Humanities, webpage, with 2014 citation (accessed 2022).

40. Trillin, foreword, Waters and Friends, *40 Years of Chez Panisse*, 7.

41. Mark Bittman, *Animal, Vegetable, Junk: A History of Food, from Sustainable to Suicidal* (Boston: Houghton Mifflin Harcourt, 2021), 191, 175; Elaine McIntosh, *American Food Habits in Historical Perspective* (Westport, CT: Praeger, 1995), 136.

42. O'Sullivan, *American Organic*, 189.

43. Freedman, *Why Food Matters*, 98–99.

44. Bittman, *Animal, Vegetable, Junk*, 293.

45. Koch, *Gender and Food*, 63.

46. Goldstein with Brown, *Inside the California Food Revolution*, 308.

47. Kauffman, *Hippie Food*, 276.

48. Freedman, *Why Food Matters*, 80; Gabaccia, *We Are What We Eat*, 8, also 3, 9.

49. Priscilla Parkhurst Ferguson, *Word of Mouth: What We Talk About When We Talk about Food* (Berkeley: University of California Press, 2014), 4.

Bibliography

ARCHIVES

Beinecke Library and Manuscripts Collections, Yale University, New Haven, CT

Chester Bowles Papers
Langston Hughes Papers
Walter Francis White and Poppy Cannon White Papers

Cornell University, Ithaca, NY

Paul Jones Chapman Papers
Cornell Cooperative Extension
Division of Nutritional Sciences, Nutrition Program Records
Expanded Food and Nutrition Education Program
Food and Recipe Booklets
Clive McCay Papers
Moosewood Collective Records
New York State College of Home Economics Records

Fales Library and Special Collections, New York University, New York, NY

Marion Nestle Papers 1970–2017
Voices from the Food Revolution: People Who Changed the Way Americans Eat, oral histories, 2011.

National Agricultural Library, Beltsville, MD

Bureau of Human Nutrition Information Service Records
Citizens Food Committee Program (1947)
Crowley Collection
Food for Victory Crusade (Ralston)
Raymond Andrew Ioanes Papers
Nancy Leidenfrost Papers
Nutrition Publications from Sandy Facinoli
National School Lunch Week Collection
People on the Farm
Riley Memorial Foundation Records

National Agricultural Library (website)
Dr. Hazel Katherine Stiebeling Collection

National Records and Archives Administration, II, College Park, MD

Record Group 16, Records of the Office of the Secretary of Agriculture

Abstracts of Meetings of the Cabinet Committee on World Food Problems, 1946–1948
Copies of Letters and Memorandums Sent to or Prepared for the signature of the President, 1964–1968
General Correspondence, 1906–1976
Records of the Immediate Offices of the Commissioner and Secretary of Agriculture, Mimeographed copies of speeches, 1953–1960
Records of John A. Schnittker
Speeches and Statements of Agriculture Secretary Edward Madigan, 1991–1993
Speeches and Statements of Agriculture Secretary Clayton Yeutter, 1989–1991
Statements and Speeches of the Secretary of Agriculture, 1959–1968

Record Group 136, Records of the Agricultural Marketing Service

Office of the Administrator, Correspondence of the Secretary of Agriculture and Asst Sec of Agriculture Relating to the AMS, 1954

Record Group 310, Records of the Agricultural Research Service

Information Division, General Records Concerning the History and Philosophy of Home Economics and Nutrition research, 1932–1970
Marketing and Nutrition Research, Research Progress Reports, 1926–1959
Nutrition Education Division, Records Relating to Family Food Plans, 1970–1975, to Food Plan Working Papers, 1974–1975

Record Group 462, Records of the Food and Nutrition Service, and Food, Nutrition, and Consumer Services, 1969–1994

Child Nutrition Division, Records Relating to the School Lunch Program, 1940–1973
Posters to Promote Healthful Eating, 1980–1990
Program Planning and Development Files, 1959–1966
White House Conference on Nutrition Records, 1969–1971

New York Public Library Manuscripts and Archives Division, New York, NY

Jefferson Market Garden Records

Schlesinger Library, Radcliffe Institute for Advanced Study, Harvard University, Cambridge, MA

Julia Child Papers

BOOKS

Ackerman, Diane. *A Natural History of the Senses*. New York: Vintage Books, 1990.
Allen, Will, with Charles Wilson. Foreword by Eric Schlosser. *The Good Food Revolution: Growing Healthy Food, People, and Communities*. New York: Avery, 2012.

Allport, Susan. *The Primal Feast: Food, Sex, Foraging, and Love.* New York: Harmony Books, 2000.
———. *The Queen of Fats: Why Omega-3s Were Removed from the Western Diet and What We Can Do to Replace Them.* Berkeley: University of California Press, 2006.
Baranski, Marci R. *The Globalization of Wheat: A Critical History of the Green Revolution.* Pittsburgh: University of Pittsburgh Press, 2022.
Barber, Dan. *The Third Plate: Field Notes on the Future of Food.* New York: Penguin, 2014.
Barnet, Andrea. *Visionary Women: How Rachel Carson, Jane Jacobs, Jane Goodall, and Alice Waters Changed Our World.* New York: Ecco, 2018.
Barr, Luke. *Provence, 1970: M. F. K. Fisher, Julia Child, James Beard, and the Reinvention of American Taste.* New York: Clarkson Potter, 2013.
Belasco, Warren. *Appetite for Change: How the Counterculture Took on the Food Industry.* 2nd updated edition. Ithaca, NY: Cornell University Press, 1989, 1993, 2007.
———. *Food: The Key Concepts.* Oxford, New York: Berg, 2008.
———. *Meals to Come: A History of the Future of Food.* Berkeley: University of California Press, 2006.
Beck, Simone, Louisette Bertholle, and Julia Child. *Mastering the Art of French Cooking.* New York: Knopf, 1961.
Bentley, Amy. *Eating for Victory: Food Rationing and the Politics of Domesticity.* Urbana: University of Illinois Press, 1998.
———. *Inventing Baby Food: Taste, Health, and the Industrialization of the American Diet.* Berkeley: University of California Press, 2014.
Berg, Joel. *All You Can Eat: How Hungry is America?* New York: Seven Stories, 2008.
Berry, Wendell. With an introduction by Michael Pollan. *Bringing It to the Table: On Farming and Food.* Berkeley: Counterpoint, 2009.
———. *The Unsettling of America: Culture and Agriculture.* San Francisco: Sierra Club Books, 1986, 1997.
Better Homes and Gardens New Cook Book. New York: Meredith, 1953.
Biltekoff, Charlotte. *Eating Right in America: The Cultural Politics of Food and Health.* Durham, NC: Duke University Press, 2013.
Bittman, Mark. *Animal, Vegetable, Junk: A History of Food, from Sustainable to Suicidal.* Boston: Houghton Mifflin Harcourt, 2021.
Bobrow-Strain, Aaron. *White Bread: A Social History of the Store-Bought Loaf.* Boston: Beacon, 2012.
Brown, Wendy. *Undoing the Demos: Neoliberalism's Stealth Revolution.* New York: Zone Books, 2015.
Cannon, Poppy. With illustrations by Byron Goto. *The Bride's Cookbook.* New York: Henry Holt, 1954.
———. *The Can-Opener Cookbook.* New York: Thomas Y. Crowell, 1951, 1952.
———. Drawings by Mircea Vasiliu. *Eating European: Abroad and At Home.* Garden City, NY, Doubleday, 1961.
———. *The Electric Epicure's Cookbook.* New York: Thomas Y. Crowell, 1961.
———. *The Frozen-Foods Cookbook.* New York: Thomas Y. Crowell, 1964.
———. *A Gentle Knight: My Husband, Walter White.* New York: Rinehart, 1956.
———. *Italian Cooking.* New York: Grosset & Dunlap, 1975.
———. *The New, New Can-Opener Cookbook.* New York: Thomas Y. Crowell, 1968.
———. *Poppy Cannon's All-Time, No-Time, Any-Time Cookbook.* New York: Thomas Y. Crowell, 1974.

———. *Unforbidden Sweets: Delicious Desserts of 100 Calories or Less.* New York: Thomas Y. Crowell, 1958.

Cannon, Poppy, and Patricia Brooks. *The Presidents' Cookbook: Practical Recipes from George Washington to the Present.* New York: Funk & Wagnalls, 1968.

Caradonna, Jeremy. *Sustainability: A History.* New York: Oxford University Press, 2014.

Carpenter, Novella. *Farm City: The Education of an Urban Farmer.* New York: Penguin, 2009.

Carroll, Abigail. *Three Squares: The Invention of the American Meal.* New York: Basic Books, 2013.

Case, Andrew N. *The Organic Profit: Rodale and the Making of Marketplace Environmentalism.* Seattle: University of Washington Press, 2018.

Child, Julia. In collaboration with E. S. Yntema. *Julia Child & Company.* New York: Ballantine Books, 1978.

Child, Julia and Simone Beck. *Mastering the Art of French Cooking, Volume Two.* New York: Knopf, 1970.

Cohen, Benjamin R. *Pure Adulteration: Cheating on Nature in the Age of Manufactured Food.* Chicago: University of Chicago Press, 2019.

Cohen, Benjamin R., Michael S. Kideckel, and Anna Zeide, eds. *Acquired Tastes: Stories about the Origins of Modern Food.* Cambridge, MA: MIT Press, 2021.

Cohen, Lizabeth. *A Consumers' Republic: The Politics of Mass Consumption in Postwar America.* New York: Knopf, 2003.

Collingham, Lizzie. *The Taste of War: World War II and the Battle for Food.* New York: Penguin, 2012.

Collins, Gail. *When Everything Changed: The Amazing Journey of American Women from 1960 to the Present.* New York: Little, Brown, 2009.

Coontz, Stephanie. *A Strange Stirring: The Feminine Mystique and American Women at the Dawn of the 1960s.* New York: Basic Books, 2011.

Coveney, John. *Food, Morals and Meaning: The Pleasure and Anxiety of Eating.* 2nd ed. London and New York: Routledge, 2006.

Cowan, Ruth Schwartz. *More Work for Mother: The Ironies of Household Technology from the Open Hearth to the Microwave.* New York: Basic Books, 1983.

Cross, Gary S., and Robert N. Proctor. *Packaged Pleasures: How Technology & Marketing Revolutionized Desire.* Chicago: University of Chicago Press, 2014.

Cullather, Nick. *The Hungry World: America's Cold War Battle against Poverty in Asia.* Cambridge, MA: Harvard University Press, 2010.

Cunningham, Marion. With Jeri Leber. *The Fannie Farmer Cookbook,* revised 12th ed. New York: Knopf, 1987.

De Beauvoir, Simone. Translated by Constance Borde and Sheila Malovany-Chevallier. Introduction by Judith Thurman. *The Second Sex.* New York: Knopf, 2010.

Deutsch, Tracey. *Building a Housewife's Paradise: Gender, Politics, and American Grocery Stores in the Twentieth Century.* Chapel Hill: University of North Carolina Press, 2010.

Diner, Hasia R. *Hungering for America: Italian, Irish, and Jewish Foodways in the Age of Migration.* Cambridge, MA: Harvard University Press, 2001.

Dreilinger, Danielle. *The Secret History of Home Economics: How Trailblazing Women Harnessed the Power of Home and Changed the Way We Live.* New York: Norton, 2021.

DuPuis, E. Melanie. *Dangerous Digestion: Politics of American Dietary Advice.* Berkeley, CA: University of California Press, 2015.

Elias, Megan J. *Food in the United States, 1890–1945*. Santa Barbara, CA: ABC Clio, 2009.

———. *Food on the Page: Cookbooks and American Culture*. Philadelphia: University of Pennsylvania Press, 2017.

———. *Lunch: A History*. Lanham, MD: Rowman & Littlefield, 2014.

———. *Stir It Up: Home Economics in American Culture*. Philadelphia: University of Pennsylvania Press, 2008.

Endres, Kathleen L., and Therese L. Lueck. *Women's Periodicals in the United States: Consumer Magazines*. Westport, CT: Greenwood Press, 1995.

Eschliman, Dwight. Text by Steve Ettlinger. *Ingredients: A Visual Exploration of 75 Additives & 25 Food Products*. New York: Regan Arts, 2015.

Ettlinger, Steve. *Twinkie, Deconstructed: My Journey to Discover How the Ingredients Found in Processed Foods Are Grown, Mined (Yes, Mined), and Manipulated into What America Eats*. New York: Hudson Street, 2007.

Finn, Maria. Illustrations by Eika Yokoyama. *A Little Piece of Earth: How to Grow Your Own Food in Small Spaces*. New York: Universe, 2010.

Fisher, M. F. K. *As They Were*. New York: Vintage, 1983.

Fitzgerald, Deborah. *Every Farm a Factory: The Industrial Ideal in American Agriculture*. New Haven, CT: Yale University Press, 2003.

Flores, H. C. Foreword by Toby Hemenway. Illustrations by Jackie Holmstrom. *Food Not Lawns: How to Turn Your Yard into a Garden and Your Neighborhood into a Community*. White River Junction, VT: Chelsea Green, 2006.

Foer, Jonathan Safran. *Eating Animals*. New York: Little, Brown, 2009.

———. *We Are the Weather: Saving the Planet Begins at Breakfast*. New York: Farrar, Straus and Giroux, 2019.

Freedman, Paul. *American Cuisine and How It Got This Way*. New York: Liveright, 2019.

———. *Why Food Matters*. New Haven, CT: Yale University Press, 2021.

Friedan, Betty. *The Feminine Mystique*. New York: Norton, 1963.

Fromartz, Samuel. *Organic, Inc.: Natural Foods and How They Grew*. Orlando, FL: Harcourt, 2006.

Fussell, Betty. Illustrated by Glenna Putt. *Food in Good Season*. New York: Knopf, 1988.

———. *Masters of American Cookery: M. F. K. Fisher, James Andrews Beard, Raymond Craig Claiborne, Julia McWilliams Child*. New York: Times Books, 1983.

———. *My Kitchen Wars*. New York: North Point/Farrar, Straus and Giroux, 1999.

Gabaccia, Donna. *We Are What We Eat: Ethnic Food and the Making of Americans*. Cambridge, MA: Harvard University Press, 1998.

Gardner, Bruce. *American Agriculture in the Twentieth Century: How It Flourished and What It Cost*. Cambridge, MA: Harvard University Press, 2002.

Goines, David Lance. *The Free Speech Movement: Coming of Age in the 1960s*. Berkeley, CA: Ten Speed, 1993.

———. Foreword by Alice Waters. *The Poster Art of David Lance Goines: A 40-Year Retrospective*. Mineola, NY: Dover, 2010.

Goldstein, Joyce. With Dore Brown. *Inside the California Food Revolution: Thirty Years That Changed Our Culinary Consciousness*. Berkley: University of California Press, 2013.

Goodman, David, E. Melanie DuPuis, and Michael K. Goodman. *Alternative Food Networks: Knowledge, Practice, and Politics*. London and New York: Routledge, 2012.

Gosse, Van. *The Movements of the New Left 1950–1975: A Brief History with Documents*. Boston: Bedford/St. Martin's, 2005.

Gray, Margaret. *Labor and the Locavore: The Making of a Comprehensive Food Ethic.* Berkeley: University of California Press, 2014.

Guthman, Julie. *Agrarian Dreams: The Paradox of Organic Farming in California.* 2nd ed. Oakland: University of California Press, 2014.

———. *Weighing In: Obesity, Food Justice, and the Limits of Capitalism.* Berkeley: University of California Press, 2011.

———. *Wilted: Pathogens, Chemicals, and the Fragile Future of the Strawberry Industry.* Oakland: University of California Press, 2019.

Hadden, Evelyn J. With photographs by Joshua McCullough. Foreword by Lauren Springer Ogden. *Hellstrip Gardening: Create Paradise Between the Sidewalk and the Curb.* Portland, OR: Timber, 2014.

Hamilton, Shane. *Supermarket USA: Food and Power in the Cold War Farms Race.* New Haven, CT: Yale University Press, 2018.

Harris, Daniel. *Cute, Quaint, Hungry and Romantic: The Aesthetics of Consumerism.* Boston: Da Capo, 2000.

Hobhouse, Henry. *Seeds of Change: Five Plants that Transformed Mankind.* New York: Harper & Row, 1985.

Holt-Giménez, Eric. *A Foodie's Guide to Capitalism: Understanding the Political Economy of What We Eat.* Foreword by Marion Nestle. New York: Monthly Review Press and Food First Books, 2017.

Hooker, Richard J. *Food and Drink in America: A History.* Indianapolis, IN: Bobbs-Merrill, 1981.

Horowitz, Roger. *Kosher USA: How Coke Became Kosher and Other Tales of Modern Food.* New York: Columbia University Press, 2016.

———. *Putting Meat on the American Table: Taste, Technology, Transformation.* Baltimore: Johns Hopkins University Press, 2006.

Imhoff, Daniel, ed. *CAFO (Concentrated Animal Feeding Operation): The Tragedy of Industrial Animal Factories.* San Rafael, CA: Earth Aware, 2010.

Inness, Sherrie A. *Dinner Roles: American Women and Culinary Culture.* Iowa City: University of Iowa Press, 2001.

Jelinek, Lawrence J. *Harvest Empire: A History of California Agriculture.* 2nd ed. San Francisco: Boyd & Fraser, 1979, 1982.

Johnson, Lorraine. *City Farmer: Adventures in Urban Food Growing.* Vancouver: Greystone Books, 2010.

Katz, Sandor Ellix. *The Revolution Will Not Be Microwaved: Inside America's Underground Food Movements.* White River Junction, VT: Chelsea Green, 2006.

Katzen, Mollie. *The Moosewood Cookbook.* Berkeley, CA: Ten Speed, 1977, and revised, new ed., 1992.

Kauffman, Jonathan. *Hippie Food: How Back-to-the-Landers, Longhairs, and Revolutionaries Changed the Way We Eat.* New York: William Morrow, 2018.

Kaufman, Frederick. *A Short History of the American Stomach.* Orlando, FL: Harcourt, 2008.

Keys, Ancel, and Margaret Keys. Foreword by Paul Dudley White, MD. *Eat Well & Stay Well.* Garden City, NY: Doubleday, 1959.

Kimball, Kristin. *The Dirty Life: A Memoir of Farming, Food, and Love.* New York: Scribner, 2010.

Kingsolver, Barbara. With Steven L. Hopp and Camille Kingsolver. Original drawings by

Richard A. Houser. *Animal, Vegetable, Miracle: A Year of Food Life.* New York: Harper Perennial, 2007.

Koch, Shelley L. *Gender and Food: A Critical Look at the Food System.* Lanham MD: Rowman & Littlefield, 2019.

Lappé, Frances Moore. *Diet for a Small Planet.* Rev. ed. Illustrated by Kathleen Zimmerman and Ralph Iwamoto. New York: Ballantine Books, 1971, 1975.

———. *EcoMind: Changing the Way We Think, to Create the World We Want.* New York: Nation Books, 2011.

———. *Getting a Grip² Clarity, Creativity and Courage for the World We Really Want.* Rev. ed. Cambridge, MA: Small Planet Media, 2007, 2010.

———. *Rediscovering America's Values: A Dialogue that Explores Our Fundamental Beliefs and How They Offer Hope for America's Future.* New York: Ballantine Books, 1989.

Lappé, Frances Moore, and Anna Lappé. *Hope's Edge: The Next Diet for a Small Planet.* New York: Penguin Putnam, 2002.

Lappé, Frances Moore, and Joseph Collins. With Cary Fowler. *Food First: Beyond the Myth of Scarcity.* Rev. and updated. New York: Ballantine Books, 1978.

Lappé, Frances Moore, Joseph Collins, and Peter Rosset. With Luis Esparza. *World Hunger: Twelve Myths.* 2nd ed. New York: Grove Press, 1998.

Lappé, Frances Moore, and Paul Martin Du Bois. *The Quickening of America: Rebuilding Our Nation, Remaking Our Lives.* San Francisco: Jossey-Bass, 1994.

Lappé, Frances Moore, and Rachel Schurman. *Taking Population Seriously* (published first as *Food First Development Report 4, September 1988: The Missing Piece in the Population Puzzle*). San Francisco: Food First Books, 1990.

Lappé, Frances Moore, Rachel Shurman, and Kevin Danaher. *Betraying the National Interest.* New York: Grove Press, Food First Books, 1987.

Laudan, Rachel. *Cuisine and Empire: Cooking in World History.* Berkeley: University of California Press, 2013.

Lautenschlager, Julie L. *Food Fight! The Battle over the American Lunch in Schools and the Workplace.* Jefferson, NC: McFarland, 2006.

Lawson, Laura J. *City Bountiful: A Century of Community Gardening in America.* Berkeley: University of California Press, 2005.

Levenstein, Harvey. *Fear of Food: A History of Why We Worry about What We Eat.* Chicago: University of Chicago Press, 2012.

———. *Paradox of Plenty: A Social History of Eating in Modern America.* Rev. ed. Berkeley: University of California Press, 2003.

———. *Revolution at the Table: The Transformation of the American Diet.* Berkeley: University of California Press, 2003.

Levine, Susan. *School Lunch Politics: The Surprising History of America's Favorite Welfare Program.* Princeton, NJ: Princeton University Press, 2008.

Lileks, James. *The Gallery of Regrettable Food: Highlights from Classic American Recipe Books.* New York: Crown, 2001.

Lovegren, Sylvia. *Fashionable Food: Seven Decades of Food Fads.* Chicago: University of Chicago Press, 1995, 2005.

Ludington, Charles C., and Mathew Morse Booker, eds. *Food Fights: How History Matters to Contemporary Food Debates.* Chapel Hill: University of North Carolina Press, 2019.

Madden, J. Patrick, and Scott G. Chaplowe, eds. *For ALL Generations: Making World*

Agriculture More Sustainable. Glendale, CA: OM Publishing and World Sustainable Agriculture Association, 1997.

Mann, Charles C. *The Wizard and the Prophet: Two Remarkable Scientists and their Dueling Visions to Shape Tomorrow's World.* New York: Knopf, 2018.

Mart, Michelle. *Pesticides, A Love Story: America's Enduring Embrace of Dangerous Chemicals.* Lawrence: University Press of Kansas, 2015.

Martin, Jacqueline Briggs. Illustrated by Hayelin Choi. Afterword by Alice Waters. *Alice Waters and the Trip to Delicious.* Bellevue, WA: Readers to Eaters, 2014.

Martschukat, Jürgen, and Bryant Simon. *Food, Power, and Agency.* London: Bloomsbury, 2017.

Mason, Jim, and Peter Singer. *Animal Factories.* New York: Crown, 1980.

McCarthy, Mary. *The Group.* San Diego, CA: Harcourt Brace, 1954, 1982.

McDonald, Bryan L. *Food Power: The Rise and Fall of the Postwar American Food System.* New York: Oxford University Press, 2017.

———. *Food Security.* Cambridge, UK: Polity Press, 2010.

McFeely, Mary Drake. *Can She Bake a Cherry Pie? American Women and the Kitchen in the Twentieth Century.* Amherst: University of Massachusetts Press, 2000.

McGrath, Maria. *Food for Dissent: Natural Foods and the Consumer Counterculture Since the 1960s.* Amherst: University of Massachusetts Press, 2019.

McIntosh, Elaine N. *American Food Habits in Historical Perspective.* Westport, CT: Praeger, 1995.

McKay, George. *Radical Gardening: Politics, Idealism & Rebellion in the Garden.* London: Francis Lincoln Limited, 2011.

McKenna, Maryn. *Big Chicken: The Incredible Story of How Antibiotics Created Modern Agriculture and Changed the Way the World Eats.* Washington, DC: National Geographic, 2017.

McNamee, Thomas. Foreword by R. W. Apple Jr. *Alice Waters & Chez Panisse: The Romantic, Impractical, Often Eccentric, Ultimately Brilliant Making of a Food Revolution.* New York: Penguin, 2007.

McWilliams, James E. *American Pests: The Losing War on Insects from Colonial Times to DDT.* New York: Columbia University Press, 2008.

———. *Just Food: Where Locavores Get It Wrong and How We Can Truly Eat Responsibly.* New York: Little, Brown, 2009.

———. *The Modern Savage: Our Unthinking Decision to Eat Animals.* New York: St. Martin's, Thomas Dunne Books, 2015.

———. *The Pecan: A History of America's Native Nut.* Austin: University of Texas Press, 2013.

———. *A Revolution in Eating: How the Quest for Food Shaped America.* New York: Columbia University Press, 2005.

Mendelson, Anne. *Stand Facing the Stove: The Story of the Women Who Gave America* The Joy of Cooking. New York: Henry Holt, 1996.

Merchant, Carolyn. *The Death of Nature: Women, Ecology, and the Scientific Revolution.* San Francisco: Harper San Francisco, 1980, 1989, 1990.

———. *Earthcare: Women and the Environment.* New York: Routledge, 1995.

Meyerowitz, Joanne, ed. *Not June Cleaver: Women and Gender in Postwar America, 1945–1960.* Philadelphia: Temple University Press, 1994.

Mintz, Sidney W. *Sweetness and Power: The Place of Sugar in Modern History.* New York: Penguin, 1985.

———. *Tasting Food, Tasting Freedom: Excursions into Eating, Culture, and the Past.* Boston: Beacon, 1996.

Mudry, Jessica J. *Measured Meals: Nutrition in America.* Albany: State University of New York Press, 2009.

Neuhaus, Jessamyn. *Manly Meals and Mom's Home Cooking: Cookbooks and Gender in Modern America.* Baltimore: Johns Hopkins University Press, 2003.

Nestle, Marion. *Food Politics: How the Food Industry Influences Nutrition and Health.* Rev. and expanded ed. Berkeley CA: University of California Press, 2007.

———. *Safe Food: Bacteria, Biotechnology, and Bioterrorism.* Berkeley: University of California Press, 2003.

———. *Slow Cooked: An Unexpected Life in Food Politics.* Oakland: University of California Press, 2022.

———. *Soda Politics: Taking on Big Soda (and Winning).* New York: Oxford University Press, 2015.

———. *Unsavory Truth: How Food Companies Skew the Science of What We Eat.* New York: Basic Books, 2018.

———. *What to Eat.* New York: North Point, 2006.

Nestle, Marion, in conversation with Kerry Trueman. *Let's Ask Marion: What You Need to Know about the Politics of Food, Nutrition, and Health.* Oakland: University of California Press, 2020.

Nestle, Marion, and Malden Nesheim. *Why Calories Count: From Science to Politics.* Berkeley: University of California Press, 2012.

Nestle, Marion, ed. *The Surgeon General's Report on Nutrition and Health.* Washington, DC: Department of Health and Human Services, 1988.

O'Neill, Molly, ed. *American Food Writing: An Anthology with Classic Recipes.* New York: Library of America, 2007.

Orr, Stephen. *Tomorrow's Garden: Design and Inspiration for a New Age of Sustainable Gardening.* New York: Rodale, 2011.

O'Sullivan, Robin. *American Organic: A Cultural History of Farming, Gardening, Shopping, and Eating.* Lawrence: University Press of Kansas, 2015.

Parkhurst Ferguson, Priscilla. *Word of Mouth: What We Talk about When We Talk about Food.* Berkeley: University of California Press, 2014.

Perkins, John H. *Geopolitics and the Green Revolution; Wheat, Genes, and the Cold War.* New York: Oxford University Press, 1997.

Petrini, Carlo. Translated by William McCuaig. *Slow Food: The Case for Taste.* New York: Columbia University Press, 2001.

Petrini, Carlo, with Ben Watson and Slow Food Editore, eds. *Slow Food: Collected Thoughts on Taste, Tradition, and the Honest Pleasures of Food.* White River Junction, VT: Chelsea Green, 2001.

Philpott, Tom. *Perilous Bounty: The Looming Collapse of American Farming and How We Can Prevent It.* New York: Bloomsbury, 2020.

Pilcher, Jeffrey M., ed. *The Oxford Handbook of Food History.* New York: Oxford University Press, 2012.

Pollan, Michael. *Cooked: A Natural History of Transformation.* New York: Penguin, 2013.

———. *In Defense of Food: An Eater's Manifesto.* New York: Penguin, 2008.

———. *The Omnivore's Dilemma: A Natural History of Four Meals.* New York: Penguin, 2006.

Poppendieck, Janet. *Free for All: Fixing School Food in America.* Berkeley: University of California Press, 2010.

Price, Jennifer. *Flight Maps: Adventures with Nature in Modern America.* New York: Basic Books, 1999.

Pringle, Peter. *Food, Inc.: Mendel to Monsanto—The Promises and Perils of the Biotech Harvest.* New York: Simon and Schuster, 2003.

Puma, Joan. Drawings by Jeryl English. *The Complete Urban Gardener.* New York: Harper & Row, 1985.

Reardon, Joan. *M. F. K. Fisher, Julia Child, and Alice Waters: Celebrating the Pleasures of the Table.* New York: Harmony Books, 1994.

———. *Poet of the Appetites: The Lives and Loves of M. F. K. Fisher.* New York: North Point, 2004.

Reichl, Ruth. *Save Me the Plums: My Gourmet Memoir.* New York: Random House, 2019.

Rombauer, Irma S., and Marion Rombauer Becker. *Joy of Cooking.* Indianapolis, IN: Bobbs-Merrill, 1964.

Ruhlman, Michael. *Grocery: The Buying and Selling of Food in America.* New York: Abrams, 2017.

Ruis, A. R. *Eating to Learn, Learning to Eat: The Origins of School Lunch in the United States.* New Brunswick, NJ: Rutgers University Press, 2017.

Rutledge, Jennifer Geist. *Feeding the Future: The Emergence of School Lunch Programs as Global Social Policy.* New Brunswick, NJ: Rutgers University Press, 2016.

Sabin, Paul. *The Bet: Paul Ehrlich, Julian Simon, and Our Gamble over Earth's Future.* New Haven, CT: Yale University Press, 2013.

Saville, Florence Rogers. *Real Food for Your Baby!* New York: Simon and Schuster, 1973.

Sayre, Laura, and Sean Clark, eds. Foreword by Frederick L. Kirschenmann. *Fields of Learning; The Student Farm Movement in North America.* Lexington: University Press of Kentucky, 2011.

Scrinis, Gyorgy. *Nutritionism: The Science and Politics of Dietary Advice.* New York: Columbia University Press, 2013.

Severson, Kim. *Spoon Fed: How Eight Cooks Saved My Life. A Memoir.* New York: Riverhead Books, 2010.

Seymour, Nicole. *Bad Environmentalism: Irony and Irreverence in the Ecological Age.* Minneapolis: University of Minnesota Press, 2018.

Shapiro, Laura. *Julia Child.* New York: Viking, 2007.

———. *Perfection Salad: Women and Cooking at the Turn of the Century.* Introduction by Michael Stern. New York: Modern Library, 1986, 2001.

———. *Something from the Oven: Reinventing Dinner in 1950s America.* New York: Viking Penguin, 2004.

———. *What She Ate: Six Remarkable Women & the Food that Tells Their Stories.* New York: Viking, 2017.

Shell, Ellen Ruppel. *Cheap: The High Cost of Discount Culture.* New York: Penguin, 2009.

Shetterly, Caitlin. *Modified: GMOs and the Threat to Our Food, Our Land, Our Future.* New York: G. P. Putnam's Sons, 2016.

Shiva, Vandana. *The Violence of the Green Revolution: Third World Agriculture, Ecology and Politics.* London and New Jersey: Zed Books, and Penang, Malaysia: Third World Network, 1991.

———. *Who Really Feeds the World? The Failures of Agribusiness and the Promise of Agroecology.* Berkeley, CA: North Atlantic Books, 2016.

Shprintzen, Adam D. *The Vegetarian Crusade: The Rise of an American Reform Movement, 1817–1921*, Chapel Hill: University of North Carolina Press, 2013.

Simon, Bryant. *The Hamlet Fire: A Tragic Story of Cheap Food, Cheap Government, and Cheap Lives.* New York: New Press, 2017.

Simon, Linda. *The Biography of Alice B. Toklas.* Garden City, NY: Doubleday 1977.

Simon, Michele. *Appetite for Profit: How the Food Industry Undermines Our Health and How to Fight Back.* New York: Nation Books, 2006.

Singer, Peter. *Animal Liberation: A New Ethics for Our Treatment of Animals.* New York: Avon Books, 1975.

Singer, Peter, and Jim Mason. *The Way We Eat: Why Our Food Choices Matter.* Emmaus PA: Rodale, 2006.

Slongwhite, Dale Finley. Foreword by Jeannie Economos. *Fed Up: The High Costs of Cheap Food.* Gainesville: University Press of Florida, 2014.

Smedshaug, Christian Anton. Translation by John Irons. *Feeding the World in the 21st Century: A Historical Analysis of Agriculture and Society.* London: Anthem, 2010.

Smith, Alisa, and J. B. MacKinnon. *The 100-Mile Diet: A Year of Local Eating.* Toronto: Vintage Canada, 2007.

Smith, Andrew F. *Eating History: 30 Turning Points in the Making of American Cuisine.* New York: Columbia University Press, 2009.

Smith, Mark M. *Sensing the Past: Seeing, Hearing, Smelling, Tasting, and Touching History.* Berkeley: University of California Press, 2007.

Smith, Nicola. With photographs by Geoff Hansen. *Harvest: A Year in the Life of an Organic Farm.* Guilford, CT: Lyons, 2004.

Smith-Howard, Kendra. *Pure and Modern Milk: An Environmental History since 1900.* New York: Oxford University Press, 2014.

Solkoff, Joel. *The Politics of Food: The Decline of Agriculture and the Rise of Agribusiness in America.* San Francisco: Sierra Club Books, 1985.

Specht, Joshua. *Red Meat Republic: A Hoof-to-Table History of How Beef Changed America.* Princeton, NJ: Princeton University Press, 2019.

Spring, Justin. *The Gourmands' Way: Six Americans in Paris and the Birth of the New Gastronomy.* New York: Farrar, Straus and Giroux, 2017.

Steinberg, Ted. *Down to Earth: Nature's Role in American History.* New York: Oxford University Press, 2002.

Stoll, Steven. *The Fruits of Natural Advantage: Making the Industrial Countryside in California.* Berkeley: University of California Press, 1998.

Strange, Marty. *Family Farming: A New Economic Vision.* Lincoln: University of Nebraska Press, and San Francisco: Institute for Food and Development Policy, 1988.

Strauss, David. *Setting the Table for Julia Child: Gourmet Dining in America, 1934–1961.* Baltimore: Johns Hopkins University Press, 2011.

Striffler, Steve. *Chicken: The Dangerous Transformation of America's Favorite Food.* New Haven, CT: Yale University Press, 2005.

Taubes, Gary. *The Case Against Sugar.* New York: Knopf, 2016.

———. *Good Calories, Bad Calories: Fats, Carbs, and the Controversial Science of Diet and Health.* New York: Anchor Books, 2007, 2008.

Theophano, Janet. *Eat My Words: Reading Women's Lives Through the Cookbooks They Wrote.* London: Palgrave Macmillan, 2002.

Toensmeier, Eric. With contributions from Jonathan Bates. *Paradise Lot: Two Plant Geeks, One-Tenth of an Acre, and The Making of an Edible Garden Oasis in the City.* White River Junction, VT: Chelsea Green, 2013.

Toklas, Alice B. *The Alice B. Toklas Cook Book.* Illustrations by Sir Francis Rose. New York: Harper & Brothers, 1954.

———. *Aromas and Flavors of Past and Present.* Introduction and comments by Poppy Cannon. New York: Harper & Brothers, 1958.

Tsing, Anna Lowenhaupt. *The Mushroom at the End of the World: On the Possibility of Life in the Capitalist Ruins.* Princeton, NJ: Princeton University Press, 2015.

Veit, Helen Zoe. *Modern Food, Moral Food: Self-Control, Science, and the Rise of Modern American Eating in the Early Twentieth Century.* Chapel Hill: University of North Carolina Press, 2013.

Vileisis, Ann. *Kitchen Literacy: How We Lost Knowledge of Where Food Comes from and Why We Need to Get It Back.* With a new Afterword. Washington, DC: Island Press/Shearwater Books, 2008.

Walker, Nancy A. *Women's Magazines, 1940–1960: Gender Roles and the Popular Press.* Boston: Bedford/St. Martin's, 1998.

Wallach, Jennifer Jensen. *Getting What We Need Ourselves: How Food Has Shaped African American Life.* Lanham, MD: Rowman & Littlefield, 2019.

Waters, Alice. *The Art of Simple Food, II.* New York: Clarkson Potter, 2013.

———. *Chez Panisse Fruit.* New York: William Morrow Cookbooks, 2002.

———. *The Chez Panisse Menu Cookbook.* New York: Random House, 1982.

———. *Chez Panisse Vegetables.* New York: Harper Collins, 1996.

———. *Fanny at Chez Panisse: A Child's Restaurant Adventures with 46 Recipes.* New York: William Morrow Cookbooks, 1997.

———. *In the Green Kitchen: Techniques to Learn by Heart.* New York: Clarkson Potter, 2010.

———. *We Are What We Eat: A Slow Food Manifesto.* New York: Penguin, 2021.

Waters, Alice, and the Cooks of Chez Panisse. In collaboration with David Tanis and Fritz Streiff. Illustrated by David Lance Goines. *Chez Panisse Café Cookbook.* New York: Harper Collins Publishers, 1999.

Waters, Alice, and Friends. Foreword by Calvin Trillin. Afterword by Michael Pollan. *40 Years of Chez Panisse: The Power of Gathering.* New York: Clarkson Potter, 2011.

Waters, Alice, with Bob Carrau, illustrations by Ann Arnold, *Fanny in France.* New York: Viking Books for Young Readers, 2016.

Waters, Alice, with Cristina Mueller and Bob Carrau. *Coming to My Senses: The Making of a Counterculture Cook.* New York: Clarkson Potter, 2017.

Waters, Alice, with Daniel Duane. Photographs by Davie Littschwager. *Edible Schoolyard, A Universal Idea.* San Francisco: Chronicle Books, 2008.

Waters, Alice, with Fanny Singer, *My Pantry: Homemade Ingredients That Make Simple Meals Your Own: A Cookbook.* New York: Clarkson Potter, 2015.

Waters, Alice, with Patricia Curtan, Kelsie Kerr, and Frtiz Streiff. Illustrations by Patricia Curtan. *The Art of Simple Food: Notes, Lessons, and Recipes from a Delicious Revolution.* New York: Clarkson Potter, 2007.

Waters, Alice, with Patricia Curtan and Martine Labro. *Chez Panisse Pasta, Pizza & Calzone.* New York: Random House, 1984.

Whorton, James. *Before Silent Spring: Pesticides and Public Health in Pre-DDT America.* Princeton, NJ: Princeton University Press, 1974.

Wicks, Judy. *Good Morning, Beautiful Business: The Unexpected Journey of an Activist Entrepreneur and Local Economy Pioneer.* White River Junction, VT: Chelsea Green, 2013.

Willett, Walter, MD, with Patrick Skerrett. *Eat, Drink, and Be Healthy; The Harvard Medical School Guide to Healthy Eating.* New York: Free Press, 2001.

Winders, Bill. Foreword by James Scott. *The Politics of Food Supply: U.S. Agricultural Policy in the World Economy.* New Haven, CT: Yale University Press, 2009.

Wurgaft, Benjamin Aldes. *Meat Planet: Artificial Flesh and the Future of Food.* Oakland: University of California Press, 2019.

Yost, Edna. *American Women of Science.* Philadelphia: Frederick A. Stokes, 1943.

Zeide, Anna. *Canned: The Rise and Fall of Consumer Confidence in the American Food Industry.* Oakland: University of California Press, 2018.

———. *US History in 15 Foods.* London: Bloomsbury Academic, 2023.

Zukin, Sharon. *Point of Purchase: How Shopping Changed American Culture.* New York: Routledge, 2004.

NEWSPAPERS, PERIODICALS, AND NEWS OUTLETS CONSULTED

American Way
Bangor Daily News
Bon Appetit
Chicago Tribune
East West
Epoch Times
Family Circle
In These Times
Ithaca Times
Jewish Advocate
Los Angeles Times
Michigan Citizen
Mother Earth News
New Age Journal
New York Amsterdam News
New York Times
New York Times Magazine
The New Yorker
Organic Gardening
People
Philadelphia Inquirer
Philadelphia Tribune
National Public Radio (NPR)
NBC News
Scholastic Scope
Time
Wall Street Journal

ARTICLES, JOURNALS, CHAPTERS, DISSERTATIONS

Anderson, J. L. "Lard to Lean: Making the Meat-Type Hog in Post-World War II America." In *Food Chains: From Farmyard to Shopping Cart*, edited by Warren Belasco and Roger Horowitz, 29–46. Philadelphia: University of Pennsylvania Press, 2009.

Barthes, Roland. "Toward a Psychosociology of Contemporary Food Consumption." In *Food and Culture: A Reader*, edited by Carole Counihan and Penny Van Esterik, 20–27. New York: Routledge, 1997.

Belasco, Warren. "Food Matters: Perspectives on an Emerging Field." In *Food Nations: Selling Taste in Consumer Societies*, edited by Warren Belasco and Philip Scranton, 2–23. New York: Routledge, 2002.

———. "How Much Depends on Dinner?" In *Food Chains*, edited by Belasco and Horowitz, 9–15.

Bentley, Amy. "Inventing Baby Food: Gerber and the Discourse of Infancy in the United States." In *Food Nations*, edited by Belasco and Scranton, 92–112.

Berry, Wendell. "The Pleasures of Eating," In Wendell Berry, *What are People For?* 145–152. New York: North Point, 1990.

Fischler, Claude. "The McDonaldization of Culture." In *Food: A Culinary History from Antiquity to the Present*, edited by Jean-Louis Flandrin and Massimo Montanari, 530–47. New York: Columbia University Press, 1999.

Flandrin, Jean-Louis and Massimo Montanari. "Conclusion: Today and Tomorrow." In *Food*, edited by Flandrin and Montanari, 548–53.

Gabaccia, Donna R. "As American as Budweiser and Pickles? Nation-Building in American Food Industries." In *Food Nations*, edited by Belasco and Scranton, 175–93.

Garcia, Matt, "Setting the Table: Historians, Popular Writers, and Food History," 656–78; respondents: E. Melanie DuPuis, "Keeping It Complex," 679–81; Madeline Y. Hsu, "On the Possibilities of Food Writing as a Bridge between the Popular and the Political," 682–85; Mark Padoongpatt, "Sitting at the Table: Food History as American History," 686–89; Monica Perales, "The Food Historian's Dilemma: Reconsidering the Role of Authenticity in Food Scholarship," 690–93; Jeremy Pilcher, "The Whole Enchilada: A Full Plate of Food History," 694–96; Matt Garcia, "Final Thoughts on Food Studies," 697–99. Food History Roundtable, *Journal of American History* 103 (3) (Dec. 2016): 656–99.

Goodyear, Dana. "Jeremiah Tower, a Forgotten Father of the American Food Revolution." *The New Yorker*, May 1, 2017.

Guthman, Julie, and Melanie DuPuis. "Embodying Neoliberalism: Economy, Culture, and the Politics of Fat." *Environment and Planning: Society and Space* 24 (2006): 427–48.

Hamilton, Shane. "Analyzing Commodity Chains: Linkages or Restraints?" In *Food Chains*, edited by Belasco and Horowitz, 16–25.

———. "The Economies and Conveniences of Modern-Day Living: Frozen Foods and Mass Marketing, 1945–1965." *Business History Review* 77 (1) (Spring 2003): 33–60.

Harper, Alfred. "Contributions of Women Scientists in the U.S. to the Development of Recommended Dietary Allowances." *Journal of Nutrition* 133 (2003): 3698–3702.

Knight, Sam. "Betting the Farm: The Obsessions of Jake Fiennes Could Change How Britain Uses It Land." *The New Yorker*, Feb. 10, 2020, 32–38.

Laudan, Rachel. "A Plea for Culinary Modernism: Why We Should Love New, Fast, Processed Food." *Gastronimica* (Feb. 2001): 36–44.

Levenstein, Harvey. "The Perils of Abundance: Food, Health, and Morality in American History." In *Food*, edited by Flandrin and Montanari, 516–29.

Mack, Adam. "'Good Things to Eat in Suburbia': Supermarkets and American Suburban Culture, 1930–1970." PhD diss. University of South Carolina, 2006.

Mead, Margaret. "The Changing Significance of Food." In *Food and Culture*, edited by Counihan and Van Esterik, 11–19.

Phillips, Sarah T. "The Price of Plenty: Getting Farm Policy Right in the 1960s." *Journal of American History* 109 (3) (Dec. 2022): 596–620.

Pollan, Michael. "The Food Movement, Rising." *New York Review of Books*, June 10, 2010.

Solnit, Rebecca. "Revolutionary Plots: On Urban Gardening." In *The Encyclopedia of Trouble and Spaciousness*, Rebecca Solnit, 285–97. San Antonio, TX: Trinity University Press, 2014.

"Special Issue: The Cycle of Food," *Audubon*, Mar.–Apr. 2011.

FILMS

Growing Cities: A Film About Urban Farming in America. Directed by Dan Susman produced by Dan Susman, Andrew Mombouquette, and Dana Altman. 2013, 93 minutes.

Truck Farm. Directed by Ian Cheney, produced by Ian Cheney and Curt Ellis, written by Ian Cheney and Simon Beins. 2010, 48 min.

Index